Foreword

Christopher Kuner has kindly asked me to write a foreword to this book, largely based on his PhD dissertation for Tilburg University in the Netherlands, and I have accepted his request with pleasure. Subsequently, he allowed me the privilege of reading the full text of the thesis on its way to finalization. On that basis, I can now confirm that this book will help its readers to become familiar with a complex and fast-expanding reality that increasingly affects us all, whether we know it or not, and this regardless of any professional interest in the regulatory aspects of the subject.

As data processing is becoming a more and more pervasive feature of our information societies, and data increasingly move around the globe at the relentless rhythm of ever more demanding economies, or merely driven by shared interest in social networks, it is natural that issues involving cross-border data flows are attracting more attention. What in the early days of privacy law may have seemed like a 'borderline' or even 'across the border' issue, is now discovered and discussed as an inconvenient truth that national borders still play a key role in legal regulations, although data flows may cross those same borders a million times every second.

It should not come as a surprise that the first interactions with the issue of data privacy also included restrictions on data flows in order to protect the integrity of national systems of carefully developed principles and procedures. This trend was followed at a higher level in the first international privacy frameworks in the context of the OECD and the Council of Europe, although this was balanced against the need to ensure a free flow of information across borders, where possible. The subsequent harmonization of national laws in the context of the EU once again followed the same logic of 'principled pragmatism'.

The ongoing review of the EU legal framework for data protection takes place against an interesting background. The right to the protection of personal data has been recognized as a separate fundamental right in the EU Charter. At the same time, there is a need to ensure a more effective protection of personal data in practice and a greater consistency of such protection within the EU. However, globalization of data flows also requires a pragmatic redefinition of the international scope of EU law and a more effective approach to the regulation of data flows across EU borders. In a wider perspective, it should be noted that 'global interoperability' of privacy frameworks has been identified by some main actors as a worthy goal in the mid-term future.

That is—in a nutshell—the stage on which the author of this book is operating in the different chapters leading up to his conclusions and recommendations. Whether the EU legislator or other international stakeholders are ready to follow his advice is of secondary importance. His contribution to the global debate is, in any case, rich and stimulating, at times thought-provoking, and well documented and worth reading.

Peter Hustinx
European Data Protection Supervisor

Brussels
December 2012

TRANSBORDER DATA FLOWS AND
DATA PRIVACY LAW

Transborder Data Flows and Data Privacy Law

CHRISTOPHER KUNER

OXFORD

UNIVERSITY PRESS

OXFORD
UNIVERSITY PRESS

Great Clarendon Street, Oxford, OX2 6DP,
United Kingdom

Oxford University Press is a department of the University of Oxford.
It furthers the University's objective of excellence in research, scholarship,
and education by publishing worldwide. Oxford is a registered trade mark of
Oxford University Press in the UK and in certain other countries

© Christopher Kuner, 2013

The moral rights of the author have been asserted

First edition published in 2013

Impression: 3

British Library Cataloguing in Publication Data

Data available

ISBN 978–0–19–967461–9

Printed in Great Britain by
CPI Group (UK) Ltd, Croydon, CR0 4YY

Preface

This book examines how the transfer of personal data across national borders is regulated under data protection and privacy law, draws conclusions about its legal nature and underlying policies, and proposes improvements based on theories of legal pluralism. Since the 1970s a number of international institutions, and over 70 countries in all regions of the world, have enacted data protection and privacy laws regulating transborder data flows, yet the topic does not seem to have received a comprehensive, internationally-oriented legal analysis since a few pioneering works in the 1980s and 1990s.

It seeks to refute the view one sometimes encounters that transborder data flow regulation is a narrow subject of interest only to data protection specialists. On the contrary, the subject has significant implications for many other areas of the law besides data protection, such as public and private international law, human rights law, and regulation of the Internet. Because of the broad scope of the topic, inspiration has been drawn from these other areas. Despite what may seem to be an emphasis on European law, I have tried to deal with the topic from a global perspective.

I have done my best to go into sufficient detail on specific topics, without covering all the intricacies of national law, and keeping in mind the maxim that 'nothing should ever be published except where the author has something new to say and can say it in such simple and clear language that all readers can understand it.'[1] The book is current as of 1 January 2013. The analysis is informed by my experience as a practising lawyer and a participant in the work of international organizations, and by information gleaned over many years from discussions with data protection regulators, diplomats, and company privacy officers. It has been written without any ideological 'agenda', and contains solely my personal views and not those of any organization with which I may be affiliated.

My first exposure to this topic occurred while working on behalf of the International Chamber of Commerce (ICC) to negotiate a set of standard contractual clauses with the European Commission. I learned much from this experience, and from colleagues such as Susan Binns, Dr Ulf Brühann, Leonardo Cevera-Navas, Pascale Gelly, Marisa Jimenez, and Rocio Mendez. I am also grateful to the ICC for the opportunity to become part of so many interesting international initiatives. Participation in meetings of the T-PD group of the Council of Europe over the last decade has been invaluable, as has the chance to prepare two reports

---

[1] F.A. Mann, unpublished manuscript, quoted in Lawrence Collins, 'F.A. Mann', in Jack Beatson and Reinhard Zimmerman (eds), *Jurists Uprooted: German-Speaking Émigré Lawyers in Twentieth-century Britain* 381 (OUP 2004), at 438.

for the OECD for which warm thanks are due to Anne Carblanc and Michael Donohue.

Many persons have provided valuable assistance and suggestions over the course of this research, in particular the following: Marty Abrams; Amit Ashkenazi; Paula Bruening; Barbara Bucknell; Cédric Burton; Prof. Fred Cate; Malcolm Crompton; Gary T. Davis; Anne-Marije Fontein-Bijnsdorp; Clarisse Girot; Prof. Graham Greenleaf; Ayesha Hassan; Dr Jörg Hladjk; Yukiko Ko; Dr Waltraut Kotschy; John Kropf; Sophie Kwasny; Olivier Matter; Pablo Palazzi; Anna Pateraki; Jörg Polakiewicz; Kenneth Propp; Olivier Proust; Florence Raynal; Anne Ruwet; Dr Eva Souhrada-Kirchmayer; Blair Stewart; Jennifer Stoddart; Dan Jerker B. Svantesson; Dr Omer Tene; Richard Thomas; Micah Thorner; and Mason Weisz. Much background research was performed during a visitorship at the Oxford Internet Institute, to which I am grateful. Ruth Anderson and her colleagues at Oxford University Press also deserve my thanks for their help in bringing this book to fruition.

I am also indebted to the law firms of Hunton & Williams and Wilson, Sonsini, Goodrich & Rosati, to the members of the European Privacy Officers Forum (EPOF) and the European Privacy Advisory Group (EPAG), and to all my clients throughout the years, for helping me to learn about the practical side of transborder data flow regulation.

Special thanks are due to the Cambridge University Centre for European Legal Studies and to Wolfson College, Cambridge, where much of this book was written while a visiting fellow. I am deeply grateful to them, and in particular to Prof. Catherine Barnard of Trinity College, Cambridge.

I would also like to express my gratitude to Peter Hustinx for taking the time from his very busy schedule to write the foreword.

This book is largely based on my PhD dissertation for Tilburg Law School of Tilburg University, the Netherlands (with some changes and updating). Many thanks are due for the valuable input provided by the members of my PhD committee, namely Dr Lee Bygrave; Prof. Paul De Hert; Dr Lokke Moerel; and Prof. Dr Spiros Simitis. And fortunate is the PhD candidate with a supervisor like Prof. Corien Prins, whose encouragement, graciousness, insight, and patience have been both crucial and exemplary.

Analysis of the legal framework for data protection has too often neglected both the practicalities of how the law actually works and its international implications. If this book succeeds in illuminating transborder data flow regulation in light of the relevant practical issues and its global impact, then it will have made a contribution to a discussion that has frequently produced more heat than light.

Christopher Kuner

Brussels
December 2012

Contents

Table of Cases

Table of Legislation

Bold references are where the legislation is reproduced in the text

DOMESTIC

List of Abbreviations

APEC	Asia-Pacific Economic Cooperation
BCR	binding corporate rules
CBPR	Cross-Border Privacy Rules
CRM	Customer Relationship Management
CSR	corporate social responsibility
DHS	Department of Homeland Security (US)
DIFC	Dubai International Financial Centre
DPA	data protection authority
DPO	data protection officer
ECJ	European Court of Justice
ECOWAS	Economic Community of West African States
EEA	European Economic Area
FTC	Federal Trade Commission (US)
GATS	General Agreement on Trade in Services
GATT	General Agreement on Tariffs and Trade
GPEN	Global Privacy Enforcement Network
ICC	International Chamber of Commerce
ICCPR	International Covenant on Civil and Political Rights
ILC	International Law Commission
ITU	International Telecommunications Union
MMOU	Multilateral Memorandum of Understanding
OAS	Organization of American States
OECD	Organisation for Economic Co-operation and Development
PIPEDA	Personal Information Protection and Electronic Documents Act (Canada)
PNR	passenger name records
SEI	Special Informatics Agency
SOX	Sarbanes–Oxley Act (US)
SWIFT	Society for Worldwide Interbank Financial Telecommunication
T-PD	Bureau of the Consultative Committee of the Convention for the Protection of individuals with Regard to the Automatic Processing of Personal Data (Council of Europe)
UAE	United Arab Emirates
UDHR	Universal Declaration of Human Rights
UNCITRAL	United Nations Commission on International Trade Law
UNESCO	United Nations Educational, Scientific and Cultural Organization
UNIDROIT	International Institute for the Unification of Private Law
W3C	World Wide Web Consortium
WTO	World Trade Organization

1

Background and Introduction

A. Growth of transborder data flows

1. The changing economic, social, and technological landscape

The global economy is undergoing an 'information explosion' that can 'unlock new sources of economic value, provide fresh insights into science and hold governments to account'.[1] There has been a 'massive growth in the complexity and volume' of global data flows, accompanied by a change in the nature of such transfers in that they no longer constitute point-to-point transmissions, but 'occur today as part of a networked series of processes made to deliver a business result'.[2] Personal data are now crucial raw materials of the global economy; data protection and privacy have emerged as issues of concern for individuals; and confidence in data

---

[1] 'Data, data everywhere—A special report on managing information', *The Economist*, 27 February 2010, at 3.

[2] See Paul M. Schwartz, 'Managing Global Data Privacy: Cross-Border Information Flows in a Networked Environment' (2009), <http://theprivacyprojects.org/wp-content/uploads/2009/08/The-Privacy-Projects-Paul-Schwartz-Global-Data-Flows-20093.pdf>, at 4.

processing and privacy protection have become important factors in enabling the acceptance of electronic commerce. The international transfer of personal data has resulted in economic growth and efficiencies that have had a positive impact around the world, while at the same time subjecting the privacy of individuals to new and increased risks.

In the 1970s, the term 'transborder data flows' was typically understood to refer to point-to-point data transfers such as the 'exchange of internal company administrative information, response to requests for service by customers, and maintenance of records concerning or describing customers or subjects'.[3] By contrast, many transborder data flows today involve multiple partners (ie, persons, organizations) communicating through networks in a distributed fashion (in particular via phenomena such as 'Web 2.0', online social networking, search engines, and cloud computing). The following are some of the main developments that have changed the landscape for transborder data flows over the last few decades.

- *The increased globalization of the world economy* As described by the World Bank, 'over the last few decades, the pace of this global integration has become much faster because of unprecedented advancements in technology, communications, science, transport and industry'.[4] This has included the wholesale reduction of capital controls (eg, exchange controls, and controls on the international sale or purchase of various financial assets),[5] and the liberalization of international trade through the succession of General Agreement on Tariffs and Trade (GATT) trade rounds and the foundation of the World Trade Organization (WTO).

- *The growing economic importance of data processing* The processing of personal data has become a vital component of economic growth. As European data protection regulators have noted, 'In some sectors, particularly in the on-line environment, personal data has become the de facto currency in exchange for on-line content'.[6] The industry for data analytics alone has been estimated to be worth over US$100 billion, and to be growing at almost 10 per cent annually.[7]

- *The social and cultural importance of online activity* With the growth of the Internet, the ability to transfer data around the world online has attained a huge importance in social and cultural terms. The Internet and other online media have become indispensable tools for individuals to communicate globally, and have furthered individual participation in the political process,

---

[3] J.M. Carroll, 'The Problem of Transnational Data Flows', in *Policy Issues in Data Protection and Privacy, Proceedings of the OECD Seminar 24th to 26th June 1974*, at 201.

[4] See <http://youthink.worldbank.org/issues/globalization/>.

[5] See International Monetary Fund, 'Capital Controls: Country Experiences with their Use and Liberalization' (17 May 2000), <http://www.imf.org/external/pubs/ft/op/op190/index.htm>.

[6] Article 29 Working Party, 'Opinion 3/2010 on the principle of accountability' (WP 173, 13 July 2010), at 5.

[7] 'Data, data everywhere' (n 1), at 4.

increased transparency of governmental activities, and promoted fundamental rights (a well-known example is the use of Internet communications and online social media in the popular 'Arab Spring' uprisings in 2011[8]).

- *The ubiquity of transborder data flows* In past decades, transborder data flows often only occurred when there was the explicit intent to transfer data internationally (eg, when a computer file was intentionally sent to a specific location in another country). Nowadays, the architecture of the Internet and technological solutions such as cloud computing mean that even a transfer to a party in the same country may result in the message or file transiting via other countries, without the sender ever being aware of this.[9] As computing devices are routinely implanted in many varieties of implements used in daily life that communicate and process personal data via the Internet (the so-called 'Internet of Things'[10]), great volumes of personal data will be transferred internationally even without the direct involvement of a human being.

- *Increase in data transfers by States and data sharing between them* States (including governments and regulatory agencies) are now transferring an ever-growing amount of personal data across national borders for purposes that can include regulatory coordination, law enforcement, and many others.

- *Interaction between the public and private sectors in the processing of personal data* There is a growing interaction between data processing by private sector organizations, governmental entities, and public authorities. For example, public authorities often seek access to commercial databases maintained by private sector entities.

- *The changing role of geography* While geography and territoriality are still the key factors for the application of data protection and privacy law, they have become less important from the business and technological points of view. Many companies structure their operations based on lines of business rather than geography, and technology allows the transfer of personal data without regard to national borders.

- *Greater direct involvement of individuals in transborder data flows* The development of new technologies and business models for processing personal data has led to a greater direct involvement of individuals in the way that their data are transferred across national borders. In particular, phenomena such

---

[8] See, eg, Journalist's Resource, 'The Arab Spring and the Internet: Research Roundup' (22 March 2012), <http://journalistsresource.org/studies/society/internet/research-arab-spring-internet-key-studies/>.

[9] See European Data Protection Supervisor, 'Opinion of the European Data Protection Supervisor on the Commission's Communication on "Unleashing the potential of Cloud Computing in Europe"', 16 November 2012, at 6, stating that cloud computing 'leads to a considerable increase of transfers of personal data over networks, involving many different parties and crossing borders between countries …', and that 'the physical location of the data is usually not known by the client …'

[10] See, eg, Commission of the European Communities, 'Communication to the European Parliament, the Council, the European Economic and Social Committee and the Committee of the Regions: The Internet of Things—An Action Plan for Europe', COM(2009) 278 final, 18 June 2009.

as electronic commerce and online social networks have made it possible for individuals to initiate the transborder transfer of personal data more easily. At the same time, it has become more difficult for individuals to determine the ways in which data are transferred, and the location where they are processed.

- *Growing danger to the privacy of individuals* These developments have all brought great economic and social benefits, but have also increased the risks of misuse of personal data and of violations of the law. For example, there has been explosive growth in the scale and sophistication of criminal attacks against users' personal data conducted via the Internet.[11] Government access to and sharing of personal data may also create risks.[12]

2. Increase in the volume of data flows

The volume of transborder data flows has grown exponentially over the last few decades, which has driven a corresponding increase in transborder data flow regulation. This growth can be seen from a few examples:

Wal-Mart, a retail giant, handles more than 1m customer transactions every hour, feeding databases estimated at more than 2.5 petabytes—the equivalent of 167 times the books in America's Library of Congress ... Facebook, a social-networking website, is home to 40 billion photos. And decoding the human genome involves analysing 3 billion base pairs—which took ten years the first time it was done, in 2003, but can now be achieved in one week. All these examples tell the same story: that the world contains an unimaginably vast amount of digital information which is getting ever vaster ever more rapidly.[13]

The application of data analytics techniques to large amounts of personal data, including processing of the data for purposes that may be different than those for which they were originally collected, is known as the phenomenon of 'big data'. Such projects typically involve the transfer of data from numerous sources without regard to geography, and can have major benefits for society:

The discovery of Vioxx's adverse drug effects, which led to its withdrawal from the market, was made possible by analysis of clinical and cost data collected by Kaiser Permanente, the California-based managed-care consortium. Had Kaiser Permanente not aggregated clinical and cost data, researchers might not have been able to attribute 27,000 cardiac arrest deaths occurring between 1999 and 2003 to use of the drug. Similarly, researchers in South Africa discovered a positive relationship between therapeutic vitamin B use and delay of progression to AIDS and death in HIV-positive patients ... Another oft-cited

---

[11] See, eg, Symantec Corp., 'Internet Security Threat Report, Volume XV' (April 2010), <http://www4.symantec.com/Vrt/wl?tu_id=SUKX1271711282503126202>.

[12] Eg, when governmental law enforcement entities access personal data held by the private sector. See, eg, 'Systematic Government Access to Private Sector Data' (special issue), 2(4) International Data Privacy Law (2012).

[13] 'Data, data everywhere' (n 1), at 3.

example is Google Flu Trends, which predicts and locates outbreaks of the flu making use of information—aggregate search queries—not originally collected with this innovative application in mind.[14]

Big data applications can have particular benefits for the developing world.[15] For example, Global Pulse, an initiative of the UN Secretary-General, conducts research and enters into partnerships with States and private sector entities to investigate how data analytics can be used to help to protect vulnerable populations, particularly in developing countries.[16] The work of Global Pulse involves data research and the development of tools all over the world, and is thus dependent on the ability to transfer data freely between different countries. A few examples of how data analytics can be used for development purposes are 'the Healthmap project ... [which] compiles disparate data from online news, eyewitness reports and expert-curated discussions, as well as validated official reports, to "achieve a unified and comprehensive view of the current global state of infectious diseases"'; and 'use of crowdsourcing following the earthquake that devastated Haiti, where a centralised text messaging system was set up to allow cell-phone users to report on people trapped under damaged buildings.'[17]

Little empirical research has been done on the exact volume of transborder data flows, but growth in Internet traffic gives an indication of the speed with which they are increasing, since much data processing is carried out on the Internet and is thus routed without regard to national borders. For example, the Cisco Visual Networking Index, a widely watched measurement of Internet usage and growth, gave the following predictions in 2011:

Annual global IP traffic will reach the zettabyte threshold (966 exabytes or nearly 1 zettabyte) by the end of 2015. In 2015, global IP traffic will reach 966 exabytes per year or 80.5 exabytes per month. Global IP traffic has increased eightfold over the past 5 years, and will increase fourfold over the next 5 years. Overall, IP traffic will grow at a compound annual growth rate (CAGR) of 32 percent from 2010 to 2015. In 2015, the gigabyte equivalent of all movies ever made will cross global IP networks every 5 minutes. Global IP networks will deliver 7.3 petabytes every 5 minutes in 2015.[18]

---

[14] Omer Tene and Jules Polenetsky, 'Big Data for All: Privacy and User Control in the Age of Analytics' (20 September 2012), at 9, <http://papers.ssrn.com/sol3/papers.cfm?abstract_id=2149364>. See also McKinsey Global Institute, 'Big data: the next frontier for innovation, competition, and productivity' (May 2011), <http://www.mckinsey.com/Insights/MGI/Research/Technology_and_Innovation/Big_data_The_next_frontier_for_innovation>, stating: 'analyzing large data sets—so-called big data—will become a key basis of competition, underpinning new waves of productivity growth, innovation, and consumer surplus'.

[15] See Global Pulse, 'Big Data for Development: Challenges and Opportunities' (May 2012), <http://www.unglobalpulse.org/sites/default/files/BigDataforDevelopment-UNGlobalPulseJune2012.pdf>, at 4, stating: 'the diffusion of data science to the realm of international development nevertheless constitutes a genuine opportunity to bring powerful new tools to the fight against poverty, hunger and disease.' See also Gillian Tett, 'Big data is watching you', *Financial Times*, 10 August 2012, <http://www.ft.com/cms/s/2/97cffaf0-e1b5-11e1-92f5-00144feab49a.html>.

[16] See <http://www.unglobalpulse.org/about-new>.

[17] Global Pulse (n 15), at 22–3.

[18] See <http://www.cisco.com/en/US/solutions/collateral/ns341/ns525/ns537/ns705/ns827/white_paper_c11-481360_ns827_Networking_Solutions_White_Paper.html>.

To give an idea of the amount of data involved in these statistics, one extabyte of data would hold approximately 36,000 years' worth of HD video, while one zet-tabyte (which is 1,000 extabytes) is the equivalent of approximately 250 billion DVDs.[19] The growth in Internet traffic is expected to be greatest in less developed regions such as Latin America, the Middle East, and Africa.[20]

Since the Internet is structured to transit data based not on geography but on technical parameters, it can be assumed that a large amount of the personal data transmitted on it must cross national borders, so that the actual route they take is unpredictable. Indeed, technological complexity and the effort required to track data sent over the Internet means that it may no longer be feasible to differentiate between transborder data flows and those that do not cross national borders. Thus, the regulatory framework for transborder data flows is in effect the same as that for data transfers on the Internet, and for the Internet itself.

The scope of data processing and its complexity have changed radically since the first regulation of transborder data flows was enacted in the 1970s. The following excerpt from an article published in 1980 described what was apparently a com-mon scenario at the time:

The health records of a Swiss national are collected by his employer in Switzerland. Using leased private (dedicated) lines procured from a series of European PTT's [Postal, Telegraph and Telephone service agencies], the employer transmits the data to corporate headquarters in Amsterdam where they are processed, stored, and aggregated with health records of other nationals working in other countries ... The employer, having received the fully processed health data, now sends it along via EURONET to the employer's insurance carrier, an Italian firm whose primary data, processing facilities are located in Spain. The insurance carrier again processes the data, stores them in Madrid on magnetic tape and issues the appropriate group health policy to the employer.[21]

The cost of transferring data over computer networks in the 1970s was so high that mainly large corporations or governments could take advantage of it.[22] The cost of Internet access today is well within the means of the ordinary citizen, and the Internet is full of free applications and services, so that cost is no longer a factor inhibiting the transborder flow of data.

In the 1970s and 1980s, transborder data flows largely took place using closed networks. This involved the use of technologies such as telephony, telefax, teletext, and Datex; international private telecommunications networks such as TYMNET and IBM1; value-added services offered on a national level such as Bildschirmtext

---

[19] Charles Arthur, 'What's a zettabyte? By 2015 the Internet will know, says Cisco', *The Guardian*, 29 June 2011, <http://www.guardian.co.uk/technology/blog/2011/jun/29/zettabyte-data-internet-cisco>.

[20] Global Pulse (n 15), at 10, stating: 'While Internet traffic is expected to grow 25–30% between 2011 and 2015 in North America, Western Europe and Japan, the figure is expected to reach or sur-pass 50% in Latin America, the Middle East and Africa ...'

[21] William L. Fishman, 'Introduction to Transborder Data Flows', 16 Stanford Journal of International Law 3, 21 (1980).

[22] Jan Freese, *International Data Flow* (Studentlitteratur 1979), at 25.

in Germany and Videotex in the UK; or corporate networks, such as SWIFT, DFN.[23] Use of these networks or services was generally limited to subscribers or closed user groups; they did not typically interact with other networks; and it was not difficult to determine the location where their use took place. By contrast, the following anonymized case studies published in 2009 indicate the current complexity of transborder data flows in the corporate world:

A marketer in Spain would use the criteria developed by the analytics vendor in India to select a list of customers from the global Customer Relationship Management (CRM) system in the U.S. which would be transferred to their call center in Mexico for execution of a telemarketing campaign to consumers in Spain. Results from the telemarketing effort from Mexico would then be fed back to the U.S. to update the information in the global CRM system.[24]

The GRP system [a global recruitment process system that a provider of technology solutions uses to recruit employees] permits interested individuals to apply for an employment position, independent of the country in which they are located or the country from which the opportunity originates ... The GRP system allows Zeta and its wholly-owned subsidiaries to assist in identification and selection of candidates, both internal and external, for employment opportunities ... [T]he GRP system leads to data transfers on demand. These data transfers cannot necessarily all be predicted in advance of a job posting. A job can be posted from South Africa to the GRP system server in Zurich, and then accessed by Zeta employees in over 100 countries. Some of these employees will send their personal data to the system. In addition, outside recruiters from these or other countries might send in data.[25]

There is a striking contrast between these scenarios, those from 1980 involving the use of proprietary communications networks and magnetic tape, and those from 2009 involving direct access to the data and an upload of the data directly using the same network. The complexity of the data flows has also changed drastically, so that it has become difficult to identify exactly which entity is initiating or controlling the data flows at a particular point in time; to localize the data flows as taking place in a specific location; and to classify the roles of the various actors involved in them.

3. Resulting legal issues

The changing landscape for transborder data flows and the dramatic growth in their volume and scope have led to a corresponding increase in the complexity of legal issues, which can be illustrated by the following examples.

- *Characterizing the activities leading to transborder data flows and the roles and obligations of the parties involved in them* Company A operates a web service

---

[23] For an overview of data transfer technologies being used at this time, see Michael Bothe and Wolfgang Kilian, *Rechtsfragen grenzüberschreitender Datenflüsse* (Verlag Dr Otto Schmidt 1992), Ch 2.
[24] Schwartz (n 2), at 13.   [25] Schwartz (n 2), at 63.

from servers located in its own country. Company A has offices in other countries, but they are only sales offices—that is, all decisions regarding the purposes and means of data processing are taken at its headquarters in its own country, and it only has servers in that country. Customers of the company in other countries go to its website and enter information, which is then processed by Company A on its servers.

Questions Is the access of the website by the individual that results in Company A processing the data in its country to be considered a 'transborder data flow'? If so, which party is exporting the data to Company A, the individual who interacts with the website, or Company A itself? If it is Company A, does it have to register or have the transfer approved by any regulatory authority, and if so, which Company A entity in which country should do so? If the exporter is Company A, how can the company ensure a legal basis for the data transfer? If the exporter is the individual, should the individual have to provide a legal basis for the transfer of his or her own data, and if so, what options are available?

- *Clarifying the policies that underlie transborder data flow regulation* A company with its headquarters in Country A is concerned about the cost of complying with the country's data protection laws. It is considering moving its company database to a newly established office in Country B, where most of its customers reside, and which would result in quicker access of its firm website by customers; Country B does not have a data protection law. Both countries have democratic systems of government, but law enforcement authorities in Country B have greater powers to compel companies to give them access to their databases.

  Questions If the company moves its data processing operations to Country B, should this be considered circumvention of the law of Country A? In answering this question, what weight should be given to the risk of law enforcement access to data in Country B?

- *Outsourcing of data processing to service providers and the interrelationship between transborder data flow regulation and applicable law issues* A data processing service provider in Country A is instructed by a company in Country B to process personal data in Country A and subsequently to transfer them back to the company in Country B. The data were sent to the service provider by the company, and originate from Country B. The data protection laws of both Country A and Country B mandate that certain protections are given to data transferred outside the country, among which is that the country's law should continue to apply to the processing.

  Questions Which country's law should apply to the processing of the data? Should the data transfer requirements of both countries apply to the transfer? Which requirements should apply if there is a conflict between them?

- *The role of technological solutions* Company A transfers personal data to Company B in a different country without data protection or privacy laws. The laws of the country where Company A is established allow transborder data flows only if the data receive an adequate level of protection in the country of data import. The data are transferred to Company B in encrypted form, so that only it can have access to them.

Questions Should the fact that the data were transferred in encrypted form satisfy the transborder data flow requirements to which Company A is subject? If so, should the encryption have to meet particular technical standards?

- *Conflicts between transborder data flow regulation and other legal requirements* 'Company X does business in many countries, including Country A, a country that lacks sufficient legal protections for personal data. It transfers personal data regarding transactions from countries all over the world to its central database located at its headquarters in Country B. Company X has taken the necessary steps so that its data processing activities are valid under the legal requirements of the countries where it does business. These legal requirements include that Company X will only process data for purposes defined at the time of collection; that it will provide a legal basis for onward transfers of the data to third parties; and that it will only transfer the data to third parties if steps are taken to provide adequate protection in the country to which the data are transferred. In addition, the consumer privacy policy of Company X states that it will use personal data only for limited specified purposes and provide adequate protection for onward transfers of personal data. Law enforcement authorities in Country A approach Company X stating that they have suspicions that certain individuals with which Company X has transacted business may be involved in illegal activities. The individuals are citizens of multiple countries, including those of Country A. These authorities then request Company X to turn over to them all records Company X holds involving transactions with such individuals over the last three years, including those stored at its database in Country B. The request is not based on a judicial order, and does not list any further details beyond the names of the individuals and the time frame in which the relevant transactions took place. The authorities state that if this request is not complied with, they will initiate criminal proceedings against the management board of Company X's subsidiary in Country A.'[26]

Questions Which legal obligations should Company X comply with, those of Country A or Country B? Should the data protection law of Country B recognize the law enforcement requirements of Country A as a legal basis to transfer the data?

These are just a few of the legal issues that arise under transborder data flow regulation, and that will be dealt with in this study.

---

[26] Quoted from International Chamber of Commerce (ICC), 'Cross-border law enforcement access to company data—current issues under data protection and privacy law', Doc. No. 373/507 (7 February 2012), <http://www.iccwbo.org/Data/Policies/2012/Cross-border-law-enforcement-access-to-company-data-current-issues-under-data-protection-and-privacy-law/>.

B. Growth of transborder data flow regulation

The growth in transborder data flows has been accompanied by a growth in rules of data protection and privacy law that regulate the transfer of personal data outside the geographical boundaries of the country of data collection and processing. Such regulation began on an international scale in the 1980s with the enactment of instruments such as the Organisation for Economic Co-operation and Development Guidelines on the Protection of Privacy and Transborder Flows of Personal Data (hereinafter: the 'OECD Guidelines');[27] the Council of Europe Convention for the Protection of Individuals with regard to Automatic Processing of Personal Data (ETS 108) (hereinafter: 'Council of Europe Convention 108');[28] the EU Data Protection Directive 95/46 (hereinafter: the 'EU Data Protection Directive' or 'the Directive');[29] and the Asia-Pacific Economic Cooperation (APEC) Privacy Framework (hereinafter: 'APEC Privacy Framework').[30] Many of these frameworks are under review; for example, on 25 January 2012 the European Commission issued a proposal for revision of the EU legal framework for data protection (including the EU Directive),[31] and similar exercises are underway in international organizations such as the Council of Europe and the OECD.

Over 70 countries have now adopted data protection or privacy laws that explicitly regulate transborder data flows. Beginning in Europe, such laws have spread to all regions of the world, including North and Latin America; the Caribbean; all Member States of the European Union and the European Economic Area, and several other European countries as well; Africa; the Near and Middle East; Eurasia; and the Asia-Pacific region. Some countries are also in the process of adopting data protection and privacy legislation that includes regulation of transborder data flows, or of amending their existing regulation. In addition, many countries are bound by international legal instruments such as the Additional Protocol to Council of Europe Convention 108, and others are eligible to participate in voluntary systems such as the APEC Privacy Framework (which by itself covers 21 countries). Transborder data flow regulation exists not only at the national level, but also at the local or regional level in a number of federal countries, and is dealt with in data sharing agreements between States. Companies and other data controllers increasingly view such regulation as a matter of high-level strategic importance, which has led to a growth of private sector regulation as well. The Appendix at the end of this

---

[27] (23 October 1980), <http://www.oecd.org/internet/interneteconomy/oecdguidelinesontheprotectionofprivacyandtransborderflowsofpersonaldata.htm>.

[28] 28 January 1981, ETS 108 (1981).

[29] Directive 95/46/EC of the European Parliament and of the Council of 24 October 1995 on the protection of individuals with regard to the processing of personal data and on the free movement of such data, [1995] OJ L281/31.

[30] APEC Privacy Framework (2005), <http://www.apec.org/Groups/Committee-on-Trade-and-Investment/~/media/Files/Groups/ECSG/05_ecsg_privacyframewk.ashx>.

[31] See <http://ec.europa.eu/justice/newsroom/data-protection/news/120125_en.htm>.

study contains English versions of provisions in data protection and privacy law instruments from around the world that regulate transborder data flows.

C. What are transborder data flows?

The application of transborder data flow regulation, and the obligations it brings, is predicated on the existence of a data transfer. There is a lack of clarity as to the meaning of the term, and regulatory instruments often use different ones without making it clear what they mean. The EU Directive refers to 'transfer to a third country of personal data' (Article 25(1)), without defining 'data transfer'; the Commission's 2012 proposal to amend the EU data protection framework[32] also fails to do so. The APEC Privacy Framework variously uses the terms 'international transfer', 'information flows across borders', 'cross-border information flow', and 'cross-border data transfer' interchangeably to refer to the movement of personal data across national borders.[33] The Canadian Personal Information Protection and Electronic Documents Act (PIPEDA) does not distinguish between domestic and international flows of data, and a 'data transfer' is considered to mean 'use' of the data by an organization.[34] The OECD Privacy Guidelines refer to 'transborder data flows', defining the term as 'movements of personal data across national borders' (§ 1(c)), while Council of Europe Convention 108 refers to 'transborder flows of personal data', defined as 'the transfer across national borders, by whatever medium, of personal data undergoing automatic processing or collected with a view to their being automatically processed' (Article 12(1)). Since the OECD Guidelines and Council of Europe Convention 108 both refer to 'transborder data flows', that is the term that is used here, but it should be understood to refer generically to all cases of data crossing national borders.

The difficulty of defining what constitutes a 'data transfer' is increased by the fact that data can cross borders not just by being actively transferred, but also by being made available to recipients in other countries.[35] The law tends to conceive of transborder data flows as if they were the result of a discrete act, such as someone pushing a button and causing data to be transferred. In fact, nowadays data transfers often take place as part of a process. This point is brought out in the following description of data flows in a system for clinical drug trials operated by a multinational pharmaceutical company:

The data flow in a clinical trial system is ongoing, and multi-directional. As the Alpha report states, data transfers 'are rarely uni-directional.' The report adds, 'The data flow

---

[32] Proposal for a Regulation of the European Parliament and of the Council on the protection of individuals with regard to the processing of personal data and on the free movement of such data (General Data Protection Regulation), COM(2012) 11 final.

[33] APEC Privacy Framework (n 30).

[34] See Office of the Privacy Commissioner of Canada, 'Guidelines for Processing Personal Data Across Borders' (2009), <http://www.priv.gc.ca/information/guide/2009/gl_dab_090127_e.pdf>, at 5.

[35] European Data Protection Supervisor (n 9), at 17.

cannot be considered a discrete event, but is rather a continuous process.' A number of interconnected systems will interact together to produce different data sets that are tailored to the specific user.[36]

In many cases, it is also not clear whether merely making personal data accessible (eg, on the Internet) should be considered to result in such a transfer, or whether this requires some active or automatic transmission of the data. This was the issue in the *Bodil Lindqvist* case[37] decided by the European Court of Justice,[38] where the defendant was charged with breach of Swedish data protection law for publishing on her Internet site personal data of a number of people working with her on a voluntary basis in a parish of the Swedish Protestant Church. The Court found that there is no data transfer to a third country within the meaning of Article 25 of the EU Data Protection Directive when an individual in a Member State loads personal data onto an Internet page which is stored on a site on which the page can be consulted and which is hosted by a natural or legal person established in that State or in another Member State, thereby making those data accessible to anyone who connects to the Internet, including people in a third country. The Court's decision was based on the fact that the information was not being sent automatically from the server to other Internet users; that there was thus no direct transfer of personal data between the person loading the information on the server and the person accessing the data from the server; that the data transfer restrictions contained in Article 25 were probably not intended to apply in such a situation; and that if a data transfer were found to exist in this case, then the restrictions of Article 25 would apply any time that information was loaded onto and made accessible via the Internet, which would make EU law applicable to the entire Internet.

The *Lindqvist* decision seems to be based partly on pragmatic considerations, such as the fact that there was no evidence that the personal data were ever actually accessed outside the EU.[39] The Court also seemed to put particular weight on the likely consequences of a contrary decision, namely that finding that a data transfer occurred in this case would effectively make the entire Internet subject to EU data protection law,[40] a consideration that has also been faced by national legislators when deciding whether to define access to data on the Internet as a 'data transfer'.[41] In addition, the Court found that the provisions on international data transfers

---

[36] Schwartz (n 2), at 41.

[37] C-101/01 [2003] ECR I-12971.

[38] The Court of Justice, the highest court of the Court of Justice of the European Union (CJEU), will be referred to throughout as the European Court of Justice (ECJ), which was its name prior to 2009.

[39] See Ulf Brühann, 'Die Veröffentlichung personenbezogener Daten im Internet als Datenschutzproblem', (2004) Datenschutz und Datensicherheit 201, 203.

[40] C-101/01 [2003] ECR I-12971, at para. 69.

[41] See, eg, Dag Wiese Schartum, 'Norway', in Peter Blume (ed), *Nordic Data Protection Law* (DJØF 2001), at 102–4, describing the concern of the Norwegian government in revising its data protection law that it should not automatically cover the entire Internet.

contained in the Directive were a 'special regime', which were never intended, in the Court's view, to have general application to the entire global Internet.[42]

Some of the Court's reasoning can be faulted. For instance, whether or not the data were actually accessed seems irrelevant, and has been largely rejected by the EU data protection authorities in their interpretation of the case;[43] rather, the key question should be whether the data *could* have been accessed. Failing to consider as data transfers situations when data were not being automatically transmitted to other countries seems untenable, given that the intention to make data available to other countries may exist just as much when they are merely made accessible as when they are actively transmitted, and that technological advancements will probably blur the distinction to a point where it can no longer be maintained.[44] But the Court's decision is praiseworthy, even visionary, in its willingness to consider the international implications of its ruling, and in its decision not to apply the EU restrictions on international data transfers past a point of reasonableness.[45]

Following the *Lindqvist* case, there continues to be a lack of clarity regarding the definition of 'data transfer', particularly with regard to situations in which individuals input their personal data onto an Internet site. The question of whether a data transfer takes place is often used as a proxy for determining whether the data protection law of a particular country or region is applicable to the processing,[46] with the boundaries of the question being that, on the one hand, data controllers should not be able to evade their responsibility by claiming that no data transfer has taken place,[47] while on the other hand, not every interaction of an individual with a website should be considered to be a data transfer;[48] within these broad parameters, the definition of data transfer depends largely on the facts of the particular case.

---

[42] C-101/01 [2003] ECR I-12971, at para. 69, stating: 'If Article 25 of Directive 95/46 were interpreted to mean that there is "transfer [of data] to a third country" every time that personal data are loaded onto an internet page, that transfer would necessarily be a transfer to all the third countries where there are the technical means needed to access the internet. The special regime provided for by Chapter IV of the directive would thus necessarily become a regime of general application, as regards operations on the internet.'

[43] See, eg, UK Information Commissioner, 'The Eighth Data Protection Principle and international data transfers' (30 May 2006), at para 1.3.4, stating: 'In practice, data are often loaded onto the internet with the intention that the data be accessed in a third country, and, as this will usually lead to a transfer, the principle in the Lindqvist case will not apply in such circumstances'.

[44] Dan Jerker B. Svantesson, 'Privacy, the Internet and Transborder Data Flows: An Australian Perspective', 4 Masaryk University Journal of Law and Technology 1, 15 (2010), stating: 'While it is true that Lindqvist could not transfer the content of her website to an Internet user that was not connected to the Internet at the time, or who did not wish to take the steps necessary to visit her website, that is no different to the fact that a TV station cannot provide TV programs to somebody who does not turn on their TV, or who does not chose the TV station's particular channel. Consequently, the Court's justification of their approach, by reference to the relevant technology, is weak indeed.'

[45] Svantesson (n 44), at 16.   [46] See Chapter 6.

[47] See Article 29 Working Party, 'Working document on determining the international application of EU data protection law to personal data processing on the Internet by non-EU based websites' (WP 56, 30 May 2002), at 9, stating that the objective of applicable law rules concerning non-EU websites is 'to ensure that individuals enjoy the protection of national data protection laws ...'

[48] Article 29 Working Party (n 47), stating: 'the Working Party is of the opinion that not any interaction between an Internet user in the EU and a web site based outside the EU leads necessarily to the application of EU data protection law'.

Since the existence of a data transfer results in obligations on the part of the data controller to provide a legal basis for the transfer, determining that one has taken place is often a type of protective measure to ensure that local data protection law will continue to apply after the data are transferred.[49] In practice, the likelihood that a data transfer will be found to have occurred is higher in circumstances when the data controller has an establishment in the country of the individual whose data are processed, when the controller is in some way targeting the individual, or when the controller has some degree of control over the means used by the individual to process the data. On the other hand, a transfer is less likely to be found when the individual has initiated contact with the controller without being targeted, when the controller does not have any operations in the individual's country, or when the controller does not exercise control over the purpose or means which the individual uses to process the data.

The definition of data transfer will be further considered later on.[50] Terms such as 'transborder data flows' and 'mere transit' will be broadly construed; technology, business models, and trends regarding online activities of users are changing so fast that a narrow definition would omit many interesting phenomena from analysis.

D. The changing role of the individual

Individuals have a much greater ability to initiate transborder data flows than ever before. For example, a person can now book a hotel room in a foreign country via an Internet website, whereas in past decades this would have required more effort and cost (eg, by telephoning the hotel or sending a letter), or could only have been done via an intermediary (eg, a travel agency or hotel booking service). Internet services such as online social networks have also given individuals a greater power to communicate across borders. But along with this increased power goes a growing concern about the role that individuals play in the online environment. For example, it is easy for individuals to communicate across borders without understanding who is processing their data and the terms under which they are processed, and to transfer the data of third parties without them ever knowing about this.

EU data protection law contains an exemption covering the processing of data 'by a natural person in the course of a purely personal or household activity'.[51]

---

[49] See, eg, European Commission, 'Communication from the Commission to the European Parliament, the Council, the European Economic and Social Committee and the Committee of the Regions, Safeguarding Privacy in a Connected World—A European Data Protection Framework for the 21st Century', COM(2012) 9/3, 25 January 2012, at 10, stating: 'Individuals' rights *must continue to be ensured when personal data is transferred* from the EU to third countries, and whenever individuals in Member States are targeted and their data is used or analysed by third country service providers' (emphasis added). See also Chapter 6.B.

[50] See Chapter 8.C.

[51] Article 3(2). See also Article 29 Working Party, 'Opinion 5/2009 on online social networking' (WP 163, 12 June 2009), at 5.

Thus, the protection of an individual's private sphere implies that they should not have to comply with data protection requirements when performing intimate personal activities such as keeping a diary or writing a private letter. This exemption applies not only to transborder data flow regulation, but also to other obligations of a data controller. However, it has special relevance to the transborder flow of data, since many of the online services in the context of which it applies involve the processing of personal data in other countries.

Application of this exemption to data processing in an online environment is becoming increasingly problematic. For example, many online services allow individuals to input their own personal data directly (which routinely involves transferring the data across borders), and data protection authorities have found that the exemption may apply to situations when individuals enter information about their 'personal, family or household affairs' into an online social networking site.[52] However, it is often difficult to determine if such processing should be considered the individual's own personal activity, a commercial activity by the website, or both.[53] In addition, an individual can violate the data protection rights of a third party more easily in the context of the Internet, such as by posting a private photo on a social networking site (and thus making it available for download around the world) without the third party expecting it. There is thus a fine line to be drawn between not overburdening intimate personal and private activities, on the one hand, and not exempting individuals who transfer personal data from all responsibility, on the other hand.

E. Differentiating data transfers from 'mere transit'

Transborder data flow regulation typically does not apply in situations where data are merely 'transiting' across territory. For example, Article 4(1)(c) of the EU Data Protection Directive provides that EU data protection law shall apply also when a data controller 'is not established on Community territory and, for purposes of processing personal data makes use of equipment, automated or otherwise, situated on the territory of the said Member State, *unless such equipment is used only for purposes of transit through the territory of the Community*' (emphasis added). The regulation of transborder data flows under the UK Data Protection Act also applies only to 'data transfers', but not to 'mere transit', defined as situations where data are routed through one country on their way to another one.[54]

This means that, for example, a telecommunications provider without a fixed place of business in the EU, but that maintains a telecommunications network over which data flow in and out of the EU, is not subject to EU data protection law (and thus also to transborder data flow regulation under the Directive) to the

---

[52] Article 29 Working Party (n 51), at 3.
[53] See the discussion in European Data Protection Supervisor (n 9), at 9–10.
[54] UK Information Commissioner (n 43), at para 1.3.2.

extent that such equipment is only used for 'transit' of data. Another example of mere transit is data routing on the Internet, which consists of a router finding the best path for a data packet to travel and then forwarding it on.[55] The policy behind this exemption is that in cases of mere transit of data the rights and freedoms of EU citizens are not affected.[56]

The Directive does not explain what constitutes 'transit', but the Article 29 Working Party has defined it as 'for example in the case of telecommunication networks (cables) or postal services which only ensure that communications transit through the Union in order to reach third countries'.[57] The Working Party goes on to note that this exception should be subject to a narrow interpretation.[58] However, the extent of the distinction between 'mere transit' and data transfers covered by data protection law remains uncertain.

F. Scope of the study

Only *legal* issues relevant to the regulation of transborder data flows will be covered, and only those that arise under data protection and privacy law (unless otherwise noted). Such regulation exists in other areas of the law as well (eg, under export control restrictions, media law, tax law) that will not be examined, since they either involve the processing of non-personal data or are only peripherally related to data protection and privacy.[59]

Many data protection laws regulate the transfer of personal data to third parties apart from specific regulation of *transborder* data flows. For example, Japanese law restricts data transfers to third parties in general,[60] without containing a specific provision on international data transfers. While such general restrictions on data transfers may restrict international transfers as well, including them would exceed

---

[55] For a description of data routing on the Internet, see 'Routing 101: the Basics', <http://www.cisco.com/en/US/netsol/ns339/ns392/ns399/ns400/networking_solutions_white_paper0900a-ecd802d5489.shtml>.

[56] See Spiros Simitis and Ulrich Dammann, *EU-Datenschutzrichtlinie* (Nomos-Verlag 1997), at 130.

[57] Article 29 Working Party, 'Opinion 8/2010 on applicable law' (WP 179, 16 December 2010), at 23.

[58] Article 29 Working Party (n 57), stating: 'As this is an exception to the equipment criterion, it should be subject to a narrow interpretation. It should be noted that the effective application of this exception is becoming infrequent: in practice, more and more telecommunication services merge pure transit and added value services, including for instance spam filtering or other manipulation of data at the occasion of their transmission. The simple "point to point" cable transmission is disappearing gradually. This should also be kept in mind when reflecting on the revision of the data protection framework.'

[59] For a discussion of transborder data flow regulation in areas such as media law, taxation, and telecommunications law, see Anne W. Branscomb, 'Global Governance of Global Networks: A Survey of Transborder Data Flow in Transition', 36 Vanderbilt Law Review 985 (1983); John M. Eger, 'Emerging Restrictions on Transnational Data Flows: Privacy Protection or Non-Tariff Trade Barriers?', 10 Law and Policy in International Business 1055 (1978).

[60] Kojinjoho no hogo ni kansuru horitsu [Japanese Personal Information Protection Act], Law No. 57 of 2003, Article 23.

the scope of this study. Thus, it is limited to examining rules that specifically regulate the flow of data across national borders, with a few exceptions.

The concept of 'regulation' will be broadly construed to include all types of conditions, limitations, and restrictions on the transfer of data across national borders. For example, some data protection laws require data exporters to register transborder data flows with a regulatory authority before they are carried out,[61] which may involve considerable effort, and can impede or slow down data transfers. It also encompasses measures that private actors take, whether or not they have binding legal force, which limit or constrain the transfer of personal data across national borders. Many actions of private parties affect, influence, or restrict the transfer of personal data across national borders, even if they may lack the overriding legal quality of governmental regulation. Private sector instruments such as contractual clauses, internal company policies, and codes of practice are becoming more widely used to structure and protect international data transfers, and may have binding legal value, such as through contract law or regulatory approval. Schemes whereby instruments used by the private sector are either drafted in advance by public authorities (eg, the EU-approved standard contractual clauses[62]) or approved by them (eg, 'binding corporate rules' or BCRs in the EU) are becoming increasingly common, resulting in a patchwork of private and public regulation.[63] Indeed, the inherently international nature of transborder data flows means that they are not easily susceptible to a single regulatory solution, and a mixture of public and private sector regulation may be the most effective way to deal with them. This broad definition of 'regulation' is in line with modern regulatory scholarship.[64]

This study is concerned mainly with international flows of *personal* data, defined as data relating to an identified or identifiable natural person (ie, an individual).[65]

---

[61] See, eg, Argentina Personal Data Protection Act 2000, Article 21(2)(e); Austrian Data Protection Act 2000, § 17 in conjunction with § 19 no. 5; Croatian Act on Personal Data Protection (12 June 2003), no. 1364-2003 (as amended by Act on Amendments to the Personal Data Protection Act, No. 2616-2006), Article 14(10); Dutch Data Protection Act, § 28 lit. e; French Data Protection Act, § 23 in conjunction with § 30; Polish Data Protection Act, § 41(7).

[62] See Commission Decision 2010/87/EU of 5 February 2010 on standard contractual clauses for the transfer of personal data to processors established in third countries under Directive 95/46/EC of the European Parliament and of the Council, [2010] OJ L39/5; Commission Decision 2004/915/EC of 27 December 2004 amending Decision 2001/497/EC as regards the introduction of an alternative set of standard contractual clauses for the transfer of personal data to third countries, [2004] OJ L385/74.

[63] See Christopher Marsden, *Internet Co-Regulation: European Law, Regulatory Governance and Legitimacy in Cyberspace* (CUP 2011), at 44, stating: 'The role of corporations, consumers and states in inter-meshed webs of regulatory activity is now accepted by legal theorists …'; Bert-Jaap Koops, 'Criteria for normative technology: the acceptability of "code as law" in light of democratic and constitutional values', in Roger Brownsword and Karen Yeung (eds), *Regulating Technologies: Legal Futures, Regulatory Frames and Technological Fixes* 161 (Hart 2008), at 161, stating: 'Traditionally, the acceptability of "private" regulation can be and has been interpreted separately from acceptability of "public" regulation, but a sharp distinction between public and private regulation can no longer be made as we are moving towards a world of polycentric governance'.

[64] See Colin J. Bennett and Charles D. Raab, *The Governance of Privacy* (MIT Press 2006), at 117–19.

[65] See EU Data Protection Directive (n 29), Article 2(a).

Thus, for the most part it does not examine flows of non-personal data, or data that can only identify a legal person (eg, a company). Distinguishing what are and are not personal data can be a difficult exercise, and the term can have different meanings in different legal systems.[66] Moreover, advances in modern computer technologies now allow an ever-increasing variety of data that may previously have been considered non-personal or anonymous to be tied to an individual, given enough time and computing power.[67] However, the limitation to personal data is necessary since most regulation focuses on it, and to make it clear that data that are clearly non-personal will not be covered (eg, data about logistics shipments, weather patterns, statistical information).

Regulatory obligations under data protection and privacy law differ based on whether the party processing personal data is deemed to be a 'data controller' (ie, a party determining the purposes and means of data processing) or a 'data processor' (ie, a party processing data on the instruction of a data controller),[68] and there is considerable disagreement about what these terms mean in practice. Data processing by both types of parties will be covered here.

Certain types of data flows carried out by the public sector (eg, those conducted for law enforcement purposes) may give rise to special issues. Warnings were already being made in the 1970s about drawing a sharp boundary between data privacy rules in the public and private sectors,[69] which are even more relevant today, since 'the distinction between activities of the private sector and of the law enforcement sector is blurring'.[70] Law enforcement entities often seek access to personal data processed by the private sector; for example, the EU Data

---

[66] *Compare* Article 29 Working Party, 'Opinion 2/2002 on the use of unique identifiers in telecommunication terminal equipments: the example of IPv6' (WP 58, 30 May 2002), at 3, concluding that IP addresses are protected by EU data protection law, *with Columbia Pictures, Inc. v Bunnell*, 245 FRD 443, 69 FedRServ3d 173 (C.D. Cal. 2007), in which a US federal court found that IP addresses were not covered by the term 'personal information' contained in the defendants' website privacy policy.

[67] See, eg, Paul Ohm, 'Broken Promises of Privacy: Responding to the Surprising Failure of Anonymization', 57 UCLA Law Review 1701, (2010), stating: 'Computer scientists have recently undermined our faith in the privacy-protecting power of anonymization, the name for techniques that protect the privacy of individuals in large databases by deleting information like names and social security numbers. These scientists have demonstrated that they can often "reidentify" or "deanonymize" individuals hidden in anonymized data with astonishing ease.'

[68] Essentially, the data controller is subject to most compliance responsibilities, while a data processor is responsible for complying with the instructions given to it by the controller. See, eg, Article 29 Working Party, 'Opinion 1/2010 on the concepts of "controller" and "processor"' (WP 169, 16 February 2010).

[69] See Frits W. Hondius, 'International Data Protection Action', in *Policy Issues in Data Protection and Privacy, Proceedings of the OECD Seminar 24th to 26th June 1974*, 208, at 216, stating: 'We should also warn against drawing too sharp a boundary between rules on data privacy in the private or the public sector. Not only do certain activities take place in one country in the private and in another country in the public sphere but there is also intensive interchange between the two sectors (for example public bodies entrusting certain operations to private firms)'.

[70] Opinion of the European Data Protection Supervisor on Communication from the Commission to the European Parliament, the Council, the Economic and Social Committee and the Committee of the Regions, 'A comprehensive approach on personal data protection in the European Union' (14 January 2011), at 9.

Retention Directive[71] mandates that Internet and telecommunications service providers retain certain types of data generated by their users, and make such data available to law enforcement authorities upon request. The volume and scope of such requests have increased, in some cases even requiring private sector entities to monitor communications of third persons on an ongoing basis.[72] Given the growing interaction between data processing in the private and public sectors, which routinely involves the transfer of personal data across national borders, it makes little sense to consider the two sectors separately with regard to the regulation of transborder data flows.

Much of the discussion will involve European Union law, since the EU has the most long-standing, influential, and complex transborder data flow regulation. However, this study is global in scope, and the analysis it provides is intended to apply to all regions of the world. It purposely does not delve into the minutiae of national regulatory requirements, and focuses on the main jurisprudential themes.

G. Towards a normative framework

1. Conceptual questions

Several factors make it difficult to develop a normative framework against which to measure the quality and success of data protection law (of which regulation of transborder data flows is a component).

First, there is disagreement between legal systems about how concepts such as 'data protection' and 'privacy' are to be understood. Data protection can be regarded as a specific aspect of privacy that gives rights to individuals in how data identifying them or pertaining to them are processed, and subjects such processing to a defined set of safeguards. 'Privacy' can be seen as a concept that is both broader than and independent from data protection, though there is significant overlap between the two. Generally speaking, data protection (sometimes also referred to as 'informational privacy') deals with the legality of processing data regarding an identified or identifiable individual, while privacy deals with protection of an individual's 'personal space';[73] however, the two are closely related and can seldom be

---

[71] Directive 2006/24/EC of the European Parliament and of the Council of 15 March 2006 on the retention of data generated or processed in connection with the provision of publicly available electronic communications services or of public communications networks and amending Directive 2002/58/EC, [2006] OJ L105/54.

[72] See ICC (n 26).

[73] See, eg, Case T-194/04 *Bavarian Lager v Commission* [2007] ECR-II 04523, para. 118 (partially reversed by the ECJ, Case C-28/08 P *Bavarian Lager* [2010] ECR I-06055), where the European Court of First Instance stated: 'it should also be emphasized that the fact that the concept of "private life" is a broad one, in accordance with the case-law of the European Court of Human Rights, and that the right to the protection of personal data may constitute one of the aspects of the right to respect for private life … does not mean that all personal data necessarily fall within the concept of "private life"'.

neatly distinguished.[74] In European law, 'privacy' includes issues relating to the protection of an individual's 'personal space' that go beyond data protection, such as 'private, family and home life, physical and moral integrity, honour and reputation, avoidance of being placed in a false light, non-revelation of irrelevant and embarrassing facts, unauthorised publication of private photographs, protection against misuse of private communications, protection from disclosure of information given or received by the individual confidentially.'[75] Privacy is also a concept that must be determined based on the social customs of the particular society in question.[76] Transborder data flow regulation relates to the processing of personal data and is thus, strictly speaking, a question of data protection rather than privacy law, though the issues involved are closely linked in many ways, and thus reference to privacy will sometimes be made.

Secondly, the legal nature of data protection law is an important factor in determining the normative framework for transborder data flow regulation. Thus, whether a particular area of the law is considered to be private law, public law, administrative law, human rights law, commercial law, or some other type of law will influence what criteria are used for determining how it should be evaluated. However, such classification is particularly difficult with regard to data protection law, since it is a mixture of various types of law:

> Data protection legislation will typically contain provisions of a public law nature, relating to an authority and its duties and decisions. But the law will also often include civil law provisions, typically on liability for data protection violations. The provisions of data protection legislation may therefore have to be qualified as belonging to different areas of law, to which different relevant connection criteria are assigned.[77]

The hybrid nature of data protection law can be seen by the example of the EU Data Protection Directive, which sets forth two goals, namely furtherance of the free flow of personal data within the EU internal market, and achievement of a high level of data protection throughout the EU.[78] Thus, the Directive has both economic motivations (promoting the free flow of data) and human rights motivations (protecting fundamental rights to data protection). The normative framework

---

[74] See, eg, James Griffin, *On Human Rights* (OUP 2008), at 229, who describes the relationship between data protection and privacy as follows: 'The right to informational privacy protects us against people's access to certain knowledge about us. The right to the privacy of space and life protects us against intrusions into that space and into that part of our life—say, into our married or family life. These two rights overlap in their protections, but, on the face of it, are different'. See also Roger Brownsword and Morag Goodwin, *Law and Technologies of the Twenty-First Century* (CUP 2012), at 308.

[75] Parliamentary Assembly of the Council of Europe, Resolution 428, para. C2 (1970).

[76] See Alan Westin, *Privacy and Freedom* (Atheneum 1970), at 12.

[77] Jon Bing, 'Data Protection, Jurisdiction and the Choice of Law', [1999] Privacy Law & Policy Reporter 92, 93, also available at <http://www.austlii.edu.au/au/journals/PLPR/1999/65.html>.

[78] See Article 1 of the Directive, stating that its object is both to 'protect the fundamental rights and freedoms of natural persons, and in particular their right to privacy with respect to the processing of personal data', and to ensure that 'Member States shall neither restrict nor prohibit the free flow of personal data between Member States for reasons connected with the protection afforded under paragraph 1.'

is determined in large part by the aim of regulation and the policies it pursues, so that it is more difficult to determine which framework should apply when regulation is motivated by diverse goals. Regulation to further economic interests is generally based on a rationale that it is necessary to overcome 'market failures',[79] but regulation may also be enacted for reasons other than economic efficiency, such as to further a desirable social policy,[80] and economic efficiency cannot serve as the sole criterion for regulation that is designed to advance fundamental rights.[81]

Thirdly, transborder data flow regulation takes a variety of divergent forms, which makes it more difficult to arrive at a scheme for its normative evaluation.[82] Such regulation is based not only on legislation, but may also include private law instruments such as contractual clauses between parties transferring personal data across borders, as well as non-binding instruments like codes of practice. With regard to one example illustrating the differences between legal systems, in the US there is a greater resistance to legal regulation of privacy and a greater reliance on private sector and technological solutions, whereas in the EU government regulation and regulatory agencies play a greater role.[83]

Fourthly, transborder data flow regulation requires consideration of many areas of law, including human rights law, contract law, public and private international law, EU law, and others. It will be necessary to go into each of these areas in sufficient detail, without dealing with them exhaustively.

2. Normative theories

Transborder data flow regulation involves norms arising from fundamental rights law, economic regulation, law enforcement requirements, and private sector practices; legal sources, such as national law, regional agreements, and international treaties; and actors such as individuals, companies, data protection regulators, national governments, and law enforcement authorities. The diversity of actors, norms, and policy goals makes it impossible to construct an overarching framework that could

---

[79] See Robert Baldwin, Martin Cave, and Martin Lodge, *Understanding Regulation: Theory, Strategy, and Practice* (2nd edn, OUP 2012), at 15, stating: 'many of the rationales for regulating can be described as instances of "market failure". Regulation in such cases is argued to be justified because the untolled marketplace will, for some reason, fail to produce behavior or results in accordance with the public interest'.

[80] Baldwin, Cave, and Lodge (n 79), at 23.

[81] Baldwin, Cave, and Lodge (n 79), at 26, stating: 'questions of justice ... cannot be answered by economists' appeals to efficiency and distributional questions ... have to be made on the basis of grounds other than efficiency.' See also Ronald Dworkin, 'Is Wealth a Value?', (1980) 9 Journal of Legal Studies 191.

[82] See Baldwin, Cave, and Lodge (n 79), at 37, stating: 'if it is the case that a regulatory regime involves numbers of regulators of different kinds—state and non-state, national and trans-national, public interest and private/commercial—there are likely to be complex interactions or legitimation claims, numbers of competing conceptions of regulatory quality, and a variety of processes for furthering legitimation claims.'

[83] See Charles D. Raab and Paul De Hert, 'Tools for Technology Regulation: Seeking Analytical Approaches Beyond Lessig and Hood', in Roger Brownsword and Karen Yeung (eds), *Regulating Technologies: Legal Futures, Regulatory Frames and Technological Fixes* 263 (Hart 2008), at 268 fn 8.

reconcile the various legal conflicts and issues. Indeed, suggesting a grand scheme to 'solve' the problems presented by transborder data flow regulation diverts attention from other possibilities which, even if they do not represent a complete solution, can help to deal with some of the major issues. This study will therefore describe systematically the relevant issues and problems through the perspective of legal pluralism, which is defined as a situation based on 'the existence of a multiplicity of distinct and diverse normative systems, and the likelihood of clashes of authority-claims and competition for primacy amongst these ... It emphasizes the value of diversity and difference amongst various national and international normative systems and levels of governance, and the undesirability and implausibility of constitutional approaches which seek coherence between these systems.'[84] Individual steps will also be suggested that could reduce the scope of the problems to a more manageable level, drawing on different areas of law.

Any regulation is enacted to further certain goals or policies,[85] and it must be asked what policies transborder data flow regulation is supposed to further; how these policies are articulated; whether such regulation actually does advance them; and whether they are justifiable. Examination of the policies and purposes for which regulation was enacted is used as a method of evaluation in other areas as well, such as EU law[86] and public international law.[87] It is also necessary to examine basic conditions of regulatory 'craftsmanship'—that is, what substantive and procedural characteristics regulation should exhibit.[88]

Theories concerning the regulation of information technology are helpful for evaluating the regulation of transborder data flows, since the two areas share a number of characteristics. In particular, both of them involve issues of economic efficiency and of fundamental rights; are subject to regulation under both traditional legislation and private sector instruments; and are inherently international in nature. Moreover, perhaps the majority of transborder data flows occurs online, making theories of technology regulation particularly relevant. Koops has summarized the views of a number of authors who have sought to develop theories of how technologies can be regulated, and has divided them into primary (eg, human rights and other moral values, the rule of law, and democracy) and secondary criteria (eg,

---

[84] Gráinne de Búrca, 'The European Court of Justice and the International Legal Order after *Kadi*', 51 Harvard International Law Journal 1, 12, 32 (2010).

[85] See Chris Reed, 'How to Make Bad Law: Lessons from Cyberspace', 73 Modern Law Review 903, 904 (2010), stating: 'a fundamental aim of any law ... is to influence behaviour to some useful end.'

[86] See Hannes Rössler, 'Interpretation of EU Law', in Jürgen Basedow, Klaus J. Hopt, Reinhard Zimmermann, and Andreas Stier (eds), *Max Planck Encyclopedia of European Private Law* (OUP 2012), at 979.

[87] See Vienna Convention on the Law of Treaties (adopted on 23 May 1969, entered into force on 27 January 1980) 1155 UNTS 331, Article 31; Nicola Vennemann, 'Application of International Human Rights Conventions to Transboundary State Acts', in Rebecca M. Bratspies and Russell A. Miller (eds), *Transboundary Harm in International Law: Lessons from the Trailsmelter Arbitration* 295 (CUP 2006), at 301–2 (note that Vennemann cites Article 27 of the Vienna Convention but seems to mean Article 31).

[88] See, eg, Baldwin, Cave, and Lodge (n 79), at 27; Lon L. Fuller, *The Morality of Law* (2nd edn, Yale University Press 1969), at 39.

transparency of rule-making, accountability, efficiency).[89] None of these criteria provide a complete answer by themselves to the questions raised by transborder data flow regulation, but they will be drawn on in combination throughout.

3. Conclusions

As will be explained in more detail in Chapter 8, transborder data flow regulation is an example of a pluralistic legal framework, and the norms, parties, and institutions that it involves are so diverse and fragmented that they cannot be analysed under a single regulatory theory. In keeping with theories of legal pluralism, various criteria (fundamental rights, efficiency, transparency, accountability, etc.) suitable to each of its constituent elements will be used to evaluate them as appropriate.

[89] Koops (n 63), at 169.

2

International Regulation of Transborder Data Flows

A. Introduction

Beginning in the 1970s in Europe, transborder data flow regulation has spread around the world. A number of instruments regulating transborder data flows have been enacted on an international scale, some legally binding, and others not. The variety of instruments, the diversity of international organizations that have enacted them, and the failure to agree on a global standard for data protection have meant that there is a lack of overall global harmonization. Some of the leading regulatory instruments are being revised, with an outcome that is uncertain. These developments have led to legal fragmentation, with different types of regulation emerging and a variety of international and regional institutions to deal with them (it should be noted that the distinction between 'international' and 'regional' regulation is to some extent arbitrary, and certain instruments could be classified in either camp).

While in some cases instruments enacted at the international level can have direct effect and thus provide a legal basis for individuals to exercise their rights,[1] in most cases the instruments discussed in this chapter either apply solely at a horizontal level between States (eg, Council of Europe Convention 108), or are not legally binding (eg, the OECD Guidelines). Thus, in practice data protection rights are generally asserted under national regulation or private sector instruments as discussed in Chapter 4.

B. Early transborder data flow regulation

The 'beginnings' of transborder data flow regulation constitute the period when the first data protection laws were enacted in the 1970s and 1980s, the first of which is considered to be that of the German federal state of Hessen that was adopted in 1970 and did not contain any provisions regulating transborder data flows.[2] Shortly thereafter, many European countries enacted data protection laws containing such regulation,[3] which fall into three main categories:

- requiring an explicit authorization from the data protection authority before transferring personal data outside the country (eg, in Austria,[4] Norway,[5] and Sweden[6]);
- adopting verbatim the provisions of Article 12 of Council of Europe Convention 108 (eg, in Irish law[7]); or

---

[1] This is the case for certain provisions of the EU Data Protection Directive. See, eg, Joined Cases C-468/10 and C-469/10 *ASNEF and FECEMD v Administración del Estado* [2011] ECR I-0000; Joined Cases C-465/00 and C-138/01 *Rechnungshof* [2003] ECR I-4989.

[2] Hessisches Datenschutzgesetz, 7 October 1970.

[3] For an overview of transborder data flow restrictions in early data protection laws, see Michael Bothe and Wolfgang Kilian, *Rechtsfragen grenzüberschreitender Datenflüsse* (Verlag Dr Otto Schmidt 1992), at 529–65.

[4] Österreichisches Datenschutzgesetz vom 18.10.1978, §§ 32, 34. The Austrian Act also required authorization for any access of a database in Austria from abroad, or if any part of the data processing was performed abroad. See Hans-Joachim Mengel, *Internationale Organisationen und transnationaler Datenschutz* (Wissenschaftlicher Autoren-Verlag 1984), at 156–7.

[5] See Mengel (n 4), at 156.   [6] Swedish Data Act of 1973, Article 11.

[7] Irish Data Protection Bill, 1987.

- requiring that either the individual whose data were transferred had to consent to the transfer, or that the country of import had to have a data protection law with a similar level of protection (eg, in Finland[8]).

Even within the same geographic region and among laws that demonstrated a number of similarities, there were important differences in the approaches taken. For example, in the 1970s, the Swedish, Norwegian, and Danish data protection acts were similar in the way that they regulated data exports, but the Swedish Act was enforced more strictly, the Norwegian Act contained a number of exceptions, and the Danish Act generally allowed transfers without restrictions.[9]

In some cases, regulation applied to data imports as well as data exports. One example was the Austrian Data Protection Act, which covered imports of data to service providers in Austria from foreign clients,[10] since it was believed that such providers would have to export the data back to their clients later on, so that data imports would necessarily lead to data exports.[11] The concept of a 'data import' also included direct access of a foreign database from Austria.[12] Similarly, the Data Protection Act of Luxembourg provided that users in the country accessing a foreign database had to obtain government approval.[13]

At the time these early laws were drafted, the transborder flow of personal data seems to have been regarded as the exception rather than the rule,[14] but there was concern about the possibility of circumventing legal protections on data processing by transferring personal data to countries without data protection laws and performing the processing there.[15] In the 1970s and 1980s, data transferred internationally tended to be predominantly non-personal, such as statistics, weather information, aeroplane traffic information, and the like.[16] At this time, concern about circumvention of the law may have been increased by public statements that companies were prepared to transfer their data processing to countries with less stringent data protection regimes.[17]

---

[8] Finnish Personal Data File Act and Personal Data File Decree, 30 April 1987, § 22.

[9] Jon Bing, 'Transnational Data Flows and the Scandinavian Data Protection Legislation', 24 Scandinavian Studies in Law 65, 75 (1980).

[10] Österreichisches Datenschutzgesetz vom 18.10.1978, § 33.

[11] See Lucius N. Wochner, *Der Persönlichkeitsschutz im grenzüberschreitenden Datenverkehr* (Schulthess Polygraphischer Verlag 1981), at 180–2.

[12] Österreichisches Datenschutzgesetz vom 18.10.1978, § 34(2).

[13] Luxembourg Data Protection Act of 31 March 1979, § 5(2). See Wochner (n 11), at 215.

[14] See Frits W. Hondius, 'International Data Protection Action', in *Policy Issues in Data Protection and Privacy, Proceedings of the OECD Seminar 24th to 26th June 1974*, at 208, stating: 'the vast majority of data processing operations take place within the limits of national frameworks, either in the private or in the public sector'.

[15] See Chapter 5.C.2.

[16] See Jan Freese, *International Data Flow* (Studentlitteratur 1979), at 19, stating: 'data flows presently consist mostly of technical, economic and scientific information and to a lesser extent personal data'.

[17] See Mengel (n 4), at 10, describing a case in 1974 in which a company announced publicly that it was going to transfer its data processing to Luxembourg because that country's data protection laws were less 'authoritarian' than those in Germany.

C. Protection of informational sovereignty

The main reason for enactment of transborder data flow regulation has been to ensure data protection rights and protect privacy, based on the policy goals discussed in Chapter 5. However, another concern only peripherally related to privacy has arisen from time to time, namely worries about the loss of a State's 'informational sovereignty'[18] through uncontrolled transborder flows of personal data.[19] The basis for these concerns was described as follows in 1974 with regard to data flows from Canada to the US:

First is the broad perspective of concern for national sovereignty and cultural identity resulting from the aggregation of transborder electronic traffic and information transfer. Second is the perspective of the administration of the affairs of the state. The territorial basis of national jurisdiction and therefore of regulatory law is probably the most immediate source of frustration for a country wishing to exercise control, for administrative reasons, over the storage and use of data about its citizens located beyond its own borders. Third, there is the perspective of the individual and the legal difficulties that may arise in his attempt to redress wrongs in respect of personal data about him stored abroad.[20]

Countries such as Sweden explicitly voiced similar concerns,[21] and a case that arose in France seemed to emphasize the risks that information dependency could pose:

The risks of dependence on foreign data-processing systems were exemplified by the case of the Dresser Corporation, a major US supplier of oil field and pipeline equipment and related technology. Dresser's French subsidiary conducted its engineering and design work by accessing a computer program located at corporate headquarters in the United States,

---

[18] See Report of the Commission on Transnational Corporations of the UN Economic and Social Council of 6 July 1981, reprinted in Mengel (n 4), at 198–9, stating: 'If a country lacks data about itself and the international system in which it finds itself—because of a very limited capacity to collect, access, or process them—it can be said to lack pertinent decision-making capacity about its own future. Seen from this angle, an extension of the concept of sovereignty to include "informational sovereignty" is not surprising.'

[19] See, eg, Mengel (n 4), at 16, quoting a statement made in 1979 by a Canadian minister calling for immediate international regulation of transborder data flows 'to ensure that we do not lose control of information vital to the maintenance of national sovereignty'.

[20] Allan Gotlieb, Charles Dalfen, and Kenneth Katz, 'The Transborder Transfer of Information by Communications and Computer Systems: Issues and Approaches to Guiding Principles', 68 American Journal of International Law 227, 246–7 (1974).

[21] See Report of the Commission on Transnational Corporations of the UN Economic and Social Council of 6 July 1981 (n 18), at 199, referring to a study carried out in 1978 by the government of Sweden stating that a lack of informational sovereignty could expose a country to 'foreign manipulation'; G. Russell Pipe, 'National Policies, International Debates', 29(3) Journal of Communications 114, 121 (1979), quoting a member of the Swedish parliament as saying that the risks inherent in the storage of data outside the country means that 'the critical mass of data concerning the Swedish economy and its citizens should never leave the national territory'; William L. Fishman, 'Introduction to Transborder Data Flows', 16 Stanford Journal of International Law 3, 10 (1980), stating: 'Fear of undue reliance on other countries, and loss of national control and ultimately sovereignty has also been expressed by the Swedes, but in a more generalized way'; Ved P. Nanda, 'The Communication Revolution and the Free Flow of Information in a Transnational Setting', 30 American Journal of Comparative Law Supplement 411, 421 (1982).

using a telecommunications link. The French subsidiary had contracts with the former Soviet Union to supply equipment to construct a gas pipeline from the Urals to Western Europe. These contracts, however, violated US export regulations. When the French government ordered Dresser France to fulfil the contracts, the US parent firm cut the data link to corporate headquarters. Because the French subsidiary was dependent upon the data link to perform its business operations, it was unable to meet its contractual obligations with the former Soviet Union. The French government was also unable to require the firm to fulfil its contracts since it could not restore access to the necessary data-processing facilities in the United States ...[22]

Cases such as this one led officials of the French government to express concern about the loss of national economic sovereignty through transborder data flows.[23]

Tensions between developed countries (particularly the US) and developing ones have also arisen based on the economic and political risks of being dependent on information flows controlled from another country.[24] This led to economic sovereignty issues being camouflaged in the language of privacy protection, as can be seen in the following excerpt from a resolution adopted by the Conference of Latin American Informatics Authorities in 1982, where the enactment of data protection laws is justified based on the need to promote local data processing capabilities:

The Third Conference of Latin American Informatics Authorities passed a resolution emphasizing the links between transborder data flows and national sovereignty, as well as issues of national security and the right to privacy ... To counteract these potential problems, the resolution recommended that countries develop national data protection laws. *Such laws could promote the local development of information resources, partly by limiting the extent to which data were stored and processed abroad.*[25]

Concerns about sovereignty also played a role in the restrictions on transborder data flows enacted by Brazil, which were perhaps the most draconian of any

---

[22] Sara Schoonmaker, *High-Tech Trade Wars: US–Brazilian Conflicts in the Global Economy* (University of Pittsburgh Press 2002), at 46–7.

[23] See John M. Eger, 'Emerging Restrictions on Transnational Data Flows: Privacy Protection or Non-Tariff Trade Barriers?', 10 Law and Policy in International Business 1055, 1065–6 (1978), quoting the following statement made by French Justice Ministry official Louis Joinet at an OECD symposium held in Vienna in September 1977: 'Information is power, and economic information is economic power. Information has an economic value and the ability to store and process certain types of data may well give one country political and technological advantage over other countries. This in turn may lead to a loss of national sovereignty through supranational data flows.'

[24] Schoonmaker (n 22), at 14, stating 'debates over ... transborder data flows were a key part of the broader struggle for a new world information order. Former Third World countries viewed the flows as part of a new form of information dependency ...' Regarding tensions concerning informational sovereignty between the US and the developing world at the time, see Fred H. Cate, 'The First Amendment and the International "Free Flow" of Information', 30 Virginia Journal of International Law 371 (1989); Nanda (n 21).

[25] Schoonmaker (n 22), at 48 (emphasis added). The resolution was the 'Recommendation Directly Pertaining to Transborder Data Flows Adopted by the Third Conference of Latin American Informatics Authorities, Recommendation Number 12', reprinted in United Nations Centre on Transnational Corporations, 'Transnational Corporations and Transnational Data Flows: A Technical Paper', ST/CTC/23, 1982, Annex III, at 114–16, <http://unctc.unctad.org/data/e82iia4a.pdf> and <http://unctc.unctad.org/data/e82iia4b.pdf>.

country. In 1976, Brazil introduced a system whereby the use of international computer networks, foreign data banks, and other computerized systems resulting in transborder data flows required prior permission of a government board.[26] Such approvals were apparently granted sparingly:

> Between May 1978 and January 1980, 19 applications were filed and decisions were taken on 16. Approval was denied for applications related to the use of time-sharing services and data banks abroad and certain types of the international operations of foreign affiliates; approval was given for airline reservation systems and demonstration systems. In general, the Government of Brazil 'does not allow the use of computers placed abroad, which through teleinformatics accomplish tasks whose solutions can be obtained in the country'.[27]

In 1979, Brazil established a Special Informatics Agency (SEI) to regulate the flow of data out of the country. According to one author, 'SEI examines potential transborder data flows and international information services on an individual basis. SEI then determines what the impact of the services will be in terms of economic, privacy, and national sovereignty concerns. Based upon this analysis, the application is either accepted, rejected, or conditionally accepted.'[28] Brazil was apparently the only developing country to institute a thorough system of transborder data flow controls on such a scale;[29] perhaps not coincidentally, a military government ruled the country at the time.

   The Brazilian restrictions were resisted by the US, which saw the ability to transfer data freely across borders as a lynchpin of its own national sovereignty.[30] As one US politician put it in 1977: 'One way to "attack" a nation such as the United States which depends heavily on information and communication is to restrain the flow of information—cutting off contact between the headquarters and the overseas branches of a multinational firm; taxing telecommunications crossing borders; building information walls around a nation.'[31] Thus, some nations saw regulation of transborder data flows as a way to protect their sovereignty, whereas others saw it as a threat to their sovereignty.

   Governments continue to regulate, or even block completely, the transborder flow of data for reasons relating to national sovereignty. For example, the government of China blocks access to many kinds of Internet content,[32] and in 2011 the Egyptian government attempted to quell internal rebellion by completely shutting down access to the Internet.[33] These actions are assertions of power to protect governmental interests, and have nothing to do with the protection of privacy.

---

[26] Mengel (n 4), at 201.   [27] Mengel (n 4), at 201.
[28] Jane Bortnick, 'International Information Flow: The Developing World Perspective', 14 Cornell International Law Journal 333, 342 (1981).
[29] See Schoonmaker (n 22), at 14, stating: 'the Brazilian military government, however, was the only one to implement a major policy in this area'.
[30] Schoonmaker (n 22), at 50–6.   [31] Schoonmaker (n 22), at 51.
[32] See Jack Goldsmith and Tim Wu, *Who Controls the Internet? Illusions of a Borderless World* (OUP 2008), at 92–100.
[33] See Ryan Singel, 'Report: Egypt Shut Down Net with Big Switch, Not Phone Calls', Wired (10 February 2011), <http://www.wired.com/threatlevel/2011/02/egypt-off-switch/>.

Recent technological developments such as cloud computing have also spurred governments to assert concerns about information sovereignty. For example, some EU Member States (eg, France and Germany[34]) have begun promoting the construction of cloud computing infrastructures located in their own countries, based on concerns that government data stored with providers in the US may be subject to access by US law enforcement authorities.[35] The ever-increasing globalization of data processing may cause a counter-reaction and motivate States to assert their sovereign interests in data processing and transborder data flow regulation more aggressively,[36] both because of privacy concerns and for economic reasons. Thus, regulation of transborder data flows to protect interests of national sovereignty remains alive and well.

D. Free flow of data and freedom of information

Transborder data flow regulation is dealt with not only in data protection and privacy law, but in a number of specialized international treaties in areas such as telecommunications, satellite transmission, and broadcasting,[37] which will generally not be dealt with in detail here since they do not focus solely on privacy and data protection.

However, such instruments demonstrate that transborder data flows have long been the subject of international lawmaking. For example, before the first International Telegraph Convention was concluded in 1865, States had concerns about the transmission of telegraphic messages across their borders, so that it was necessary to cable a message to the last territorial station of the sending State, carry it across the border in written form, and then transmit it further telegraphically in the adjoining State.[38] During negotiation of the Convention, agreement to allow the transfer of telegrams across national borders was only reached by incorporating into it the possibility for States to restrict their transfer for reasons such as State security, compliance with law, and public order—that is, by allowing States to regulate the transborder flow of telegraphic data.[39]

---

[34] See 'Innenminister Friedrich will sichere "Bundescloud" aufbauen' (18 December 2011), <http://www.teltarif.de/bundes-cloud-friedrich-regierung-telekom-sichere-speicherung/news/45000.html>.

[35] See Kristina Irion, 'Government cloud computing and the policies of data sovereignty' (September 2011), <https://www.econstor.eu/dspace/bitstream/10419/52197/1/672481146.pdf>.

[36] See Zachary N.J. Peterson, Mark Gondree, and Robert Beverly, 'A Position Paper on Data Sovereignty: The Importance of Geolocating Data in the Cloud', <http://rbeverly.net/research/papers/soverign-hotcloud11.pdf>.

[37] A number of these are discussed in Edward W. Ploman, *International Law Governing Communications and Information* (Frances Pinter Ltd 1982), at 143 and 228–32.

[38] Gotlieb, Dalfen, and Katz (n 20), at 228.

[39] Gotlieb, Dalfen, and Katz (n 20). See also Anne W. Branscomb, 'Global Governance of Global Networks: A Survey of Transborder Data Flow in Transition', 36 Vanderbilt Law Review 985, 995–6 (1983).

Of particular relevance are the principles of the 'free flow of information' and 'freedom of information'.[40] Both terms refer to the open and free exchange of information, and derive from basic human rights instruments under public international law. Thus, the Universal Declaration of Human Rights of 1948 (UDHR) and the International Covenant on Civil and Political Rights of 1966 (ICCPR) both protect the right to privacy or private life[41] and mention the freedom to transfer data 'regardless of frontiers'.[42] This indicates that the ability to transfer data freely across national borders is essential to freedom of expression and freedom of opinion, as the negotiating history of the ICCPR shows.[43] At the same time, the free flow of information is not unlimited, and is subject to a balancing against other rights, including the right to privacy.[44]

Further instruments under international law support the free exchange of data globally. For example, Article 1(2) of the Constitution of the United Nations Educational, Scientific and Cultural Organization (UNESCO) of 1945 states that the Organization will 'promote the free flow of ideas by word and image', and the Agreement on the Importation of Educational, Scientific and Cultural Materials of 1950 (Florence Agreement) aims to facilitate 'the free flow of books, publications and educational, scientific and cultural materials'[45] by obligating signatory States not to impose customs duties or charges on their importation.[46] In the 1940s and 1950s, proposals were made in the United Nations for an international convention (or series of conventions) dealing with freedom of information, access to information, and its transmission between countries, but they did not gain the requisite support.[47]

---

[40] Note that in this context, 'freedom of information' has a different meaning than the right of citizens to gain access to data held by the public sector. Ploman (n 37), at 125, states that the distinction between the concepts of 'freedom of information' and 'free flow of information' is 'to some extent arbitrary', and rests on the fact that the UN has been dealing with the 'politico-juridical aspects' of the issue under the heading of freedom of information, while UNESCO has been dealing with 'practical measures to promote the flow of information'.

[41] See UDHR, Article 12; ICCPR, Article 17. Neither instrument explicitly mentions data protection.

[42] See UDHR, Article 19, stating: 'Everyone has the right to freedom of opinion and expression; this right includes freedom to hold opinions without interference and to seek, receive and impart information and ideas through any media and *regardless of frontiers*' (emphasis added); ICCPR, Article 19(2), stating: 'Everyone shall have the right to freedom of expression; this right shall include freedom to seek, receive and impart information and ideas of all kinds, *regardless of frontiers*, either orally, in writing or in print, in the form of art, or through any media of his choice' (emphasis added).

[43] See Lauri Hannikainen and Kristian Myntti, 'Article 19', in Asbjørn Eide et al. (eds), *The Universal Declaration of Human Rights: A Commentary* (Scandinavian University Press 1992), at 278, analysing the negotiating history of Article 19 of the UDHR and concluding that its aim 'was to promote an unobstructed flow of information in all directions and regardless of frontiers'.

[44] See Manfred Nowak, *UN Covenant on Civil and Political Rights (CCPR Commentary)* (N.P. Engel 1993), at 354, who states in commentary on Article 19 of the ICCPR that: 'The freedom to seek information may be limited in the interest of the rights of others. Principally conceivable here is the protection of privacy and intimacy pursuant to Art. 17'.

[45] Preamble to the Florence Agreement.

[46] These documents are all reproduced in Ploman (n 37), at 142–67, who cites several other international agreements promoting the free flow of information, some of them going back to the 19th century (eg, the Convention for the International Exchange of Official Documents and of Scientific and Literary Publications, Brussels, 1886).

[47] See Plowman (n 37), at 127–8.

E. Transborder data flows in international law

The regulation of transborder data flows for data protection or privacy reasons has not traditionally received much attention in public international law.[48] The normative basis of data protection law ultimately rests on human rights treaties such as the UDHR and the ICCPR that protect the right to privacy or private life[49] but do not mention data protection. Council of Europe Convention 108,[50] which is discussed later, is the only binding international treaty dealing with data protection, but so far is more of regional than global application. There have been calls for an international convention dealing with data protection and privacy; for example, in 2005 the 27th International Conference of Data Protection and Privacy Commissioners issued the 'Montreux Declaration', in which it appealed to the United Nations 'to prepare a binding legal instrument which clearly sets out in detail the rights to data protection and privacy as enforceable human rights'.[51] Some companies have made similar appeals; for example, in 2007, Google called for the creation of 'global privacy standards'.[52] However, so far 'there does not exist a truly global convention or treaty dealing specifically with data privacy'.[53]

The International Law Commission (ILC) of the United Nations has stated that 'the international binding and non binding instruments, as well as the national legislation adopted by States, and judicial decisions reveal a number of core principles' of data protection.[54] However, the ILC goes on to say that data protection is an area 'in which State practice is not yet extensive or fully developed'.[55] Since most data protection legislation relies on the same international documents, the fundamental, high-level principles of the law are similar across regions and legal systems,[56] but once one descends from the highest level of abstraction, there can be significant differences in detail. There is also considerable divergence in the details of regulation, their aims, and their legal nature.[57]

---

[48] See on the status of data protection under public international law Christopher Kuner, 'An International Legal Framework for Data Protection: Issues and Prospects', 25 Computer Law and Security Review 307, 309–11 (2009).

[49] See UDHR, Article 12 and ICCPR, Article 17.

[50] 28 January 1981, ETS 108 (1981).

[51] 27th International Conference of Data Protection and Privacy Commissioners, 'The protection of personal data and privacy in a globalised world: a universal right respecting diversities' (2005), <www.privacyconference2005.org/fileadmin/PDF/montreux_declaration_e.pdf>.

[52] See <http://googlepublicpolicy.blogspot.com/2007/09/call-for-global-privacy-standards.html>.

[53] See Lee Bygrave, 'Privacy Protection in a Global Context—A Comparative Overview', in Peter Wahlgren (ed), *Scandinavian Studies in Law* 319 (Stockholm Institute for Scandinavian Law 2004), at 333.

[54] International Law Commission, 'Report on the Work of its Fifty-Eighth Session' (1 May to 9 June and 3 July to 11 August 2006) UN Doc. A/61/10, Annex D, para. 11.

[55] ILC (n 54), Annex D, para. 12.

[56] Bygrave (n 53), at 347, stating: 'data privacy laws in the various countries expound broadly similar core principles and share much common ground in terms of enforcement patterns.'

[57] See Chapter 3.

Various organs of the United Nations have dealt with the subject of data protection since the late 1960s.[58] Most work on transborder data flow regulation has been done by the 'Commission on Transnational Corporations' of the UN Economic and Social Council, which in 1981 issued a report that gives much useful information on the way the subject was viewed at the time.[59] The report stresses both the risks and benefits of transborder data flows, and mentions that, while relatively few networks for data communication existed then, their growth was proceeding at a rapid pace,[60] with many of the transborder data flows that were taking place being carried out by corporations in the course of their business.[61]

In 1990, the United Nations issued its Guidelines concerning Computerized Personal Files, which take the form of a non-binding guidance document.[62] The UN General Assembly has requested 'governmental, intergovernmental and non-governmental organisations to respect those guidelines in carrying out the activities within their field of competence'.[63] The Guidelines state in paragraph 9 that 'when the legislation of two or more countries concerned by a transborder data flow offers comparable safeguards for the protection of privacy, information should be able to circulate as freely as inside [sic] each of the territories concerned. If there are no reciprocal safeguards, limitations on such circulation may not be imposed unduly and only in so far as the protection of privacy demands'.

Since adoption of the UN Guidelines, the United Nations has not been very active with regard to transborder data flow regulation, and issues under public international law have been dealt with mostly in regional organizations such as the EU or the Council of Europe rather than by UN institutions. It is thus not surprising that national data protection legislation tends to be more influenced by the OECD Guidelines, the EU Directive, or Council of Europe Convention 108 than by anything issued by the United Nations. Moreover, there seems to be little political will of UN member States to enact a multilateral convention dealing with data protection or transborder data flows.

---

[58] For an overview, see Mengel (n 4), at 183–244.

[59] Report of the Commission on Transnational Corporations of the Economic and Social Council of 6 July 1981, reprinted in Mengel (n 4), at 185–207.

[60] Mengel (n 4), at 188–90.

[61] Mengel (n 4), at 198, stating as an example that 'in the case of Canada, for instance, approximately 90 per cent of total net transborder data flows involve data flows from foreign affiliates in Canada to parent corporations abroad.'

[62] UN Guidelines concerning Computerized Personal Data Files of 14 December 1990, UN Doc. E/CN.4/1990/72, <http://www.unhcr.org/refworld/docid/3ddcafaac.html>.

[63] UN Doc. A/RES/45/95 (14 December 1990).

F. OECD Privacy Guidelines of 1980

The OECD is an international organization based in Paris that deals with economic and social policy and currently has 34 member countries[64] from various regions, including many EU Member States and countries from North America (eg, Canada and the US), the Asia-Pacific region (eg, Australia and Korea), and Latin America (eg, Chile and Mexico). This global membership gives the group's work on privacy considerable geographic reach. But the fact that the members of the OECD are largely developed, industrialized States raises questions about the legitimacy of its work for the less developed world.[65]

Discussion of transborder data flows began in the OECD in 1970, and culminated in publication of the OECD Privacy Guidelines in 1980. The Guidelines are a non-binding set of principles that member countries may enact, and have the dual aim of achieving acceptance of certain minimum standards of privacy and personal data protection, and of eliminating, as far as possible, factors which might induce countries to restrict transborder data flows.[66]

The Guidelines contain the following main provisions dealing with transborder data flows:

15. Member countries should take into consideration the implications for other Member countries of domestic processing and re-export of personal data.
16. Member countries should take all reasonable and appropriate steps to ensure that transborder flows of personal data, including transit through a Member country, are uninterrupted and secure.
17. A Member country should refrain from restricting transborder flows of personal data between itself and another Member country except where the latter does not yet substantially observe these Guidelines or where the re-export of such data would circumvent its domestic privacy legislation. A Member country may also impose restrictions in respect of certain categories of personal data for which its domestic privacy legislation includes specific regulations in view of the nature of those data and for which the other Member country provides no equivalent protection.
18. Member countries should avoid developing laws, policies and practices in the name of the protection of privacy and individual liberties, which would create obstacles to transborder flows of personal data that would exceed requirements for such protection.

---

[64] Member countries are Australia; Austria; Belgium; Canada; Chile; Czech Republic; Denmark; Estonia; Finland; France; Germany; Greece; Hungary; Iceland; Ireland; Israel; Italy; Japan; Korea; Luxembourg; Mexico; Netherlands; New Zealand; Norway; Poland; Portugal; the Slovak Republic; Slovenia; Spain; Sweden; Switzerland; Turkey; the United Kingdom; and the US.

[65] See Michael Kirby, 'The history, achievement and future of the 1980 OECD guidelines on privacy', 1 International Data Privacy Law 6, 13–4 (2011).

[66] OECD Guidelines, Explanatory Memorandum, para. 25.

The OECD Guidelines represent the most global consensus yet achieved in the area of data protection and transborder data flow regulation, but were purposely written at a high level, and are focused on the facilitation of global data flows for economic purposes rather than on human rights.[67] The Guidelines may be implemented by law in the OECD member countries, but are not legally binding. At the time they were finalized, there was optimism that the Guidelines could lead to greater harmonization of data protection law;[68] in fact, since their enactment, the regulation of transborder data flows has become more diverse, reflecting differences in national and regional legal frameworks for privacy protection.

In 2010 the OECD initiated a process to review the Guidelines, to determine if they require amendment; this process had not been completed at the time this study was finalized.

G. Council of Europe Convention 108 and Additional Protocol

1. Background

The Council of Europe is an international organization with currently 47 State members working in the areas of human rights, the rule of law, and democracy.[69] Preparatory work on data protection law in the Council of Europe began as early as 1968, when the Committee of Ministers began a study on the protection of individuals' private sphere in light of developments in modern technology.[70] In 1981, the Council of Europe enacted its Convention 108,[71] which is 'the hereto sole international treaty dealing specifically with data protection',[72] and which entered into force on 1 October 1985. The Convention is also open for signature by countries that are not member States of the Council of Europe; no non-member has so far acceded to it, although on 31 March 2011 Uruguay officially requested permission to accede,[73] and several other non-members (particularly African and

---

[67] See Frits W. Hondius, 'A Decade of International Data Protection', 30 Netherlands International Law Review 103, 106 (1983), stating: 'the thrust of the Council of Europe's Convention is the protection of human rights; that of the OECD Guidelines the facilitation of transborder data flows'.

[68] See, eg, Michael D. Kirby, 'Transborder Data Flows and the "Basic Rules of Data Privacy"', 16 Stanford Journal of International Law 27, 65–6 (1980).

[69] Member countries are Albania; Andorra; Armenia; Austria; Azerbaijan; Belgium; Bosnia and Herzegovina; Bulgaria; Croatia; Cyprus; Czech Republic; Denmark; Estonia; Finland; France; Georgia; Germany; Greece; Hungary; Iceland; Ireland; Italy; Latvia; Liechtenstein; Lithuania; Luxembourg; the former Yugoslav Republic of Macedonia; Malta; Moldova; Monaco; Montenegro; Netherlands; Norway; Poland; Portugal; Romania; Russia; San Marino; Serbia; Slovakia; Slovenia; Spain; Sweden; Switzerland; Turkey; Ukraine; and the United Kingdom.

[70] Mengel (n 4), at 25.

[71] Convention for the Protection of Individuals with regard to Automatic Data Processing of Personal Data, 28 January 1981, ETS 108 (1981).

[72] Lee Bygrave, *Data Protection Law: Approaching its Rationale, Logic and Limits* (Kluwer Law International 2002), at 32.

[73] See 'Convention for the Protection of Individuals with regard to Automatic Processing of Personal Data (ETS No. 108)—Request by Uruguay to be invited to accede, 6 July 2011', in which the deputies invited Uruguay to accede; Consultative Committee of the Convention for the Protection

Latin American countries) are known to be considering doing so. Convention 108 is a high-level instrument that does not create rights for individuals[74] and is not directly applicable against private parties, but obligates States to implement in their law the protections that it provides.[75] It leaves considerable leeway for States to implement its provisions in different ways in light of their legal and constitutional systems.[76]

The Convention was an important milestone in the development of data protection as a fundamental right. Unlike the European Convention on Human Rights, membership of Convention 108 does not give rise to jurisdiction of the European Court of Human Rights, so that there is no direct judicial enforcement of the Convention. However, in some cases the European Court of Human Rights has referred to Convention 108,[77] and Article 8 of the European Convention on Human Rights probably includes the obligation to give effect to the provisions of Convention 108.[78] The EU has also committed to ensure that its law is consistent with the relevant conventions of the Council of Europe (though EU law may provide more extensive protection);[79] for example, the EU Charter of Fundamental Rights is to be interpreted in the same way as the European Convention on Human Rights.[80]

Article 12 of Convention 108 provides as follows:

1. The following provisions shall apply to the transfer across national borders, by whatever medium, of personal data undergoing automatic processing or collected with a view to their being automatically processed.
2. A Party shall not, for the sole purpose of the protection of privacy, prohibit or subject to special authorisation transborder flows of personal data going to the territory of another Party.

---

of Individuals with regard to Automatic Processing of Personal Data [ETS No. 108], 'Opinion on Uruguay's request to be invited to accede to Convention 108 and its additional Protocol', T-PD (2011) 08 rev en (26 May 2011), <http://www.coe.int/t/dghl/standardsetting/dataprotection/TPD_documents/T-PD%20BUR_2011_08%20en.pdf>; 'Consultative Committee of the Convention for the Protection of Individuals with regard to Automatic Processing of Personal Data (ETS No. 108) (T-PD)—Abridged report of the 24th plenary meeting', 2 July 2008, in which the deputies of the Committee of Ministers agreed to take account of the T-PD's recommendation that countries that are not members of the Council of Europe be allowed to accede to Convention 108.

[74] Council of Europe Convention 108, Explanatory Report, para. 38.

[75] Council of Europe Convention 108, Article 3.

[76] Council of Europe Convention 108, Explanatory Report, at para. 39, stating that implementing measures 'can take different forms, depending on the legal and constitutional system of the State concerned: apart from laws they may be regulations, administrative guidelines, etc. Such binding measures may be usefully reinforced by measures of voluntary regulation in the field of data processing, such as codes of good practice or codes of professional conduct.'

[77] See, eg, *Amann v Switzerland* (2000) ECHR 87, para. 65; *Rotaru v Romania* (2000) ECHR 191, para. 43.

[78] See Paul De Hert and Serge Gutwirth, 'Data Protection in the Case law of Strasbourg and Luxembourg: Constitutionalisation in Action', in Serge Gutwirth et al. (eds), *Reinventing Data Protection?* 3 (Springer 2009), at 27.

[79] See Memorandum of Understanding between the Council of Europe and the European Union, May 2007, at para. 27.

[80] EU Charter of Fundamental Rights, Article 52(3).

3. Nevertheless, each Party shall be entitled to derogate from the provisions of paragraph 2:
   a. insofar as its legislation includes specific regulations for certain categories of personal data or of automated personal data files, because of the nature of those data or those files, except where the regulations of the other Party provide an equivalent protection;
   b. when the transfer is made from its territory to the territory of a non-contracting State through the intermediary of the territory of another Party, in order to avoid such transfers resulting in circumvention of the legislation of the Party referred to at the beginning of this paragraph.

In 2001 the Council of Europe adopted an Additional Protocol to the Convention, which may only be signed by the signatories to the Convention itself.[81] The relevant Article 2 of the Additional Protocol provides as follows:

1. Each Party shall provide for the transfer of personal data to a recipient that is subject to the jurisdiction of a State or organisation that is not Party to the Convention only if that State or organisation ensures an adequate level of protection for the intended data transfer.
2. By way of derogation from paragraph 1 of Article 2 of this Protocol, each Party may allow for the transfer of personal data:
   a. if domestic law provides for it because of:
      – specific interests of the data subject, or
      – legitimate prevailing interests, especially important public interests, or
   b. if safeguards, which can in particular result from contractual clauses, are provided by the controller responsible for the transfer and are found adequate by the competent authorities according to domestic law.

As of January 2013, the Convention had been ratified or acceded to by 44 Council of Europe member States, and the Additional Protocol by 33 of them, most of which are located in Europe or border on it. In addition to being in force in all (in the case of the Convention) or most (in the case of the Additional Protocol) EU Member States, both the Convention and the Additional Protocol are in force in several non-EEA (European Economic Area) and non-EU countries as well,[82] thus providing a source of legally binding regulation of transborder data flows beyond what is applicable in those regional groups.

---

[81] See Additional Protocol, Explanatory Report, para. 34.

[82] Non-EEA and non-EU Member States that have enacted the Convention include Albania; Andorra; Armenia; Azerbaijan; Bosnia and Herzegovina; Croatia; Georgia; the former Yugoslav Republic of Macedonia; Moldova; Monaco; Montenegro; Serbia; Switzerland; and the Ukraine, and those that have enacted the Additional Protocol include Albania; Andorra; Armenia; Bosnia and Herzegovina; Croatia; the former Yugoslav Republic of Macedonia; Moldova; Monaco; Montenegro; Serbia; Switzerland; and the Ukraine.

The Council of Europe has also adopted a Recommendation regulating the use of personal data in the police sector, which contains rules for the international transfer of personal data, as follows:[83]

5.4. International communication

Communication of data to foreign authorities should be restricted to police bodies. It should only be permissible:

a. if there exists a clear legal provision under national or international law,

b. in the absence of such a provision, if the communication is necessary for the prevention of a serious and imminent danger or is necessary for the suppression of a serious criminal offence under ordinary law, and provided that domestic regulations for the protection of the person are not prejudiced.'

2. Modernization

In 2010 the Council of Europe began an ongoing process to modernize the Convention and update it in light of the many social, economic, and technological changes that have occurred since it was originally enacted. The proposals for modernization have been discussed for several years in the Council of Europe's Bureau of the Consultative Committee of the Convention for the Protection of individuals with regard to the Automatic Processing of Personal Data (known as the 'T-PD Bureau', and referred to throughout as the 'T-PD'), an expert group made up of representatives of Council of Europe member States, data protection authorities, and observers. The T-PD has built up a substantial body of expertise on the legal issues presented by the Convention, and on international data protection law in general.

The T-PD considered a number of drafting proposals for revision of Article 12 of the Convention and Article 2 of the Additional Protocol in the period from September 2011 to June 2012 (this period has been selected as representative since it is between when consideration of proposals to modernize these instruments began and the date of the group's first 2012 plenary meeting). Four of the texts were prepared by the Secretariat of the T-PD (most are available on the Internet[84]), and two were presented for discussion by the International Chamber of Commerce (ICC, which has official observer status in the group). These texts are the following:

- ICC proposal of 2 September 2011;
- Secretariat version of 15 November 2011;[85]
- Secretariat version of 18 January 2012;[86]
- ICC proposal of 31 January 2012;

---

[83] Council of Europe, Recommendation No. R(87)15 of the Committee of Ministers to Member States regulating the use of personal data in the police sector (17 September 1987), Principle 5.4.

[84] See <http://www.coe.int/t/dghl/standardsetting/dataprotection/Modernisation_En.asp>.

[85] T-PD-BUR(2011) 27_en (15 November 2011), <http://www.coe.int/t/dghl/standardsetting/dataprotection/TPD_documents/T-PD-BUR_2011_27_en.pdf>.

[86] T-PD-BUR(2012)01EN (18 January 2012), <http://www.coe.int/t/dghl/standardsetting/dataprotection/TPD_documents/T-PD-BUR_2012_01_EN.pdf>.

- Secretariat version of 5 March 2012;[87]
- Secretariat version of 27 April 2012.[88]

These proposals illustrate the issues at stake, and excerpts from them will be cited throughout to illustrate specific points.

The T-PD concluded its work on modernization at the end of November 2012,[89] but the final text is subject to approval of the Council of Europe member States, so that the final outcome and timescale of the process are uncertain.

H. EU Data Protection Directive 95/46

1. Current rules

Perhaps the most influential[90] legal instrument regulating transborder data flows is the EU Data Protection Directive 95/46,[91] which was adopted in 1995 and came into force in 1998. The European Commission began conducting studies on the regulation of transborder data flows as early as 1973,[92] spurred by cases in which the free flow of data between the Member States of the European Communities was threatened by the varying levels of data protection applicable in them. For example, an Austrian government ordinance signed in 1980 by Federal Chancellor Bruno Kreisky required the prior authorization of the Austrian Data Protection Commission before personal data of legal persons could be transferred to France, Germany, or Sweden, since the data protection laws of those countries did not cover such data.[93] In the 1970s, the Swedish Data Protection Board refused to authorize the transfer of personal data to the United Kingdom in several cases.[94] And in a famous case that occurred in 1989, the French subsidiary of the Italian automobile company Fiat was only allowed by the French data protection authority to transfer

---

[87] T-PD-BUR(2012)01Rev_en (5 March 2012), <http://www.coe.int/t/dghl/standardsetting/dataprotection/TPD_documents/T-PD-BUR_2012_01Rev_en.pdf>.

[88] T-PD-BUR(2012)01Rev2_en (27 April 2012), <http://www.coe.int/t/dghl/standardsetting/dataprotection/TPD_documents/T-PD-BUR_2012_01Rev2FIN_en.pdf>.

[89] See <http://www.coe.int/t/dghl/standardsetting/DataProtection/default_en.asp>.

[90] See Corien Prins, 'Should ICT regulation be undertaken at an international level?', in Bert-Jaap Koops, Miriam Lips, Corien Prins, and Maurice Shellekens (eds), *Starting Points for ICT Regulation: Deconstructing Prevalent Policy One-Liners* 151 (TMC Asser Press 2006), at 162, 172, stating that the EU Directive has had a 'considerable impact' on regulation in other States.

[91] Directive 95/46/EC of the European Parliament and of the Council of 24 October 1995 on the protection of individuals with regard to the processing of personal data and on the free movement of such data, [1995] OJ L281/31. See regarding the background of transborder data flow regulation in the Directive, Paul M. Schwartz, 'European Data Protection Law and Restrictions on International Data Flows', 80 Iowa Law Review 471 (1995).

[92] See Mengel (n 4), at 52.

[93] Verordnung des Bundeskanzlers vom 18. Dezember 1980 über die Gleichwertigkeit ausländischer Datenschutzbestimmungen, Bundesgesetzblatt für die Republik Österreich, 30 December 1980, at 3403, <http://www.ris.bka.gv.at/Dokumente/BgblPdf/1980_612_0/1980_612_0.pdf>. See also Mengel (n 4), at 14.

[94] See Bing (n 9), at 73.

employee data to Italy once a data transfer agreement between the two companies had been signed, owing to a lack of data protection legislation in Italy.[95]

Under the Directive, which is legally binding in the 27 EU Member States[96] and the three EEA member countries (Iceland, Liechtenstein, and Norway[97]), the transfer of personal data within the EU and EEA may not be restricted based on the level of data protection in the country of data export.[98] However, data transfers to other countries are prohibited unless such countries provide 'an adequate level of data protection' as determined by the European Commission.[99] Thirteen such Commission adequacy decisions have so far been issued.[100] International agreements between the EU and three other countries have resulted in transfers to the latter of airline passenger name record (PNR) data being declared as offering adequate protection,[101] and such an agreement has also been reached with the US regarding the transfer of financial messaging data (the SWIFT Case).[102]

The rules requiring a legal basis for international data transfers apply in addition to those requiring a legal basis for data processing.[103] Thus, deciding whether personal data may be transferred outside the EU is a two-step process: personal data must first be legally collected and processed under the Directive and, secondly, there must be a legal basis for the transfer outside the EU under Article 25 or 26.

Article 25 of the Directive reads as follows:

1. The Member States shall provide that the transfer to a third country of personal data which are undergoing processing or are intended for processing after transfer may take place only if, without prejudice to compliance with the national provisions adopted pursuant to the other provisions of this Directive, the third country in question ensures an adequate level of protection.

2. The adequacy of the level of protection afforded by a third country shall be assessed in the light of all the circumstances surrounding a data transfer operation or set

---

[95] See Commission nationale de l'informatique et des libertés, 10e rapport d'activité, at 32 (1989).

[96] Austria; Belgium; Bulgaria; Cyprus; Czech Republic; Denmark; Estonia; Finland; France; Germany; Greece; Hungary; Ireland; Italy; Latvia; Lithuania; Luxembourg; Malta; the Netherlands; Poland; Portugal; Romania; Slovakia; Slovenia; Spain; Sweden and the United Kingdom. Croatia is expected to join the EU on 1 July 2013.

[97] See Decision of the EEA Joint Committee No 83/1999 of 25 June 1999 amending Protocol 37 and Annex XI (Telecommunication services) to the EEA Agreement, [2000] OJ L296/41.

[98] EU Data Protection Directive, Article 1(2).　　　[99] EU Data Protection Directive, Article 25.

[100] Ie, covering Andorra; Argentina; Canadian organizations subject to the Canadian Personal Information Protection and Electronic Documents Act (PIPEDA); the Faroe Islands; the Bailiwick of Guernsey; Israel; the Bailiwick of Jersey; the Isle of Man; New Zealand; Switzerland; Uruguay; transfers under the US Safe Harbor agreement; and transfers of airline passenger data to the US Department of Homeland Security (DHS). See <http://ec.europa.eu/justice/data-protection/document/international-transfers/adequacy/index_en.htm>.

[101] Ie, covering Australia, Canada, and the US.

[102] Agreement between the European Union and the United States of America on the processing and transfer of Financial Messaging Data from the European Union to the United States for purposes of the Terrorist Finance Tracking Program, [2010] OJ L8/11.

[103] Agreement between the European Union and the United States of American (n 102), Article 25(1).

of data transfer operations; particular consideration shall be given to the nature of the data, the purpose and duration of the proposed processing operation or operations, the country of origin and country of final destination, the rules of law, both general and sectoral, in force in the third country in question and the professional rules and security measures which are complied with in that country.

3. The Member States and the Commission shall inform each other of cases where they consider that a third country does not ensure an adequate level of protection within the meaning of paragraph 2.

4. Where the Commission finds, under the procedure provided for in Article 31(2), that a third country does not ensure an adequate level of protection within the meaning of paragraph 2 of this Article, Member States shall take the measures necessary to prevent any transfer of data of the same type to the third country in question.

5. At the appropriate time, the Commission shall enter into negotiations with a view to remedying the situation resulting from the finding made pursuant to paragraph 4.

6. The Commission may find, in accordance with the procedure referred to in Article 31(2), that a third country ensures an adequate level of protection within the meaning of paragraph 2 of this Article, by reason of its domestic law or of the international commitments it has entered into, particularly upon conclusion of the negotiations referred to in paragraph 5, for the protection of the private lives and basic freedoms and rights of individuals.

Member States shall take the measures necessary to comply with the Commission's decision.

As derogations, Article 26(1) permits data transfers under the following conditions:

1. By way of derogation from Article 25 and save where otherwise provided by domestic law governing particular cases, Member States shall provide that a transfer or a set of transfers of personal data to a third country which does not ensure an adequate level of protection within the meaning of Article 25(2) may take place on condition that:

   (a) the data subject has given his consent unambiguously to the proposed transfer; or

   (b) the transfer is necessary for the performance of a contract between the data subject and the controller or the implementation of precontractual measures taken in response to the data subject's request; or

   (c) the transfer is necessary for the conclusion or performance of a contract concluded in the interest of the data subject between the controller and a third party; or

   (d) the transfer is necessary or legally required on important public interest grounds, or for the establishment, exercise or defence of legal claims; or

   (e) the transfer is necessary in order to protect the vital interests of the data subject; or

   (f) the transfer is made from a register which according to laws or regulations is intended to provide information to the public and which is open to consultation either by the public in general or by any person who can demonstrate legitimate interest, to the extent that the conditions laid down in law for consultation are fulfilled in the particular case.[104]

---

[104] EU Data Protection Directive, Article 26(1).

Such derogations may only be relied on to a limited extent; for example, the Article 29 Working Party (a consultative body composed of the various EU Member State data protection authorities, the European Commission, and the European Data Protection Supervisor) has indicated that 'consent is unlikely to provide an adequate long-term framework for data controllers in cases of repeated or even structural transfers for the processing in question'.[105]

In addition, Article 26(2) allows for the transfer of personal data in certain cases where 'adequate safeguards' have been used:

> 2. Without prejudice to paragraph 1, a Member State may authorize a transfer or a set of transfers of personal data to a third country which does not ensure an adequate level of protection within the meaning of Article 25 (2), where the controller adduces adequate safeguards with respect to the protection of the privacy and fundamental rights and freedoms of individuals and as regards the exercise of the corresponding rights; such safeguards may in particular result from appropriate contractual clauses.

This provision foresees the use of binding contractual commitments between the data exporter and data importer that obligate both to provide certain enumerated protections for the data processing. Two types of clause may be used, namely so-called 'standard contractual clauses', which are pre-approved by the European Commission and are supposed to be used without change,[106] and 'ad hoc' clauses, which are custom-drafted in each specific case by the parties and often must be approved by the local data protection authorities (DPAs).

Although it is not explicitly mentioned in the Directive, Member State DPAs also recognize the possibility for companies in the EU to use 'binding corporate rules' (BCRs) as a legal basis to export personal data, based on a recognition of them as providing 'adequate safeguards' under Article 26(2) of the Directive. BCRs are legally binding data processing rules adopted by a company or group of companies and which grant rights to data subjects.[107] BCRs are regarded as an example of the principle of 'accountability',[108] since they are based on the concept that a data controller should assume responsibility for its data processing anywhere in the world, and should put in place procedures to ensure that it does so.[109] Through the use of BCRs, the entire corporate group becomes a 'safe haven' in which personal

---

[105] Article 29 Working Party, 'Working document on a common interpretation of Article 26(1) of Directive 95/46/EC of 24 October 1995' (WP 114, 25 November 2005), at 11.

[106] See, eg, Commission Decision 2010/87/EU of 5 February 2010 on standard contractual clauses for the transfer of personal data to processors established in third countries under Directive 95/46/EC of the European Parliament and of the Council, [2010] OJ L39/5, Clause 11; Commission Decision 2004/915/EC of 27 December 2004 amending Decision 2001/497/EC as regards the introduction of an alternative set of standard contractual clauses for the transfer of personal data to third countries, [2004] OJ L385/74, Clause 2.

[107] For an exhaustive analysis of the use of BCRs, see Lokke Moerel, *Binding Corporate Rules: Corporate Self-Regulation of Global Data Transfers* (OUP 2012).

[108] See Chapter 3.B.2.d.

[109] See Article 29 Working Party, 'Opinion 3/2010 on the principle of accountability' (WP 173, 13 July 2010), at 7.

data can be freely transferred from one corporate member to another, receiving the same protection wherever they go, regardless of whether the country in which the data are processed is considered to offer adequate protection. BCRs are not mentioned in the Directive, and the European Commission has no authority to issue adequacy decisions for them; thus, BCRs are approved by the national data protection authorities instead. Most (but not all) DPAs recognize BCRs and are willing to approve them, but the conditions for approval are not identical in all EU Member States. The DPAs have created a procedure designed to lead to mutual recognition of national approvals, though not all DPAs recognize it yet.[110]

The Directive thus allows international transfers of personal data based on three types of possible legal base, namely (1) an 'adequacy' decision of the European Commission; (2) one of the derogations of Article 26(1); or (3) 'adequate safeguards' under Article 26(2) (meaning contractual clauses or BCRs). Use of the derogations is subject to various limitations and restrictions, which in practice are particularly important with regard to the use of consent. Thus, in order to be valid, consent must be a clear and unambiguous indication of wishes, freely given, specific, and informed.[111]

EU data protection law regulates not only the initial transfer of data from the EU to a third country but also so-called 'onward transfers', meaning further transfers of the data from the country of import. This situation can arise in many different instances: for example, the operation of a human resources database may be outsourced to a service provider with affiliates in many countries which access the database to perform routine maintenance. In such a case, the initial transfer to the service provider is an international data transfer, and the further access to the database by its affiliates is considered an onward transfer. Articles 25 and 26 of the EU Directive do not explicitly address what precautions should be taken, if any, when data importers transfer the data to other third parties, whether in the same or in another country. However, the Article 29 Working Party has stated that 'further transfers of the personal data from the destination third country to another third country should be permitted only where the second recipient country also affords an adequate level of protection. The only exceptions permitted should be in line with Article 26 of the Directive.'[112]

Member State implementations of the Directive result in considerable differences in national legal approaches to international data transfers.[113] Compliance

---

[110] See <http://ec.europa.eu/justice/data-protection/document/international-transfers/binding-corporate-rules/index_en.htm>.

[111] See Article 29 Working Party (n 105), at 11–12.

[112] Article 29 Working Party, 'First orientations on Transfers of Personal Data to Third Countries— Possible Ways Forward in Assessing Adequacy' (WP 4, 26 June 1997), at 6.

[113] See Christopher Kuner, *European Data Protection Law: Corporate Compliance and Regulation* (2nd edn, OUP 2007), at 162–6. See also European Commission (DG Justice), 'Comparative Study on Different Approaches to New Privacy Challenges in Particular in the Light of Technological Developments' (20 January 2010), <http://ec.europa.eu/justice/policies/privacy/docs/studies/new_privacy_challenges/final_report_working_paper_2_en.pdf>, at 92, stating that the EU legal rules on international data transfers are 'complex' and 'not uniformly applied' by the EU Member States.

with international data transfer requirements in the EU involves the successful completion of a number of steps, which may vary in each individual case based on the data transfer mechanism used, but generally includes at least the following.

- The data controller that seeks to export the personal data (ie, the data exporter) must first determine the Member State law applicable to the data processing, and ensure that national requirements applicable to data collection and processing have been complied with. This can include matters such as providing notice to individuals about the processing of their data; ensuring that there is a legal basis for data collection and processing; and notification of processing to the DPAs.

- The data exporter must then evaluate the various legal bases for transfer (eg, consent, a Commission adequacy decision, use of the standard contractual clauses) to decide which one it wants to use.

- The exporter must ensure that both it and the data importer(s) that will receive the personal data can comply with whatever obligations are incumbent on it based on the selected legal basis for transfer, and, if not, take steps to rectify the situation.

- The exporter must then take whatever steps are required under applicable national law to legitimize the data export. This can include obtaining signature of standard contractual clauses by the data importer; updating privacy policies to be sure that they reflect the fact that personal data will be exported from the EU; notifying the export to the relevant DPAs; and, if necessary, obtaining authorization for the export from the DPA.

- The data exporter may also take further internal steps that, though they may not all be legally required, will serve to limit its legal risk. This can include appointing a company privacy officer; performing due diligence checks on the original data importer and those parties to whom the data may be transferred later on; keeping adequate documentation relating to the export; and conducting regular data security audits.

In practice, successful completion of all these steps will usually take a few weeks at a minimum, and may even extend for years in extreme cases.

The EU has adopted a regulation applicable to data processing by the EU institutions that contains rules similar to those of the Directive.[114] It has also enacted a decision to provide a common level of data protection for the cross-border exchange of personal data within the framework of police and judicial cooperation. Under Article 13 of the Council Framework Decision on the protection of personal data processed in the framework of police and judicial cooperation in

---

[114] See Regulation (EC) No. 45/2001 of the European Parliament and of the Council of 18 December 2000 on the protection of individuals with regard to the processing of personal data by the institutions and bodies of the Community and on the free movement of such data, [2001] OJ L8/1.

criminal matters, personal data may only be transferred from Member State law enforcement authorities to third countries or international bodies if certain conditions are fulfilled, including that such country or international body ensures an adequate level of protection for the data processing (though a number of exceptions to this requirement are provided).[115]

2. Proposed changes

On 25 January 2012, the European Commission officially adopted a proposal for a General Data Protection Regulation[116] (the 'Proposed Regulation') that would, if enacted, replace the EU Data Protection Directive 95/46. The Commission also adopted a proposal for a directive (the 'Proposed Directive') containing rules for data processing 'with regard to the processing of personal data by competent authorities for the purposes of prevention, investigation, detection or prosecution of criminal offences or the execution of criminal penalties'[117] that would replace the Council Framework Decision. The Proposed Directive contains rules for the transborder exchange of personal data in the area of police and judicial cooperation, but its rules are generally more lenient than those of the Proposed Regulation,[118] and the focus here will be on the latter instrument. These proposals were still subject to EU legislative procedures at the time this study was finalized, and both are thus subject to change.

The Proposed Regulation would make a number of major changes to the existing EU legal regime for transborder data flows. In particular, Article 40 abandons the presumption under Directive 95/46 that personal data may not be transferred

---

[115] Council Framework Decision 2008/977/JHA of 27 November 2008 on the protection of personal data processed in the framework of police and judicial cooperation in criminal matters, [2008] OJ L350/60.

[116] Proposal for a Regulation of the European Parliament and of the Council on the protection of individuals with regard to the processing of personal data and on the free movement of such data (General Data Protection Regulation), COM(2012) 11 final. See Christopher Kuner, 'The European Commission's Proposed Data Protection Regulation: A Copernican Revolution in European Data Protection Law', (6 February 2012) Bloomberg BNA Privacy & Security Law Report 6; Paul M. Schwartz, 'The E.U.–U.S. Privacy Collision: A Turn to Institutions and Procedures', Harvard Law Review Symposium 2012: Privacy & Technology, <http://www.harvardlawreview.org/symposium/papers2012/schwartz.pdf>.

[117] Proposal for a Directive of the European Parliament and of the Council on the protection of individuals with regard to the processing of personal data by competent authorities for the purposes of prevention, investigation, detection or prosecution of criminal offences or the execution of criminal penalties, and the free movement of such data, COM(2012) 10/3, Article 1(1).

[118] Eg, Article 35(1)(b) of the Proposed Directive states that when an adequacy decision has not been issued, a transfer of personal data to a recipient in a third country or to an international organization is permissible when 'the controller or processor has assessed all the circumstance surrounding the transfer of personal data and concludes that appropriate safeguards exist with respect to the protection of personal data', thus in effect allowing the data exporter to make its own determination of whether the transfer should proceed. See also European Data Protection Supervisor, 'Opinion of the European Data Protection Supervisor on the data protection reform package' (7 March 2012), <http://www.edps.europa.eu/EDPSWEB/webdav/site/mySite/shared/Documents/Consultation/Opinions/2012/12-03-07_EDPS_Reform_package_EN.pdf>, at 64.

absent an 'adequate level of protection' in the recipient country, and instead requires compliance with all provisions of the Regulation, including those on international transfer. There are three categories of mechanism that may legalize international data transfers, namely a Commission adequacy decision under Article 41; the use of 'appropriate safeguards' under Article 42 (which include binding corporate rules under Article 43); or the application of a derogation under Article 44.

Article 41 expands the scope of Commission adequacy decisions somewhat, by explicitly providing that they may cover not only an entire country, but also a territory within a third country, a processing sector, or an international organization (Articles 41(1) and (3)). The Proposed Regulation also gives the Commission increased power to decide that a territory, processing sector, or international organization does not provide adequate protection, and to enforce such decision by prohibiting data transfers to it (Article 41(5) and (6)).

International data transfers are also possible if 'appropriate safeguards' are in place (Article 42(2)), meaning either binding corporate rules; 'standard data protection clauses' approved by the Commission (the counterpart of the present 'standard contractual clauses'); standard data protection clauses adopted by a DPA in accordance with a new 'consistency mechanism'; or 'ad hoc' contractual clauses authorized by a DPA. Of these, transfers based on ad hoc contractual clauses and those using other appropriate safeguards not provided for in a legally binding instrument require further authorization by the DPA (Article 42(4) and (5)). The Commission may also declare generally valid standard contractual clauses that have been adopted by DPAs (Article 42(2)(c)).

Articles 41(8) and 42(5), together with Recital 134, confirm that despite repeal of Directive 95/46, Commission decisions (such as adequacy decisions, and those approving the standard contractual clauses) and those of DPAs remain in force, but also raise some important questions about the functioning of certain adequacy decisions. For example, Article 40 seems to suggest that the conditions for data processing, and in particular those governing international data transfers, must also be applied to onward transfers of personal data that are sent to a third country and then subject to further transfers. Some Commission adequacy decisions already contain rules for conducting onward transfers,[119] and it is not clear how such rules would interact with the rules of the Proposed Regulation.

Any remaining legal barriers to the use of binding corporate rules under Member State law will be removed (Article 43). Use of BCRs is limited to companies in 'the same corporate group of undertakings' (Recital 85). The Proposed Regulation also explicitly recognizes the use of BCRs for data processors. The requirements for BCRs contained in Article 43 are generally similar to those that have been set forth already by the Article 29 Working Party. The Commission also retains important powers to adopt delegated and implementing acts with regard

---

[119] See, eg, Safe Harbor Onward Transfer Principle. See also Christopher Kuner, 'Onward Transfers of Personal Data under the US Safe Harbor Framework', (17 August 2009) Bloomberg BNA Privacy & Security Law Report 1211.

to the format, procedures, and requirements for approval of BCRs (Article 43(3) and (4)).

The use of derogations to transfer personal data is possible under Article 44, though their scope has been changed somewhat in comparison with Article 26 of the Directive. In particular, new restrictions on the use of consent to transfer personal data are introduced (Article 44(1)(a)). This may be because there are growing concerns that individuals may not understand what they are consenting to, and that they may not have a meaningful opportunity to refuse consent.[120] One significant change is introduced in Article 44(1)(h), which provides that 'a data transfer may, under limited circumstances, be justified on a legitimate interest of the controller or processor, but only after having assessed and documented the circumstances of that transfer operation'.[121] This would require that data transfers are notified to the DPAs but not approved by them (Article 44(6)). However, the fact that it cannot be used when the transfers can be described as 'frequent or massive' (Article 44(1)(h)) would seem to rule it out in scenarios such as cloud computing.

The Commission Proposal can be criticized on a number of grounds. For one thing, there are few improvements to the existing system for issuing adequacy decisions, which has proved to be slow and cumbersome. It would be advisable to include concrete goals, steps, and time limits to increase the efficiency and transparency of the procedures, which could be accomplished through the insertion of language such as the following to proposed Article 41(3):

The Commission shall adopt and make public binding procedures for reaching decisions concerning the adequacy of protection, which shall contain at least the following information:

(a) the procedures by which a third country, territory, a processing sector within that third country (which can be represented by an association or group of data controllers or data processors), or an international or regional organization may request that an adequacy decision be issued;

(b) the steps of the decision-making procedure, including time limits within which each step must be completed;

(c) the rights of the party or parties that have requested an adequacy decision to present their case in the various steps of the procedure;

(d) how interested parties (including individuals, consumer organizations, academic experts, government entities, data controllers and processors, and others) may express their opinion concerning the proposed decision.

The Commission shall either approve or refuse an application for a decision regarding the adequacy of protection within one year of its submission.

The Proposal also does not sufficiently take into account the enactment by third countries of regional and international instruments (eg, Council of Europe

---

[120] See, eg, Fred H. Cate, 'The Failure of Fair Information Practice Principles', in Jane K. Winn (ed), *Consumer Protection in the Age of the Information Economy* 341 (Ashgate 2006), also online at <http://papers.ssrn.com/sol3/papers.cfm?abstract_id=1156972>.
[121] Explanatory memorandum, at 12.

Convention 108) when assessing the adequacy of protection. To deal with this issue, Article 41(1) could be reformulated as follows:

A transfer may take place where the Commission has decided that the third country, a territory or a processing sector within that third country, or an international organization, a legally binding convention or instrument under human rights law or international law, or a system of data protection adopted under the auspices of a regional organization in question ensures an adequate level of protection. Such transfer shall not require any further authorization.

And finally, the Proposal contains insufficient grounds for transfers in scenarios such as cloud computing. Binding corporate rules are useful mostly for large multinational companies, and there is a need for alternative grounds of transfer that are flexible enough to cover many Internet scenarios and that could be used by smaller companies. The derogation provided by Article 44(1)(h) seems designed at least in part for such scenarios, but it is more appropriate to cover them based on the use of adequate safeguards rather than by including them under a derogation. Since Chapter IV of the Regulation already includes comprehensive accountability obligations for controllers and processors, the best solution would be to allow transfers based on the use of appropriate accountability systems,[122] such as under an addition to Article 42(2) that would consider the following steps to constitute 'appropriate safeguards':

implementation by the data controller or data processor transferring personal data of appropriate and effective measures for protecting them that respect the provisions of this Regulation, in particular Chapter IV (such as through the use of legally-binding internal privacy rules or other similar measures), provided that the data controller or data processor can demonstrate such measures, and their effectiveness, on request from the relevant supervisory authority. The controller or processor shall give particular consideration to the nature of the data, the purpose and duration of the proposed processing operation or operations, as well as the situation in the country of origin, the third country and the country of final destination, and adduced appropriate safeguards with respect to the protection of personal data, where necessary. The controller or the processor shall document the measures referred to in the documentation referred to in Article 28.

This addition would allow for transfers based on measures giving effect to the accountability provisions of the Regulation, which could cover a variety of internal compliance measures that stop short of full-scale BCRs. Transfers would be allowed without prior authorization, but would be subject to control by the DPAs.

---

[122] See Chapter 3.B.2.d regarding the concept of accountability.

I. APEC Privacy Framework

In 2005, the 21 member economies of the Asia-Pacific Economic Cooperation (APEC) group agreed on the APEC Privacy Framework.[123] The Framework is a voluntary set of standards designed to protect personal data transferred outside the APEC member States by use of the principle of 'accountability'.[124] The relevant provision of the Framework reads as follows:

Principle IX (Accountability)

A personal information controller should be accountable for complying with measures that give effect to the Principles stated above. When personal information is to be transferred to another person or organization, whether domestically or internationally, the personal information controller should obtain the consent of the individual or exercise due diligence and take reasonable steps to ensure that the recipient person or organization will protect the information consistently with these Principles.

The Framework foresees that organizations (such as companies) may adopt Cross-Border Privacy Rules (CBPRs) as a way to apply protections across the organization no matter where the data are processed.[125] Like BCRs, CBPRs are internal corporate codes that bind the company to provide a certain level of data protection throughout all its affiliates around the world. A paper released by the US government explains how CBPRs are to work:

One example of an initiative to facilitate transnational mutual recognition is the Asia-Pacific Economic Cooperation's (APEC) voluntary system of Cross Border Privacy Rules (CBPR), which is based on the APEC Privacy Framework and includes privacy principles that APEC member economies have agreed to recognize. Codes of conduct based on these principles could streamline the data privacy policies and practices of companies operating throughout the vast APEC region. Upon implementation, APEC's CBPR system will require interested applicants to demonstrate that they comply with a set of CBPR program requirements based on the APEC Privacy Framework. Moreover, the commitments an applicant makes during this process, while voluntary, must be enforceable under laws in member economies.

---

[123] The APEC member economies include Australia; Brunei Darussalam; Canada; Chile; the People's Republic of China; Hong Kong, China; Indonesia; Japan; the Republic of Korea; Malaysia; Mexico; New Zealand; Papua New Guinea; Peru; the Republic of the Philippines; the Russian Federation; Singapore; Chinese Taipei; Thailand; the US; and Vietnam.

[124] See APEC Privacy Framework (2005), <http://www.apec.org/Groups/Committee-on-Trade-and-Investment/~/media/Files/Groups/ECSG/05_ecsg_privacyframewk.ashx>, Principle 9, providing that a personal information controller 'should be accountable for complying with measures that give effect to the Principles … When personal information is to be transferred to another person or organization, whether domestically or internationally, the personal information controller should obtain the consent of the individual or exercise due diligence and take reasonable steps to ensure that the recipient person or organization will protect the information consistently with these Principles'. See also Chapter 3.B.2.d.

[125] See APEC Data Privacy Pathfinder Projects Implementation Work Plan (Revised), APEC Doc. 2009/SOM1/ECSG/SEM/027, <http://aimp.apec.org/Documents/2009/ECSG/SEM1/09_ecsg_sem1_027.doc>.

Successful CBPR certification will entitle participating companies to represent to consumers that they are accountable and meet stringent and globally recognized standards, so facilitating the transfer of personal data throughout the APEC region.[126]

The Framework grants countries considerable flexibility to implement it in a way that takes into account their social, cultural, and other differences.[127] In addition, the Framework's provisions are subject to derogation by mandatory rules of national law,[128] and there has not yet been extensive experience with mechanisms to implement it in practice (such as CBPRs). Implementation of the Framework may not necessarily require legislation, but can also be accomplished through mechanisms such as industry self-regulation,[129] meaning that divergence is likely to continue even between those countries that have implemented it. The lack of binding effect and the divergence of the Framework from principles of EU data protection law have led to accusations that the level of protection under it is too low;[130] only time will tell how it functions in practice. Still, the APEC Framework has resulted in useful work to develop the concept of accountability and explore how privacy rules can function across a highly diverse region.

J. ECOWAS

The Economic Community of West African States (ECOWAS) is a group of 15 African countries founded in 1975 that promotes regional economic integration.[131] On 16 February 2010, the group adopted a Supplementary Act on Personal Data Protection, which is a model privacy law that the member States may adopt, the relevant provision of which reads as follows:

Article 36

1) The data controller shall transfer personal data to a non-member ECOWAS country only where such a country provides an adequate level of protection for privacy, freedoms and the fundamental rights of individuals in relation to the processing or possible processing of such data.
2) The data controller shall inform the Data Protection Authority prior to any transfer of personal data to such a third country.

Several ECOWAS member countries have enacted data protection legislation that regulates transborder data flows (eg, Benin, Burkina Faso, and Senegal).

---

[126] White House, 'Consumer Data Privacy in a Networked World' (February 2012), <http://www.whitehouse.gov/sites/default/files/privacy-final.pdf>, at 32.

[127] APEC Privacy Framework (n 124), at 7.   [128] APEC Privacy Framework (n 124), at 8.

[129] APEC Privacy Frameworth (n 124), at 31.

[130] See, eg, Graham Greenleaf, 'Five Years of the APEC Privacy Framework: Failure or Promise?', 25 Computer Law and Security Review 28 (2009).

[131] ECOWAS member countries include Benin; Burkina Faso; Cape Verde; the Ivory Coast; Gambia; Ghana; Guinea; Guinea-Bissau; Liberia; Mali; Niger; Nigeria; Senegal; Sierra Leone; and Togo.

K. World trade law

Many companies need to transfer personal data across borders in order to provide services. The General Agreement on Trade in Services (GATS),[132] a treaty of the World Trade Organization (WTO) that entered into force in 1995, has liberalized the provision of many types of services. The obligations of the GATS might seem to conflict with legislative regulation of transborder data flows, since the latter can inhibit or even prevent the provision of services internationally by restricting the transfer of personal data needed to perform them.[133] However, the GATS contains exemptions for rules protecting privacy and for those maintaining 'public order'.[134]

The scope and application of these exemptions is anything but clear, given that no dispute resolution panel rulings have yet construed them, and any regulation seeking to fall under them would still have to satisfy a proportionality or balancing test.[135] Thus, while transborder data flow regulation is, generally speaking, permissible based on the exemptions to the GATS, it is possible that it could violate world trade law in certain circumstances, for example if it were arbitrary or represented a disguised restriction on trade,[136] so that its permissibility will depend largely on an evaluation of the particular circumstances in which it is applied.

L. Organization of American States (OAS)

The Organization of American States (OAS) is the world's oldest regional organization, dating from 1948, and includes 35 countries.[137] The OAS has set forth policy

---

[132] General Agreement on Trade in Services, 15 April 1994, Marrakesh Agreement Establishing the World Trade Organization, Annex 1B, The legal texts: The results of the Uruguay Round of multilateral trade negotiations 284 (1999), 1869 UNTS 183, 33 International Legal Materials 1167 (1994).

[133] See Peter P. Swire and Robert E. Litan, *None of Your Business: World Data Flows, Electronic Commerce, and the European Privacy Directive* (Brookings Institution Press 1998), at 189–96; Maria Verónica Perez Asinari, 'Is there any Room for Privacy and Data Protection within the WTO Rules?', 9 Electronic Commerce Law Review 249 (2002); Rolf H. Weber, 'Regulatory Autonomy and Privacy Standards under GATS', 7 Asian Journal of WTO and International Health Law and Policy 25 (2012). See also Gregory Shaffer, 'Globalization and Social Protection: the Impact of EU and International Rules in the Ratcheting Up of US Privacy Standards', 25 Yale Journal of International Law 1, 46–51 (2000).

[134] GATS, Article XIV, stating: 'Subject to the requirement that such measures are not applied in a manner which would constitute a means of arbitrary or unjustifiable discrimination between countries where like conditions prevail, or a disguised restriction on trade in services, nothing in this Agreement shall be construed to prevent the adoption or enforcement by any Member of measures ... (a) necessary to protect public morals or to maintain public order ... (c) necessary to secure compliance with laws or regulations which are not inconsistent with the provisions of this Agreement including those relating to ... (ii) the protection of the privacy of individuals in relation to the processing and dissemination of personal data and the protection of confidentiality of individual records and accounts ...'

[135] See Weber (n 133), at 39–40.   [136] Weber (n 133), at 43–4.

[137] The member countries are Antigua and Barbuda; Argentina; Barbados; Belize; Bolivia; Brazil; Canada; Chile; Colombia; Costa Rica; Cuba; Commonwealth of Dominica; Dominican Republic; Ecuador; El Salvador; Grenada; Guatemala; Guyana; Haiti; Honduras; Jamaica; Mexico; Nicaragua;

options for member States in the area of data protection, which includes the following one concerning international data transfers:[138]

International transfers of personal data should only be carried out if the receiving country, which is the destination country, offers, at a minimum, the same level of personal data protection, afforded by these principles ... Moreover, transit countries, which are countries where information is routed through and not processed, do not have to be in compliance ... However, the transfer of the personal data should still be secure. To determine whether minimum data protection standards are afforded by a receiving country, the following factors should be analyzed: 1) the nature of the data; 2) the country of origin; 3) the receiving country; 4) the purpose for which the data is being processed; and 5) the security measures in place for the transfer and processing of the personal data ... In the event that the receiving country does not afford the same level of protection, the transfer of personal data may still occur if one of the following conditions exists and the processing is fair and lawful ... [139]

The OAS has indicated that it is 'committed to exploring a potential Model Inter-American Law on Data Protection',[140] which presumably may contain rules dealing with transborder data flows.

M. Data transfers by States, governments, and regulatory agencies

1. Introduction

When the first transborder data flow regulation was enacted in the 1970s, most data transfers carried out by States, governments, and regulatory agencies did not involve personal data (ie, names, addresses, and other information that could be tied to an identifiable person).[141] Provisions in international agreements dealing with the transfer of personal data have traditionally tended to be broad and lacking in detail; for example, the following provision is contained in the US Social Security Administration's Totalization Agreements, which have been entered into between the US and numerous States:

Unless otherwise required by the national statutes of a Party, information about an individual which is transmitted in accordance with this Agreement to that Party by the other Party

---

Panama; Paraguay; Peru; Saint Kitts and Nevis; St Lucia; Saint Vincent and the Grenadines; Suriname; The Bahamas; Trinidad and Tobago; the US; Uruguay; and Venezuela.

[138] See Permanent Council of the Organization of American States, Committee on Juridical and Political Affairs, Draft: Preliminary Principles and Recommendations on Data Protection (The Protection of Personal Data), CP/CAJP-2921/10, 19 November 2010.

[139] Draft: Preliminary Principles and Recommendationson Data Protection (n 138), at 12.

[140] OAS, Department of International Law Newsletter, 'Department of International Law Advances Cooperation with Organizations and Authorities on Privacy and Data Protection' (November 2011), <http://www.oas.org/dil/Newsletter/newsletter_api_ppd_NOV-2011.html>.

[141] See, eg, Freese (n 16), at 32, stating in 1979 that 'there seems to be little to indicate that extensive transfers of personal data are made by public authorities. The flow of technical data, on the other hand, is quite considerable.'

shall be used exclusively for purposes of implementing this Agreement. Such information received by a Party shall be governed by the national statutes of that Party for the protection of privacy and confidentiality of personal data.[142]

However, this situation has changed completely in the last few years, and States and public authorities now routinely transfer personal data to other countries. Many of these transfers involve the sharing of data between States for purposes that can include corporate governance, pharmaceutical regulation, taxation, anti-money laundering, law enforcement, among others.

Data transfers between States can give rise to special concerns. First, States have unmatched power over the life and liberty of individuals, so misuse of data by them can have the most serious repercussions.[143] Secondly, in some cases government processing of personal data may not be fully subject to data protection and privacy law. For example, until a few years ago data processing relating to national defence, security, and criminal law was exempt from the scope of the EU Data Protection Directive[144] (this situation changed under the Lisbon Treaty which entered into force on 1 December 2009,[145] and the European Commission has also proposed a General Data Protection Directive that would apply to data processing for criminal justice purposes but has not yet been enacted[146]). As can be seen in the Appendix, many data protection laws regulating transborder data flows also contain exemptions covering transfers for governmental or law enforcement purposes.[147]

Details about data processing by States and data sharing between them are often not officially published, and can be difficult to locate. Discussions with government officials and DPAs indicate that many transborder data flows taking place between governments are removed from legal and public scrutiny.

2. Law enforcement data access and data sharing

Data sharing between governments for law enforcement purposes has increased greatly following the terrorist attacks of 11 September 2001. This was spurred in particular by the recommendations of the '9/11 Commission' of the US government issued in 2004, which found that the effective combating of terrorism

---

[142] Quoted in John W. Kropf, *Guide to U.S. Government Practice on Global Sharing of Personal Information* (American Bar Association 2012), at 5. The Agreement is available at <http://www.ssa.gov/international/agreement_descriptions.html>.

[143] See regarding the potential of misuse of data processing to lead to large-scale human rights abuses by governments, William Seltzer and Margo Anderson, 'The Dark Side of Numbers: The Role of Population Data Systems in Human Rights Abuses', 68(2) Social Research 481 (2001).

[144] EU Data Protection Directive, Article 3(2).

[145] Treaty of Lisbon amending the Treaty on European Union and the Treaty establishing the European Community, [2007] OJ C306/1.

[146] See n 116.

[147] See, eg, Argentina Personal Data Protection Act (4 October 2000), Act No. 25,326, Section 12(2)(e); Dubai International Financial Centre Data Protection Law 2007, Law No. 1 of 2007, Article 12(1)(j); Macao Personal Data Protection Act (Act 8/2005), Article 20(3); Mauritius Data Protection Act 2004, Act No. 13 of 2004, Article 31(2)(b)(iii).

required a much greater sharing of data both between US government agencies, and between the US government and other governments:

The U.S. government cannot meet its own obligations to the American people to prevent the entry of terrorists without a major effort to collaborate with other governments. We should do more to exchange terrorist information with trusted allies, and raise U.S. and global border security standards for travel and border crossing over the medium and long term through extensive international cooperation.[148]

The US government then enacted a series of mandates to share personal data with its allies and friends.[149]

In the wake of the 9/11 Commission's report, the US has been seeking to conclude agreements with other States and regional bodies to facilitate the sharing of personal data for law enforcement purposes.[150] Such agreements have been concluded between the EU and the US covering the transfer of PNR data of airline passengers[151] and of financial messaging data (the SWIFT Case).[152] The 'High Level Contact Group', which is comprised of officials from various entities of the EU and the US government, has agreed on a set of high-level principles to provide privacy protections for data transferred between the two.[153] The EU and the US are currently attempting to negotiate a treaty to govern information sharing. While such agreements to share data for law enforcement purposes with the US contain protections for privacy and personal data, they have been criticized as in effect 'watering down' the protections contained in EU law.[154] The EU has also created a number of

---

[148] See 'The 9/11 Commission Report' (2004), at 390, <http://www.911commission.gov/report/911Report.pdf>.

[149] See Kropf (n 142), at 3 fn 1, who mentions the US Secretary of State's authorization under the USA PATRIOT Act of 2011 to enter into agreements with foreign governments to share information from the visa lookout database for the purpose of fighting terrorism, and Homeland Security Presidential Directive 6 (HSPD-6) that mandated the Secretary of State to seek ways to access terrorist screening information from foreign States.

[150] See John W. Kropf, 'The Golden Rule of Privacy: A Proposal for a Global Privacy Policy on Government-to-Government Sharing of Personal Information', (15 January 2007) Bloomberg BNA Privacy & Security Law Report 90, stating that 'the US government is on the cusp of implementing a series of international agreements to share personally identifiable information (PII) with its allies and friends'.

[151] Agreement between the United States of America and the European Union on the use and transfer of passenger name records to the United States Department of Homeland Security, [2012] OJ L215/5, containing safeguards for the processing of PNR data by the DHS, and providing under Article 19 that 'In consideration of this Agreement and its implementation, DHS shall be deemed to provide, within the meaning of relevant EU data protection law, an adequate level of protection for PNR processing and use. In this respect, carriers which have provided PNR to DHS in compliance with this Agreement shall be deemed to have complied with applicable legal requirements in the EU related to the transfer of such data from the EU to the United States.'

[152] See n 102. Article 5 provides protections to personal data transferred from the EU to the US for the purposes of the US Terrorist Finance Tracking Program, and Article 6 declares that they result in an adequate level of data protection.

[153] Reports by the High Level Contact Group (HLCG) on information sharing and privacy and personal data protection (23 November 2009), Principle 12, <http://register.consilium.europa.eu/pdf/en/09/st15/st15851.en09.pdf>.

[154] See, eg, 'Opinion of the European Data Protection Supervisor on the Proposal for a Council Decision on the conclusion of the Agreement between the United States of America and the European

intra-governmental systems for the sharing of law enforcement-related data, such as the Schengen Information System for the sharing of data for the purpose of law enforcement and immigration control.[155]

Government use of personal data and data sharing increasingly involves data originally collected by the private sector. The purposes for such data access are highly varied, and can include 'to deliver social services, administer tax programmes and collect revenue, issue licenses, support hundreds of regulatory regimes ranging from voter registration to employee identity verification, operate public facilities such as toll roads and national parks, and for law enforcement and national security'.[156] There is also a growing number of cases in which governments obligate businesses to collect, retain, and share with them data about their customers and clients, in order to combat offences such as money laundering, drug trafficking, tax evasion, and terrorism.[157] This may include access by governments to personal data stored by companies in other countries,[158] including data on the Internet.[159] States and regional organizations in many areas of the world sometimes conclude treaties that provide protections to personal data transferred between them for law enforcement purposes; for example, the EU has concluded an agreement with the Australian government providing protections for EU PNR data transferred to Australia.[160]

The conditions under which such data access and data sharing by law enforcement takes place are highly diverse, untransparent, and largely subject to national law, meaning that there is little harmonization of them, even within regional groups like the EU whose Member States are subject to the same overarching

Union on the use and transfer of Passenger Name Records to the United States Department of Homeland Security' (9 December 2011), <http://www.edps.europa.eu/EDPSWEB/webdav/site/mySite/shared/Documents/Consultation/Opinions/2011/11-12-09_US_PNR_EN.pdf>; Chris Jones (Statewatch Analysis), 'Making fundamental rights flexible: the European Commission's Approach to negotiating agreements on the transfer of passenger name record (PNR) data to the USA and Australia' (March 2012), <http://www.statewatch.org/analyses/no-169-eu-pnr-us-aus-comparison.pdf>.

155   Convention implementing the Schengen Agreement of 14 June 1995 between the Governments of the States of the Benelux Economic Union, the Federal Republic of Germany and the French Republic on the gradual abolition of checks at their common borders, [2000] OJ L239/19. See Franziska Boehm, *Information Sharing and Data Protection in the Area of Freedom, Security and Justice* (Springer 2012), at 260–319; Els De Busser, *Data Protection in EU and US Criminal Cooperation* (Maklu 2009).

156   Fred H. Cate, James X. Dempsey, and Ira S. Rubenstein, 'Systematic government access to private-sector data', 2 International Data Privacy Law 195, 195 (2012).

157   Cate, Dempsey, and Rubenstein (n 156).

158   For examples of such situations, see ICC, 'Cross-border law enforcement access to company data—current issues under data protection and privacy law', Doc. No. 373/507 (7 February 2012), <http://www.iccwbo.org/Data/Policies/2012/Cross-border-law-enforcement-access-to-company-data-current-issues-under-data-protection-and-privacy-law/>.

159   See European Data Protection Supervisor, 'Opinion of the European Data Protection Supervisor on the Commission's Communication on "Unleashing the potential of Cloud Computing in Europe"', 16 November 2012, at 22.

160   See, eg, Agreement between the European Union and Australia on the processing and transfer of European Union-sourced passenger name record (PNR) data by air carriers to the Australian Customs Service, [2008] OJ L213/49.

framework of fundamental rights law.[161] The access to personal data by foreign law enforcement authorities has led to international political tensions, particularly between the EU and the US.[162]

3. Other international agreements

There are also innumerable bilateral and multilateral agreements concluded between countries that cover the exchange of data in specific governmental contexts and that may contain privacy protections. It is impossible here systematically to analyse the thousands of international agreements that involve the exchange of personal data, which are not all accessible and are often available only in various local languages. Taking just one country as an example, the US is party to 'dozens of government-to-government (G2G) information-sharing agreements on a spectrum of topics, including taxes, pension payments, securities enforcement, airline passenger data, lost or stolen travel documents, and law enforcement'.[163] Privacy-related provisions in these agreements range from short, generic paragraphs[164] to lengthier, custom-drafted provisions based on the US Fair Information Practices Principles.[165] Anecdotal evidence and discussion with diplomats, data protection regulators, and other government officials indicate that in many countries provisions related to data protection and privacy contained in treaties lack any kind of harmonization.

Some of the multilateral agreements that regulate the sharing of personal data would not be thought of as instruments of data protection and privacy law, and thus fall outside this study. For example, in 2002 the International Organization of Securities Commissions (IOSCO) concluded a 'Multilateral Memorandum of Understanding (MMOU) concerning Consultation and Cooperation and the Exchange of Information' governing the exchange of information between securities regulators in 82 countries as of May 2012.[166] The MMOU does not mention the words 'data protection' or 'privacy', but contains protections for personal data exchanged across borders between securities regulators, and implements

---

[161] See Boehm (n 155), at 425, stating with regard to data sharing by law enforcement within the EU that 'information exchange ... is still an unregulated field above all in respect of the protection of fundamental rights'.

[162] See, eg, Fred H. Cate, 'Government data mining: the need for a legal framework', 43 Harvard Civil Rights-Civil Liberties Law Review 435 (2008); Joel R. Reidenberg, 'E-commerce and transatlantic privacy', 38 Houston Law Review 717 (2001); Yesha Yadav, 'Separated by a common language? An examination of the transatlantic dialogue on data privacy law and policy in the fight against terrorism', 36 Rutgers Computer and Technology Law Journal 73 (2009). See also Chapter 6.D.3.

[163] Kropf (n 142), at 2.

[164] See, eg, Article 15 of the US–German Social Security Agreement, 7 January 1976, which provides: 'The use of information furnished under the Agreement by one Contracting State to another with regard to an individual shall be governed by the respective national statutes for the protection of privacy and confidentiality of personal data.'

[165] See examples cited in Kropf (n 142), at 17–27.

[166] See <http://www.iosco.org/library/index.cfm?section=mou_siglist>.

various principles such as confidentiality that are essential to privacy protection as well.[167]

N. Madrid Resolution

Because of the diversity of national data protection and privacy legislation, there have been growing calls for a global legal instrument on data protection, resulting in the drafting of proposed standards by a group of DPAs from around the world under the leadership of the Spanish Data Protection Authority. In November 2009, the group published the 'Madrid Resolution', which is a set of international standards for data protection and privacy.[168] The Madrid Resolution contains a provision dealing with international data transfers, which provides that they may generally be carried out when the country of data import affords the level of protection provided in the Resolution.[169] In addition, the document allows such level of protection to be afforded by other means, such as contractual clauses, binding corporate rules,[170] or in situations similar to those covered in the exceptions in Article 26(1) of the EU Directive (eg, when the data subject consents).[171] Finally, national DPAs are empowered to make such data transfers subject to authorization before being carried out.[172]

O. Conclusions

Transborder data flow regulation has developed from a national phenomenon in the 1970s to one dealt with by a variety of international instruments. The various instruments demonstrate a number of similarities, but there are also important differences between them (eg, as to whether they are legally binding, and whether they treat data protection as a fundamental right). Many of them are being revised, so that they may change in the coming years.

 While privacy protection has been the main motivation for enacting transborder data flow regulation, States have sometimes also used it as a way to further their sovereignty. Regulation also implicates other important rights and values, particularly freedom of expression and the free flow of data, which sometimes have not been sufficiently considered. The nature of the data transferred has also changed fundamentally since the first international instruments were enacted; for example, there is now much more sharing of personal data between governments

---

[167] See, eg, sections 10 and 11 of the MMOU.
[168] Madrid Resolution, 'International Standards on the Protection of Personal Data and Privacy' (2009).
[169] Madrid Resolution (n 168), para. 15(1).   [170] Madrid Resolution (n 168), para. 15(2).
[171] Madrid Resolution (n 168), para. 15(3).   [172] Madrid Resolution (n 168).

(often for law enforcement purposes), though the details of such transfers are often unclear.

In order to understand transborder data flow regulation, it is necessary to identify the different ways in which regulation can be classified. The analysis in the next chapter will demonstrate further the diversity of such regulation, and will discuss the different levels at which transborder data flow regulation operates.

3

Typology of Regulatory Approaches

A. Introduction

Over the last few decades numerous countries have adopted data protection or privacy laws that regulate transborder data flows, based on one or more of the international and regional instruments surveyed in Chapter 2; national laws are discussed in more detail in Chapter 4.

This activity has led to a diverse body of regulation that can be characterized in different ways, such as whether it follows a geographic or an organizational approach; what the default regulatory position is; which types of organization promulgate or enact it; its legal nature; and the forms that it takes. In many cases these characteristics overlap, so that regulation cannot always be classified as belonging solely to one category or the other.

B. Differences between regulatory systems

1. Data protection as a fundamental right

In some countries, such as the Member States of the European Union and those that adhere to the European Convention on Human Rights and the Council of

Europe Convention 108, data protection is regarded as a fundamental human right. This is expressly stated, for example, in the EU Data Protection Directive,[1] the European Convention on Human Rights as interpreted by the European Court of Human Rights,[2] EU treaties,[3] the EU Charter of Fundamental Rights,[4] Council of European Convention 108,[5] several national constitutions of European countries,[6] and case law of the European Court of Justice (ECJ).[7]

The classification of data protection as a fundamental right has important implications. Taking the EU as an example, protection of fundamental rights is considered to be one of the general principles of EU law, against which all regulation must be evaluated, and breach of which may give rise to liability in damages.[8] As a fundamental right and general principle of law, data protection has the same legal status as the EU treaties.[9]

In other legal systems, data protection and privacy may have a different status. For example, the terms 'fundamental right' and 'human right' are not used at all in the APEC Privacy Framework, and the purpose of the Framework is described instead in terms of realizing the benefits of electronic commerce.[10] In the US, privacy is protected by a myriad of state and sector-specific federal laws, with constitutional protections limited to governmental intrusion.[11] In legal systems without overarching protection for privacy as a fundamental right, its status is thus determined by the type of legal basis on which protection rests in a particular case (ie, federal law, state law, case law, administrative regulation).

Even in those legal systems that regard data protection as a fundamental right, the regulation of transborder data flows may not necessarily be considered a 'core'

---

[1] Article 1(1), stating: 'Member States shall protect the fundamental rights and freedoms of natural persons, and in particular their right to privacy with respect to the processing of personal data'.

[2] See Article 8 of the Convention, together with case law interpreting it, such as *Rotaru v Romania* (2000) ECHR 191. See also Robin C.A. White and Claire Ovey, *The European Convention on Human Rights* (5th edn, OUP 2010), at 374–7.

[3] See Consolidated version of the Treaty on the Functioning of the European Union, [2010] OJ C83/47, Article 16(1), stating: 'Everyone has the right to the protection of personal data concerning them'.

[4] Charter of Fundamental Rights of the European Union, [2010] OJ C83/2, Article 8(1), stating: 'Everyone has the right to the protection of personal data concerning him or her'.

[5] Article 1, referring to the individual's 'right to privacy, with regard to automatic processing of personal data relating to him'.

[6] See, eg, Belgian Constitution of 7 February 1831, last revised in July 1993, Article 22; Portuguese Constitution of 2 April 1976, Article 26; Spanish Constitution of 27 December 1978, Article 18; Swedish Constitution of 1 January 1975, Article 2.

[7] See, eg, Joined Cases C-465/00, C-138/01, and C-139/01 *Rechnungshof* [2003] ECR I-4989, at para. 68.

[8] See Takis Tridimas, *The General Principles of EU Law* (2nd edn OUP 2009), at 29–35.

[9] Tridimas (n 8), at 51.

[10] See APEC Privacy Framework (2005), <http://www.apec.org/Groups/Committee-on-Trade-and-Investment/~/media/Files/Groups/ECSG/05_ecsg_privacyframewk.ashx>, at 3, stating: 'APEC economies realize that a key part of efforts to improve consumer confidence and ensure the growth of electronic commerce must be cooperation to balance and promote both effective information privacy protection and the free flow of information in the Asia Pacific region'.

[11] See Paul M. Schwartz and Daniel Solove, *Privacy Law Fundamentals* (International Association of Privacy Professionals 2011), at 2–7.

principle of the law. For example, in the *Bodil Lindqvist* case, the ECJ held that the restrictions on transborder data flows contained in Article 25 of the EU Directive did not apply, partly because it found them to constitute a 'regime of special application', which it contrasted with the 'general regime' under Chapter II of the Directive that sets forth the conditions for the lawful processing of personal data.[12] Thus, in the EU Directive, the provisions on transborder data flows are not included in the section containing the core rules of data processing ('Chapter II: General Rules on the Lawfulness of the Processing of Personal Data'), but in a separate section ('Chapter IV: Transfer of Personal Data to Third Countries'). This suggests that the restrictions of Articles 25 and 26 of the Directive have a subsidiary function, and are not of the same status as the general rules for data processing contained elsewhere in the Directive. Likewise, the Madrid Resolution[13] refers throughout to data protection as a 'right', but the regulation of transborder data flows is included not in Part II, which lists 'basic principles' of data protection (lawfulness and fairness, purpose specification, proportionality, data quality, openness, and accountability), but instead in a separate section (section 15).

It is permissible under human rights law both to recognize data protection as a fundamental human right, and to find that regulation of transborder data flows plays a subsidiary role in it. Regarding a topic as a fundamental right does not mean that every detail of its implementation is fundamental to its nature.[14] Thus, for example, the EU Charter of Fundamental Rights refers to the 'essence' of fundamental rights and freedoms,[15] and mentions as essential elements of data protection the requirement that data are processed based on consent or some other legal basis, the rights of access and rectification, and control of data protection rules by an independent authority,[16] but without mentioning regulation of transborder data flows. The European Court of Human Rights generally interprets rights in terms of their object and purpose in the context of the European Convention on Human Rights as a whole,[17] and (as will be discussed later) it is the object and purpose of transborder data flow regulation to act as a kind of conflict of laws regime that seeks to apply the core principles of data protection law no matter where data are processed.[18] Thus, such regulation does not itself constitute a core substantive rule of data protection law.

---

[12] C-101/01 [2003] ECR I-12971, paras. 63 and 69.

[13] Madrid Resolution, 'International Standards on the Protection of Personal Data and Privacy' (2009).

[14] See Peter Hustinx, Concluding Remarks made at 3rd Annual Symposium of the European Union Agency for Fundamental Rights, Vienna (10 May 2012), <http://www.edps.europa.eu/EDPSWEB/webdav/site/mySite/shared/Documents/EDPS/Publications/Speeches/2012/12–05–10_Speech_Vienna_EN.pdf>, at 5.

[15] Charter of Fundamental Rights of the European Union (n 4), Article 52(1).

[16] Charter of Fundamental Rights of the European Union (n 4), Article 8(2) and (3).

[17] See White and Ovey (n 2), at 65.   [18] See Chapter 6.

2. Geographically-based versus organizationally-based regulation

(a) Introduction

A further distinction can be made between transborder data flow regulation based on the location to which the data are to be transferred (the geographically-based approach), and that based on the organizations that receive the data abroad (the organizationally-based approach). Many countries have adopted the geographical-ly-based approach, which is based on whether an 'adequate level of data protection' is offered by the importing country. Council of Europe Convention 108 uses this standard, along with all the EU Member States; other European countries such as Albania, Andorra, Bosnia and Herzegovina, and Russia; Latin American countries such as Argentina; African countries like Benin, Morocco, and Senegal; and some Asian countries such as Macau.

The organizationally-based approach makes data exporters accountable for ensur-ing the continued protection of personal data transferred to other organizations no matter what their geographic location. The Canadian Personal Information Protection and Electronic Documents Act (PIPEDA) implements the account-ability approach,[19] as does the law of Mexico, which allows data transfers without the consent of the data subject 'where the transfer is made to holding companies, subsidiaries or affiliates under common control of the data controller, or to a par-ent company or any company of the same group as the data controller, operating under the same internal processes and policies'.[20] The law of Colombia also allows transfer when either the country of import or the recipient of the data provides sufficient guarantees for their protection.[21]

(b) Geographically-based approach (adequacy)

The geographically-based approach regulates data transfers based on the standard of data protection in the country of import. This requires both that a certain level of protection is assured by the legal system of the country in question, and that such protections are actually complied with, since 'data protection rules only con-tribute to the protection of individuals if they are followed in practice'.[22] Since the geographically-based approach is closely associated with the concept of an 'adequate level of data protection' contained in Article 25 of the EU Data Protection Directive, it will also be referred to here as the 'adequacy approach'.

---

[19] See Office of the Privacy Commissioner of Canada, 'Guidelines for Processing Personal Data across Borders' (2009), <http://www.priv.gc.ca/information/guide/2009/gl_dab_090127_E.pdf>, at 5, stating: 'PIPEDA does not prohibit organizations in Canada from transferring personal informa-tion to an organization in another jurisdiction for processing. However under PIPEDA, organizations are held accountable for the protection of personal information transfers under each individual out-sourcing arrangement'.

[20] Decree issuing the Federal Law on Protection of Personal Data Held by Private Parties (2010), Article 37(III).

[21] Law 1266 of 2008, Article 5.

[22] Article 29 Working Party, 'Working Document: Transfers of personal data to third countries: Applying Articles 25 and 26 of the EU data protection directive' (WP 12, 24 July 1998), at 5.

Regional and national legislation in countries following the adequacy approach apply a variety of formulations to measure the level of protection, such as the following:

- 'an adequate level of protection' (EU Directive[23]);
- 'an equivalent protection' (Council of Europe Convention 108[24])
- 'an adequate level of protection' (Additional Protocol to Council of Europe Convention 108[25]);
- 'a level of protection for personal data equivalent, at least, to that established by this Law' (Andorra[26]);
- 'the same principles of data protection' (Bosnia and Herzegovina[27]);
- 'a sufficient level of protection for privacy rights, rights and freedoms of data subjects in relation to the processing of personal data' (Senegal[28]).

In EU law, the substantive requirements for adequacy include adherence of the legal system to certain basic data processing requirements (namely the principles of purpose limitation, data quality and proportionality, transparency, security, rights of data subjects, and restrictions on onward transfers), as well as to other legal requirements that are considered 'additional' (restrictions on processing sensitive data, on direct marketing, and on automated individual decisions).[29] A finding of adequacy by the EU is a complex process that typically takes several years, and involves the following steps:[30]

- a formal request from the country involved that it seeks to be considered adequate;
- a proposal from the European Commission (made on the basis of a legal study prepared by an academic institution);
- an opinion of the Article 29 Working Party;
- an opinion of the Article 31 Committee delivered by a qualified majority of the Member States;
- a 30-day period of scrutiny for the European Parliament, to check if the Commission has exercised its powers properly (the Parliament may also issue a recommendation if it wishes); and
- an opinion adopted by the College of Commissioners.

---

[23] Article 25(1).   [24] Article 12(3)(a).   [25] Article 2(1).
[26] Qualified Law 15/2003 of December 18, on the Protection of Personal Data, 2003, Article 35.
[27] Law on the Protection of Personal Data, Article 8.
[28] Law No. 2008–12 of January 25, 2008, on the Protection of Personal Data, Article 49.
[29] Article 29 Working Party (n 22), at 6–7.
[30] See European Commission, 'Commission decisions on the adequacy of the protection of personal data in third countries', <http://ec.europa.eu/justice/data-protection/document/international-transfers/adequacy/index_en.htm>.

The adequacy approach can serve as a motivation for States to enact transborder data flow regulation, in order to attract data exports from other countries and thus support the data processing sector of their economies.[31] Encouragement of other States to adopt similar regulation was one of the motivations for the adequacy standard contained in the EU Directive.[32]

In practice, it can be difficult for a State or regional organization to pass judgement on a foreign regulatory system without political considerations playing some role. For example, in July 2010 the government of Ireland delayed an EU adequacy decision for Israel based on alleged Israeli government involvement in the forging of Irish passports.[33] In addition, members of the Article 29 Working Party have told the author that politics entered into that group's decision to approve Argentina as providing an adequate level of data protection,[34] and a failed bid for adequacy by Australia in the early 2000s caused tensions between that country and the EU. There is thus a risk that a determination of adequacy may become entangled in political issues.

(c) Crafting an adequacy system: the example of Convention 108

The Additional Protocol to Council of Europe Convention 108 provides that data may only be transferred to a non-party if an 'adequate level of protection for the intended data transfer' applies (Article 2(1)), making it a prime example of the adequacy approach. The work on modernization of Convention 108 undertaken by that organization's Bureau of the Consultative Committee of the Convention for the Protection of individuals with Regard to the Automatic Processing of Personal Data (T-PD) illustrates the difficulties of devising a geographically-based standard for data imports that is logically coherent, provides sufficient protection, and is flexible in its application.

Both the Council of Europe Secretariat and the International Chamber of Commerce (ICC) have made drafting suggestions to modernize the text. Section 1 of the ICC proposal of 2 September 2011 would define an adequate level of protection as follows:

---

[31] See, eg, Amiti Sen and Harsimran Julka, 'India seeks "Data Secure Nation" status, more Hi-end business from European Union', *The Economic Times*, 16 April 2012, <http://articles.economictimes.indiatimes.com/2012-04-16/news/31349813_1_data-security-council-data-protection-laws-standard-contractual-clauses>, explaining that the Indian government is seeking to persuade the EU that it offers adequate data protection in order to entice more data processing business to India from European customers.

[32] See, eg, Lokke Moerel, *Binding Corporate Rules: Corporate Self-Regulation of Global Data Transfers* (OUP 2012), at 19 fn 9.

[33] See 'Ireland blocks EU data sharing with Israel' (8 July 2010), <http://jta.org/news/article/2010/07/08/2739965/ireland-backs-out-of-data-sharing-with-israel>. Israel later received an adequacy decision from the European Commission; see Commission Decision 2011/61/EU of 31 January 2011 pursuant to Directive 95/46/EC of the European Parliament and of the Council on the adequate protection of personal data by the State of Israel with regard to automated processing of personal data, [2011] OJ L27/39.

[34] Commission Decision C (2003) 1731 of 30 June 2003 pursuant to Directive 95/46/EC of the European Parliament and of the Council on the adequate protection of personal data in Argentina, [2003] OJ L168.

2. An adequate level of protection based on the protections stipulated in this Convention under section 1 may be provided as follows:
   a. the State in which the organisation processing the personal data is located has been found under applicable domestic or international law to offer adequate protection based on the protections stipulated in this Convention; or
   b. the organisation or organisations processing the personal data have been found to offer such protection; or
   c. the organisation or organisations processing the personal data have implemented appropriate and effective measures for ensuring such protection (such as through the use of contractual clauses, legally-binding internal privacy rules, or other similar measures), and can demonstrate such measures, and their effectiveness, on request from the relevant supervisory authority.
3. By way of derogation from sections 1 and 2, adequate protection need not be provided in the following cases:
   a. the individual has given his consent unambiguously to the processing; or
   b. the processing is necessary for the performance of a contract between the individual and the organisation processing the data or the implementation of pre-contractual measures taken in response to the individual's request; or
   c. the processing is necessary for the conclusion or performance of a contract concluded in the interest of the individual between the organisation processing the data and a third party; or
   d. the processing is necessary or legally required on important public interest grounds, or for the establishment, exercise or defence of legal claims; or
   e. the processing is necessary in order to protect the vital interests of the individual.

In this draft, the notion of an 'adequate level of protection' is tied to the protections of Convention 108, as specified further in sections 2 and 3; the term 'protections stipulated in this Convention' in section 2 is taken from current Article 11 of the Convention. These provisions would cover situations where either the State in which the organization is located, or the organization processing the data, has been found to offer adequate protection. Adequacy could be determined nationally or internationally (such as via an EU adequacy decision). The provision does not distinguish between data flows to State parties to the Convention and those to States that are not parties. Section 2(c) implements the concept of accountability, and recognizes the use of mechanisms such as standard contractual clauses and binding corporate rules (BCRs). Provided that suitable and effective measures are in place, it is intended to cover situations where processing occurs within or across a single organization or where the data are transferred to a third party. The reference to 'organisation or organisations' in sections 2(b) and 2(c) allows for transfers to multiple entities that have separately or jointly implemented effective protections to cover the data processing.

The draft of the Council of Europe Secretariat dated 15 November 2011 also contains principles for determining adequacy, and provides as follows:

3. By way of derogation from paragraph 1, each Party may also allow for the communication and disclosure of personal data, for the purpose of processing, to a recipient which is not subject to the jurisdiction of a Party to the Convention, where,

in light of the present Convention, the adequate level of protection is ensured by measures adopted and implemented by the person communicating or disclosing personal data, and by the recipient, in so far as:

a. those persons can demonstrate, to a competent supervisory authority within the meaning of Article 12ter of this convention, prior to the communication or disclosure of data, the quality and effectiveness of the measures taken, notably by means of contractual clauses, binding internal rules or similar measures, and

b. the national authorities can only have access to data according to rules safeguarding, in light of the present Convention, an adequate protection of the data subjects, and

c. the competent supervisory authority within the meaning of Article 12ter of this convention, be informed in a reasonable period of time and prior to the measures referred to in litera a [sic], and that it can suspend, forbid or subject to condition the communication or disclosure of data.[35]

The Secretariat's next draft (of 18 January 2012) is too lengthy to quote here in full. The main provision concerning adequacy reads as follows:

2. When the recipient is subject to the jurisdiction of a Party to the Convention, the law applicable to this recipient is presumed to provide an adequate level of protection and a Party shall not prohibit or subject to special authorisation their communication or making available, as referred to in paragraph 1 bis.[36]

Article 12(3) of the draft goes on to provide that the presumption of adequacy of protection shall not apply when data are communicated or made accessible through a party to the Convention which is a mere intermediary for communicating data to a non-party such that the legislation of the party is circumvented; the legislation of the party to which the data are communicated includes specific data processing rules that do not find their equivalent in the legislation of the party to which the recipient of the data is subject; or the party to which the recipient is subject has not implemented all of the rights and obligations of the Convention as determined in a proceeding before the T-PD. Section 12(4) provides that when the recipient is not subject to the jurisdiction of a party to the Convention, an adequate level of protection can be ensured by other means, such as contract clauses and other mechanisms that will be discussed later.

The draft then states (Article 12(5)) that when a service not subject to the law of a party to the Convention is provided to an individual habitually resident in the territory of a party and processes data 'beyond what is necessary to deliver the service', the parties shall provide that the service cannot be carried out unless the law applicable to it provides for an adequate level of protection; this proposal would use applicable law rules to protect data processed abroad. Finally, Article 12(7) allows transfers without an adequate level of protection when the data subject has given his or her consent, the specific interests of the data subject require it in a

---

[35] T-PD-BUR(2011) 27_en (15 November 2011), <http://www.coe.int/t/dghl/standardsetting/dataprotection/TPD_documents/T-PD-BUR_2011_27_en.pdf>.

[36] T-PD-BUR(2012)01EN (18 January 2012), <http://www.coe.int/t/dghl/standardsetting/dataprotection/TPD_documents/T-PD-BUR_2012_01_en.pdf>.

particular case, or 'the legitimate interests, in particular important public interests, prevail in the specific case'.

The ICC draft of 31 January reads as follows with regard to the standard of protection:

2. When the recipient is subject to the jurisdiction of a Party to the Convention, the law applicable to this recipient is presumed to provide an adequate level of protection and a Party shall not prohibit or subject to special authorisation their communication or making available, as referred to in paragraph 1. However, the presumption of adequacy of protection provided for in paragraph 1 shall not apply when, as determined by the Consultative Committee provided for in Chapter V by a majority vote, one of the following conditions applies with regard to the Party to whose jurisdiction the recipient is subject:
   a. the Party has not implemented in law some or all of the rights and obligations enshrined in the Convention, or
   b. the Party does not generally observe such rights and obligations in practice.

It also provides that parties not subject to the Convention may transfer data based on 'appropriate safeguards' (as discussed later), and that transfers may be made under grounds identical to those of Article 26(1) of the Directive, with an important addition (section 12(4)(f)), taken from Article 44(1)(h) of the Commission proposal for a General Regulation allowing a transfer when 'the transfer is necessary for the purposes of the legitimate interests pursued by the controller or the processor, which cannot be qualified as frequent or massive, and the controller or processor has assessed all the circumstances surrounding the data transfer operation or the set of data transfer operations and based on this assessment adduced appropriate safeguards with respect to the protection of personal data, where necessary.' Allowing international data transfers based on the legitimate interest of the data controller is already foreseen in the Additional Protocol to the Convention (Article 2(2)(a)), but is otherwise a novelty in European data protection law. The exclusion of transfers that are 'frequent or massive' would seem to rule out use of this provision in scenarios such as cloud computing.

The next version is that of the Secretariat of 5 March 2012, which features two alternative texts, one similar to the Secretariat draft of 18 January, and the second similar to the ICC proposal of 31 January. Following this, the Secretariat then issued a new version on 27 April, the relevant portions of which read as follows:

2. When the recipient is subject to the jurisdiction of a Party to the Convention, the law applicable to this recipient is presumed to provide an adequate level of protection and a Party shall not, for the sole purpose of data protection, prohibit or subject to special authorisation the disclosure or making available of data. The Conventional Committee may nevertheless conclude that the level of protection is not adequate.
3. When the recipient is subject to the jurisdiction of a State or international organisation which is not Party to the Convention, an adequate level of protection can be ensured by:
   a) the law of that State or organisation, in particular by applicable international treaties or agreements, or

     b) standardised or ad hoc legal measures, such as contract clauses, internal rules or similar measures that are binding, effective and capable of effective remedies, implemented by the person who discloses or makes personal data accessible and by the recipient ...

4. Notwithstanding paragraphs 2 and 3, each Party may provide that the disclosure or making available of data may take place without the law applicable to the recipient ensuring, for the purposes of this Convention, an adequate level of protection of data subjects, if in a particular case:

     a) the data subject has given his/her specific, free and explicit consent, after being informed of risks arising in the absence of appropriate safeguards, or

     b) the specific interests of the data subject require it in the particular case, or

     c) legitimate interests protected by law and meeting the criteria of Article 9, prevail ...

6. Each Party may foresee in its domestic law derogations to the provisions set out in this Chapter, providing they constitute a measure necessary in a democratic society to protection of freedom of expression and information.[37]

The version of 27 April includes the following explanatory note to these provisions:

The proposed provisions are still be based [sic] on the well-known notion of an adequate level of protection. The Convention shall continue to require such protection, in particular if data is communicated or disclosed to recipients not subject to the jurisdiction of a Party to the Convention, recognising that this rule has promoted the development of data protection laws around the world. The starting point is that any external communication or disclosure (any communication or disclosure of data to a recipient who is not subject to the jurisdiction of the concerned Party), whether the recipient concerned be a Party or not to the Convention, can only be made on the condition that an adequate level of protection can be guaranteed. This adequate level of protection will be presumed to exist between Parties of the Convention (the Conventional Committee having been asked to give an opinion on this issue), whereas, as regards recipients that are not subject to the jurisdiction of a Party to the Convention, it will be able to be guaranteed by several mechanisms. The use of standard contractual clauses and binding corporate rules (BCRs) will also be foreseen and encouraged, provided that suitable and effective control measures by supervisory authorities are in place.[38]

Significantly, the 27 April draft no longer includes circumvention of the law as a justification for requiring an adequate level of data protection.

    The proposals contained in the various drafts to modernize Convention 108 illustrate the issues that must be addressed in a regulatory system based on the adequacy approach. These include what standards and procedures should be used to define an 'adequate level of protection'; what, if any, exemptions should be provided; and how to deal with onward transfers from a State with adequate protection. The drafters must steer a difficult course between not weakening data protection standards, on the one hand, and providing sufficient flexibility for data

---

[37] T-PD-BUR(2012)01Rev2_en (27 April 2012), <http://www.coe.int/t/dghl/standardsetting/dataprotection/TPD_documents/T-PD-BUR_2012_01Rev2FIN_en.pdf>.
[38] T-PD-BUR(2012)01Rev2_en (n 37), at 6.

transfers, on the other hand; careful legal craftsmanship is required to construct a system that both provides a sufficient level of data protection and does not create unnecessary burdens on data flows.

(d) Organizationally-based approach (accountability)

The geographically-based approach is often contrasted with the organizationally-based approach, which focuses on measures taken by data exporters and importers to make them 'accountable' for their processing of personal data. The concept of accountability was originally applied to determine how government officials can best be made to account to the public for their actions.[39]

Accountability is mentioned in various data protection instruments, including the OECD Guidelines,[40] the APEC Privacy Framework,[41] the Madrid Resolution,[42] the Canadian federal privacy legislation,[43] the draft privacy legislation that was being considered by the Australian government in 2012,[44] and others.[45] In the context of transborder data flow regulation, it 'ensures that the original collector of the personal information remains accountable for compliance with the original privacy framework that applied when and where the data was collected, regardless of the other organisations or countries to which the personal data travels subsequently'.[46] The accountability approach does not base the protection granted on a specific standard such as 'an adequate level of protection', but instead obliges data controllers to comply with certain privacy principles, no matter where the geographical location of the data processing. As such, it requires that the protections applicable under the law of the data controller continue to apply to processing of the

---

[39] See Robert Baldwin, Martin Cave, and Martin Lodge, *Understanding Regulation: Theory, Strategy, and Practice* (2nd edn, OUP 2012), at 338–55; Moerel (n 32), at 178–86.

[40] OECD Guidelines, Accountability Principle (Paragraph 14), which reads: 'A data controller should be accountable for complying with measures which give effect to the principles stated above'.

[41] See, eg, APEC Privacy Framework (n 10), Accountability Principle, para. 26: 'A personal information controller should be accountable for complying with measures that give effect to the Principles stated above. When personal information is to be transferred to another person or organization, whether domestically or internationally, the personal information controller should obtain the consent of the individual or exercise due diligence and take reasonable steps to ensure that the recipient person or organization will protect the information consistently with these Principles.'

[42] Madrid Resolution (n 13), Article 11: 'The responsible person shall: a. take all the necessary measures to observe the principles and obligations set out in this Document and in the applicable national legislation, and b. have the necessary internal mechanisms in place for demonstrating such observance both to data subjects and to the supervisory authorities in the exercise of their powers, as established in section 23.'

[43] PIPEDA, Schedule 1, section 4.1 Principle 1: Accountability: 'An organization is responsible for personal information under its control and shall designate an individual or individuals who are accountable for the organization's compliance with the following principles ...'

[44] Parliament of the Commonwealth of Australia, House of Representatives, 'Privacy Amendment (Enhancing Privacy Protection) Bill 2012, Explanatory Memorandum', at 70–1 (discussing Section 16C of the proposed legislation).

[45] See Moerel (n 32), at 175–7 for a listing of data protection instruments that use the accountability concept.

[46] Malcolm Crompton, Christine Cowper, and Christopher Jefferis, 'The Australian *Dodo* Case: An Insight for Data Protection Regulation', (26 January 2009) Bloomberg BNA Privacy & Security Law Report 180, at 181.

data after they are exported.[47] The principles on which protection is based differ among the variations of the approach; thus, BCRs, which are an expression of the accountability principle developed in the EU, contain protections based on EU law, while the possibility of transferring data in the APEC region is based on the APEC Framework that was agreed by the member countries of that organization.

Accountability does not specifically restrict transborder data flows, but imposes compliance responsibilities on parties that transfer personal data internationally. As the Office of the Privacy Commissioner of Canada has explained with regard to application of the accountability principle under PIPEDA, 'PIPEDA does not prohibit organizations in Canada from transferring personal information to an organization in another jurisdiction for processing. However under PIPEDA, organizations are held accountable for the protection of personal information transfers under each individual outsourcing arrangement.'[48] On a practical level, accountability may require organizations to take steps such as implementing appropriate privacy policies that are approved by senior management and implemented by a sufficient number of staff; training employees to comply with these policies; adopting internal oversight and external verification programmes; providing transparency to individuals as to the policies and compliance with them; and adopting mechanisms to enforce compliance.[49] Widespread experience with accountability as a basis for transborder data flow regulation is lacking, but some countries seem to have used it with success (eg, Canada), whereas other expressions of it have been criticized based on their allegedly providing too low a level of protection.[50]

EU data protection law also recognizes the principle of accountability, for example in instruments such as the revised set of standard contractual clauses for data transfers adopted by the European Commission in 2004.[51] The initial set of clauses adopted in 2001 mandated that the data exporter and data importer remain jointly and severally liable for damages resulting from violations of certain provisions.[52] Discussions with the ICC and other business associations led the Commission to change this clause in the 2004 set and replace joint and several liability with the

---

[47] APEC Privacy Framework (n 10), at 28, stating: 'information controllers should take reasonable steps to ensure the information is protected, in accordance with these Principles, after it is transferred'; Paula Bruening and Bridget Treacy, 'Privacy, Security Issues Raised by Cloud Computing', (9 March 2009) Bloomberg BNA Privacy & Security Law Report 425, 427, stating that organizations that implement accountability take measures to ensure that obligations under law 'attach to the data', and that such obligations are to be met in whatever jurisdiction the data are processed.

[48] Office of the Privacy Commissioner of Canada, 'Guidelines for Processing Personal Data across Borders' (2009), <http://www.priv.gc.ca/information/guide/2009/gl_dab_090127_E.pdf>, at 5.

[49] Galway Project and Centre for Information Policy Leadership, 'Data Protection Accountability: The Essential Elements, A Document for Discussion' (2009), <http://www.huntonfiles.com/files/webupload/CIPL_Galway_Accountability_Paper.pdf>, at 11–14.

[50] See Graham Greenleaf, 'Five Years of the APEC Privacy Framework: Failure or Promise?', 25 Computer Law and Security Review 28 (2009).

[51] Commission Decision 2004/915/EC of 27 December 2004 amending Decision 2001/497/EC as regards the introduction of an alternative set of standard contractual clauses for the transfer of personal data to third countries, [2004] OJ L385/74.

[52] Commission Decision 2001/497/EC of 15 June 2001 on standard contractual clauses for the transfer of personal data to third countries, under Directive 95/46/EC, [2001] OJ L181/19, Clause 6(2).

imposition of 'due diligence' requirements on both importer and exporter: for example, in the new set, the data exporter warrants that it has used reasonable efforts to determine that the data importer is able to satisfy its legal obligations under the Clauses (Clause I.(b)), and at the request of the data exporter the data importer must provide the exporter with evidence of financial resources sufficient to fulfil its responsibilities under Clause III (Clause II.(f)). Such obligations represent a concretization of the concept of accountability, although they do not use the term. Some data protection authorities (DPAs) have questioned the adequacy of protection provided by use of the accountability principle in the 2004 clauses.[53]

Another prominent example of the accountability principle in EU law is binding corporate rules,[54] which produce a zone of protection for data transfers within the company by obliging the data exporter and its affiliated entities to introduce protections for the data no matter where the geographic location of processing. The requirements for BCRs, which were initially articulated by the Article 29 Working Party in a series of papers,[55] are designed to ensure that companies transferring personal data from the EU to their various entities throughout the world take adequate steps to protect them, and that they remain answerable and responsible for them. The Proposed Data Protection Regulation that the European Commission issued in 2012 indicates that BCRs must be legally binding on the controller's or processor's group of undertakings, including their employees, must expressly confer enforceable rights on individuals, and must specify the following:

(a) the structure and contact details of the group of undertakings and its members;
(b) the data transfers or set of transfers, including the categories of personal data, the type of processing and its purposes, the type of data subjects affected and the identification of the third country or countries in question;

---

[53] Eg, the German data protection authorities refuse to recognize use of the 2004 clauses with regard to the transfer of employee data unless extra protections are implemented. Abgestimmte Positionen der Aufsichtsbehörden in der AG 'Internationaler Datenverkehr' am 12./13. Februar 2007—Bezug: Protokoll der Sitzung mit Wirtschaftsvertretern am 23. Juni 2006 (28 March 2007), Section II.2.

[54] Article 29 Working Party, 'Opinion 3/2010 on the principle of accountability' (WP 173, 13 July 2010), at 15, stating: 'Binding corporate rules is an example of a way to implement data protection principles on the basis of the accountability principle. It is a way identified and accepted by the Article 29 Working Party to provide adequate safeguards for transfers outside the European Union'. Moerel (n 32), at 175–227, provides an exhaustive analysis of the use of BCRs as an expression of the accountability approach.

[55] Article 29 Working Party, 'Working Document on Frequently Asked Questions (FAQs) related to Binding Corporate Rules' (WP 155 rev. 4, 24 June 2008); 'Working Document setting up a framework for the structure of Binding Corporate Rules' (WP 154, 25 June 2008); 'Working Document setting up a table with the elements and principles to be found in Binding Corporate Rules' (WP 153, 24 June 2008); Article 29 Working Party, 'Recommendation 1/2007 on the Standard Application for Approval of Binding Corporate Rules for the Transfer of Personal Data' (WP 133, 10 January 2007); 'Working Document Establishing a Model Checklist Application for Approval of Binding Corporate Rules' (WP 108, 14 April 2005); 'Working Document Setting Forth a Co-Operation Procedure for Issuing Common Opinions on Adequate Safeguards Resulting From "Binding Corporate Rules"' (WP 107, 14 April 2005); 'Model Checklist, Application for approval of Binding Corporate Rules' (WP 102, 25 November 2004); 'Working Document on Transfers of personal data to third countries: Applying Article 26(2) of the EU Data Protection Directive to Binding Corporate Rules for International Data Transfers' (WP 74, 3 June 2003).

(c) their legally binding nature, both internally and externally;

(d) the general data protection principles, in particular purpose limitation, data quality, legal basis for the processing, processing of sensitive personal data; measures to ensure data security; and the requirements for onward transfers to organisations which are not bound by the policies;

(e) the rights of data subjects and the means to exercise these rights, including the right not to be subject to a measure based on profiling in accordance with Article 20, the right to lodge a complaint before the competent supervisory authority and before the competent courts of the Member States in accordance with Article 75, and to obtain redress and, where appropriate, compensation for a breach of the binding corporate rules;

(f) the acceptance by the controller or processor established on the territory of a Member State of liability for any breaches of the binding corporate rules by any member of the group of undertakings not established in the Union; the controller or the processor may only be exempted from this liability, in whole or in part, if he proves that that member is not responsible for the event giving rise to the damage;

(g) how the information on the binding corporate rules, in particular on the provisions referred to in points (d), (e) and (f) of this paragraph is provided to the data subjects in accordance with Article 11;

(h) the tasks of the data protection officer designated in accordance with Article 35, including monitoring within the group of undertakings the compliance with the binding corporate rules, as well as monitoring the training and complaint handling;

(i) the mechanisms within the group of undertakings aiming at ensuring the verification of compliance with the binding corporate rules;

(j) the mechanisms for reporting and recording changes to the policies and reporting these changes to the supervisory authority;

(k) the co-operation mechanism with the supervisory authority to ensure compliance by any member of the group of undertakings, in particular by making available to the supervisory authority the results of the verifications of the measures referred to in point (i) of this paragraph.[56]

At least in theory, a widespread use of accountability can replace more bureaucratic mechanisms (eg, registrations of data processing with the DPAs and authorizations of data transfers by them); it is no secret in the data protection community that some data controllers view accountability as a justification for them to be freed from such burdens.

The accountability approach may mean different things to different people, based on different understandings of its consequences. Thus, data controllers may understand it as a way of giving them greater control over how they structure their compliance responsibilities and reduce bureaucratic burdens, whereas regulators may understand it as adding an extra layer of responsibility with which data

---

[56] Proposal for a Regulation of the European Parliament and of the Council on the protection of individuals with regard to the processing of personal data and on the free movement of such data (General Data Protection Regulation), COM(2012) 11 final, Article 43(2).

controllers must comply.[57] In its Proposed Regulation, the European Commission took the latter position, as the draft provides for strengthened accountability of data controllers by requiring in Article 5(f) that personal data are processed under the responsibility and liability of the controller, which is also responsible for compliance, and Article 22 of the draft 'describes in detail the obligation of responsibility of the controller to comply with this Regulation and to demonstrate this compliance, including by way of adoption of internal policies and mechanisms for ensuring such compliance.'[58]

The European Commission and the Article 29 Working Party seem to view accountability as a mechanism for ensuring that the original data controller remains responsible for the processing after data are transferred.[59] However, accountability should not result in perpetual vicarious liability of the original data exporter. For example, consider the case of a data exporter that has taken all reasonable and required steps to investigate the suitability of a business partner in another region before transferring personal data to it for processing. If the business partner turns out to be a criminal who sells the data to a third party without authorization, who then sells it to another third party etc., it is reasonable to require the data exporter to compensate the individuals whose data were misused for damage caused by the original data importer, and to serve as the contact point for inquiries. But elementary principles of tort law mean that the data exporter should not be subject to unlimited liability for a chain of malfeasances committed by third parties that it could not have foreseen.[60] Indeed, such unlimited liability may violate the requirement in fundamental rights law that an interference with rights is foreseeable as to its effects—that is, that it is 'formulated with sufficient precision to enable any individual … to regulate his conduct'.[61] Thus, liability for data processing should cease under certain pre-defined circumstances (eg, when data have been transferred to a sole data controller, or when data have been misused through no fault of the original controller), even if other obligations (eg, a responsibility to provide

---

[57] *Compare*, eg, the descriptions of an accountability approach in Galway Project and Centre for Information Policy Leadership (n 49), at 8, stating: 'An accountability-based approach to data governance is characterised by its focus on setting privacy-protection goals for organisations based on criteria established in current public policy and on allowing organisations discretion in determining appropriate measures to reach those goals', *with* the description in Article 29 Working Party, 'The Future of Privacy' (WP 168, 1 December 2009), at 20, stating: 'Pursuant to this principle, data controllers would be required to carry out the necessary measures to ensure that substantive principles and obligations of the current Directive are observed when processing personal data'.

[58] Proposal for a Regulation of the European Parliament and of the Council (n 56), Explanatory memorandum, at 10.

[59] Article 29 Working Party (n 57), at 12, suggesting that 'a new provision could be included in the new legislative framework pursuant to which data controllers would remain accountable and responsible for the protection of personal data for which they are controllers, even in the case the data have been transferred to other controllers outside the EU'.

[60] See European Group on Tort Law, 'Principles of European Tort Law' (2005), <http://civil.udg.edu/php//templates/PUBLIC/img/egtl/icon_doc.gif>, Article 4.102, basing the required standard of conduct under tort law on, among other things, 'the foreseeability of the damage' and 'the availability and the costs of precautionary or alternative methods'.

[61] *Rotaru v Romania* (2000) ECHR 191, at para. 55.

information to individuals and to facilitate contacts with other parties as far as possible) could remain in force.

The accountability approach is less a standard of data protection than a process for structuring compliance and responsibility. There is no conflict per se between the accountability and adequacy approaches, and it is unthinkable that an approach based on adequacy could function without the controller being accountable for its actions. There seems to be confusion surrounding the concept of accountability, based on the fact that data controllers see it as a way to free them from bureaucratic requirements, while regulators see it as a way to strengthen responsibility; in fact, if it is properly implemented, it can do both. The accountability approach will no doubt be refined as greater experience with it is gained.

(e) Conclusions

There is overlap between the geographically-based and organizationally-based approaches, so that they are not mutually exclusive. For example, the EU legal framework, which is based on the adequacy approach, also recognizes instruments that legitimize transborder data flows within organizations under the accountability approach, like binding corporate rules and standard contractual clauses. Most countries in other regions that have implemented the EU-style adequacy approach also allow the use of such accountability-based mechanisms as a legal basis for the transfer of data.[62] It is likely that the two approaches will continue to grow closer together, and only a combination of them can cope with the increasing complexity of data transfer issues posed by the Internet.

3. Default regulatory position

The laws and instruments regulating transborder data flows also differ in the 'default position' that they take. Many (in particular those based on the adequacy standard deriving from EU law) require that personal data may not flow outside the jurisdiction unless a legal basis for the transfer is present,[63] which in some cases requires regulatory authorization. Some others (eg, the OECD Guidelines[64] and the legislation in New Zealand[65]) generally permit data flows, but give regulators the power to block or limit them in certain circumstances, and require parties

---

[62] A few examples include the laws of the Faroe Islands, Israel, Macau, Mauritius, and Moldova.

[63] See, eg, EU Data Protection Directive, Article 25(1), providing: 'The Member States shall provide that the transfer to a third country of personal data which are undergoing processing or are intended for processing after transfer may take place *only if, without prejudice to compliance with the national provisions adopted pursuant to the other provisions of this Directive, the third country in question ensures an adequate level of protection*' (emphasis added).

[64] See OECD Privacy Guidelines, paras. 16–18.

[65] See Privacy (Cross-border Information) Amendment Bill 221-2 (2008), Part 11A, <http://www.legislation.govt.nz/bill/government/2008/0221/latest/DLM1362819.html>, providing that the New Zealand Privacy Commissioner *may* prohibit transborder data flows under certain circumstances (ie, that the default rule is that data may flow absent action being taken by the Commissioner).

exporting personal data to remain accountable or responsible for them once they have crossed national borders.[66]

However, the default position is not necessarily a black-or-white choice, and, as explained earlier,[67] many examples of transborder data flow regulation show the influence of multiple approaches. For example, the European Commission has called for the concept of accountability to be anchored in the European data protection legal framework,[68] and some jurisdictions using the accountability approach also recognize that the flow of personal data across national borders may raise concerns about the level of privacy protection.[69]

The factors relevant to setting the default position have been considered in detail in the proposals to modernize Council of Europe Convention 108.[70] Some of the drafts seem to assume that transfers can proceed automatically and without authorization in cases of transfers to countries with adequate protection, meaning in most cases countries that have acceded to the Convention.[71] Other drafts, such as the ICC proposal of 31 January, would let transfers proceed also without prior authorization when certain safeguards are in place (eg, under contractual clauses and BCRs), but would give regulators the power to intervene to question or block transfers. For example, the 18 January draft of the Council of Europe Secretariat provides as follows:

4. When the recipient is not subject to the jurisdiction of a Party to the Convention, an adequate level of protection can be ensured by:
   a) the domestic legislation of that State or that organisation, or
   b) legal standards such as contract clauses, internal rules or similar measures that are binding, effective and capable of effective remedies, implemented by the person who communicates or makes personal data accessible and by the recipient, provided that:
      i) *the competent supervisory authority within the meaning of Article 12 bis of the Convention is informed in advance and within a reasonable time of the measures implemented and that this authority may suspend, prohibit or subject to condition the communication or making available of data;* (emphasis added)
      ii) the person who communicates or makes data available or the recipient can demonstrate to a supervisory authority within the meaning of Article 12

---

[66] See Office of the Privacy Commissioner of Canada (n 48), at 4, stating: 'Canada has chosen an organization-to-organization approach that is not based on the concept of adequacy', and that Canadian law 'does not prohibit organizations in Canada from transferring personal information to an organization in another jurisdiction', but that 'organizations are held accountable for the protection of personal information transfers …'

[67] See Section B.2.

[68] See Proposal for a Regulation of the European Parliament and of the Council (n 55), Article 5(f) (requiring that personal data be processed under the responsibility and liability of the controller), and Article 22 (imposing duties of responsibility and accountability on data controllers).

[69] Office of the Privacy Commissioner of Canada (n 47), at 3, stating that cross-border transfers 'do raise some legitimate concerns about where the personal information is going as well as what happens to it while in transit and after it arrives at some foreign destination'.

[70] See Section B.2.c.

[71] See, eg, 18 January draft, Article 12(2); 31 January ICC draft, Article 12(2).

      bis of the Convention and at the request of that authority, the quality and
      effectiveness of actions taken; and

   iii) that the national authorities of the Party to which the recipient is subject
      can only access the data in accordance with the rules ensuring, under the
      Convention, an adequate protection of the data subjects, [or if this is not
      the case that the recipient implements all relevant legal remedies, likely to
      contribute to the protection of the data subjects].[72]

This proposal requires that a legal basis is present before data may be transferred
(eg, via adequate protection of the country to which data are transferred, contractual clauses). At the same time, section 4.b)i) foresees that data transfers can
proceed without prior authorization of the regulatory authorities, but that the
authorities can step in to suspend them. Thus, this proposal represents a mixture
of the two default positions.

    The ICC draft of 31 January states as follows regarding the default position:

   3. When the recipient is not subject to the jurisdiction of a Party to the Convention,
      personal data can be communicated or made accessible to a recipient that has
      adduced appropriate safeguards with respect to the protection of personal data
      when the organisation or organisations processing the personal data have imple-
      mented appropriate and effective measures for ensuring such protection (such as
      through the use of contractual clauses, legally-binding internal privacy rules, or
      other similar measures), and can demonstrate such measures, and their effective-
      ness, on request from the relevant supervisory authority.

    ...

   6. With regard to appropriate safeguards under paragraph 3 or derogations under
      paragraph 4, *the competent supervisory authority may require that the person who
      communicates or makes data available or the recipient can demonstrate to a supervisory
      authority within the meaning of Article 12 of the Convention and at the request of
      that authority, the quality and effectiveness of actions taken, and may suspend, prohibit
      or subject to condition the communication or making available of data.* (Emphasis
      added)

This ICC proposal allows data to be transferred without prior regulatory approval,
but gives regulators the power to stop transfers if necessary.

    And finally, the 27 April draft of the Secretariat states the following:

   3.b. The competent supervisory authority within the meaning of Article 12 bis of the
      Convention [*shall*] [*may*] be informed of the ad hoc measures implemented and
      may request that the person who discloses or makes data available, or the recipi-
      ent, demonstrate the quality and effectiveness of actions taken. This authority
      may suspend, prohibit or subject to condition the disclosure or making available
      of data. (Emphasis added)

    ...

   5. The competent supervisory authority within the meaning of Article 12 bis of
      the Convention, may suspend, prohibit or subject to condition the disclosure or
      making available of data within the meaning of Articles 12.3.b and 12.4.[73]

[72] See n 36.   [73] See n 37.

The 27 April draft leaves the question of whether the regulatory authorities 'shall' or 'may' be informed of measures implemented in square brackets, indicating that a firm position on the default rule was still open. Remembering that the Convention is drafted at a high level and is to be implemented in a large number of countries with diverse approaches to transborder data flows, it would seem preferable to leave the question of whether prior authorization for transfers is required up to national law.

C. Conclusions

A variety of regulatory approaches to transborder data flows have arisen over the past decades. Regulation can be classified in various ways, such as whether it regards data protection as a fundamental right; whether it is based on the level of data protection in the country to which the data are imported (adequacy approach), or the measures taken by the organization that receives the data (organizational approach); and whether it requires a separate legal basis for transborder data flows or generally allows them without one. In addition to international instruments, transborder data flows can be regulated by other mechanisms, such as national and regional legislation, private sector regulation, or technology; the details of such regulation will be explored in the following chapter.

4

National, Private Sector, and Technological Approaches

A. Introduction

Beginning in Europe, data protection laws have spread to all regions of the world, and a survey published in early 2012 named 89 countries worldwide as having them.[1] While not all data protection or privacy laws contain restrictions on transborder data flows,[2] the Appendix lists a minimum of 73 countries with laws that do so (ie, the 27 EU and three EEA member States, and 43 other countries),

---

[1] Graham Greenleaf, 'Global data privacy laws: 89 countries, and accelerating', Queen Mary University of London, School of Law Legal Studies Research Paper No. 98/2012 (2012), <http://ssrn.com/abstract=2000034>.

[2] An example of a data protection law that does not regulate transborder data flows is the Azerbaijani Law on Personal Data No. 998-IIIQ (2010).

representing approximately 38 per cent of the current 193 UN member States. This number does not include those countries that have not enacted such regulation at the level of national law but that are parties to international legal instruments such as the Additional Protocol to Council of Europe Convention 108, and those eligible to participate in voluntary systems such as the APEC Privacy Framework (which by itself covers 21 countries). In addition, transborder data flow regulation exists not only at the national level, but also at the state level in a number of federal countries.[3] If one includes all such instruments, then the number of countries regulating transborder data flows by means of data protection and privacy law is closer to 100. In addition to legislation, there is an increasing variety of private sector regulation such as contract clauses, codes of conduct, internal corporate rules, and others.

National legislation demonstrates a wide variety of approaches. The most influential model is the EU Directive: besides being directly applicable in the 27 EU and three EEA member States, it has significantly influenced transborder data flow regulation in other European countries (eg, Albania, Bosnia and Herzegovina, Serbia, and Switzerland), and in other regions like South America (eg, Argentina, Colombia, and Peru), Africa (eg, Angola, Benin, and Morocco), and Asia (eg, Macau and New Zealand). The influence of the EU Directive has been due at least in part to the perceived economic benefit that can accrue to countries that enact it and are then able to import personal data under an EU 'adequacy decision',[4] and the fact that it presents a single, clearly structured document that is seemingly easy to adopt (when participating in the work of international organizations dealing with legal harmonization, the author has observed that States often find it easier to use an existing regional text as a model rather than draft a new legal instrument from scratch). However, modelling transborder data flow regulation on the EU Directive raises complex issues, since the Directive is based on constitutional principles and fundamental rights under EU law. Other newer regional models (eg, the APEC Privacy Framework, and a potential model law being developed by the Organization of American States (OAS)) will no doubt gain influence as time goes on. Some countries show the influence of multiple approaches; for example, Russia

---

[3] Eg, in the German federal states and a number of Canadian provinces. See, eg, Hessisches Datenschutzgesetz, § 17; Alberta Freedom of Information and Protection of Privacy Act, § 40(1)(g); British Columbia Freedom of Information and Protection of Privacy Amendment Act, § 30.1. See also Fred H. Cate, 'Provincial Canadian Geographic Restrictions on Personal Data in the Public Sector' (2008), <http://www.hunton.com/files/tbl_s47Details/FileUpload265/2312/cate_patriot-act_white_paper.pdf>.

[4] See New Zealand Privacy Commissioner, 'Privacy amendment important for trade and consumer protection' (26 August 2010), <http://www.privacy.org.nz/media-release-privacy-amendment-important-for-trade-and-consumer-protection/>, quoting the New Zealand Privacy Commissioner as follows regarding amendments to the New Zealand Privacy Act that restrict international data transfers: 'An EU adequacy finding is also likely to satisfy data export requirements of other countries. I believe New Zealand businesses are already losing some trading opportunities through a gap in our privacy laws. This change will allow New Zealand to compete on a secure basis for international data business.'

is part of APEC, but it bases the possibility of transferring personal data on the adequacy test derived from the EU Directive.[5]

Conspicuous by their absence from the list of countries with transborder data flow regulation are some of the major world economies such as China and the US, which together represent approximately one-third of global gross domestic product.[6] However, economic growth over the long term is likely to be higher in developing countries than in the more developed economies,[7] and many developing countries have adopted regulatory frameworks for transborder data flows, so that the economic power of countries that have enacted legislation will probably increase over time. Among the motivations for developing countries to enact such frameworks are the promotion of electronic commerce,[8] the protection of private life,[9] and the protection of privacy in connection with large-scale government data collection projects (such as digitalization of the electoral rolls).[10]

B. Listing of national approaches

The following overview of national transborder data flow regulation is organized by region, with comments on some provisions of particular interest; the Appendix contains English versions of all texts.

1. North America

Countries: Canada (federal and provincial level)
Canadian federal law does not explicitly regulate transborder data flows, but Canadian regulators have interpreted the Personal Information Protection and Electronic Documents Act (PIPEDA)[11] to require that data controllers within

---

[5] See Federal Law of the Russian Federation of 27 July 2006 No. 152-FZ on Personal Data (as amended by Law of 25 July 2011 No. 261-FZ), Article 12.

[6] See the Conference Board, 'Global Economic Outlook 2012', <http://www.conference-board.org/data/globaloutlook.cfm>, stating that in 2011 the US represented 18.6 per cent and China 15.8 per cent of global gross domestic product.

[7] See, eg, Carnegie Endowment for International Peace, 'The World Order in 2050' (April 2010), <http://www.carnegieendowment.org/files/World_Order_in_2050.pdf>, at 1, predicting that by 2050, 'traditional Western powers will remain the wealthiest nations in terms of per capita income, but will be overtaken as the predominant world economies by much poorer countries'.

[8] See Government of Mauritius, Debate No. 12 of 01.06.04, Second Reading of the Data Protection Bill (No. XV of 2004), at 2, stating that adoption of a data protection bill 'will also constitute a strong incentive for prospective overseas agencies to do business in Mauritius in the ICT sector proper, or in businesses where personal data is used routinely'.

[9] See Burkina Faso, Assemblée Nationale, Dossier No. 06 relatif au projet de loi portant sur la protection des données à caractère personnel, at 3.

[10] See République du Sénégal, Rapport sur le projet de loi No. 32/2007 portant sur la protection des données à caractère personnel, at 3.

[11] See PIPEDA, Schedule 1, section 4.1 Principle 1: Accountability: 'An organization is responsible for personal information under its control and shall designate an individual or individuals who are accountable for the organization's compliance with the following principles ...'

Canada remain accountable for personal data they transfer to other countries.[12] The Canadian provinces of Alberta,[13] British Colombia,[14] Nova Scotia,[15] and Québec[16] have also enacted such legislation.

The European Commission has found that an adequate level of data protection exists for transfers of personal data to Canadian organizations subject to PIPEDA,[17] and for transfers of airline passenger name record (PNR) data to the Canada Border Services Agency,[18] as well as for transfers under the EU–US Safe Harbor agreement.[19] Bilateral agreements have been reached between the EU and the US finding that adequate protection exists for transfers of PNR data to the US Department of Homeland Security (DHS),[20] and providing protections for financial data accessed in the US for anti-terrorism purposes.[21]

---

[12] See Office of the Privacy Commissioner of Canada, 'Guidelines for Processing Personal Data across Borders' (2009), <http://www.priv.gc.ca/information/guide/2009/gl_dab_090127_E.pdf>, at 5: 'PIPEDA does not prohibit organizations in Canada from transferring personal information to an organization in another jurisdiction for processing. However under PIPEDA, organizations are held accountable for the protection of personal information transfers under each individual outsourcing arrangement.'

[13] The Alberta Personal Information Protection and Electronic Documents Act, § 40(1)(g), permits the disclosure of personal information controlled by a public body in response to a subpoena, warrant, or order issued by a court only when the court has 'jurisdiction in Alberta'.

[14] The British Colombia Freedom of Information and Protection of Privacy Amendment Act, § 30.1, requires each public body to ensure that 'personal information in its custody or under its control is stored only in Canada and accessed only in Canada'; some exceptions are provided.

[15] The Nova Scotia Personal Information International Disclosure Protection Act (2006), § 5(1), requires that a public body ensure that 'personal information in its custody or under its control ... is stored only in Canada and accessed only in Canada'; some exceptions are provided.

[16] The Québec Act Respecting Access to Documents Held by Public Bodies and the Protection of Personal Information (2006), § 70.1, requires that before 'releasing personal information outside Québec or entrusting a person or a body outside Québec with the task of holding, using or releasing such information on its behalf', public bodies must ensure that the information receives protection 'equivalent' to that afforded under provincial law. In addition, the Act Respecting the Protection of Personal Information in the Private Sector, § 17, provides that an organization doing business in Québec that entrusts a person outside Québec with 'holding, using or communicating such information on its behalf' must take 'all reasonable steps to ensure' that the information will be used only for the purposes for which consent was obtained and will not be 'communicated to third parties' without such consent.

[17] Commission Decision 2002/2/EC of 20 December 2001 pursuant to Directive 95/46/EC of the European Parliament and of the Council on the adequate protection of personal data provided by the Canadian Personal Information Protection and Electronic Documents Act, [2002] OJ L2/13.

[18] Commission Decision 2006/253/EC of 6 September 2005 on the adequate protection of personal data contained in the Passenger Name Record of air passengers transferred to the Canada Border Services Agency, [2005] OJ L91/49.

[19] Commission Decision 2000/520/EC of 26 July 2000 pursuant to Directive 95/46/EC of the European Parliament and of the Council on the adequacy of the protection provided by the safe harbor privacy principles and related frequently asked questions issued by the US Department of Commerce, [2000] OJ L215/7.

[20] Agreement between the United States of America and the European Union on the use and transfer of passenger name records to the United States Department of Homeland Security, [2012] OJ L215/5.

[21] Agreement between the European Union and the United States of America on the processing and transfer of Financial Messaging Data from the European Union to the United States for purposes of the Terrorist Finance Tracking Program, [2010] OJ L8/11.

2. Latin America

Countries: Argentina,[22] Colombia,[23] Mexico,[24] Peru,[25] and Uruguay[26]
Provisions in Latin American countries show a strong influence of the EU Directive. Of particular interest is the Mexican Decree, which combines elements of the EU approach (eg, the use of consent) with other legal bases that would allow data transfer more liberally than is possible under existing EU law (eg, Article 37III, which would allow data transfers freely within corporate groups). The law of Peru creates broad exceptions for the transfer of data internationally between intelligence agencies to combat certain criminal phenomena, including 'the fight against terrorism, illegal drug trafficking, money laundering, corruption, human trafficking and other forms of organized crime'.[27]

The European Commission has found that an adequate level of data protection exists for data transfers to Argentina[28] and Uruguay.[29]

3. Caribbean countries

Countries: Bahamas,[30] Costa Rica,[31] St Lucia,[32] and Trinidad and Tobago[33]
Four Caribbean countries so far have enacted data protection legislation regulating transborder data flows. Barbados has been working on a data protection law that includes transborder data flow regulations, but it has not yet been passed. The Cayman Islands, which are a British Overseas Territory, have published a consultation document about potentially enacting data protection legislation.[34] The number of Caribbean countries with such laws may well grow, spurred on by activity of the OAS in this area.

---

[22] Personal Data Protection Act (4 October 2000), Act No. 25,326, Section 12.

[23] Law 1266 of 2008, Article 5; Law 1581 of 17 October 2012.

[24] Decree issuing the Federal Law on Protection of Personal Data Held by Private Parties (2010), Articles 36 and 37.

[25] Law No. 29733/2011 on the Protection of Personal Data, Articles 11 and 15.

[26] Data Protection Act, No. 18.331 (2008), Article 23.

[27] Law No. 29733/2011 on the Protection of Personal Data, Article 15.3.

[28] Commission Decision C (2003) 1731 of 30 June 2003 pursuant to Directive 95/46/EC of the European Parliament and of the Council on the adequate protection of personal data in Argentina, [2003] OJ L168.

[29] Commission Implementing Decision 2012/484/EU of 21 August 2012 pursuant to Directive 95/46/EC of the European Parliament and of the Council on the adequate protection of personal data by the Eastern Republic of Uruguay with regard to automated processing of personal data, [2012] OJ L227/11.

[30] Data Protection (Privacy of Personal information) Act (11 April 2003), Section 17.

[31] Law no. 8968/2011 on the Protection of Personal Data, Articles 14 and 31.

[32] Data Protection Act 2011, Article 28.

[33] Act No. 13/2011 on the Protection of Personal Privacy and Information, Section 72.

[34] See Consultation on the draft Data Protection Bill 2012 (September 2012), <http://www.dataprotection.ky/images/downloads/general%20public%20consultation%20paper.pdf>.

4. EU and EEA member States

As stated earlier, the EU Data Protection Directive (including restrictions on transborder data flows) is legally binding in the 27 EU and three EEA member States.[35] Implementation of Articles 25 and 26 of the Directive shows considerable divergence in detail,[36] as the following examples from Member State practice with regard to use of the EU standard contractual clauses illustrate.

- A number of Member States require prior approval by the data protection authority (DPA) for transfers using the standard contractual clauses (including Austria, Denmark, France, Luxembourg, Poland, Spain, and Slovenia). In some other Member States where approval of the clauses is not mandatory, the DPA may nevertheless require that a copy of them is submitted to it for review as part of the process of notifying data processing (these include Belgium, Cyprus, Czech Republic, Estonia, Italy, and Portugal).

- In Austria, the DPA requires that the annexes to the standard contractual clauses are drafted in a detailed manner and that all elements of the data that are to be transferred are listed in detail. In addition, applicants must enter into a new set of clauses and obtain additional DPA approval each time a single new item of data is to be transferred.

- In Poland, the DPA requests copies of the applicant's IT and data protection policy, and charts showing how the data will flow. The DPA has also asked applicants for information about the level of protection in the third country of import, including detailed information on the legal system in that country, and the possibility of access by government and public authorities.

- In Slovenia, the DPA requires that separate applications are filed for each country to which the data are to be transferred. Thus, if the data are to be transferred to 30 corporate subsidiaries around the world, it is necessary to file 30 applications. The DPA also requests copies of the commercial register of the data importers to prove that they are actually a member of the data exporter's corporate group.

Local or regional data protection laws in many EU Member States may also regulate transborder data flows.[37]

---

[35] See Chapter 2.H.1.

[36] See European Commission, 'Working Paper No. 2: Data protection laws in the EU' (20 January 2010), <http://ec.europa.eu/justice/policies/privacy/docs/studies/new_privacy_challenges/final_report_working_paper_2_en.pdf>, at 92–4.

[37] See, eg, § 17 of the German federal state of Hessen (Hessisches Datenschutzgesetz 1999), which applies only to the public law sector and entities subject to public law.

5. Other European countries

Countries: Albania,[38] *Andorra,*[39] *Bosnia and Herzegovina,*[40] *Croatia,*[41] *Faroe Islands,*[42] *Guernsey,*[43] *the Isle of Man,*[44] *Jersey,*[45] *the former Yugoslav Republic of Macedonia,*[46] *San Marino,*[47] *Serbia,*[48] *Switzerland,*[49] *and Ukraine*[50]

The transborder data protection regulations of most other (non-EU and non-EEA) European countries are similar to those under EU law, which is not surprising since most of them have either received an 'adequacy decision' from the European Commission (eg, Andorra,[51] the Faroe Islands,[52] Guernsey,[53] the Isle of Man,[54] Jersey,[55] and Switzerland[56]), are EU candidate countries (eg, the former Yugoslav Republic of Macedonia and Serbia), or potential candidates (eg, Albania and Bosnia and Herzegovina) that will have to adapt their data protection laws to EU law in order to gain membership.[57] An adequate level of data protection is provided for transfers of personal data from Switzerland to the US that fall within the Safe Harbor agreement between those two countries.[58]

[38] Law No. 9887 on the Protection of Personal Data (10 March 2008), Article 8.

[39] Qualified Law 15/2003 of December 18, on the Protection of Personal Data, 2003, Article 35.

[40] Law on the Protection of Personal Data (27 July 2001), Article 8.

[41] Act on Personal Data Protection (12 June 2003), no. 1364-2003 (as amended by Act on Amendments to the Personal Data Protection Act, No. 2616-2006), Article 13.

[42] Act on Processing of Personal Data, Act No. 73 of 8 May 2001, as amended by Act No. 24 of 17 May 2004, Articles 16 and 17.

[43] Data Protection (Bailiwick of Guernsey) Law (2001), as amended by the Data Protection (Bailiwick of Guernsey) (Amendment) Ordinance (2010), 8th Principle.

[44] Data Protection Act (2002), 8th Principle.

[45] Data Protection (Jersey) Law, 2005 (L.2/2005), 8th Principle.

[46] Law on Personal Data Protection (25 January 2005), Articles 27, 31–3.

[47] Act on Collection, Elaboration and Use of Computerised Personal Data, 1983, as amended by Act No. 70/95 (1995), Article 4.

[48] Law on Personal Data Protection (October 2008), Article 53.

[49] Federal Act on Data Protection (as amended April 2011), Article 6.

[50] Law of Ukraine No. 2297-VI of 1 June 2010 on Protection of Personal Data, Article 29(3).

[51] Commission Decision of 19 October 2010 pursuant to Directive 95/46/EC of the European Parliament and of the Council on the adequate protection of personal data in Andorra, [2010] OJ L277/27.

[52] Commission Decision of 5 March 2010 pursuant to Directive 95/46/EC of the European Parliament and of the Council on the adequate protection provided by the Faeroese Act on the processing of personal data, [2010] OJ L58/17.

[53] Commission Decision 2003/821 of 21 November 2003 on the adequate protection of personal data in Guernsey, [2003] OJ L308.

[54] Commission Decision 2004/411 of 28 April 2004 on the adequate protection of personal data in the Isle of Man, [2004] OJ L151/1.

[55] Commission Decision 2008/393/EC of 8 May 2008 pursuant to Directive 95/46/EC of the European Parliament and of the Council on the adequate protection of personal data in Jersey, [2008] OJ L138/21.

[56] Commission Decision 2005/518/EC of 26 July 2000 pursuant to Directive 95/46/EC of the European Parliament and of the Council on the adequate protection of personal data provided in Switzerland, [2000] OJ L215/1.

[57] See <http://ec.europa.eu/enlargement/index_en.htm>.

[58] Letter from Swiss Federal Data Protection and Information Commissioner FDPIC Hans-Peter Thür of 9 December 2008, <http://export.gov/static/sh_swiss_FDP_Commissioner_Latest_eg_main_018520.pdf>.

6. Africa

Countries: Angola,[59] Benin,[60] Burkina Faso,[61] Gabon,[62] Ghana,[63] Mauritius,[64] Morocco,[65] Senegal,[66] and Tunisia[67]

A growing number of African countries with data protection laws regulate transborder data flows; many of these laws show the influence of the EU Directive. Many of the African countries with data protection laws are part of the 'Francophonie' and are being assisted by the French data protection authority (CNIL) to promote data protection based on EU standards.[68] These laws restrict data flows to countries that do not provide a sufficient or adequate level of protection (eg, the laws of Benin and Morocco), or simply state that data may not be transferred abroad unless the transfer complies with the applicable legal requirements of the national law (eg, the law of Burkina Faso) or has received authorization of the data protection authority (eg, the law of Mauritius). Article 50 of the law of Tunisia, providing that 'the transfer of personal data to a foreign country is prohibited when it may endanger public security or Tunisia's national vital interests', demonstrates how transborder data flow restrictions may be used to advance a country's national security interests. The Data Protection Act of Ghana, enacted in 2012, also regulates data imports, and provides that the law of the foreign country from which data are imported shall continue to apply when data are sent to Ghana for processing.[69]

7. Near and Middle East

Countries: Dubai International Financial Centre (DIFC)[70] and Israel[71]

The DIFC, which is a self-legislating free financial zone administered by the government of Dubai, has enacted data transfer restrictions similar to those under the UK Data Protection Act and the EU Directive. The Israeli law and regulations show a clear influence of EU law, but add some interesting additional grounds for data transfer; for example, data transfer outside Israel is permitted to countries that have implemented Council of Europe Convention 108.

---

[59] Law No. 22/11 on the Protection of Personal Data, Articles 33 and 34.
[60] Law No. 2009-09 on the Protection of Personal Data (27 April 2009), Articles 9 and 43(h).
[61] Law No. 010-2004/AN Regarding the Protection of Personal Data (20 April 2004), Article 24.
[62] Law No. 001/2011 (25 September 2011) on the Protection of Personal Data, Articles 94–6.
[63] Data Protection Act 2012, Sections 18(2) and 47(1).
[64] Data Protection Act 2004, Act No. 13 of 2004, Article 31.
[65] Law No. 09-08 Relative to the Protection of Individuals with regards to their personal data (5 March 2009), Chapter 5, Articles 43–44.
[66] Law No. 2008-12 of January 25, 2008, on the Protection of Personal Data, Articles 49–51.
[67] Law No. 2004-63 of July 27, 2004, on the Protection of Personal Data (2004), Articles 50–2.
[68] See <http://www.cnil.fr/la-cnil/nos-defis/a-linternational/francophonie/>, referring to one of the accomplishments of the group as 'à l'adoption, par des pays de l'espace francophone tels que le Burkina-Faso, la Tunisie, le Maroc, d'une législation de protection de la vie privée'.
[69] Data Protection Act 2012, Section 18(2).
[70] DIFC Data Protection Law 2007, Law No. 1 of 2007, Articles 11 and 12.
[71] Protection of Privacy Law, 5741-1981 (2001), Article 36(2); and Privacy Protection (Transfer of Data to Databases Abroad) Regulations, 5761-2001, implementing Article 36(2) of the Protection of Privacy Law 5741-1981.

The European Commission has found that an adequate level of personal data exists for transfers of personal data to Israel.[72]

8. Eurasia

Countries: Armenia,[73] Russia,[74] and Ukraine[75]

The laws of these countries demonstrate some influence of the EU Directive, but also contain some wide-ranging exceptions. The Armenian law permits transborder data flows on the basis of international treaties entered into by Armenia, and based on the general criteria for legality of data processing, which include 'the protection of state and public security from imminent peril'[76] (as in the Tunisian law discussed in Section 6). The Russian provision largely adopts the EU approach, but also adds some extra situations in which data transfers may be permitted (eg, under Article 12(4)(3) 'in the cases provided by Federal Laws, if this is necessary for the purpose of protection of the principles of the constitutional regime of the Russian Federation and ensuring the country's defence and the State's security'). Under amendments adopted in 2011, the Russian law also allows the transfer of personal data to countries that have ratified Council of Europe Convention 108.

9. Indian subcontinent

India lacks a comprehensive legislative framework for privacy protection.[77] In 2011, the Indian Ministry of Communications and Information Technology issued Rules under Section 43A of the Information Technology Act 2000 covering the processing of 'sensitive data' by the private sector, that also contains rules on transborder data flows.[78] Under Rule 3, the term 'sensitive data' is defined so broadly that it could seemingly cover most kinds of personal data processed by a company.[79] Rule 7 allows transfers of such data both inside and outside India only if the corporate body or persons to whom the data are transferred ensures the 'same

---

[72] Commission Decision 2011/61/EU of 31 January 2011 pursuant to Directive 95/46/EC of the European Parliament and of the Council on the adequate protection of personal data by the State of Israel with regard to automated processing of personal data, [2011] OJ L27/39.

[73] Law of the Republic of Armenia on Personal Data (8 October 2002), Articles 6 and 13.

[74] Federal Law of the Russian Federation of 27 July 2006 No. 152-FZ on Personal Data (as amended by Law of 25 July 2011 No. 261-FZ).

[75] Law of Ukraine No. 2297-VI of 1 June 2010 on Protection of Personal Data, Article 29(3).

[76] Law of the Republic of Armenia on Personal Data, Article 6(4).

[77] See Graham Greenleaf, 'Promises and illusions of data protection in Indian Law', 1 International Data Privacy Law 47 (2011).

[78] Information Technology (Reasonable security practices and procedures and sensitive personal data or information) Rules (2011).

[79] Under Rule 3, 'sensitive personal data' includes: a) passwords; b) financial information such as bank account or credit card or debit card or other payment instrument details; c) physical, psychological and mental health conditions; d) sexual orientation; e) medical records and history; f) biometric information; g) any detail relating to (a)–(f) above received by the corporate body for provision of services; or h) any information relating to (a)–(g) that is received, stored or processed by the corporate body under a lawful contract or otherwise.

level of data protection' as provided under the Rules, the transfer is necessary for the performance of a contract between the corporate body or a person and the information provider, or the individual has consented to the transfer. The application of these rules in practice is as yet unclear.

10. Asia-Pacific countries

Countries: Australia,[80] *Macau (Macau Special Administrative Region (MSAR) of the People's Republic of China),*[81] *New Zealand,*[82] *and South Korea*[83]

Countries in the Asia-Pacific region have a wide variety of approaches to privacy, which may also differ from those of western countries like the US and the EU Member States.[84] It is thus not surprising that there are many divergent approaches to the regulation of transborder data flows, ranging from the absence of such regulation in most countries, to those influenced by the EU Directive (eg, New Zealand). The Australian Privacy Act allows transborder data flows under a number of conditions, such as when the data exporter 'reasonably believes that the recipient of the information is subject to a law, binding scheme or contract which effectively upholds principles for fair handling of the information that are substantially similar to the National Privacy Principles', the individual has consented to the transfer, or certain other conditions apply.[85] However, the Australian government was considering amendments to the Privacy Act in 2012 that would implement the accountability principle.[86] The South Korean Personal Information Protection Act, which was enacted in 2011, imposes a duty on data exporters to provide individuals with information about the transfer and to obtain their consent:

> (3) When a personal information manager provides a third person at any overseas location with personal information, he/she shall notify a subject of information of the matters referred to in each subparagraph of paragraph (2) and obtain the consent thereto, and shall not enter into a contract concerning the trans-border transfer of personal information stipulating any details contravening this Act.[87]

The European Commission has found that an adequate level of data protection exists for data transfers to New Zealand.[88] An agreement has been concluded

---

[80] Privacy Act 1988, as amended on 14 September 2006, Schedule 3, Principle 9.
[81] Personal Data Protection Act (Act 8/2005), Articles 19 and 20.
[82] Privacy Act 1993, Part 11A.
[83] Personal Information Protection Act, Law 10465 (2011), Article 17(3).
[84] See Hiroshi Miyashita, 'The evolving concept of data privacy in Japanese law', 1 International Data Privacy Law 229, 230 (2011).
[85] Schedule 3, Principle 9.
[86] See 'Privacy law reform: challenges and opportunities', remarks by Timothy Pilgrim, Australian Privacy Commissioner (23 February 2012), <http://www.oaic.gov.au/news/speeches/timothy_pilgrim/timothy_pilgrim_emerging_challenges_feb12.html>.
[87] Personal Information Protection Act, Law 10465 (2011), Article 17(3).
[88] European Commission, 'EU approves New Zealand's data protection standards in step to boost trade' (EU RAPID press release) (19 December 2012), <http://europa.eu/rapid/press-release_IP-12-1403_en.htm>.

between the EU and the Australian government finding that an adequate level of data protection is provided for transfers of PNR data to Australia.[89]

11. Other countries

Some countries are considering the adoption of data protection and privacy legislation that includes regulation of transborder data flows (eg, Barbados,[90] Malaysia,[91] and South Africa[92]), or the amendment of their existing regulation (eg, Australia[93]). In Hong Kong (which is a Special Administrative Region of the People's Republic of China), privacy legislation is in force, but the specific provision dealing with transborder data flows is not.[94] The Singapore parliament has approved data protection legislation containing regulation of transborder data flows, but would allow any organization to be exempted from such requirements by the Singapore Data Protection Commission.[95]

Certain governmental entities in China may be preparing to enact transborder data flow restrictions. In 2011, the Chinese Ministry of Industry and Information Technology (MIIT) issued a proposed national standard entitled 'Information Security Technology—Guidelines for Personal Information Protection'. According to reports, the draft standard 'would prohibit the transfer of personal data abroad without explicit legal authorization or regulatory approval. It is not clear whether the standard would be mandatory for at least some industries, and whether any regulatory authority would issue guidelines or establish an approval procedure.'[96] In addition, 'Jiansu Province (where many foreign manufacturing joint ventures operate) has gone ahead on its own with a "Regulation of Information Technology" that came into force in January 2012. This ordinance generally requires consent or official approval for data transfers outside the province. The municipal government of Shenzen, near Hong Kong, has announced that it is preparing a similar ordinance.'[97]

---

[89] Agreement between the European Union and Australia on the processing and transfer of European Union-sourced passenger name record (PNR) data by air carriers to the Australian Customs Service, [2008] OJ L213/49.

[90] Data Protection Act (draft bill), § 4(2)(h).

[91] Personal Data Protection Bill (2010) (enacted but not yet in force), § 129.

[92] Protection of Personal Information Bill (2012) (still in the legislative process), Chapter 9, clause 72.

[93] See Parliament of the Commonwealth of Australia, House of Representatives, 'Privacy Amendment (Enhancing Privacy Protection) Bill 2012, Explanatory Memorandum', at 70–1 (discussing Section 16C of the proposed legislation).

[94] Personal Data (Privacy) Ordinance, § 33.

[95] Personal Data Protection Bill (Bill No 24/2012), Article 26.

[96] See W. Scott Blackmer, 'Transborder data flows at risk', Lexology 20 February 2012, <http://www.infolawgroup.com/2012/02/articles/cloud-computing-1/transborder-data-flows-at-risk/>.

[97] Scott Blackmer (n 96).

C. Private sector initiatives

1. Introduction

There has been an increasing number of initiatives in the private sector regulating transborder data flows, driven by factors including the value that customers and business partners place on data protection; greater enforcement of data protection law; and legal incentives for the use of specific regulatory mechanisms. Private sector initiatives may not be as visible as legislation, since often they are only known to the parties to a transaction or to the individuals affected by it, but they can be implemented by the parties more quickly than legislation or other regulatory measures that need to be enacted into law. They may be legally binding on the parties under private law (eg, contractual clauses), or may be voluntary. But even codes of practice and other mechanisms that are not legally binding may become widely used by parties that transfer personal data across national borders. The European Commission's proposed General Data Protection Regulation would encourage the drafting of codes of conduct in relation to 'the transfer of data to third countries or international organisations', which could be approved by the Commission as having 'general validity' within the EU.[98]

The ease of using such private sector initiatives means that they may create a 'web' of data transfer regulation that applies in countless transactions across organizations as well as between countries. They can never completely replace regulation under public law, but can be a valuable complement to it, and can also plug regulatory gaps that legislation cannot fill (eg, by applying also to transfers of data between countries without data protection or privacy laws). There is a growing trend towards relying on private sector practices and principles as a form of regulation, which is variously referred to as 'co-regulation' or 'self-regulation', a distinction that will not be examined further here.[99]

2. Examples

In some cases, public authorities have approved specific mechanisms for the transfer of personal data to be used by private parties engaged in transborder data flows. Regulatory 'backup' by the State through approval of private sector mechanisms or potential enforcement of them can prove decisive in having them generally accepted.[100] Such mechanisms often provide legal incentives for their use, such as

---

[98] Proposal for a Regulation of the European Parliament and of the Council on the protection of individuals with regard to the processing of personal data and on the free movement of such data (General Data Protection Regulation), COM(2012) 11 final, Article 38.

[99] Regarding the distinction between these terms, see Christopher Marsden, *Internet Co-Regulation: European Law, Regulatory Governance and Legitimacy in Cyberspace* (CUP 2011), at 54.

[100] See Kalypso Nicolaidis and Gregory Shaffer, 'Transnational mutual recognition regimes: governance without global government', 68 Law and Contemporary Problems 263, 282 (2005), explaining

allowing data transfers without a need for further regulatory approvals and author-izations. For example, the EU–US Safe Harbor framework, which can be adopted voluntarily by organizations based in the US that import personal data from the EU, was agreed between the US government and the EU, and has since been sub-ject to an adequacy decision by the European Commission, so that data transfers to Safe Harbor members are presumed to enjoy adequate protection in compliance with EU requirements[101] (a similar framework has also been agreed to between the US and Switzerland[102]).

The EU has formally approved standard contractual clauses that parties transfer-ring personal data from the EU can use to satisfy EU data transfer requirements; such clauses can be entered into voluntarily but then become legally binding. The clauses provide protections for data transferred under the clauses, including require-ments that data are transferred only after applicable local legal requirements have been complied with;[103] obligations on the parties to grant rights to individuals;[104] and data security obligations.[105] In the EU, the DPAs also approve binding corpor-ate rules (BCRs) before companies can use them, which leads to a standardization of their substantive data protection obligations.[106] BCRs provide a legal basis for the transfer of personal data from the EU, and thus constitute a private sector data transfer mechanism that can be used once endorsed by the regulator.

A variety of codes of practice, best practices, and other voluntary mechanisms may also regulate transborder data flows. For example, the Voluntary Model Data Protection Code for the Private Sector of the Infocomm Development Authority of Singapore (IDA) and the National Trust Council of Singapore (NTC) provides that where data are to be transferred to someone (other than the individual or the organization or its employees) inside or outside Singapore, the organization shall take reasonable steps to ensure that they are not processed inconsistently with

---

that enforcement of the Safe Harbor arrangement through the US Federal Trade Commission (FTC) ultimately proved decisive in the EU and the US being able to reach agreement on the system in 2000. See also Katie W. Johnson, 'APEC Cross-Border Data Transfer Rules Aren't a Safe Harbor, FTC's Ramirez Says', (19 March 2012) Bloomberg BNA Privacy & Security Law Report 503, explaining that in the US, enforcement of CBPRs under the APEC system will also ultimately be subject to action by the FTC.

[101] See Commission Decision 2000/520/EC of 26 July 2000 pursuant to Directive 95/46 of the European Parliament and of the Council on the adequacy of the protection provided by the safe harbor privacy principles and related frequently asked questions issued by the US Department of Commerce, [2000] OJ L215/7. For further information on the Safe Harbor, see <http://export.gov/safeharbor/>.

[102] See <http://export.gov/safeharbor/swiss/index.asp>.

[103] See, eg, Commission Decision 2004/915/EC of 27 December 2004 amending Decision (EC) 2001/497 as regards the introduction of an alternative set of standard contractual clauses for the trans-fer of personal data to third countries, [2004] OJ L385/74, Clause I(a).

[104] Commission Decision 2004/915/EC (n 103), Clause II(e).

[105] Commission Decision 2004/915/EC (n 103), Annex A(4).

[106] See, eg, Article 29 Working Party, 'Working Document setting up a framework for the structure of Binding Corporate Rules' (WP 154, 25 June 2008), giving a template for the elements that BCRs should contain in order to be approved.

the Code.[107] The Treasury Board of Canada has adopted guidance setting data processing standards for public bodies that contract for services (including situations where this will result in personal data being transferred outside Canada).[108]

Many companies and private sector entities now routinely include language on data protection and transborder data flows in their commercial agreements. Such clauses may be drafted on an ad hoc basis, which has the advantage that they can be tailored to fit the particular transfer situation, and can also be used in cases where no data protection legislation is otherwise applicable. Besides the need to comply with the requirements of applicable data protection and privacy law, such clauses can help to protect a company's business interest, since they are increasingly demanded by customers, and misuse of data transferred abroad can result in adverse publicity and action by regulators.

The following are just two examples of such clauses, which typify ones that companies have actually used in practice. Some such clauses can be implemented at strategic level, to provide an overall framework for data transferred by a company, while others can be used with regard to individual transfers or projects. The following example falls into the first category, and is a set of clauses concluded between the members of a global group of companies designed to facilitate data flows and protect data transferred between them:

Each Member signing this Agreement agrees and warrants as follows:

I. To cooperate with any other Member concerning inquiries about processing of the Personal Data.

II. To process the Personal Data solely on behalf of the Data Controller and in compliance with the following:

    (i) The applicable data protection legislation of the country where the Provider that processes Personal Data has its establishment (the 'Applicable Data Protection Law');

    (ii) This Agreement and any Company global privacy practices or policies; and

    (iii) Any requirements that have been agreed to pursuant to a written, contractual agreement with a Data Controller, unless such instructions would not be in compliance with the Applicable Data Protection Law.

III. That it shall promptly notify the Contracting Party about:

    (i) An inability to comply for whatever reason with this para.;

    (ii) Any conflict about which it becomes aware between the Applicable Data Protection Law and any requirements agreed to pursuant to a written, contractual agreement with a Data Controller which has a substantial adverse affect on compliance with this Agreement;

    (iii) Any legally binding request for disclosure of the Personal Data by a law enforcement authority unless otherwise prohibited, such as a prohibition

---

[107] Voluntary Model Data Protection Code for the Private Sector (Version 1.3 final), Principle 4.1.1.

[108] Treasury Board of Canada, 'Taking Privacy into Account Before Making Contracting Decisions' (2006).

under criminal law to preserve the confidentiality of a law enforcement investigation;

(iv) Any discovery of accidental or unauthorised disclosure of the information; and

(v) Any request by a Data Subject or Supervisory Authority relating to the Personal Data, without responding to such request unless it has been otherwise authorised to do so.

IV. To the extent that it is a Contracting Party, to deal expeditiously with inquiries from Data Controllers relating to processing of the Personal Data.

V. To work cooperatively with other Members to resolve any privacy-related issues under this Agreement.

VI. Not to enter into agreements with Data Controllers or third parties which contradict this Agreement or any Company global privacy practices or policies or stand in conflict with granting the protections for Personal Data contained herein.

VII. To ensure that its agents or employees with access to the Personal Data are informed of their obligation to comply with the protections given to the Personal Data in this Agreement.

VIII. To have in place appropriate technical and organisational measures to protect the Personal Data against accidental or unlawful destruction or accidental loss, alteration, unauthorised disclosure or access, and which provide a level of security appropriate to the risk represented by the processing and the nature of the data to be protected, as specified further in the Processing Contract.

The second example is of a set of clauses used by a data controller to outsource processing to a data processor in a specific case. The clauses indicate the respective roles of data controller and data processor, and emphasize in particular the responsibilities of the processor:

The Processor agrees and warrants the following:

A. to process Personal Data only on behalf of the Controller and in accordance with the Controllers' instructions;

B. that it has implemented appropriate operational, technical and organizational measures to protect Personal Data against accidental or unlawful destruction or accidental loss, alteration, unauthorized disclosure or access, in particular where the Processing involves the transmission of Personal Data over a network, and against all other unlawful forms of Processing, and appropriate supplementary measures aimed at protecting Personal Data against the specific risks presented by the Processing.

C. that it shall inform its employees and agents having access to Personal Data of the confidentiality and security requirements set out in this Agreement, and that such employees and agents may process Personal Data only if they are informed of their obligation to comply with the protections given to the Personal Data.

In many cases, companies use a combination of mechanisms to comply with data protection law. Corporate structures and cultures are very different, and what works in one company may not work in others. Thus, a company may use a combination of internal corporate codes, contractual clauses, mandatory employee training, regular data protection audits, and other mechanisms to ensure that data it transfers to other locations receive the appropriate degree of protection and that data protection requirements are complied with.

D. Regulation through technology

Professor Lessig famously proclaimed that 'code is law'—that is, that 'the software and hardware that make cyberspace what it is constitute a set of constraints on how you can behave'[109]—and Professor Reidenberg has stated that 'creation and implementation of information policy are embedded in network designs and standards as well as in system configurations'.[110] In this regard, bodies such as the International Telecommunications Union (ITU) and the World Wide Web Consortium (W3C) have promulgated technical standards that have proven influential for the processing of personal data.[111] Effective regulation of transborder data flows requires more than the use of a particular technology, and factors such as the process by which regulation is implemented and the people who implement it are also crucial. But technology could play a greater role in transborder data flow regulation than is now the case. For example, the European Commission's proposed General Data Protection Regulation requires the use of 'privacy by design'[112] by data controllers,[113] which could include the use of technologies to regulate transborder data flows.

Data controllers routinely configure information technology systems so as to regulate the transborder flow of data, and it is not uncommon for an international company to structure its IT system so that certain types of data may not be accessed by its employees outside a specific country or region. Such action is often taken voluntarily by the company as a way to prevent unnecessary access and processing of personal data as part of its effort to comply with applicable legal requirements. For example, a company engaged in the production of chemicals may be required under national law to regularly test its employees for exposure to certain harmful substances, and may keep a database with this information. In many cases, there will be little need for anyone outside the country where the employees work to have access to this database. The most effective way of protecting the database, and

---

[109] Lawrence Lessig, *Code (version 2.0)* (Basic Books 2006), at 124, <http://codev2.cc/download+remix/Lessig-Codev2.pdf>.

[110] Joel R. Reidenberg, 'Lex Informatica: the Formulation of Information Policy Rules through Technology', 76 Texas Law Review 553, 554 (1998).

[111] Eg, the ITU's international allocation of radio-frequency spectrum has established a de facto standard which is followed in 191 ITU member States; and W3C has published over 110 technical standards for the World Wide Web, see <http://www.w3.org/Consortium/>.

[112] Privacy by design is defined as the implementation of 'appropriate technical and organizational measures and procedures in such a way that the processing will meet the requirements of this Regulation and ensure the protection of the rights of the data subject'. Proposal for a Regulation of the European Parliament and of the Council (n 98), Article 23(1), which refers to the principle as 'data protection by design'.

[113] Proposal for a Regulation of the European Parliament and of the Council (n 98). Article 23(1) states that data controllers 'shall' implement such measures.

of complying with the company's obligations under transborder data flow regulation, would be to configure it so that access is limited to only a few employees located in the same country who need to be able to use it to do their jobs.

In addition, geolocation technologies can be implemented so as to identify the location of users and servers in order to make it possible to regulate transborder data flows more easily.[114] Indeed, providers may begin to offer such services as customers demand greater transparency about how their data are being processed.[115] However, using geolocation to control access to data can also undermine data protection, since determining the location of users can make them more identifiable. Thus, geolocation can be useful in specific cases, but also raises data protection concerns.

Another possible avenue for technology to regulate transborder data flows is the use of encryption technologies, which involves making personal data that are transferred impossible to access or read except by the intended recipients. Suggestions have been made that application of 'strong' (ie, nearly unbreakable) encryption to data that are transferred internationally would make transborder data flow regulation unnecessary, since unauthorized persons will not be able to gain access to them in intelligible form.[116]

Encryption cannot guard against all threats. It protects data from unauthorized access while they are being transferred and stored, but not against, for example, illegal use by the authorized recipients who can decrypt them. The fact that data are encrypted may also limit their utility by restricting or eliminating the ability of various parties involved in their processing to read or process them. But it can be argued that data transferred to another country in encrypted form are better protected than data that are not transferred but are stored in unencrypted form,[117] thus turning on its head the argument that transborder data flows create extra risks.

The law can create incentives for encrypting personal data that are to be transferred; for example, the proposed General Data Protection Regulation of the European Commission provides that 'the principles of data protection should not apply to data rendered anonymous in such a way that the data subject is no longer identifiable',[118] thus suggesting that data transferred in encrypted form might not be subject to the Proposed Regulation. Another incentive included in the Proposed Regulation states that a data subject does not have to be notified of a data security breach if appropriate technological measures are taken by which the data are rendered unintelligible to any person not authorized to access them.[119] Some data

---

[114] See Dan Jerker B. Svantesson, 'How does the accuracy of geolocation technologies affect the law?', 7 Masaryk University Journal of Law and Technology 11 (2008).

[115] W. Kuan Hon and Christopher Millard, 'Data Export in Cloud Computing—How can Personal Data be Transferred outside the EEA? (The Cloud of Unknowing, Part 4)', Queen Mary University of London, School of Law (4 April 2012), <http://www.cloudlegal.ccls.qmul.ac.uk/Research/researchpapers/55649.html>, at 7–8.

[116] Hon and Millard (n 115), at 27.   [117] Hon and Millard (n 115).

[118] Proposal for a Regulation of the European Parliament and of the Council (n 98), Recital 23.

[119] Proposal for a Regulation of the European Parliament and of the Council (n 98), Article 32(3).

protection authorities also require that personal data are encrypted when they are transferred; for example, in one case the Danish Data Protection Authority refused to authorize data transfers from a Danish municipal authority to Google in the US partly because data stored at Google's data centres were not encrypted.[120] US security breach notification laws that provide 'safe harbors' for data controllers using encryption have also proved to be a powerful motivation for its use;[121] the EU E-Privacy Directive also includes such a provision.[122]

The working group of German data protection authorities ('Düsseldorfer Kreis') has stated that German data protection law, as well as regulation of transborder data flows, should not apply in certain circumstances to data that have been encrypted. The scenario is described as follows:

A data processing service provider 1 resident in the EU/EEA is instructed by a client company resident in a third country to process personal data and subsequently transfer them to the client. The data originate from the EU or the EEA. They were collected there either by the client itself or on his instruction by a data processing service provider 2.... [T]he EU/EEA data processing service provider receives the data in encrypted form and has no knowledge of the contents.[123]

In this situation, the Düsseldorfer Kreis concluded that 'German substantive law is applicable neither to the data processing service providers nor to the client if the German data processor cannot access data submitted by the client (because the data processing occurs in the closed system or is encrypted, without the data processor having access to the key).'[124]

Data protection law in some States recognizes pseudonymization, which involves replacing a name or other identifying factor by a code for the purpose of eliminating identification of the individual or making identification substantially more difficult.[125] Pseudonymization is used on a wide scale in some important areas (eg, in clinical trials of pharmaceutical products), and can be regarded as a form of encryption, since it allows identification of an individual only under limited

---

[120] Datatilsynet, 'Processing of sensitive personal data in a cloud situation' (3 February 2011), <http://www.datatilsynet.dk/english/processing-of-sensitive-personal-data-in-a-cloud-solution/>.

[121] See Mark Burdon, Jason Reid, and Rouhshi Low, 'Encryption safe harbours and data breach notification laws', 26 Computer Law and Security Review 520 (2010). See also Ponemon Institute, '2011 Global Encryption Trends Survey', <http://www.ponemon.org>, at 8, (requires registration), in which 39 per cent of the companies surveyed stated that they used encryption technology to comply with privacy and data security regulations and requirements.

[122] Directive 2002/58/EC of the European Parliament and of the Council of 12 July 2002 concerning the processing of personal data and the protection of privacy in the electronic communications sector, [2002] OJ L201/37, amended by Directive 2009/136/EC of the European Parliament and of the Council of 25 November 2009, [2009] OJ L337/11, Article 4(3).

[123] Düsseldorfer Kreis, 'Fallgruppen zur Internationalen Auftragsdatenverarbeitung, Handreichung des Düsseldorfer Kreises zur rechtlichen Bewertung' (28 March 2007), <http://www.bfdi.bund.de/SharedDocs/Publikationen/Entschliessungssammlung/ErgaenzendeDokumente/HandreichungApril2007.pdf?__blob=publicationFile>, at 12, 14 (translation by the author).

[124] Düsseldorfer Kreis (n 123), at 14 (translation by the author).

[125] See, eg, the German federal Bundesdatenschutzgesetz, § 3(6a).

conditions and by certain parties; it should be encouraged by relaxing restrictions on transborder data flows under appropriate circumstances.

The use of technology to regulate transborder data flows is not a panacea. Technological or 'code-based' solutions to regulatory problems can raise questions about democratic legitimacy and discrimination;[126] for example, States can adopt national technical standards to disadvantage foreign providers, or mandate the use of domestic products.[127] Procedures would thus have to be developed to ensure accountability and transparency in the implementation of technological solutions. But greater use should be made of technology in the context of transborder data flow regulation, such as by the creation of 'safe harbours' to ease regulatory approval of transborder flows of encrypted data.

E. Conclusions

Transborder data flow regulation at the national and local level is largely based on the international and regional instruments surveyed in Chapter 2. There are a variety of different approaches under which regulation can be classified. Many approaches regard data protection as a fundamental right, while some do not; some are based on the level of protection in the geographic entity to which data are transferred, while others focus on the protections implemented in the organizations that process the data; and some have a default rule that does not allow data transfers without a separate legal basis, while others generally allow transfers but give regulators the power to intervene. These various approaches are not mutually exclusive, and some regulation can be classified in more than one category. In addition, there is an increasing amount of regulation in the private sector. Technology can also be used to regulate transborder data flows.

The result of this variety of regulation is a fragmented legal situation, with many different instruments administered by different regulators and parties in different legal systems around the world. Because of the high level of divergence in regulation, it is important to examine the policies on which it is based. The aims and rationales of the different systems, and their advantages and disadvantages, will be dealt with in the next chapter.

---

[126] See Lessig (n 109), at 138.
[127] See John Palfrey and Urs Gasser, *Interop, The Promise and Perils of Highly Interconnected Systems* (Basic Books 2012), at 189.

5

Analysis of Underlying Policies

A. Introduction

When the first transborder data flow regulation was enacted in the 1970s, few countries had data protection laws; since then, many more have enacted them, and cooperation between data protection authorities (DPAs) is increasing. The benefits of transborder data flows have become more apparent as the Internet has led to the growth of services that depend on data processing, while at the same time cybercrime, data security risks, and concerns about data access by governments are greater now than ever before. All these factors have increased the significance of transborder data flow regulation, making it important to identify the benefits and risks of transborder data flows, and the policies upon which regulation is based.

B. Benefits and risks of transborder data flows

1. Introduction

The policies underlying regulation should be designed to maximize the benefits and minimize the risks of transborder data flows. However, little empirical research has been conducted about how transborder data flows are perceived by the public. As an example, in 2008 the European Commission conducted a lengthy survey on the attitudes to data protection of 28,000 citizens around the EU, but the only question asked about transborder data flows was whether respondents knew of the EU restrictions on transferring personal data to countries without an adequate level of protection (in fact only 17 per cent had heard of them);[1] no question was asked about, for example, whether citizens were concerned about such transfers, or whether they thought regulation of them was effective.

2. Benefits

The benefits of transborder data flows can be categorized based on the parties involved.[2]

- *Society* Society is benefited by the possibility of transferring personal data across national borders. Rights such as the freedom of expression can only be fully realized if they can be exercised internationally, and expression of opinions often involves the processing of personal data. Many important social values (eg, enforcement of the law, promoting economic growth, disaster relief, protection of public health) require the ability to transfer personal data.

- *Individuals* Individuals benefit from the chance to use the huge variety of online services that have been developed in recent years and that involve transferring data across borders. These services allow individuals to stay in touch with friends and relatives, pursue their leisure interests, apply for jobs, and conduct a myriad of other beneficial activities.

- *Governments and public authorities* Governments and public authorities increasingly cooperate in a variety of areas such as law enforcement, financial supervision, disaster relief, and many others that require the transfer of personal data.

- *Companies* With the globalization of the economy, many companies have structured their operations based on lines of business rather than geography, so that the ability to transfer data is instrumental to their success.

---

[1] European Commission, 'Data Protection in the European Union: Citizens Perceptions, Analytical Report' (February 2008), <http://ec.europa.eu/public_opinion/flash/fl_225_en.pdf>, at 33.
[2] Not all of these benefits are solely related to privacy, but some are, and they will all be mentioned for the sake of completeness.

The societal value of ensuring the free flow of data has been recognized from the time the first data protection laws were drafted in the 1970s. As one author has stated:

Computerised transborder data flows contribute to interdependence between countries and individuals. They promote health, learning, employment as well as communication and understanding. They are a novel form of the freedom to receive and convey information and ideas regardless of borders.[3]

The OECD Privacy Guidelines also recognize that 'transborder flows of personal data contribute to economic and social development',[4] and the World Economic Forum has stated that the use of information and communication technologies, many of which operate via the Internet and thus rely on the ability to conduct transborder data flows, 'is a key element of infrastructure for efficient industries and a critical productivity enhancer'.[5]

The ability to conduct transborder data flows may also facilitate the exercise of fundamental rights beyond the control of authoritarian governments. For example, in 2010 the government of the United Arab Emirates (UAE) threatened to ban use of the BlackBerry messaging service, since it results in messages being encrypted during transmission to the service's central servers in Canada, so that they could not be accessed in the UAE by government agencies;[6] the Indian government also made similar threats.[7] Since Canada has privacy laws at both the federal and provincial levels, whereas neither the emirates making up the UAE nor India have omnibus privacy laws, the transfer of data to the BlackBerry servers in Canada may result in a higher level of privacy protection than in those countries.

3. Risks

The risks of transborder data flows can be categorized as follows, based on the parties put at risk.

- *Society* The protection of data as a societal value can be endangered if personal data are transferred for purposes that are illegal or against public policy, or if

---

[3] Frits W. Hondius, 'A Decade of International Data Protection', 30 Netherlands International Law Review 103, 110 (1983). See also Frits W. Hondius, *Emerging Data Protection in Europe* (North-Holland 1975), at 125, stating: 'Freedom of information is a fundamental right of the individual and a precondition for the functioning of democratic society. It includes the freedom to receive and to impart information.'

[4] See Recommendation of the Council concerning Guidelines governing the Protection of Privacy and Transborder Flows of Personal Data (23 September 1980).

[5] World Economic Forum, 'Global Information Technology Report 2009–2010', <http://www.weforum.org/pdf/GITR10/GITR%202009-2010_Full%20Report%20final.pdf>, at vii.

[6] Margaret Coker, Tim Falconer, and Phred Dvorak, 'UAE Puts the Squeeze on Blackberry', *Wall Street Journal*, 31 July 2010, <http://online.wsj.com/article/SB10001424052748704702304575402493300698912.html?mod=WSJEUROPE_hpp_LEFTTopStories>.

[7] See Zack Whittaker, 'Blackberry encryption "too secure"; national security vs. consumer privacy', ZDNet (29 July 2010), <http://www.zdnet.com/blog/igeneration/blackberry-encryption-too-secure-national-security-vs-consumer-privacy/5732>.

data transfers result in the national standard of data protection being weakened. The widespread processing and transfer of personal data for monitoring purposes can also result in the creation of a 'surveillance society'.[8]

- *Individuals* The transfer of personal data across borders may adversely affect the exercise of individuals' data protection rights by making it more difficult for them to bring claims and identify the responsible parties.

- *Governments and public authorities* The ability of governments and public authorities to function effectively can be put at risk if data that they process (including data about their citizens) are accessed abroad by foreign governments and law enforcement authorities.

- *Companies* Companies can be harmed if data that they need to conduct business are not sufficiently protected, or if transfers of data to other countries cause individuals and business partners to lose trust in them.

Throughout the history of transborder data flow regulation, there has been a persistent fear that the absence of such regulation would lead to the creation of 'data havens'—that is, 'that computer users in countries having a strict regulation will move their data processing operations to countries having a more liberal regime'.[9] However, doubts have been expressed about whether such data havens really exist.[10] Moreover, the transfer of personal data beyond national borders need not always result in a 'race to the bottom' (ie, transfers to countries with lower data protection standards), but may also involve flows of data from countries with lower standards to those with higher ones—that is, a 'race to the top'. While it has often been assumed that data controllers would seek to process data in countries without data protection laws, there is a growing recognition that data protection can be a way of building trust and a business enabler,[11] so that there are also incentives to process personal data in places with strong data protection laws.

The Article 29 Working Party has identified the following categories of international data transfer that it regards as posing 'particular risks to privacy':

- transfers involving sensitive data;

- transfers which carry the risk of financial loss (eg, credit card payments over the Internet);

---

[8] See Surveillance Studies Network for the UK Information Commissioner, A Surveillance Society (September 2006), <http://www.ico.gov.uk/~/media/documents/library/Data_Protection/Practical_application/SURVEILLANCE_SOCIETY_FULL_REPORT_2006.ashx>.

[9] Hondius, *Emerging Data Protection in Europe* (n 3), at 247.

[10] See Colin J. Bennett and Charles D. Raab, *The Governance of Privacy* (MIT Press 2006), at 279, stating: 'despite the relative ease with which companies in electronic commerce could locate in jurisdictions with lax privacy safeguards, there has been no discernible attempt to escape from the advanced industrial states—at least not for reasons that relate to privacy protection'.

[11] See International Chamber of Commerce (ICC), 'Privacy Toolkit, An International Business Guide for Policymakers' (2003), <http://intgovforum.org/Substantive_1st_IGF/privacy_toolkit.pdf>, at 3: 'Effective and appropriate privacy protection is a business enabler, not a barrier. It is a way to ensure consumer confidence and trust, and an enabler of lasting and fruitful customer relationships.'

- transfers carrying a risk to personal safety;
- transfers leading to a decision that significantly affects the individual (eg, recruitment or promotion decisions, the granting of credit, etc);
- transfers which carry a risk of serious embarrassment or tarnishing of an individual's reputation;
- transfers which may result in specific actions which constitute a significant intrusion into an individual's private life, such as unsolicited telephone calls;
- repetitive transfers involving massive volumes of data (eg, transactional data processed over telecommunications networks, the Internet); and
- transfers involving the collection of data in a particularly covert or clandestine manner (eg, Internet cookies).[12]

4. Distinguishing the specific risks of transborder data flows

It is not always clear which risks are specific to *transborder* data flows, and which ones are connected with transfers of data in general. For example, the risks of transborder data flows have been listed in a report issued by the State Services Commission of New Zealand, and can be paraphrased as follows:[13]

- non-compliance with national law;
- unauthorized release of personal information;
- inability to provide individuals with access to their personal information;
- inability to cooperate with national regulators regarding complaints;
- inability of the national regulator to investigate or enforce the law;
- inability to guarantee the protection of personal information in countries without privacy or data protection laws;
- conflicts between foreign laws and national law;
- possible access to data by foreign governments;
- overseas judicial decisions that might require the disclosure of data;
- problems with recovery or secure disposal of data;
- loss of trust if data are transferred and misused.

While some of these risks seem specific to transborder data flows (eg, an inability of the national regulator to enforce the law because its enforcement jurisdiction ends at the national borders), others can occur in any type of data transfer (eg, a loss of trust when data are transferred and misused can occur also when data are transferred within national borders). This illustrates the fact that the general risks of data protection, or of transferring data between parties, are often not

---

[12] Article 29 Working Party, 'Working Document: Transfers of personal data to third countries: Applying Articles 25 and 26 of the EU data protection directive' (WP 12, 24 July 1998), at 28.
[13] See State Services Commission of New Zealand, 'Government Use of Offshore Information and Communication Technologies (ICT) Service Providers: Advice on Risk Management' (2009), <http://www.e.govt.nz/library/offshore-ICT-service-providers-april-2007.pdf>, at 6–7, 14–15, and 26–7.

clearly distinguished from the specific risks of transferring data across national borders.

5. Advantages and disadvantages of regulation

Transborder data flow regulation may itself bring specific advantages and disadvantages, although no large-scale empirical research on this question appears to be available. For example, it has been stated that enactment of regulation by a country may make other countries more willing to transfer personal data to it.[14] In particular, States have sought to obtain an 'adequacy' finding from the European Commission under the EU Directive on the assumption that this would result in an increased flow of data to the country and thus in increased economic activity as well. An example of such a country is Uruguay, which received an EU adequacy finding in 2012, and where a number of European and US companies have operations that require the ability to receive data from other countries:

Spain's mammoth telecommunications company, Telefónica, provides client support to customers in Spain from a call center in Uruguay, where costs are much lower, but the prior lack of EC adequacy recognition meant that some sensitive information could not be transferred to the call center ... Other major international companies that have been managing part of their regional administration, finance, and other services from Uruguay—either from their own offices or using third-party service providers based in the South American country—include Bank of America, PricewaterhouseCoopers, construction equipment maker Caterpillar, and online air travel ticket seller Sabre Holdings.[15]

Transborder data flow regulation may thus attract business to a country. On the other hand, a study of the impact of Canadian provincial legislation restricting transborder data flows states that it caused 'fewer services available to Canadian public bodies and residents, increased bureaucracy and significantly reduced efficiency, higher financial costs, the threat of tangible harms to health and safety, and the undermining of competition for public bodies' business and of Canada's burgeoning services industry.'[16]

The recognition of a State's data protection framework as 'adequate' also gives leverage to the recognizing State, as adequacy status can always be withdrawn or limited if the political or legal situation changes.[17] While withdrawal of adequacy status from a State never seems to have occurred, it can be a tool to ensure that the

---

[14] See New Zealand Privacy Commissioner, 'Privacy amendment important for trade and consumer protection' (26 August 2010), <http://www.privacy.org.nz/media-release-privacy-amendment-important-for-trade-and-consumer-protection/>.

[15] David Haskel, 'EC finds Uruguay's data protection regime adequate; move may generate new business', (10 September 2012) Bloomberg BNA Privacy & Security Law Report 1369.

[16] Fred Cate, 'Provincial Canadian Geographic Restrictions on Personal Data in the Public Sector' (2008), <http://www.hunton.com/files/tbl_s47Details/FileUpload265/2312/cate_patriotact_white_paper.pdf>, at 2.

[17] Eg, adequacy decisions of the European Commission routinely include a clause stating that such status may be amended. See, eg, Commission Decision 2002/2/EC of 20 December 2001 pursuant to Directive 95/46/EC of the European Parliament and of the Council on the adequate protection of

recognized State's regulatory framework remains consistent with that of the State granting recognition.

C. Underlying policies and corresponding risks

1. Introduction

The purposes of transborder data flow regulation are most often articulated as preventing circumvention of the law, guarding against data protection risks abroad, ameliorating the difficulty of asserting rights abroad, and enhancing confidence. Even when these are not made explicit, they can be identified from the text of legislation, background materials, and statements by regulators. Other motivations for regulation tend to be subsets of these four main policies (eg, preventing circumvention of the law seems to underlie the encouragement for other States to adopt the forum's data protection standards[18]), or to be tautological.[19] These four main policy goals are analysed in detail in the following sections.

2. Preventing circumvention of the law

(a) Introduction

The most frequently cited motivation for regulation of transborder data flows has been to avoid circumvention of national regulation.[20] At the time the first legislation was passed, only a few countries had data protection and privacy laws, and circumvention of the law was a real concern. Taking Austrian law as an example, the explanatory report to its data protection legislation states that restrictions on transborder data flows were intended to counter the risk of evasion of Austrian data protection law.[21]

---

personal data provided by the Canadian Personal Information Protection and Electronic Documents Act, [2002] OJ L2/13, Article 4(1), providing: 'this Decision may be amended at any time in the light of experience with its functioning or of changes in Canadian legislation ...'

[18] See Lee Bygrave, *Data Protection Law: Approaching its Rationale, Logic and Limits* (Kluwer Law International 2002), at 79–80, stating that the chief aim of restrictions on transborder data flows is 'to hinder data controllers from avoiding the requirements of data protection laws by shifting their data-processing operations to countries with more lenient requirements'; European Commission, Amended Proposal for a Council Directive on the protection of individuals with regard to the processing of personal data and on the free movement of such data, COM(92) 422 final, 15 October 1992, at 34, stating that without restrictions on international data transfers, 'the Community's efforts to guarantee a high level of protection for individuals could be nullified by transfers to other countries in which the protection provided is inadequate'.

[19] See, eg, EU Data Protection Directive, Recital 57, stating: 'Whereas, on the other hand, the transfer of personal data to a third country which does not ensure an adequate level of protection must be prohibited', without explaining why this is so.

[20] See generally Hague Conference on Private International Law, 'Cross-Border Data Flows and Protection of Privacy' (13 March 2010), <http://www.hcch.net/upload/wop/genaff2010pd13e.pdf>.

[21] See Hondius, *Emerging Data Protection in Europe* (n 3), at 248.

Circumvention of data protection law is only possible if there are differences between various laws.[22] Thus, the need for regulation of transborder data flows is reduced to the extent that divergences between data protection and privacy law are reduced. For example, Article 1(1) of the EU Directive obliges all EU Member States to protect the fundamental rights and freedoms of natural persons regarding their right to privacy with respect to the processing of personal data, and Article 1(2) then requires Member States not to restrict the free flow of personal data between them for reasons relating to the level of protection.

There is considerable diversity in data protection and privacy laws around the world. Most data protection legislation is based on the same international documents (eg, the OECD Guidelines, Council of Europe Convention 108, the APEC Privacy Framework), so that the fundamental, high-level principles of the law are similar across regions and legal systems. However, the differences in the cultural, historical, and legal approaches to data protection mean that once one descends from the highest level of abstraction, there are significant differences in detail. Certain areas of divergence may exist between different national laws even within a regional group; for example, in the EU there is no harmonization of applicable law rules as they relate to non-contractual obligations arising out of privacy rights, so that rules of each Member State apply in such situations.[23]

The number of data protection laws has increased dramatically since the first ones were passed, thus reducing the chances that data can be transferred to a jurisdiction where no privacy protection applies. There has also never been a clear explanation of what constitutes 'circumvention' of the law in the context of transborder data flows, and whether the term should be understood in a subjective sense, such as when a party transfers data with the primary purpose of evading application of the law, or in an objective one, such as when the primary purpose of transferring the data is a business factor (eg, optimization of business processes, cost considerations, factors relating to IT infrastructure).

Principles such as freedom of contract and freedom of expression generally allow parties to structure their relations so that a particular law is applicable,[24] unless this would thwart an important socio-economic policy of the forum.[25] For example, in some legal systems consumers may not be deprived of the protection of the law

---

[22] See OECD Privacy Guidelines, Explanatory Memorandum, para. 8, stating that a consensus on data privacy principles 'would obviate or diminish reasons for regulating the export of data and facilitate resolving problems of conflict of laws'; Hondius, 'A Decade of International Data Protection' (n 3), at 118–19; Lucius N. Wochner, *Der Persönlichkeitsschutz im grenzüberschreitenden Datenverkehr* (Schulthess Polygraphischer Verlag 1981), at 220–36.

[23] See European Commission, 'Comparative study on the situation in the 27 Member States as regards the law applicable to non-contractual obligations arising out of violations of privacy and rights relating to personality', JLS/2007/C4/028, Final Report, February 2009, at 5.

[24] In the EU, eg, this is provided by the Convention on the law applicable to contractual relations (the 'Rome Convention'), [2005] OJ C334/1, Article 3(1), providing: 'A contract shall be governed by the law chosen by the parties'.

[25] Rome Convention (n 24), Article 16. See J.J. Fawcett, 'Evasion of Law and Mandatory Rules in Private International Law', 49 Cambridge Law Journal 44, 62 (1990).

of their own country,[26] and the character of data protection law as a fundamental right could argue for mandating continued protection of individuals under their home law.[27] Regulation of data transfers to other countries seems to be motivated in part by the same policy against evasion of the law as protects consumers against entering into contracts that derogate from their local law, in which case legislators and regulators should clearly explain the conditions under which transborder data flows are considered to be an evasion.

However, over the last few decades States have generally removed restrictions on the free flow of goods, services, and ideas, all of which require the exchange of data, and it seems inconsistent to then consider the transfer of data as a 'circumvention' of the law. As has been stated with regard to the doctrine of abuse of rights under EU law, 'it therefore becomes difficult to distinguish between an evasion of national law (to be considered abusive) and a choice of law that is intended or protected by EU law itself'.[28] Concerns about circumvention of the law seem to assume that data will always flow to countries with little or no data protection legislation, whereas actually they may also flow to countries with greater protection, as the BlackBerry example cited earlier shows.[29]

Effective and coherent application of the policy against circumvention would require a complex two-part inquiry, namely, first, an objective examination of whether a transfer of data has prevented the purpose of transborder data flow regulation from being achieved and, secondly, a subjective inquiry into whether the parties had the intention to benefit from an evasion.[30] Such an inquiry is impractical to carry out with any reasonable degree of certainty, and it is thus not surprising that New Zealand has already eliminated mention of preventing circumvention from its data protection law,[31] and that in its final proposal the Bureau of the Consultative Committee of the Convention for the Protection of individuals with Regard to the Automatic Processing of Personal Data (T-PD) of the Council of

---

[26] See Rome Convention (n 24), Article 5(2).

[27] See Jon Bing, 'Data Protection, Jurisdiction and the Choice of Law', [1999] Privacy Law & Policy Reporter 92, 93, also available at <http://www.austlii.edu.au/au/journals/PLPR/1999/65. html>, arguing that in some cases data protection rights may be considered to constitute *ordre publique*; Maria Vérónica Pérez Asinari, 'International Aspects of Personal Data Protection: *Quo Vadis EU?*', in Maria Vérónica Pérez Asinari and Pablo Palazzi (eds), *Challenges of Privacy and Data Protection Law* (31 Cahiers du CRID) 381, 405 (Bruylant 2008), stating that Article 4 of the EU Directive 'could be considered, in principle, as a mandatory rule'.

[28] Miguel Poiares Maduro, 'Foreword', in Rita de la Feria and Stefan Vogenauer (eds), *Prohibition of Abuse of Law: A New General Principle of EU Law?* vii (Hart 2011), at vii. See also Case C-212/97 *Centros Ltd v Erhverus- og Selskabsstyrelsen* [1999] ECR I-1459, para. 27, holding that exercise of the right of freedom of establishment does not constitute an abuse of rights under EU law.

[29] See Chapter 5.B.2.

[30] This two-step test is used in EU law to determine whether there has been an abuse of rights. See Case 110/99 *Emsland-Stärke v. Hauptzollamt Hamburg-Jonas* [2000] ECR-I-11569, paras. 52–3; Case C-255/02 *Halifax plc* [2006] ECR I-1609, paras. 74–5.

[31] The Privacy (Cross-border Information) Amendment Bill 221-2 (2008), Part 11A, <http://www. legislation.govt.nz/bill/government/2008/0221/latest/DLM1362819.html>, deletes section 114B(1)(b), which allows the New Zealand Privacy Commissioner to prohibit data exports when 'the transfer of the information may circumvent the privacy or data protection laws of the State from which it has been, or will be, received ...'

Europe did not retain Article 12(3)(b) of Convention 108 allowing States to restrict transborder data flows when they are made to circumvent the law of the State party from which data are transferred.[32] Preventing circumvention of the law thus no longer seems to be valid as a policy goal itself; rather, regulators should consider it as an aggravating factor in particular cases,[33] such as when a data transfer would demonstrate bad faith[34] or violate some strong public policy of the forum.

(b) Options for future harmonization

The risks of circumvention are closely related to the prospects for greater harmonization[35] of data protection law. Legal harmonization is most difficult in areas where law and policy differ,[36] and the details of data protection law differ substantially between different regions and legal systems. The likelihood that a legally binding data protection instrument of global application will be enacted in the foreseeable future appears slim, for a variety of reasons.[37] While a number of principles are widely accepted in different legal systems, the different cultural and legal conceptions of data protection around the world, together with the lack of any data protection law in many States, would make it difficult to reach broad international agreement on a defined set of standards. It would also have to be agreed whether such an instrument should take the form of an existing treaty (such as Council of Europe Convention 108) or whether a new one should be drafted. An international organization would have to be selected to coordinate the work, which would necessitate either the creation of a new organization or extending the mandate of an existing one. And even if a treaty were enacted, it might still not produce harmonization, since national enactment or implementation of a treaty can differ

---

[32] See Chapter 2.G.2.

[33] The Office of the New Zealand Privacy Commissioner has indicated to the author that circumvention of the law will continue to be taken into account in particular cases when deciding whether regulatory intervention is called for.

[34] See Nicola Vennemann, 'Application of International Human Rights Conventions to Transboundary State Acts', in Rebecca M. Bratspies and Russell A. Miller (eds), *Transboundary Harm in International Law: Lessons from the Trailsmelter Arbitration* 295 (CUP 2006), at 300–1, stating with regard to the European Convention on Human Rights: 'If a state intentionally places a situation that is normally governed by the ECHR outside of the scope of the ECHR, for example, by bringing persons to foreign countries in order to commit convention violations there, and by this means attempts to circumvent the ECHR's provisions, it cannot be claimed that the state is fulfilling its obligation to apply the ECHR standards in good faith as required by Article 17 of the ECHR and more generally by Article 26 of the Vienna Convention on the Law of Treaties. As a consequence of this abuse of rights, the state will be regarded as having violated the substantive provisions of the ECHR.'

[35] A reduction in the differences between various data protection and privacy laws will here be generally referred to as 'harmonization', although it is recognized that, strictly speaking, there are distinctions between the 'harmonization' and 'unification' of the law. See Katharina Boele-Woelki, 'Unifying and Harmonizing Substantive Law and the Role of Conflict of Laws', 340 *Recueil des Cours de l'Académie de Droit International* 271, 298–300 (2009).

[36] John Goldring, 'Globalisation, National Sovereignty and the Harmonisation of Laws', (1998) Uniform Law Review 435, 451, stating: 'where the policies of nations are not perceived by the governments as being identical, efforts to harmonize or unify the municipal legal rules have been less successful'.

[37] See Christopher Kuner, 'An International Legal Framework for Data Protection: Issues and Prospects', 25 Computer Law and Security Review 307 (2009).

substantially in detail. For example, Council of Europe Convention 108 is not self-executing,[38] and permits derogations in some significant areas.[39]

There is a tension in fundamental rights law between harmonization and subsidiarity,[40] which is brought into focus in the area of data protection. On the one hand, a lack of harmonization can undermine the data protection rights of individuals.[41] On the other hand, under the principle of subsidiarity, matters should be handled first at the lowest level or by the least centralized authority,[42] and protection of fundamental rights is often viewed as most effective if it takes place at the lowest level.[43] For example, the incorporation of the actual text of Article 1 of the European Convention on Human Rights into national law is generally viewed as the most effective way to implement it,[44] while the European Court of Human Rights requires that all efforts to resolve a dispute at the national level must have been undertaken before a complaint may be brought before it.[45] Moreover, variations in the law can help to take cultural and legal nuances into account; to this end, the Court has also developed a 'margin of appreciation' doctrine to allow for differing interpretations of human rights law in different States.[46]

The EU is attempting to attain greater harmonization of the laws of its Member States through its proposal to modernize the EU data protection framework,[47] and

---

[38] See Council of Europe Convention 108, Explanatory Report, para. 38.

[39] See Bygrave (n 18), at 34, citing Articles 3, 6, and 9 of the Convention.

[40] With regard to the tension between harmonization and subsidiarity in international human rights law, see Paolo G. Carozza, 'Subsidiarity as a structural principle of international human rights law', 97 American Journal of International Law 38 (2003).

[41] See Article 29 Working Party, 'The Future of Privacy' (WP 168, 1 December 2009), at 17–18, stating: 'Currently the empowerment of data subjects is being undermined by the lack of harmonisation amongst the national laws implementing Directive 95/46/EC ... As globalisation increases, these differences more and more weaken the position of the data subject....'

[42] See, eg, regarding subsidiarity as a fundamental principle of EU law, Consolidated version of the Treaty on the Functioning of the European Union, [2010] OJ C83/47, Article 5(3).

[43] See Robin C.A. White and Claire Ovey, *The European Convention on Human Rights* (5th edn, OUP 2010), at 85–6, stating: 'The protection of the individual is more effective if the substantive rights guaranteed by the Convention can be enforced by the national courts' (ie, as opposed to enforcement by the European Court of Human Rights).

[44] White and Ovey (n 43), at 85, finding that incorporation of the European Convention on Human Rights (ie, the actual text of Article 1) into national law is now 'the standard means by which effect is given to the Convention in the national legal orders'.

[45] European Convention on Human Rights, Article 26; White and Ovey (n 43), at 84, stating: 'Subsidiarity refers to the role of the Strasbourg Court as secondary to the institutions of national legal systems in adjudicating on claims that Convention rights have been violated. It is partly for this reason that a complaint cannot be made to the Strasbourg Court until all efforts to resolve the dispute have been undertaken within the national legal order.'

[46] See, eg, *Handyside v United Kingdom* (1976) 1 EHRR 737; White and Ovey (n 43), at 79–81.

[47] See Proposal for a Regulation of the European Parliament and of the Council on the protection of individuals with regard to the processing of personal data and on the free movement of such data (General Data Protection Regulation), COM(2012) 11 final, at 5, stating: 'the direct applicability of a Regulation in accordance with Article 288 TFEU will reduce legal fragmentation and provide greater legal certainty by introducing a harmonised set of core rules ...' See also European Commission, 'A comprehensive approach on personal data protection in the European Union', COM(2010) 609 final (4 November 2010), at 10, referring to 'divergences between the national laws implementing the Directive, which run counter to one of its main objectives, i.e. ensuring the free flow of personal data within the internal market'.

organizations like the Economic Community of West African States (ECOWAS) and the Organization of American States (OAS) continue to be active in promoting further harmonization in their geographic regions. The participation of many States, DPAs, and private sector entities from around the world in the drafting of non-binding instruments such as the OECD Privacy Guidelines and the Madrid Resolution may also make such instruments influential in gradually leading to greater harmonization. Indeed, participation by States and regulators in various international fora and initiatives may eventually produce a convergence of law as they better get to know each other's legal systems.

A number of other potential vehicles for harmonization could be used aside from conclusion of an international treaty. These could include, for example, (1) the spontaneous growth of norms that become used in practice (eg, *lex mercatoria*); (2) one jurisdiction's law becoming the rule in other places because of regulatory arbitrage; (3) regulatory competition, which can result in a race to the top or to the bottom; (4) communal law reform projects under the auspices of an organization such as the United Nations Commission on International Trade Law (UNCITRAL) that produce model laws; or (5) the work of supranational organizations that have legal authority to harmonize laws (eg, the EU).[48]

More uniform implementation of regional and global standards would also help to produce greater harmonization. The divergence in implementation of the EU Directive among the EU Member States has already been discussed; another relevant example is Council of Europe Convention 108, which has to be implemented in the Council of Europe member States in accordance with their own national legal and regulatory systems. Convention 108 currently contains no 'quality control' regarding the data protection standards of the States that have acceded to it—that is, even when a State has acceded, there is no mechanism to ensure that its national implementation complies with the Convention, and that its standards are actually complied with in practice. The drafts to modernize Convention 108 have attempted to deal with this issue, of which two examples will be given here. The Secretariat version of 18 January provides for the following:

> 6. At the request of a State or an international organisation, the Consultative Committee can evaluate whether the rules of its domestic law ensure an adequate level of protection for the purposes of this Convention. At the request of a Party, the Consultative Committee may also advise on the legal standards set out in paragraph 4 (b), in particular to assess whether these standards offer sufficient guarantees to ensure an adequate level of protection for the purposes of this Convention.[49]

---

[48] See A. Michael Froomkin, 'Of governments and governance', 14 Berkeley Technology Law Journal 617, 624 (1999).
[49] See <http://www.coe.int/t/dghl/standardsetting/dataprotection/TPD_documents/T-PD-BUR_2012_01_EN.pdf>.

And the ICC proposal of 31 January states in part:

2. [H]owever, the presumption of adequacy of protection provided for in paragraph 1 shall not apply when, as determined by the Consultative Committee provided for in Chapter V by a majority vote, one of the following conditions applies with regard to the Party to whose jurisdiction the recipient is subject:
   a. the Party has not implemented in law some or all of the rights and obligations enshrined in the Convention, or
   b. the Party does not generally observe such rights and obligations in practice.
   Such Party subject to a vote by the Consultative Committee shall have the opportunity to present its views before the Committee, unless the urgency of the situation requires taking immediate action. The Committee may make use of expert advice in considering the above questions.

The existence of some control over States' implementation of the Convention is of crucial importance in producing greater harmonization. Ideally this would take the form of a prior vetting of a State's national implementation and constant monitoring of its data protection practices before it accedes to the Convention, but the Council of Europe does not have the resources to perform such tasks on an ongoing basis. Thus, the proposals include procedures to allow States to challenge the quality and effectiveness of another State's laws and practices after the fact.

3. Guarding against data processing risks abroad

Transborder data flow regulation may also be motivated by specific concerns about data processing risks in particular countries.[50] Such concerns have existed, for example, in Canada since the 1970s with regard to data transfers from that country to the US, based on concerns about a loss of informational sovereignty.[51] Since then, some Canadian provinces have enacted such regulation specifically because of concerns that the US government could gain access to data of Canadian citizens and residents for law enforcement purposes when such data are outsourced for data processing in the US or to 'US-linked' companies in Canada.[52]

---

[50] See, eg, Article 29 Working Party, 'Opinion 05/2012 on Cloud Computing' (WP 196, 1 July 2012), at 5, referring to one of the risks of cloud computing as 'a risk that personal data could be disclosed to (foreign) law enforcement agencies without a valid EU legal basis and thus a breach of EU data protection law would occur'.

[51] See Hans-Joachim Mengel, *Internationale Organisationen und transnationaler Datenschutz* (Wissenschaftlicher Autoren-Verlag 1984), at 228; Allan Gotlieb, Charles Dalfen, and Kenneth Katz, 'The Transborder Transfer of Information by Communications and Computer Systems: Issues and Approaches to Guiding Principles', 68 American Journal of International Law 227, 245 (1974), referring to 'the increasing fears of Canadians about the establishment of data banks in the United States in which information about Canadians would be located'. See Chapter 2.C.

[52] See, eg, Information & Privacy Commissioner for British Columbia, 'Privacy and the USA Patriot Act: Implications for British Columbia Public Sector Outsourcing' (October 2004), <http://www.oipc.bc.ca/images/stories/sector_public/archives/usa_patriot_act/pdfs/report/privacy-final.pdf>, recommending the enactment of restrictions on the outsourcing of data under the control of Canadian public bodies based on concerns about access to such data by the US government under the Patriot Act; such restrictions have been enacted in Alberta, British Columbia, Nova Scotia, and Québec.

Companies and associations in the private sector have also taken steps to reorganize the way that they transfer data based on concerns about access to the data by law enforcement authorities of other countries. For example, on 15 June 2007, the Society for Worldwide Interbank Financial Telecommunication (SWIFT), a cooperative association located in Belgium providing worldwide secure message and payment services, announced that it would change the architecture of its data processing system so that data flowing between European countries would be stored only in Europe (rather than being mirrored in the US as was previously the case), based on considerations of data protection arising out of access to the database by US law enforcement.[53]

Trepidation about foreign law enforcement access to data transferred and stored abroad is being driven by technological phenomena like cloud computing. Data controllers may be concerned that by transferring the processing of data they hold to foreign cloud providers, the chance that foreign law enforcement authorities may gain access to such data are increased.[54] These concerns involve not only the US, but also countries such as China, where service providers have been compelled to reveal data to Chinese law enforcement authorities.[55] Such concerns are particularly pronounced in the case of public authorities that act as data controllers, since they hold a great deal of particularly sensitive data (eg, tax records, medical information, information relevant to national security).[56] Some countries (eg, France and Germany) have begun building their own national cloud infrastructures to avoid having to transfer personal data to foreign cloud providers.[57]

These concerns may be based in part on the underlying constitutional and jurisprudential principles of data protection and privacy law, in particular concerning the protective duty of the State. For example, in some civil law countries such as Germany, data protection is considered to be a personality right deriving from basic concepts of human dignity,[58] and under EU fundamental rights law the State has an active duty to protect the fundamental rights of its citizens even against

[53] See SWIFT press release of 4 October 2007, <http://www.swift.com/about_swift/legal/compliance/statements_on_compliance/swift_board_approves_messaging_re_architecture/index.page?>.

[54] See Kristina Irion, 'Government cloud computing and the policies of data sovereignty' (September 2011), <https://www.econstor.eu/dspace/bitstream/10419/52197/1/672481146.pdf>.

[55] See Luke O'Brien, 'Yahoo betrayed my husband', Wired (15 March 2007), <http://www.wired.com/politics/onlinerights/news/2007/03/72972>, regarding a case in which the Chinese government arrested a political dissident based on information that was provided to it by Yahoo; Jonathan Zittrain, 'Lost in the Cloud', *New York Times*, 19 July 2009, <http://www.nytimes.com/2009/07/20/opinion/20zittrain.html?_r=1>.

[56] See Article 29 Working Party (n 50), at 23, stating with regard to cloud computing by public authorities that: 'A special caveat is to be added as to the need for a public body to first assess whether the communication, processing and storage of data outside national territory may expose the security and privacy of citizens and national security and economy to unacceptable risks—in particular if sensitive databases (e.g., census data) and services (e.g. health case) are involved'.

[57] See 'Innenminister Friedrich will sichere "Bundescloud" aufbauen' (18 December 2011), <http://www.teltarif.de/bundes-cloud-friedrich-regierung-telekom-sichere-speicherung/news/45000.html>.

[58] See, eg, Paul M. Schwartz and Karl-Nikolaus Peifer, 'Prosser's Privacy and the German Right of Personality: Are Four Privacy Torts Better than One Unitary Concept?', 98 California Law Review 1925, 1946 (2010).

violations by third parties.[59] Restrictions on transborder data flows in early data protection laws seem to be based on the idea that the State has a duty to protect the personality rights, and thus the dignity, of individuals within its borders, and that allowing untrammelled data flows out of the country could jeopardize this protection.[60] In addition, the European Convention on Human Rights has been interpreted to include positive obligations on behalf of States with regard to the protection of private life (which the European Court of Human Rights has interpreted to include data protection).[61] While the Court has not rendered any decisions interpreting the Convention in the context of transborder data flows, it is conceivable that this duty of protection might be construed to include restrictions on transborder data flows such as those contained in Council of Europe Convention 108, which the Court has sometimes referred to in data protection cases.[62] Other legal systems with privacy law may not recognize this protective function of the State; for example, 'the American constitutional system, as opposed to the European one, rejects any protective duty of the state or any corresponding constitutional right of protection for the individual',[63] a position that fits with the fact that the US has traditionally been a strong opponent of any regulation of transborder data flows.[64]

The risks giving rise to the protective approach are often expressed in terms of the inability of the State to protect data once they have crossed its borders.[65] This may indicate that transborder data flow regulation focusing on data processing risks in specific countries is largely based on an extension of the protective duty of the State to data processing beyond its borders, which would be consistent with the increasing trend for States to use applicable law rules to extend the application of their law to data transferred to other countries.[66]

Finally, it can be questioned whether there is not a degree of hypocrisy in States expressing concern about the risks of government access to personal data transferred to other countries, when many of them provide substantial powers for law enforcement to access private sector data in their own countries. While reliable information about government practices in this area is hard to come by, it seems that such access is routinely carried out by a number of States with transborder

---

[59] See *Z v United Kingdom* (2002) 34 EHRR 97; Dieter Grimm, 'The Protective Function of the State', in Georg Nolte (ed), *European and US Constitutionalism* 137 (CUP 2005), at 137. See also Robert Uerpmann-Wittzack, 'Internetvölkerrecht', 47 Archiv des Völkerrechts 261, 271 (2009), stating that the State's duty of protection includes the obligation to provide reasonable means to exercise claims for injunctive relief, withdrawal, and damages.

[60] See Wochner (n 22), at 24.

[61] See, eg, *Case of Dickson v United Kingdom* (2008) 46 EHRR 927, para. 70. See also White and Ovey (n 43), at 361–2.

[62] See, eg, *Z v Finland* (1997) 25 EHRR 371.

[63] Heike Krieger, 'Comment' in Nolte (n 59), at 181.

[64] See Sara Schoonmaker, *High-Tech Trade Wars: US–Brazilian Conflicts in the Global Economy* (University of Pittsburgh Press 2002), at 50, stating: 'the US has consistently advocated the free flow of information as a central element of transborder data-flow policy'.

[65] See Mengel (n 51), at 8–11.

[66] See Chapter 6.B.

data flow regulation, such as Germany[67] and the UK.[68] Concern about access to data by law enforcement agencies in other countries may be used as a way to deflect attention from such access by domestic authorities.

4. Difficulty of asserting rights abroad

The difficulty of asserting data protection rights outside the country of export has often been cited as an important policy rationale underlying regulation of trans-border data flows.[69] Organizations like the OECD have recognized that individuals need to be able to enforce data protection and privacy rights across national borders.[70] The ability of individuals to assert their rights concerning the processing of personal data is a requirement of fundamental rights law, so that the inability to enforce rights with regard to data transferred abroad may create legal issues.[71]

These difficulties are based on the fact that it is easier to enforce rights within a national or regional legal system than on a global level. Taking the EU as an example, various legal instruments and obligations provide individuals and regulators with a framework that allows the assertion of rights between the EU Member States. Thus, EU DPAs are obliged to cooperate with each other,[72] and court decisions from one EU Member State can also be enforced in another Member State with relative ease;[73] however, taking regulatory action with regard to data processing carried out in another region is much more difficult.[74] In its proposal for a General Data Protection Regulation, the European Commission has proposed changes to the EU legal framework designed to further improve cooperation between DPAs and the enforceability of court and administrative decisions in the area of data protection.[75]

---

[67] See Paul M. Schwartz, 'Systematic Government Access to Private-Sector Data in Germany', 2(4) International Data Privacy Law 289 (2012).

[68] See Ian Brown, 'Government Access to Private-Sector Data in the United Kingdom', 2(4) International Data Privacy Law 230 (2012).

[69] See, eg, Article 29 Working Party, 'Opinion 7/2001 on the Draft Commission Decision (version 31 August 2001) on Standard Contractual Clauses for the Transfer of Personal Data to Data Processors Established in Third Countries under Article 26(4) of Directive 95/46' (WP 47, 13 September 2001), at 3, stating that 'the physical location of the data in third countries makes the enforcement of the contract or the decisions taken by Supervisory Authorities considerably more difficult'; Gotlieb, Dalfen, and Katz (n 51), at 247; Hondius, *Emerging Data Protection in Europe* (n 3), at 247.

[70] See OECD, 'Recommendation on Cross-border Co-operation in the Enforcement of Laws Protecting Privacy' (2007), <http://www.oecd.org/dataoecd/43/28/38770483.pdf>.

[71] See Chapter 6.C.

[72] EU Data Protection Directive, Article 28(6). A DPA of a large EU Member State has informed the author that it receives 20 to 30 cooperation requests annually from other EU DPAs.

[73] Eg, under Council Regulation (EC) 44/2001 of 22 December 2000 on jurisdiction and the recognition and enforcement of judgments in civil and commercial matters, [2001] OJ L12/1.

[74] See European Data Protection Supervisor, 'Opinion of the European Data Protection Supervisor on the Commission's Communication on "Unleashing the potential of Cloud Computing in Europe"', 16 November 2012, at 21.

[75] See Proposal for a Regulation of the European Parliament and of the Council (n 47), in particular Articles 63 and 74.

There is no overarching legal basis allowing the *global* enforcement and recognition of regulatory determinations and judgments under data protection law. However, the difficulty of asserting legal rights abroad is not unique to data protection and privacy law, but results from the fact that there is currently no global legal framework for the recognition and enforcement of judgments in other countries.[76] To combat this problem, regulators have established informal cooperation mechanisms outside traditional legal assistance channels,[77] such as the Global Privacy Enforcement Network[78] (GPEN, comprised of regulatory authorities from 21 countries) and the APEC Cross-Border Privacy Enforcement Arrangement (with initial members from three APEC countries).[79] The GPEN allows privacy regulators to cooperate in the following ways:

— Take part in periodic conference calls and meetings with other participating privacy enforcement authorities to discuss enforcement issues, trends, and experiences;

— Share information about effective investigative techniques and enforcement strategies and about each other's privacy enforcement regimes;

— Share information about similarities and differences in procedural, substantive and evidentiary rules to address challenges to cooperation;

— Coordinate and cooperate with other organizations or networks involved with related activities;

— Consider consumer and business education projects addressing privacy and data security-related issues;

— Provide content for a GPEN website to be operated by the Secretariat as described below; and

— Organize and participate in training sessions on privacy and data security-related matters with non-governmental advisors, such as representatives from industry, academia, international organizations or professional associations.

— Participants may also seek opportunities for providing assistance to one another on a bilateral basis, in appropriate privacy investigations and enforcement matters, prioritizing cases for cooperation that are the most serious in nature.[80]

Privacy regulators have also established cooperation mechanisms on a bilateral basis. For example, in October 2012 the German Federal Data Protection

---

[76] See Dan Jerker B. Svantesson, *Private International Law and the Internet* (Kluwer Law International 2007), at 282–3.

[77] See, eg, OECD, 'Report on the Cross-Border Enforcement of Privacy Laws' (2006), <http://www.oecd.org/dataoecd/17/43/37558845.pdf>, at 23–4.

[78] See <http://www.privacyenforcement.net/>.

[79] See 'APEC launches new Cross-border Data Privacy Initiative', <http://www.apec.org/Press/News-Releases/2010/0716_ecsg_cpea.aspx>.

[80] See <http://www.privacyenforcement.net/public/activities>.

Commissioner and the Canadian Federal Privacy Commissioner signed an agreement to cooperate in cases of cross-border enforcement.[81]

There is also ever-increasing use of internal dispute resolution mechanisms in both the private and public sectors,[82] which may enhance the ability of individuals to assert their rights in other countries. Anecdotal evidence suggests that few individuals bring formal complaints involving transborder data flows to privacy regulatory authorities.[83] Many such complaints may also be resolved through internal complaint handling procedures and other non-legislative mechanisms. Thus, the practical importance of formal enforcement of data protection rights across national borders may be less than is sometimes assumed.

5. Enhancing confidence

The need to enhance confidence in data processing has been cited as a motivation for data protection law. By providing a framework of rules that applies across national borders and requires assurances by the parties which process personal data, regulation of transborder data flows may reassure individuals about the protection of their data, and thus lead to increased e-commerce activity and economic growth.[84]

There is little empirical data about the effect of transborder data flow regulation on the confidence of businesses and individuals. DPAs have received some complaints from individuals regarding data transfers abroad,[85] but the number does not seem to be large.[86] Many parties involved in transborder data flows seem not properly to understand what they are or when they take place; for example, in a study

---

[81] Der Bundesbeauftragte für den Datenschutz und die Informationsfreiheit, 'Deutsche und kanadische Datenschutzbehörden schaffen Grundlage für verstärkte Zusammenarbeit' (15 October 2012), <http://www.bfdi.bund.de/DE/Oeffentlichkeitsarbeit/Pressemitteilungen/2012/21_DCANDSBehoerdenSchaffenGrundlageZurZusammenarbeit.html?nn=408908>.

[82] See OECD, 'Report on Compliance with, and Enforcement of, Privacy Protection Online' (12 February 2003), <http://www.oecd.org/officialdocuments/displaydocument/?doclanguage=en&cote=dsti/iccp/reg(2002)5/final>, at 14.

[83] See OECD (n 77), at 9.

[84] See European Commission, 'Communication from the Commission to the European Parliament, the Council, the European Economic and Social Committee and the Committee of the Regions, Safeguarding Privacy in a Connected World—A European Data Protection Framework for the 21st Century', COM(2012) 9/3, 25 January 2012, at 2, stating: 'Lack of confidence makes consumers hesitant to buy online and accept new services. Therefore, a high level of data protection is also crucial to enhance trust in online services and to fulfil the potential of the digital economy, thereby encouraging economic growth and the competitiveness of EU industries.'

[85] See, eg, OECD (n 77), at 8–9. See also Office of the Privacy Commissioner of Canada, 'Revisiting the Privacy Landscape a Year Later' (March 2006), <http://www.priv.gc.ca/information/survey/2006/ekos_2006_e.cfm>, in which 94 per cent of respondents express either moderate or high concern about Canadian companies transferring personal information on customers to other countries.

[86] See, eg, OECD (n 77), at 9, stating: 'privacy and data protection authorities do not report receiving cross-border complaints in significant number. It is certainly the case that few individual complaints have a cross-border element, with spam being a notable exception. Although this may suggest that there are not many privacy breaches with a cross-border dimension, it could just as well indicate that we lack good information on this topic.'

by the European Commission published in 2008, only a small percentage (10 per cent) of EU data controllers stated that their companies transferred personal data outside the EU,[87] a figure that must be far too low given the widespread use by companies of email and the Internet. And in a similar study from the same year, only 17 per cent of EU individuals were aware that such regulation existed.[88]

Individuals sometimes express contradictory attitudes about transborder data flows, the motivation for which may be difficult to understand rationally. For instance, the author has encountered cases in which groups of individuals in Poland expressed concern about the level of data protection in Germany (although both are EU Member States and provide an adequate level of protection), and groups in Germany did so about the data protection level in Switzerland (although the latter country has received an EU adequacy decision). Such concerns often seem to be based on anecdotes or isolated news reports rather than on objective evidence. A meta-analysis of various public opinion surveys in 2012 found that the European public is 'uncertain as to how to approach the increasing globalisation of data flows', and that few people 'seemed aware of the issues arising from extra-territorial transfers or the risks this brought'.[89]

The growing popularity of online services and social networks, nearly all of which result in the transfer of personal data across national borders, raises the question of why individuals use them so frequently if they are concerned about such transfers. It may well be that some users are not aware that their data are being transferred internationally. But to take one example, by June 2012, Facebook (which is well known as a company based in the US) had over 900 million users worldwide, many of whom reside in countries with transborder data flow regulation; such widespread usage must be at least partially an indication of a lack of interest in, or acceptance by, individuals of the fact that their data are being transferred abroad.

Studies have shown that trust is difficult to build, particularly with regard to online activities,[90] and it is not clear why transborder data flow regulation would significantly increase it. The available evidence suggests that individuals are mainly unaware that such regulations exist, do not often complain about perceived violations of them, and sometimes misunderstand them. These considerations make it seem questionable that transborder data flow regulation would by itself have a significant impact on confidence in data processing.

[87] Eurobarometer Study (for the European Commission), 'Data Protection in the European Union—Data Controllers' Perceptions—Analytical Report' (February 2008), <http://ec.europa.eu/public_opinion/flash/fl_226_en.pdf>, at 7.
[88] Eurobarometer Study (for the European Commission), 'Data Protection in the European Union—Citizens' Perceptions—Analytical Report' (February 2008), <http://ec.europa.eu/public_opinion/flash/fl_225_en.pdf>, at 33.
[89] Dara Hallinan, Michael Friedewald, and Paul McCarthy, 'Citizens' perceptions of data protection and privacy in Europe', 28 Computer Law and Security Review 263, 268 (2012).
[90] See, eg, Ye Diana Wang and Henry H. Emurian, 'An overview of online trust: Concepts, elements, and implications', 21 Computers in Human Behavior 105, 107 (2005).

D. Conclusions

There is a need to reassess the policies underlying transborder data flow regulation. Given the fundamental social, economic, and technological changes that have occurred since the first regulation was passed, international organizations, States, and governments should carefully consider the policies upon which it is based, particularly since some of them have declined in importance (eg, preventing circumvention of the law), while the significance of others has increased (eg, guarding against data processing risks abroad).

The use of transborder data protection regulation as a mechanism for protecting informational sovereignty in the past[91] demonstrates that regulation may sometimes be motivated by protection of a State's economic and political interests rather than by privacy protection. There is a risk that regulation of transborder data flows may be used by States not to promote individual rights, but to thwart them, such as when an authoritarian government prevents data from being transferred to another country with higher standards of privacy protection.

The policies underlying transborder data flow regulation are closely connected with the issues of what law applies to data processing, and which countries' authorities have regulatory power authority over it; these are dealt with next.

---

[91] See Chapter 2.C.

6

Applicable Law, Extraterritoriality, and Transborder Data Flows

A. Introduction

The topics of transborder data flow regulation, applicable law, and jurisdiction are intertwined, and countries may use rules on applicable law and jurisdiction to pursue the same policies for which they use those concerning transborder data flows.[1] Such rules are all designed to protect the rights of individuals when data are processed beyond national borders, and rules on transborder data flows often function as a kind of conflict of laws regime that seeks to apply the forum's law to data processed abroad.

In data protection law, the terms 'applicable law' (ie, which law applies to a particular act of data processing) and 'jurisdiction' (ie, which State or entity has regulatory power over it) are often conflated. For example, the Article 29 Working Party has explained the applicability of EU data protection law to non-EU websites in terms of an individual in the EU being able to complain about them to their own national regulator.[2] More recently, the Working Party has recognized

---

[1] See Christopher Kuner, 'Data Protection Law and International Jurisdiction on the Internet' (Part 1), 18(2) International Journal of Law and Information Technology 176, 178–81 (2010).

[2] Article 29 Working Party, 'Working document on determining the international application of EU data protection law to personal data processing on the Internet by non-EU based websites' (WP 56, 30 May 2002), at 15.

that applicable law and jurisdiction are distinct concepts,[3] but has also stated that they coincide in most cases,[4] and in practice data protection regulators are often reluctant to apply any law but their own. Since determination of applicable law and jurisdiction often go hand in hand in the context of transborder data flows, the two terms will generally be used interchangeably here unless otherwise noted.

The application of transborder data flow regulation depends on there being a 'data transfer' between two territorial jurisdictions, which presupposes the ability to determine when personal data have crossed national borders and thus what their location is at a specific point in time.[5] This is in line with traditional theories of jurisdiction based on the principle of territoriality.[6] Any personal data processed on the Internet will have to be stored on a computer in a physical location,[7] as indicated in the following statement regarding data processing in cloud computing services:

> While the popular view seems to be that in cloud computing data moves around the world continuously and almost randomly, so that it's not possible to know where a specific user's data are located at any one time ..., in practice this is often not so. In most cases, data are usually copied or replicated to different data centres, for business continuity/backup purposes, rather than being 'moved' by being deleted from one data centre and re-created in another. Often the provider will know where a user's data fragments (e.g. for a particular application) are stored, at the data centre if not equipment level.[8]

However, an individual data subject can often have difficulty determining the location of data processing, particularly in the online context.[9] This can be caused by various factors, such as the data controller's reluctance to disclose such information based on concerns about data security; that the controller has poor informational policies; or that the number of parties involved in the processing complicates a determination about who is processing particular data at a particular time. It can

---

[3] See Article 29 Working Party, 'Opinion 8/2010 on applicable law' (WP 179, 16 December 2010), at 10.

[4] Article 29 Working Party (n 3).   [5] Eg, EU Directive, Article 25.

[6] See, eg, Cedric Ryngaert, *Jurisdiction in International Law* (OUP 2008), at 42.

[7] See Robert Gellman, *Privacy in the Clouds: Risks to Privacy and Confidentiality from Cloud Computing* (World Privacy Forum, 23 February 2009), <http://www.worldprivacyforum.org/pdf/WPF_Cloud_Privacy_Report.pdf>, at 7, stating regarding cloud computing: 'any information stored in the cloud eventually ends up on a physical machine owned by a particular company or person located in a specific country. That stored information may be subject to the laws of the country where the physical machine is located.'

[8] W. Kuan Hon and Christopher Millard, 'Data Export in Cloud Computing—How can Personal Data be Transferred outside the EEA? (The Cloud of Unknowing, Part 4)', Queen Mary University of London, School of Law (4 April 2012), <http://www.cloudlegal.ccls.qmul.ac.uk/Research/researchpapers/55649.html>, at 7.

[9] Hon and Millard (n 8), stating: 'In most cases, whether for security or other reasons, providers do not disclose to users their data's location'. See also European Data Protection Supervisor, 'Opinion of the European Data Protection Supervisor on the Commission's Communication on "Unleashing the potential of Cloud Computing in Europe"', 16 November 2012, at 6; Article 29 Working Party, 'Opinion 05/2012 on Cloud Computing' (WP 196, 1 July 2012), at 17, stating: 'the cloud client is therefore rarely in a position to be able to know in real time where the data are located or stored or transferred'.

also be unclear *which* location should control applicable law and jurisdiction—that is, the location of the business establishment of the data controller, the location of the data, etc.[10]

The difficulty of determining when data have crossed national borders has led States and regulators to apply their own law to the processing in other countries of data concerning their own nationals and residents. One way of viewing this development is as a modern application of the doctrine of personality, under which applicable law is determined by the law of the nationality or residence of the individuals whose data are processed, which continues to apply to the data as they are transferred. While data protection rights generally apply without regard to nationality or residence,[11] in practice transborder data flow regulation has resulted in the application of national law to protect residents or nationals of the regulator's own country.

The Internet is causing a convergence of various jurisdictional bases,[12] and the designation of the jurisdictional theory used to apply to transborder data flow regulation is less important than is a determination of the circumstances in which it applies. There are other jurisdictional theories under which transborder data flow regulation could be classified, such as an application of a State's law to conduct occurring outside the State but that has effects in it (the so-called 'effects' doctrine[13]). However, designating it as an example of the personality principle seems particularly appropriate, since data protection law applies to data 'relating' to an identified or identifiable natural person[14]—that is, data the processing of which is likely to have an impact on their rights and interests[15]—and thus assumes a close link between personal data and the individuals to whom they pertain; it is a natural step to extend the personality principle from an actual person to data relating to them. In the Internet age, the personal data that render a person identifiable could be viewed as a manifestation of their personality, and many regulatory systems envision the applicable law attaching to data and following them as they are transferred around the world, just as the law of a person's nationality or tribe did to an individual in earlier centuries.

The personality principle was used extensively as a jurisdictional basis in the ancient world and in medieval Europe, where foreigners were often allowed to

---

[10] See Hon and Millard (n 8), at 8.

[11] See, eg, Article 29 Working Party (n 3), at 8.

[12] See Ian Brownlie, *Principles of Public International Law* (7th edn, OUP 2008), at 308; Mika Hayashi, 'The Information Revolution and the Rules of Jurisdiction in Public International Law', in Myriam Dunn, Sai Felicia Krishna-Hensel, and Victor Mauer (eds), *The Resurgence of the State* 59 (Ashgate 2007), at 74–5.

[13] See, eg, Case C-366/10 *The Air Transport Association of America and Others* [2011] ECR 00000, paras. 148–9. See also Jack Goldsmith, 'Against Cyberanarchy', 65 University of Chicago Law Review 1199, 1208 (1998); *Restatement of the Law (Third), The Foreign Relations Law of the United States* (American Law Institute Publishers 1987), vol 1, at 239, stating: 'a state may exercise jurisdiction based on effects in the state, when the effect or intended effect is substantial and the exercise of jurisdiction is reasonable under § 403'.

[14] See EU Directive, Article 2(a).

[15] See Article 29 Working Party, 'Opinion 4/2007 on the concept of personal data' (WP 136, 20 June 2007), at 11.

settle their disputes under the law of their own country.[16] In ancient Greece, resident aliens were under the jurisdiction of special magistrates who tried civil suits
involving foreigners,[17] and in ancient Rome, aliens were often allowed to have their
disputes settled under the law of their place of origin.[18] This system continued into
the Middle Ages, and so we read about 'in the same country, and frequently even
in the same city, the Lombard living under the Lombardic law, and the Roman
under the Roman law; and the same distinction applied to the different races of
Germans, Goths, Franks, Burgundians, and diverse other peoples who, though
residing in the same territory, yet enjoyed their respective national laws'.[19] Thus,
in the ancient and medieval worlds, 'effectively, each person carried their own law
with them'.[20]

Under the modern revival of the personality principle in data protection law,
the law is not applied to the individual him or herself, but to the personal data
relating to the individual that are processed outside the individual's country of
nationality or residence. For example, the Data Protection Act of Ghana, enacted
in 2012, mandates that the law of the country from which data are transferred to
Ghana should continue to apply to the processing.[21] Greek law also used to extend
the jurisdiction of the Greek data protection authority (DPA) over data controllers
outside the country which processed data on Greek residents by requiring them
to appoint a representative in Greece which would be liable for such data processing.[22] Since Greek residents are overwhelmingly likely to also be Greek citizens,[23]
this requirement seemed effectively to base jurisdiction on the nationality of the
data subject, whereas under Article 4(1)(c) of the EU Directive application of
national data protection law to non-EU data controllers is based on the use of
'equipment' in the EU, not on nationality or residency; the Greek provision was
changed in 2006 following objections by the European Commission.[24]

---

[16] See Kurt Lipstein, 'The General Principles of Private International Law', 135 *Recueil des Cours de l'Académie de Droit International* 72, 107–9 (1972); Paul Schiff Berman, 'Global legal pluralism', 80 Southern California Law Review 1155, 1204–5 (2007); Shalom Kassan, 'Extraterritorial Jurisdiction in the Ancient World', 29 American Journal of International Law 237 (1935).

[17] Kassan (n 16), at 245.

[18] See Coleman Phillipson, *The International Law and Custom of Ancient Greece and Rome* (Macmillan 1911), vol. 1, at 277.

[19] Phillipson (n 18), at 284.

[20] Alex Mills, 'The Private History of International Law', 55 International and Comparative Law Quarterly 1, 7 (2006).

[21] Data Protection Act 2012, Section 18(2).

[22] See European Commission, 'Analysis and impact study on the implementation of Directive EC 95/46 in Member States' (2003), <http://ec.europa.eu/justice_home/fsj/privacy/docs/lawreport/consultation/technical-annex_en.pdf>, at 8, stating: 'As regards the provision in the Directive by which controllers have to designate a representative in case they make use of such equipment, the Greek law extends this requirement beyond the situation envisaged in the Directive when it requires all controllers outside Greece to appoint a representative if they process data on Greek residents'.

[23] In 2010, eg, 91.7 per cent of Greek residents were also Greek citizens. See <http://www.guardian.co.uk/news/datablog/2010/sep/07/immigration-europe-foreign-citizens#data>.

[24] Information known to the author. For the new wording, see <http://www.dpa.gr/pls/portal/docs/PAGE/APDPX/ENGLISH_INDEX/LEGAL%20FRAMEWORK/LAW%202472-97-MARCH08-EN.PDF>, at 4.

Applying national law in other countries to the processing of data of a State's own nationals and residents can lead to conflicts of law, which have been occurring with increasing frequency.[25] The current revision of a number of international instruments presents an opportunity to adopt more coherent and unified rules concerning applicable law and transborder data flows.

B. Transborder data flow regulation and applicable law rules

In many cases, transborder data flow regulation serves the same function as do rules on applicable law. Taking the EU as an example, personal data may generally not be transferred outside the geographic boundaries of the EU without a legal basis for both their processing and international transfer.[26] Legal bases for international data transfers (eg, signature of EU-approved standard contractual clauses between data exporter and data importer that impose data processing obligations based on EU law) routinely require the application of EU data protection standards in other countries where personal data are processed;[27] EU standards are then applied to onward transfers from the data importer to third parties.[28] Decisions concerning the adequacy of data protection in the country of data import are also based on whether the country's law complies with the standards of the one from which the data are transferred. Similarly, rules on applicable law cover the processing of personal data transferred outside the EU; for example, the Article 29 Working Party has found that Article 4(1)(c) of the EU Directive applies when an individual in the EU enters data in an Internet search engine or uploads data to an online social network operated from a server in another region.[29] The issues of the protection granted to data transferred to another country, and whether the law of the country of data transfer continues to apply to the processing, also became intertwined in the Society for Worldwide Interbank Financial Telecommunication (SWIFT) case.[30]

---

[25] See Section D.   [26] EU Directive, Articles 6 and 25(1).

[27] See, eg, Commission Decision 2004/915/EC of 27 December 2004 amending Decision 2001/497/EC as regards the introduction of an alternative set of standard contractual clauses for the transfer of personal data to third countries, [2004] OJ L385/74, Clauses II(i) and III.

[28] Commission Decision 2004/915/EC (n 27), Clause II(i).

[29] See Article 29 Working Party, 'Opinion 5/2009 on online social networking' (WP 163, 12 June 2009), at 5–7.

[30] The Article 29 Working Party and the Belgian Privacy Commission could not reach complete agreement on the extent to which Belgian data protection law should continue to apply to data transferred by SWIFT to the US. See Article 29 Working Party, 'Opinion 10/2006 on the processing of personal data by the Society for Worldwide Interbank Financial Telecommunication (SWIFT)' (WP 128, 22 November 2006), at 9, stating: 'The processing of personal data by SWIFT is subject to Belgian law, implementing the Directive, regardless of where the data processing takes place ...'; and Belgian Privacy Commission, Decision of 9 December 2008 in the SWIFT Affair, unofficial English translation at <http://www.privacycommission.be/sites/privacycommission/files/documents/swift_decision_en_09_12_2008.pdf>, at para. 167, stating: 'It does not appear relevant to search for a qualification of the processing carried out by SWIFT in the U.S. on data localized physically in this country in order to respond to the binding injunctions of a U.S. authority. In any case Belgian law does not apply on U.S. territory ...'. See regarding the SWIFT case, Section D.3 and Chapter 5.C.3.

The EU rules on applicable law (contained in Article 4 of the Directive) and those concerning the regulation of transborder data flows (contained in Articles 25 and 26) are also largely based on the same underlying policies. Preventing circumvention of the law is one of the main purposes of transborder data flow regulation, which is also the purpose of Article 4(1)(c) of the EU Directive dealing with applicable law.[31]

The close relationship between applicable law and transborder data flow rules is demonstrated in the European Commission's proposal of January 2012 to reform the EU data protection rules. The Commission's Communication announcing its proposal discusses issues regarding applicable law and data transfer restrictions in the same section without distinguishing between them, implying that they are similar measures both designed to protect EU residents when their data are processed outside the EU:[32]

To respond to these challenges, the Commission is proposing a system which will ensure a level of protection *for data transferred out of the EU similar to that within the EU. This will include clear rules defining when EU law is applicable to companies or organisations established outside the EU*, in particular by clarifying that whenever the organisation's activities are related to the offering of goods or services to EU individuals, or to the monitoring of their behaviour, EU rules will apply.[33]

This statement indicates that the purpose of the proposed new rules is to protect the personal data of residents and nationals of their own countries when the data are transferred elsewhere in the world.

Regulation in regions besides the EU may also apply data protection and privacy law to the processing of data outside the country. The APEC Privacy Framework seems to provide that the protections of the law of the place from which the data were transferred 'attach to' the data and continue to be applicable as they are transferred abroad, based on the principle of accountability.[34] Further examples are provided by the Privacy Act of New Zealand, certain provisions of which apply to information held outside that country,[35] and the draft Privacy Principles of the

---

[31] See Cecile de Terwagne and Sophie Louveaux, 'Data Protection and Online Networks', 13 Computer Law and Security Report 234, 238 (1997).

[32] See European Commission, 'Communication from the Commission to the European Parliament, the Council, the European Economic and Social Committee and the Committee of the Regions, Safeguarding Privacy in a Connected World—A European Data Protection Framework for the 21st Century', COM(2012) 9/3, 25 January 2012, at 11–12, describing in the same section proposals to apply EU data protection standards 'whenever individuals in Member States are targeted and their data is used or analysed by third country service providers' and to introduce 'an improvement in current mechanisms for transferring data to third countries'.

[33] European Commission, 'How will the EU's data protection reform make international cooperation easier?', <http://ec.europa.eu/justice/data-protection/document/review2012/factsheets/5_en.pdf>. Emphasis added.

[34] APEC Privacy Framework (2005), <http://www.apec.org/Groups/Committee-on-Trade-and-Investment/~/media/Files/Groups/ECSG/05_ecsg_privacyframewk.ashx>, Principle IX Accountability, at 31, stating: 'Thus, information controllers should take reasonable steps to ensure the information is protected, in accordance with these Principles, after it is transferred'.

[35] New Zealand Privacy Act 1993, section 10; Law Commission of New Zealand, 'Review of the Privacy Act 1993' (March 2010), <http://www.lawcom.govt.nz/sites/default/files/publications/2010/03/Publication_129_460_Part_17_Chapter-14-Trans-border%20Data%20Flows.pdf>, at 389–90.

Australian government, which make the entity transferring data abroad liable for breaches of the Principles committed outside Australia by the data importer.[36] The US Children's Online Privacy Protection Act (COPPA) also applies to any website anywhere in the world that collects personal information from children in the US,[37] and in particular to websites operated outside the US but that 'are directed to children in the United States or knowingly collect information from children in the United States'.[38] And US state privacy laws may also apply to the processing anywhere in the world of personal data of residents of the state.[39] Whether these examples are seen as applications of the principle of personality, the effects doctrine, or some other jurisdictional theory, the purpose behind them is the same, namely protection of the data of citizens and residents that are transferred abroad.

Countries and regional organizations seem to be striving to use a combination of applicable law rules and transborder data flow regulation to ensure that personal data are protected under their own standards no matter where in the world they are processed. However, this may result in the application of regulation to data processing that has little or no connection with the State asserting regulatory jurisdiction; such situations are particularly likely with regard to online technologies such as cloud computing. For example, Article 4(1)(c) of the EU Directive may cause the application of EU data protection law (including data transfer restrictions) to data processing outside the EU, since it applies to non-EU data controllers which use 'equipment' located in the EU.[40] Thus, 'combining the jurisdictional provisions with the provisions on data export may mean that a cloud provider with no establishment in the EEA may nevertheless be subject to the EU data export regime when attempting to transfer data back from the EEA to its place of establishment or some other location outside the EEA, even if the data were originally collected outside the EEA and relate to non-EEA individuals'.[41] This sort of situation can be avoided by requiring some connection between the data processing and the State seeking to exercise jurisdiction, so that regulation does not apply to the entire world in an unpredictable fashion.

---

[36] See Australian Government, 'Australian Privacy Principles, Companion Guide' (June 2010), <http://www.smos.gov.au/media/2010/docs/100622-privacy-part-1-Companion-Guide.pdf>, at 13.

[37] 15 USC § 6501–6506. See Joel Reidenberg, 'Technology and Internet Jurisdiction', 153 University of Pennsylvania Law Review 1951, 1957 (2004–05).

[38] See letter from Timothy J. Muris, Chairman, Federal Trade Commission, to Congressman Edward J. Markey, United States House of Representatives, 7 May 2004, p 3 (unpublished).

[39] See, eg, Massachusetts Standards for the Protection of Personal Information of Residents of the Commonwealth, 201 Mass. Code Regs 17.00–17.05, that apply to any processing of data of Massachusetts residents, whether or not the data controller has a presence in Massachusetts. See also Theodore P. Augustinos and Socheth Sor, 'March 1 Compliance Deadline Looms for Companies With Personal Information of Massachusetts Residents', (20 February 2012) Bloomberg BNA Privacy & Security Law Report 317.

[40] The meaning of Article 4(1)(c), as well as important related questions under Article 4 of the EU Directive, is due to be clarified by the European Court of Justice in proceedings referred to it by a Spanish court that had not been completed at the time this study was finalized. Reference for a preliminary ruling from the Audiencia Nacional (Spain) lodged on 9 March 2012—Case C-131/12 *Google Spain, SL, Google Inc. v Agencia Española de Protección de Datos, Mario Costeja González.*

[41] Hon and Millard (n 8), at 6.

Transborder data flow regulation and applicable law rules should be regarded as two weapons in the same arsenal to protect the processing of data outside the individual's home jurisdiction. This is illustrated by the proposal of the International Chamber of Commerce (ICC) of 2 September 2011 for revision of Council of Europe Convention 108, which contains the following text determining the scope of the Convention:

> 1. Each Party shall provide that personal data relating to individuals who are located in its territory shall receive an adequate level of protection based on the protections stipulated in this Convention when the data are processed outside its territory, provided that the processing results from an activity directed to such individuals or that otherwise manifests a sufficient connection to such Party.

The ICC proposal obliges State parties to the Convention to provide adequate protection to data processed outside their territory, and thus regulates both transborder data flows and the law that applies to them. The second part of the sentence (beginning 'provided that the processing results ...') specifies that the Convention's provisions on transborder data flows do not apply when there is not a sufficient link between a State party and a data processing activity outside its territory. Determining whether there is a meaningful link or connection with the forum is the classic approach to evaluating the propriety of a jurisdictional basis.[42] A wide variety of terms have been used to describe such a link, such as 'seat of a legal relationship', 'centre of gravity', or 'closest connection', but they all have the same meaning and effect.[43] Under the ICC proposal, questions such as whether a data processing activity is directed to individuals located in the territory of a party, or is sufficiently connected to such party, would be determined under the applicable national law implementing the Convention. The proposal was not accepted, but demonstrates how it is possible to combine rules on applicable law and transborder data flows in the same provision.

Aiming for protection of data processed abroad by mandating continued application of the law of the place of data collection or data export also risks raising unrealistic expectations of individuals that their data can receive the same legal protection when they are processed abroad as they can be in their own country. The lack of a seamless method of asserting individual rights around the world exists not only in data protection law, but in other related areas such as consumer law, based on the sovereignty of States and on differences between national legal systems and cultures. States have in the past refused opportunities to enact global legal instruments protecting consumers in electronic commerce,[44] and it is unrealistic

---

[42] See International Law Commission (ILC), 'Report on the Work of its Fifty-Eighth Session' (1 May–9 June and 3 July–11 August 2006) UN Doc. A/61/10, Annex D, para. 42; Dan Jerker B. Svantesson, *Private International Law and the Internet* (Kluwer Law International 2007), at 246.

[43] See F.A. Mann, 'The Doctrine of Jurisdiction in International Law', 111 *Recueil des Cours de l'Académie de Droit International* 9, 45 (1964); Svantesson (n 42), at 248.

[44] See, eg, United Nations Commission on International Trade Law (UNCITRAL), Report of the Working Group IV (Electronic Commerce) on the work of its fortieth session, Vienna, 14–18 October 2002, UN Doc. A/CN.9/527, at 20, in which countries decided against including consumer matters

to expect that seamless legal protection around the world can be achieved under data protection and privacy law when this has not been realized in other areas of consumer protection law.

C. Extraterritorial application of fundamental rights law

In those countries that regard data protection as a fundamental right, regulation of transborder data flows is regarded as part of the State's protective duty. By regulating the transborder flow of personal data, a State is thus taking steps to ensure that they are not deprived of the protection of law after transfer. However, this leaves open the question of the scope of this protective duty.

In many countries, data protection law is based on fundamental rights treaties that define their scope by reference to the concept of 'jurisdiction'.[45] Council of Europe Convention 108 defines jurisdiction based on territoriality,[46] but proposals have been made to expand it to have the same coverage as the European Convention on Human Rights.[47]

The European Court of Human Rights has extended the concept of jurisdiction under the European Convention on Human Rights outside the territorial boundaries of the State parties, but this has so far been limited to cases in which the regulating State has authority or control over a territory or individual where the violation occurred, such as in cases involving the extraterritorial deprivation of life or liberty (eg, in military operations), extraterritorial law enforcement, or transboundary environmental harm.[48]

Such cases differ fundamentally from those involving transborder data flow regulation. Under human rights law, jurisdiction is 'a question of fact, of actual authority and control' of a State over the territory where the alleged violation took place or the actors that committed it.[49] While jurisdiction in fundamental

---

in the scope of the 2005 United Nations Convention on the Use of Electronic Communications in International Contracts.

[45] See, eg, International Covenant of Civil and Political Rights, Article 2(1), stating: 'Each State Party to the present Covenant undertakes to respect and to ensure to all individuals within its territory and subject to its *jurisdiction* the rights recognized in the present Covenant ...' (emphasis added); European Convention on Human Rights, Article 1, stating: 'The High Contracting Parties shall secure to everyone within their *jurisdiction* the rights and freedoms defined in Section I of this Convention' (emphasis added).

[46] Article 1, stating: 'the purpose of this convention is to secure *in the territory* of each Party for every individual, whatever his nationality or residence, respect for his rights and fundamental freedoms, and in particular his right to privacy, with regard to automatic processing of personal data related to him ("data protection")' (emphasis added).

[47] See Section E.

[48] See, eg, *Al-Jedda v United Kingdom* (2011) ECHR 1092; *Al-Skeini v United Kingdom* (2011) 53 EHRR 18. See also Robin C.A. White and Claire Ovey, *The European Convention on Human Rights* (5th edn, OUP 2010), at 91–2.

[49] Marko Milanovic, *Extraterritorial Application of Human Rights Treaties* (OUP 2011), at 53.

rights law is to be broadly construed,[50] States typically apply their transborder data flow regulation extraterritorially in situations such as when a company is legally required to extend the protection of its home country's law to personal data transferred for processing abroad. If the data are then misused after transfer, there is no question of either the State where the alleged violation occurred, or the persons or entities who committed them, being under the authority or control of the State from which the data were exported.

In addition, many alleged violations of transborder data flow regulation involve data processing by private parties. Generally speaking, non-State actors 'have no clear legal obligations to respect human rights apart from compliance with the law of the particular country in which they are operating',[51] and human rights obligations are generally not directly enforceable against natural or legal persons,[52] nor may actions by private parties be imputed to States such as to give rise to liability of the State under human rights law (apart from some exceptions which are not relevant here).[53]

Thus, the European Convention on Human Rights does not generally require State parties to control the activities abroad of companies incorporated under their laws or having their headquarters in their territories;[54] in the present context, this means that States are not required under fundamental rights law to regulate the processing of personal data that have been transferred outside their territory by private parties.

However, the responsibility of private actors under fundamental rights law is evolving, and States may have the obligation to protect individuals from activities by private actors,[55] which could be extended in the future to situations involving transborder data flows. At present, regulatory frameworks such as corporate social responsibility (CSR) generally do not have binding legal character, but they may evolve so as to create a legal duty on private actors to protect data protection rights.[56] This is apart from liability based on private law, such as contractual obliga-

---

[50] See Theodor Meron, 'Extraterritoriality of Human Rights Treaties', 89 American Journal of International Law 78, 82 (1995), stating: 'Narrow territorial interpretation of human rights treaties is anathema to the basic idea of human rights, which is to ensure that a state should respect human rights of persons over whom it exercises jurisdiction'.

[51] Philip Alston, 'The "not-a-cat" syndrome: can the international human rights regime accommodate non-state actors?', in Philip Alston (ed), *Non-State Actors and Human Rights* 3 (OUP 2005), at 36.

[52] Jörg Polakiewicz, 'Corporate Responsibility to Respect Human Rights: Challenges and Opportunities for Europe and Japan', CALE Discussion Paper No. 9 (October 2012), <http://cale.law.nagoya-u.ac.jp/_src/sc618/CALE20DP20No.209-121010.pdf>, at 8–9.

[53] Nicola Vennemann, 'Application of International Human Rights Conventions to Transboundary State Acts', in Rebecca M. Bratspies and Russell A. Miller (eds), *Transboundary Harm in International Law: Lessons from the Trailsmelter Arbitration* 295 (CUP 2006), at 306.

[54] Polakiewicz (n 52), at 14.

[55] Polakiewicz (n52); Olivier De Schutter, 'Globalization and jurisdiction: lessons from the European Convention on Human Rights', 6 Baltic Yearbook of International Law 185, 217 (2006).

[56] See Lokke Moerel, *Binding Corporate Rules: Corporate Self-Regulation of Global Data Transfers* (OUP 2012), at 276–90.

tions or adoption of CSR standards by means of unilateral declaration, which may already give rise to liability on the part of companies.[57]

In practice, applying jurisdictional criteria under public international law to situations involving transborder data flows may result in a *broader* application of human rights law to data processing in other countries, and thus greater protection, than is the case if criteria under human rights treaties are applied. Since the judgment of the Permanent Court of International Justice in the *SS Lotus* case[58] in 1921, it has become accepted that law can apply to conduct taking place beyond the borders of a State that produces an effect in it.[59] While most authorities find that some limitations on international legislative jurisdiction do exist,[60] there is little agreement on where they lie. By contrast, jurisdiction under human rights treaties has only been extended extraterritorially in situations in which the State in question had actual control over the territory where the violation occurred or the parties who committed it.

Application of the concept of jurisdiction under public international law to transborder data flows should be accompanied by a test to manage jurisdictional conflicts, such as by requiring some substantial connection to the forum before jurisdiction may be asserted.[61] This is necessary because of the risk of multiple regulators asserting jurisdiction over the same data processing.[62] Various concepts could serve as a jurisdictional 'safety valve' in this regard, such as a requirement that

---

[57] See Moerel (n 56), at 277; Polakiewicz (n 52), at 68–70.

[58] *SS Lotus* (*France v Turkey*), PCIJ Reports, Series A, No. 10, p 19 (1927), stating at 18–19 with regard to international law: 'Far from laying down a general prohibition to the effect that States may not extend the application of their laws and the jurisdiction of their courts to persons, property and acts outside their territory, it leaves them in this respect a wide measure of discretion, which is only limited in certain cases by prohibitive rules; as regards other cases, every State remains free to adopt the principles which it regards as best and most suitable.'

[59] See n 13.

[60] See, eg, *Case concerning Barcelona Traction, Light and Power Co. Ltd* (*Belgium v Spain*), [1970] ICJ Reports 65, 105, where Judge Fitzmaurice stated with regard to limits on jurisdiction that international law does: '(a) postulate the existence of limits—though in any given case it may be for the tribunal to indicate what these are for the purposes of that case; and (b) involve for every State an obligation to exercise moderation and restraint as to the extent of the jurisdiction assumed by its courts in cases having a foreign element, and to avoid undue encroachment on a jurisdiction more properly appertaining to, or more appropriately exercisable by, another State'; Brownlie (n 12), at 299; Jonathan Hill, 'The Exercise of Jurisdiction in Private International Law', in Patrick Capps, Malcolm Evans, and Stratos Konstadinidis (eds), *Asserting Jurisdiction: International and European Legal Perspectives* 39 (Hart 2003), at 43; Mann (n 43), at 30; *Restatement (Third)* (n 13), vol 1, at 235; Ryngaert (n 6), at 21; Svantesson (n 42), at 89.

[61] See, eg, *Restatement (Third)* (n 13), vol 1, § 403(3), reading: 'When it would not be unreasonable for each of the two states to exercise jurisdiction over a person or activity, but the prescriptions by the two states are in conflict, each state has an obligation to evaluate its own as well as the other state's interest in exercising jurisdiction, in light of all the relevant factors; a state should defer to the other state if that state's interest is clearly greater'; Ryngaert (n 6), at 137, recommending that: 'States limit the reach of their laws, and defer to other States that may have a stronger, often territorial nexus to a situation'; Svantesson (n 42), at 284–8, suggesting 'foreseeably' that jurisdiction would be asserted as a possible test. See also Chapter 8.C.7.

[62] See Section D.

data protection law not apply to a transfer when this would not be 'reasonable'[63] or 'proportionate'.[64] The Article 29 Working Party has hinted at this sort of approach in calling on DPAs to be cautious in asserting jurisdiction under Article 4(1)(c) of the EU Directive:

The Working Party would advocate a cautious approach to be taken in applying this rule of the data protection directive to concrete cases. Its objective is to ensure that individuals enjoy the protection of national data protection laws and the supervision of data processing by national data protection authorities in those cases where it is necessary, where it makes sense and where there is a reasonable degree of enforceability having regard to the cross-frontier situation involved.[65]

In its decision in the SWIFT case, the Belgian Privacy Commission also took into account the extent to which it could enforce compliance extraterritorially in deciding whether Belgian data protection law should apply to data processing in the US.[66]

Under Article 13 of the European Convention on Human Rights, individuals must be provided with 'an effective remedy before a *national* authority notwithstanding that the violation has been committed by persons acting in an official capacity' (emphasis added), raising the question of whether it must always be possible for an individual to assert their rights before a court or regulatory authority in their own country. However, the purpose of Article 13 is not to extend the jurisdictional reach of the Convention to the entire world, but to 'provide a means whereby individuals can obtain relief at national level for violations of their Convention rights before having to set in motion the international machinery of complaint before the Court'.[67] That is, Article 13 is intended to obligate State parties to provide an effective remedy so that individuals are not forced automatically to bring any alleged violation before the European Court of Human Rights. The fact that national courts and regulators are limited in their ability to provide a remedy for data protection violations that take place in other regions of the world

---

[63] See, eg, *Restatement (Third)* (n 13), vol 1, § 403, stating: 'territoriality and nationality remain the principle bases of jurisdiction to prescribe, but in determining their meaning rigid concepts have been replaced by broader criteria embracing principles of reasonableness and fairness to accommodate overlapping or conflicting interests of states, and affected private interests'. See also Christopher Kuner, 'Data Protection Law and International Jurisdiction on the Internet' (Parts 1 and 2), 18(3) International Journal of Law and Information Technology 227, 244–5 (2010).

[64] See Ryngaert (n 6), at 180, arguing that proportionality is one of a number of principles of international law 'that may be seen as buttressing an international rule of reason informed by interest-balancing'.

[65] Article 29 Working Party (n 2), at 9.

[66] See Belgian Privacy Commission, Decision of 9 December 2008 in the SWIFT Affair, unofficial English translation at <http://www.privacycommission.be/sites/privacycommission/files/documents/swift_decision_en_09_12_2008.pdf>, at para. 167, stating: 'It does not appear relevant to search for a qualification of the processing carried out by SWIFT in the U.S. on data localized physically in this country in order to respond to the binding injunctions of a U.S. authority. In any case Belgian law does not apply on U.S. territory, and any qualification would remain purely theoretical and without effect: none of the obligations of Belgian law could be imposed on this ground.' See regarding the SWIFT case, Section D.3 and Chapter 5.C.3.

[67] *Kudla v Poland* (2002) 35 EHRR 198, para. 152, quoted in White and Ovey (n 48), at 131.

is not owing to any failure of State parties to implement the Convention properly, but to basic principles of public international law that restrict the ability of States to conduct enforcement actions outside their borders.[68]

Furthermore, Article 13 does not require that a remedy is always judicial, merely that it is effective as determined in the legal order of the respective State party in question; this means that ombudsman procedures and other non-judicial remedies may be sufficient to satisfy Article 13.[69] Thus, if an individual brings a claim with regard to data protection violations that allegedly occurred in a third country following a data transfer, Article 13 should be satisfied if the individual is able to bring a complaint before the DPA in his or her own country, with the authority then entering into negotiations or informal discussions with the regulatory authorities in the third country or with the party that committed the alleged violation. Likewise, Article 1 of the Additional Protocol to Council of Europe Convention 108, which requires that data protection supervisory authorities with powers of investigation and intervention are established, should be interpreted to mean that such powers need only be exercised within the limits that public international law places on them.[70]

D. Conflict of laws involving transborder data flow regulation

1. Conflicts of legal regimes

The growing fragmentation of international law in recent years has been well documented,[71] and this phenomenon is true of transborder data flow regulation as well. Along with the increase in the amount and variety of regulation has gone an increase in conflicts between different regulatory systems. For example, a company may have agreed with business partners in different countries to transfer personal data to them based on certain contractual protections, but may then be subject to conflicting legal obligations under the law of the countries to which the data are transferred; a State may be subject to data transfer requirements based on the law of a regional organization to which it is party, and then accede to an international

---

[68] See, eg, Brownlie (n 12), at 309, stating: 'the governing principle is that a state cannot take measures on the territory of another state by way of enforcement of national laws without the consent of the latter'; Mann (n 43), at 145–6.

[69] White and Ovey (n 48), at 135–6.

[70] See *Al-Jedda v United Kingdom* (n 48), at para. 76, in which the European Court of Human Rights noted that in interpreting and applying the European Convention on Human Rights, it had to 'take into account relevant rules of international law'.

[71] See, eg, ILC, 'Fragmentation of International Law: Difficulties arising from the Diversification and Expansion of International Law, Report of the Study Group of the International Law Commission finalized by Martti Koskenniemi', UN Doc. A/CN.4/L.682 (13 April 2006), <http://daccess-ods.un.org/access.nsf/Get?OpenAgent&DS=A/CN.4/L.682&Lang=E>; Ralf Michaels and Joost Pauwelyn, 'Conflict of Norms or Conflict of Laws? Different Techniques in the Fragmentation of International Law', Duke Law Scholarship Repository, 4/2012, <http://scholarship.law.duke.edu/cgi/viewcontent.cgi?article=2933&context=faculty_scholarship>.

treaty that has different requirements; and a company may be obliged under data protection law to abide by certain obligations when transferring personal data, only to be ordered to transfer the data to a different country for law enforcement purposes.

Conflicts concerning data protection in transborder data flows are not just a problem for governments and companies, but can unwittingly ensnare individuals as well. For example, in 2010 the US government enacted the Foreign Account Tax Compliance Act (FATCA),[72] which requires large-scale transfers of data concerning US citizens holding accounts in foreign countries to the US tax authorities, and has been criticized as not complying with European data protection requirements.[73] As a result, some non-US banks have decided to refuse to deal with customers who are US citizens, thus denying them access to essential banking services.[74]

Some parties have objected to the application of data protection law to data transferred abroad as an improper assertion of extraterritorial jurisdiction; such complaints have been made most often with regard to the EU Directive,[75] but have also been made about US privacy law.[76] However, the threshold for finding an exercise of jurisdiction to be improper under international law is high,[77] and claims that particular types of jurisdiction 'violate international law' should thus be taken with a pinch of salt, particularly when it now seems that both the US and the EU apply their data protection and privacy law to acts occurring outside their borders.

The conflicts that have emerged regarding transborder data flow regulation typically involve different types of actor, legal regimes at different levels (national, regional, and international), and legal requirements that stand in tension to each other (eg, data protection and law enforcement requirements). These are forms of regulation 'which define the external reach of their jurisdiction along issue-specific rather than territorial lines, and which claim a global validity for

---

[72] Enacted on 18 March 2010 as part of the Hiring Incentives to Restore Employment (HIRE) Act.

[73] See Eidgenössischer Datenschutz- und Öffentlichkeitsbeauftragter, '19. Tätigkeitsbericht 2011/2012' [19th annual report of the Swiss Federal Data Protection Commissioner], at para. 1.9.1.

[74] See Bill Hinchberger, 'European banks shut Americans out over U.S. tax rules' (27 September 2012), <http://www.usatoday.com/story/money/business/2012/09/27/american-expats/1594695/>.

[75] See, eg, Jack Goldsmith and Tim Wu, *Who Controls the Internet? Illusions of a Borderless World* (OUP 2008), at 175, referring to the 'aggressive jurisdictional scope' of the EU Data Protection Directive; Patrick Ross, 'Congress fears European privacy standards' CNET News (8 March 2001), <http://news.cnet.com/2100-1023-253826.html>, quoting the chairman of the Commerce Committee of the US House of Representatives as stating that the EU Data Protection Directive is 'an effort to impose the EU's will on the US'.

[76] See Article 29 Working Party (n 2), at 4, defending EU data protection law against accusations that it is extraterritorial by stating: 'in other countries, for example in the United States of America, courts and laws apply similar reasoning in order to subject foreign websites to local rules'.

[77] See Ryngaert (n 6), 17, stating that, while rules of conflict of laws seek to identify the State with the strongest nexus to the situation, rules of public international law cast aside only the most outrageous assertions of jurisdiction.

themselves'.[78] Thus, they go beyond simple conflict of laws, and can be viewed as conflicts between different social sectors and normative regimes.[79]

Such conflicts are much more difficult to resolve when they involve multiple systems between which there is no interface or overriding 'rule of recognition' that would set the priority between them. In such situations, conflicts cannot be solved by a single regulatory theory, or by applying rules governing conflict of laws.[80] A certain number of such conflicts are inevitable in a pluralistic legal system, but they should be avoided when they lead to unnecessary international tensions.

2. Conflicts between different data protection regulations

Conflicts may also arise when different sets of transborder data flow regulations apply to the same data processing and the same parties. The interaction between Council of Europe Convention 108 and other types of transborder flow regulation to which Council of Europe member States may be parties (eg, the EU Data Protection Directive) provides one example. For example, the Convention does not presently provide a legal basis for transfers between contracting States, but if it were amended in the future to do so, then EU Member States that are also parties to the Convention would, on the one hand, be obliged under the Convention to allow the free flow of data between parties but, on the other hand, under EU law could not permit the free flow of data to countries that had not been determined by the European Commission to provide an 'adequate level of data protection'.

There can also be divergences between the data protection law of the country of data import and that of the country of data export that continue to apply to the data once they have been transferred, so that if a country allows transborder data flows only on the condition that its data protection standards continue to apply to the processing, then those standards may come into conflict with the data protection laws of the country to which data are exported. Such conflicts can arise regarding issues such as the length of time that personal data may be retained before being deleted; the conditions under which onward transfer of the data to third parties may be made; and whether valid consent has been given for processing the data. When these sorts of conflicts arise, there will often be a party caught in the middle, for example a data controller subject to conflicting legal obligations, and an individual unsure of which law applies to the processing of their data. The continued application of home country law as data are transferred around the world will make it necessary to 'tag' the data and indicate which data protection

---

[78] Andreas Fischer-Lescano and Gunther Teubner, 'Regime-Collisions: the Vain Search for Legal Unity in the Fragmentation of Global Law', 25 Michigan Journal of International Law 999, 1009 (2003).

[79] Fischer-Lescano and Teubner (n 78), at 1000, noting the emergence of 'an "intersystemic conflicts law", derived not from collisions between the distinct nations of private international law, but from collisions between distinct global sectors.'

[80] See Michaels and Pauwelyn (n 71).

regime attaches to them,[81] which will require international agreement on standards for data tagging, and will have to be done in a way that does not enable data to be tied to a particular individual.

3. Conflicts with other legal requirements

In a growing number of cases, conflicts arise between transborder data flow regulation in a particular jurisdiction and legal requirements in another. In such cases, data controllers (meaning mainly companies) are often caught between conflicting legal obligations that cannot be resolved. EU data protection law including a legal basis for the international transfer of personal data in cases involving 'important public interest grounds or for the establishment, exercise or defence of legal claims',[82] but these are generally not held to allow the international transfer of data to a non-EU country when the purpose is to comply with a foreign (ie, a non-EU) statute or legal obligation.[83]

The following are some examples of conflicts that frequently arise in practice.

- *E-discovery* US courts may order parties in other countries to transfer evidence to them under so-called 'discovery orders', with the risk that the parties will be compelled to violate their own national rules restricting transborder data flows.[84] It is the author's experience that some of these cases are resolved by negotiation and never become public. For example, a court may ask a party for an affidavit of legal counsel confirming that a conflict with foreign transborder data flow regulation exists, and may then decline to order production of the evidence, but whether it does so is entirely within the court's discretion. One case where this occurred was *Volkswagen v Valdez*,[85] in which the Texas Supreme Court vacated the order of a lower court that had ordered Volkswagen to transfer a company phone book to it in violation of German restrictions on transborder data flows. However, such a clear resolution of the conflict depends on one of the parties convincing the court that consideration should be paid to the party's obligations under foreign data protection or privacy law.

- *PNR data* Following the terrorist attacks of 11 September 2001, the US government enacted legislation requiring air carriers operating flights to or from the US or across US territory to provide it with electronic access to personal

---

[81] See Paula J. Bruening and K. Krasnow Waterman, 'Data tagging for new models of information governance', 8 IEEE Security & Privacy 64 (Sept.–Oct. 2010).

[82] EU Directive, Article 26(1)(d).

[83] See, eg, Article 29 Working Party, 'Working Document 1/2009 on pre-trial discovery for cross border civil litigation' (WP 158, 11 February 2009), at 9, stating: 'An obligation imposed by a foreign legal statute or regulation may not qualify as a legal obligation by virtue of which data processing in the EU would be made legitimate'. See also Chapter 8.C.7.

[84] See 'The Sedona Conference International Principles on Discovery, Disclosure & Data Protection' (December 2011) <https://thesedonaconference.org/download-pub/495>.

[85] 909 SW2d 900 (Tex. 1995).

information regarding the passengers on these flights (so-called passenger name record (PNR) data). EU airlines and others complained that there was no legal basis under EU rules to transfer this data. Following intense negotiations between the EU and the US that featured various legal challenges and political disagreements, the European Parliament and the Council of Ministers finally approved an agreement reached with the US government in 2012 allowing transfer of the data to US authorities, conditioned on the US observing certain protections for the data based on EU data protection law.[86]

- *Sarbanes–Oxley whistleblowing requirements* The US Congress enacted the Sarbanes–Oxley Act ('SOX') in 2002 in response to a series of corporate scandals. SOX imposes compliance obligations not only on publicly traded companies in the US, but also on non-US entities listed on US exchanges, and the European affiliates of US-listed companies. These obligations include measures designed to protect individuals who make anonymous complaints about corporate mismanagement (known as 'whistleblowers'). Companies typically comply with this requirement by establishing telephone hotlines or web-based complaint systems, many of which are also answered by operators in the US for calls originating in Europe, resulting in data transfers from the EU to the US. Anonymous reporting of alleged violations of law and policy may constitute a violation of EU data protection law, and is thus tightly regulated.[87] The conflict between SOX requirements and EU data protection law entered the public consciousness in 2005 when the French data protection authority (CNIL) refused to authorize the whistleblowing hotlines of two US-based companies.[88]

- *SWIFT* In the summer of 2006 it became known that US law enforcement authorities were accessing a US-based financial database run by SWIFT, a cooperative association located in Belgium that provides secure message and payment services to thousands of banks worldwide. The database was located in Belgium but mirrored in the US. The EU and US later reached agreement

---

[86] See Agreement between the United States of America and the European Union on the use and transfer of passenger name records to the United States Department of Homeland Security, [2012] OJ L215/5.

[87] Article 29 Working Party, 'Opinion 1/2006 on the application of EU data protection rules to internal whistleblowing schemes in the fields of accounting, internal accounting controls, auditing matters, fight against bribery, banking and financial crime' (WP 117, 1 February 2006).

[88] Délibération no. 2005-111 du 26 mai 2005 relative à une demande d'autorisation de la Compagnie européenne d'accumulateurs pour la mise en œuvre d'un dispositif de ligne éthique; Délibération no. 2005-110 du 26 mai 2005 relative à une demande d'autorisation de McDonald's France pour la mise en œuvre d'un dispositif d'intégrité professionnelle. In December 2005, the CNIL issued a decision in which it set forth conditions under which whistleblower systems could operate in France. See CNIL, Délibération no. 2005-305 du 8 décembre 2005 portant autorisation unique de traitements automatisés de données à caractère personnel mis en œuvre dans le cadre de dispositifs d'alerte professionnelle, <http://www.cnil.fr/en-savoir-plus/deliberations/deliberation/delib/83/>.

on a treaty allowing access to the data by US law enforcement authorities based on protections under EU data protection law.[89]

Conflicts can also arise with private sector instruments. For example, if a company promises in its online privacy policy to keep data secure and only use them for specified purposes, and then is required by a law enforcement authority in another country to turn the data over to it, the company may be in breach of its privacy policy.

Not all conflicts between transborder data flow regulation and other legal requirements involve the EU and the US. A number of countries (including China, some in the Gulf Region, and India) may oblige companies to allow them access to corporate databases, which can include requirements that data are transferred to them from other countries in violation of regulations on transborder data flows. These requirements were the subject of a critical report issued by the ICC in 2012, which stated in part:

Companies processing data in multiple countries face increasing government pressure to comply with law enforcement and other regulatory requests for access to personal data that conflict with data protection and privacy laws in other countries in which they operate. The growing number of such cases is caused in part by the explosive growth in phenomena such the use of multi-locational servers for cloud computing, which provide efficient, lower-cost services for individuals and businesses....[90]

As the report goes on to say, 'In many cases law enforcement requests may conflict with data protection and privacy laws ... and ... violate legal requirements regarding international data transfers.'[91] Unfortunately there is no clear solution to such conflicts, and their number and extent will probably increase in the coming years.

E. Example of Council of Europe Convention 108

The difficulty of applying regulation based on territoriality to a phenomenon that is essentially borderless has substantial implications for transborder data flow regulation. The Council of Europe's Bureau of the Consultative Committee of the Convention for the Protection of individuals with Regard to the Automatic Processing of Personal Data (T-PD) has been dealing with these issues in its work to modernize Council of Europe Convention 108, which provides a useful example of their implications.

---

[89] Agreement between the European Union and the United States of America on the processing and transfer of Financial Messaging Data from the European Union to the United States for purposes of the Terrorist Finance Tracking Program, [2010] OJ L8/11.

[90] See ICC, 'Cross-border law enforcement access to company data—current issues under data protection and privacy law', Doc. No. 373/507 (7 February 2012), <http://www.iccwbo.org/Data/Policies/2012/Cross-border-law-enforcement-access-to-company-data-current-issues-under-data-protection-and-privacy-law/>, at 1.

[91] ICC (n 90), at 1.

The current text of Article 1 of the Convention reads that 'The purpose of this convention is to secure in the *territory* of each Party for every individual, whatever his nationality or residence, respect for his rights and fundamental freedoms, and in particular his right to privacy, with regard to automatic processing of personal data relating to him ("data protection")' (emphasis added). In its proposal of 15 November 2011,[92] the Council of Europe Secretariat suggested revising Article 1 to read 'The purpose of this convention is to secure within the *jurisdiction* of each Party for every individual, whatever his nationality or residence, the right to data protection, namely respect for his rights and fundamental freedoms, and in particular his right to privacy, with regard to automatic processing of personal data relating to him' (emphasis added). The substitution of 'jurisdiction' for 'territory' is designed to bring Convention 108 into accordance with the wording of Article 1 of the European Convention on Human Rights, and with the jurisprudence of the European Court of Human Rights, which in certain circumstances has applied the protections of the European Convention on Human Rights outside the territory of the contracting parties.[93]

On 2 September 2011, the ICC submitted to the T-PD a proposal for a revision that would combine Article 12 of the Convention and Article 2 of the Additional Protocol.[94] In contrast to the European Commission's proposal for a General Data Protection Regulation, which limits the application of EU data protection law to the data of EU 'residents' processed by non-EU data controllers,[95] the ICC proposal would apply to individuals 'located' in the territory of a contracting State, thus covering not only residents, but temporary visitors, etc., and anyone located in a contracting party.

The ICC proposal attempts to minimize the difficulty of defining a 'data transfer' by not referring to the transfer of personal data and focusing instead on any situation in which personal data are processed outside the territory of the contracting State. However, it is nearly impossible to avoid any reference to territoriality in a provision regulating transborder data flows, since the very notion of a transborder data flow presupposes that data have changed location; in the ICC proposal this is reflected in the reference to the processing of data 'outside the territory' of a State party, which would have to be further defined. The text does not refer to the 'data controller', so that it also applies to data processors.

On 15 November 2011, the Council of Europe published a first preliminary draft to revise the international data transfer provisions of both Convention 108 and the Additional Protocol, the relevant provision of which reads as follows:

1. Each Party shall provide for the communication and disclosure of personal data, to a recipient which is not subject to the jurisdiction of a Party to the Convention, only if the national law applicable to that recipient ensures, in light of the present Convention, an adequate level of protection of the data subjects.

---

[92] See T-PD-BUR(2011) 27_en (15 November 2011), <http://www.coe.int/t/dghl/standardsetting/dataprotection/TPD_documents/T-PD-BUR_2011_27_en.pdf>.
[93] See, eg, *Al-Jedda v United Kingdom* (n 48); *Al-Skeini v United Kingdom* (n 48). See also Section C.
[94] See the text quoted in Section B.   [95] See Article 3(2).

The 15 November draft avoids mentioning 'data transfers', and its territorial scope is instead based on whether the recipient of the data is 'subject to the jurisdiction of a Party to the Convention'. The next version was issued by the Secretariat on 18 January 2012,[96] and reads:

> 1. Each Party shall ensure the free flow of personal data. Personal data can be communicated or made accessible to a recipient who is not subject to its jurisdiction on the condition that the law applicable to this recipient ensures, with respect to the Convention, an adequate level of protection of data subjects concerned by these data.

This version began with a requirement to 'ensure the free flow of data', which is explained as follows in the document:

> This key question will have to be further examined 'recognising that it is necessary to reconcile the fundamental values of the respect for privacy and the free flow of information between peoples' (preamble Convention 108). The co-existence of provisions on transborder data flows in both the Convention and article 2 of the additional Protocol (transfer of data to States which are not Parties) will have to be revised and the current provisions need to be examined with a view to agreeing on a new approach which would amend both the Convention and the Protocol.[97]

On 31 January 2012, the ICC then proposed a further version, reading:

> 1. Each Party shall ensure the free flow of personal data. Personal data can be communicated or made accessible to a recipient who is not subject to its jurisdiction if the other provisions of the Convention are fulfilled, and one of the following applies: the recipient is subject to the jurisdiction of a Party to this Convention, subject to the conditions of paragraph 2; or the recipient has adduced appropriate safeguards with respect to the protection of personal data pursuant to paragraph 3; or one of the derogations is applicable pursuant to paragraph 4.

This version lists the various legal bases for data transfer, but does not mention the adequacy standard. In this regard it was inspired by Article 40 of the European Commission's proposed General Data Protection Regulation, which does not specifically require an 'adequate level of protection' in the recipient country, and instead sets forth general principles that must be fulfilled when data are transferred outside the EU. It also explicitly recognizes that in addition to providing a legal basis for international data transfers, the data being transferred must be initially collected in accordance with applicable legal requirements.

On March 5, the Council of Europe Secretariat then circulated a new version of the text, which had two options regarding transborder data flows: the second one is based on the ICC proposal given earlier, while the first one reads:

> 1. Each Party shall ensure the free flow of personal data. Personal data may be communicated or made accessible to a recipient who is not subject to its jurisdiction,

---

[96] T-PD-BUR(2012)01EN (18 January 2012), <http://www.coe.int/t/dghl/standardsetting/dataprotection/TPD_documents/T-PD-BUR_2012_01_EN.pdf>.
[97] T-PD (n 96), at 4.

on the condition that the law applicable to this recipient ensures, with respect to the Convention, an adequate level of protection of data subjects.[98]

And, finally, in preparation for a meeting of the plenary of the T-PD in June 2012, the Secretariat circulated the following draft dated 27 April 2012:

> 1. Each Party shall ensure that personal data will only be disclosed or made available to a recipient who is not subject to its jurisdiction on condition that an adequate level of data protection is ensured.[99]

The tension between the need to indicate that regulation covers the flow of data across national borders, while at the same time taking account of the fact that it is difficult to localize data processing as occurring in a particular place, is illustrated by the examples from the work on modernizing Convention 108. The proposal to expand the Convention's coverage from the concept of 'territory' to that of 'jurisdiction' takes into account the diminishing role of territoriality, but still leaves certain questions open (eg, what constitutes 'disclosing' or 'making available' data to a recipient). There can be no perfect solution to the drafting of a jurisdictional provision covering transborder data flows, but the evolution of the texts in the context of the Council of Europe discussion shows how States are gradually coming to terms with the reality that transborder data flows can no longer be defined solely in terms of territoriality.

F. Conclusions

For years it has been assumed that the EU Directive is the only international data protection instrument containing a set of rules on applicable law.[100] However, at least with regard to personal data transferred abroad, transborder data flow regulation performs much the same function as applicable law rules, namely extending the protection of national law extraterritorially. Treating it as a separate form of regulation, rather than as a way of extending applicable law to other States, has led to contradictions: for example, transborder data flow regulation has been justified based on the difficulty that individuals have in asserting rights under their own data protection law once data are transferred abroad[101] but, if that is true, then it is hard to understand why it is important for such law to apply to data processing in other countries.

---

[98] See T-PD-BUR(2012)01Rev_en (5 March 2012), <http://www.coe.int/t/dghl/standardsetting/dataprotection/TPD_documents/T-PD-BUR_2012_01Rev_en.pdf>.

[99] See T-PD-BUR(2012)01Rev2_en (27 April 2012), <http://www.coe.int/t/dghl/standardsetting/dataprotection/TPD_documents/T-PD-BUR_2012_01Rev2FIN_en.pdf>.

[100] See, eg, Lee Bygrave, 'Determining applicable law pursuant to European Data Protection Legislation', 16 Computer Law and Security Report 252, 253 (2000), noting that the applicable rules of the Directive 'constitute the first and only set of rules in an international data protection instrument to deal specifically with the determination of applicable law'.

[101] See Chapter 5.C.4.

States and regional organizations have concentrated on extending the applicability of their own regulation to the processing of data in other countries, rather than on developing global standards for transborder data flows. This reflects the fact that transborder data flow regulation is still often viewed as a way to protect the rights and interests of a State's own citizens, rather than as a matter of international importance.

One of the consequences of applying data protection law across national borders in the guise of transborder data flow regulation is the chance of conflicts between data protection regimes, and between the rules of data protection law and those of other legal regimes; while this possibility has existed from the earliest days of such regulation,[102] the growth of the Internet has increased the risks it poses. The application of data protection law to data processing abroad is further complicated by its status in many States as fundamental rights law, which brings with it a protective duty of the State towards individuals; such duty cannot be extended in an unlimited fashion without causing conflicts with different legal regimes, other data protection rules, and other types of legal requirement. There are three types of loser in such conflicts: individuals, who become confused about which regulation applies to the processing of their data; data controllers, which are placed in the middle of contradictory requirements; and the law itself, which can lose respect when it makes contradictory demands or has no practical chance of being enforced. The increasing extraterritorial application of data protection law is another sign of the fragmentation of transborder data flow regulation.

States seem to want to have it both ways, namely having their local requirements apply all over the world to the processing of data originally collected in their territory, while having a seamless means of enforcing such requirements across borders. However, it is unrealistic to expect that local standards can apply globally, and cross-border enforcement is more effective if the standards under which it is conducted are shared between multiple jurisdictions. Both compliance and enforcement leave much to be desired, as will be seen in the next chapter.

---

[102] See Jon Bing, 'Transnational Data Flows and the Scandinavian Data Protection Legislation', 24 Scandinavian Studies in Law 65, 92–3 (1980).

7

Compliance and Enforcement

A. Introduction

The levels of compliance and enforcement of transborder data flow regulation are important indicators of its effectiveness.[1] A lack of enforcement, or inconsistent enforcement, may reduce respect for a particular rule, and for a regulatory system in general.[2]

Regulators face formidable challenges in enforcing transborder data flow regulation. Generally speaking, enforcement is carried out in accordance with general provisions of data protection law (eg, the sections of national data protection acts dealing with enforcement). It is easy to transfer personal data to other countries and regions of the world using the Internet; indeed, such transfers routinely occur without any particular intent to transfer data abroad merely through the use of

---

[1] See Robert Baldwin, Martin Cave, and Martin Lodge, *Understanding Regulation: Theory, Strategy, and Practice* (2nd edn, OUP 2012), at 34–7.

[2] See Chris Reed, *Making Laws for Cyberspace* (OUP 2012), at 49: 'The enforcement of a law also plays an important role in engendering respect for that law. If a state consistently fails to enforce a law it sends a message to the law's subjects that the state does not expect them to obey it. This diminishes their respect for that law, often to such an extent that any subsequent attempt to enforce it produces outrage and opposition ... Where a state wishes to enforce a law but is unable to do so in any consistent and effective way, the message is rather different but equally damaging to respect. Here the state desires that its commands should be obeyed, but is important to force individuals to do so. This weakens respect not merely for the particular law but for *all* that state's laws.'

technologies that have become commonplace.[3] In many cases the authorities may also not have sufficient resources or personnel to monitor compliance properly. For example, one study revealed that 11 out of 27 national data protection authorities (DPAs) in the EU Member States were unable to carry out the entirety of their tasks because of a lack of financial and human resources.[4]

B. Compliance responsibilities and informational requirements

Parties transferring personal data across borders are typically faced with a variety of compliance responsibilities. Some countries (particularly those subject to the EU Directive) require that a separate legal basis is present for transborder data flows, and that certain formalities are observed before they are carried out, such as that the transfer is registered with the data protection regulator; that certain protections are implemented (eg, the use of contractual clauses between data exporter and data importer); or that in certain cases the regulator has the possibility of approving the transfer.[5] Other countries that do not specifically restrict transborder data flows may still impose ongoing compliance responsibilities on entities that transfer personal data outside the country's borders. For example, under Canadian law data controllers are expected to take steps so that data transferred outside Canada will receive protection in the country of import, for example by confirming that the data importer provides training to its staff on privacy protection, has adopted effective data security measures, and grants the data exporter rights of audit and inspection.[6]

Data protection law may require data controllers to inform individuals about transborder data flows explicitly,[7] or about data transfers in general (which can include information about transborder transfers).[8] For example, the South Korean

---

[3] Reed (n 2), stating: 'enforcers face extreme difficulties in detecting errant behavior when the regulated community is extensive ... and where breaching rules is cheap and easily carried out in a clandestine manner'.

[4] European Union Agency for Fundamental Rights, 'Data Protection in the European Union: the Role of National Data Protection Authorities' (2010), <http://fra.europa.eu/fraWebsite/attachments/Data-protection_En.pdf>, at 42.

[5] See RAND Europe, 'Review of the European Data Protection Directive' (2009), <http://www.rand.org/pubs/technical_reports/2009/RAND_TR710.pdf>, at 34–5.

[6] Office of the Privacy Commissioner of Canada, 'Guidelines for Processing Personal Data across Borders' (2009), <http://www.priv.gc.ca/information/guide/2009/gl_dab_090127_e.pdf>, at 6. See also Galway Project and Centre for Information Policy Leadership, 'Data Protection Accountability: The Essential Elements, A Document for Discussion' (2009), <http://www.huntonfiles.com/files/webupload/CIPL_Galway_Accountability_Paper.pdf>, at 11, stating: 'An accountable organisation demonstrates commitment to accountability, implements data privacy policies linked to recognised outside criteria, and establishes performance mechanisms to ensure responsible decision-making about the management of data consistent with organisation policies'.

[7] French Data Protection Act, Section 32(7).

[8] See, eg, German Federal Data Protection Act, Section 33(1); Greek Data Protection Act, Section 11(1) lit. c.

Personal Information Protection Act of 2011 requires data exporters to inform individuals of the following at a minimum:

1. A recipient of personal information;
2. Purposes for which a recipient of personal information uses such information;
3. Items of personal information to provide;
4. Period for which a recipient of personal information holds and uses such information;
5. The fact that a subject of information has a right to reject to give his/her consent and details of a disadvantage, if any, due to his/her rejection to give consent.[9]

Data controllers and processors often post privacy policies on the Internet as a way to provide information about how they transfer personal data; the quality of such policies varies widely. The following is an example of a section of a policy dealing with transborder data flows (the language has been edited in order to anonymize it):

The company complies with the EU Safe Harbor framework as set forth by the Department of Commerce regarding the collection, use, and retention of data from the European Union. To view our certification, visit the US Department of Commerce's Safe Harbor Website [hyperlink] … We give your information to the people and companies that help us provide, understand and improve the services we offer.

This policy gives users little information about how the data are transferred around the world by the company, which third parties they are given to, and what those parties do with the data, so that it would be difficult for an individual to make a decision about, for example, whether to consent to the processing of data by the company.

Even when information about the geographic location of data transfer and data processing is given, it is often so vague as to be of little value for individuals whose data are processed, as can be seen from a review of the terms of service of some popular cloud computing providers:

For example, Microsoft's European sub-regions for its Windows Azure PaaS [Platform as a Service] service are simply designated as 'North Europe' and 'Western Europe', while Google Storage for Developers only offers a choice of 'Europe' or 'United States'. Amazon for EC2 does specify US East (Northern Virginia), US West (Northern California), EU (Ireland), Asia Pacific (Singapore), and Asia Pacific (Tokyo). Furthermore, even providers that allow customers to choose regions do not commit contractually, in their terms of service, to keep the relevant data or applications in the chosen region.[10]

This lack of transparency often extends to the chain of service providers used in a typical cloud computing service (ie, various data processors and subcontractors).[11]

---

[9] South Korean Personal Information Protection Act, Law 10465 (2011), Article 17(2).
[10] W. Kuan Hon and Christopher Millard, 'Data Export in Cloud Computing—How can Personal Data be Transferred outside the EEA? (The Cloud of Unknowing, Part 4)', Queen Mary University of London, School of Law (4 April 2012), <http://www.cloudlegal.ccls.qmul.ac.uk/Research/researchpapers/55649.html>, at 25.
[11] See Article 29 Working Party, 'Opinion 05/2012 on Cloud Computing' (WP 196, 1 July 2012), at 2.

The value of providing information is dependent on the attitudes and expectations of the individuals to whom it is directed, and it is unclear how much they care about the transfer of their personal data to other countries.[12] It may not always be technically and logistically possible to give highly detailed information such as which entity at what location in the world is processing personal data at a particular time. The focus of informational requirements should be on providing information to an extent and in a form useful to data subjects. The quality of information provided is also crucial when consent is used as a basis for data processing or data transfer, since the validity of consent is dependent on the individual having been given information about the processing before consenting.[13]

C. Level of compliance and enforcement

Transborder data flow regulation can be enforced by various mechanisms, which differ from country to country. The available empirical evidence indicates that the level of compliance is low in proportion to the amount of data being transferred, and that enforcement is highly selective. In its first report on transposition of the Data Protection Directive published in 2003, the European Commission noted with regard to compliance with the Directive's provisions on international data transfers that 'many unauthorised and possibly illegal transfers are being made to destinations or recipients not guaranteeing adequate protection. Yet there is little or no sign of enforcement action by the supervisory authorities.'[14]

As another example, the Spanish DPA has stated that up to 2007 it had received notification from data controllers of 8,483 international data transfers.[15] However, all the telephone calls, emails, faxes, corporate data transfers, data transfers via the Internet, etc. carried out between Spain and countries outside the EU in a year, many of which may be considered 'international data transfers' in the sense of data protection law and may therefore be subject to a duty of notification, must number in the millions or even billions. In the early 2000s, the Norwegian Data Inspectorate was receiving only 30 to 40 notifications of transborder data flows a year, even though such notification is mandatory for transfers of data abroad.[16] These examples illustrate the fact that compliance with regulation of transborder data flows lags behind the amount of personal data being transferred internationally.

---

[12] See Chapter 5.C.5.   [13] See, eg, EU Directive, Article 2(h).

[14] European Commission, 'First Report on the implementation of the Data Protection Directive (95/46/EC)', COM(2003) 265 final (15 May 2003), <http://eur-lex.europa.eu/LexUriServ/LexUriServ. do?uri=CELEX:52003DC0265:EN:NOT>, at 19.

[15] Spanish Data Protection Agency, 'Report on International Data Transfers' (July 2007), <https:// www.agpd.es/portalwebAGPD/jornadas/transferencias_internacionales_datos/common/pdfs/report_ Inter_data_transfers_colombia_en.pdf>, at 5.

[16] Dag Wiese Schartum, 'Norway', in Peter Blume (ed), *Nordic Data Protection Law* (DJØF 2001), at 102.

The European Commission has suggested several reasons for the poor state of compliance with data protection law in the EU, which could apply to regulation of transborder data flows as well:

An under-resourced enforcement effort and supervisory authorities with a wide range of tasks, among which enforcement actions have a rather low priority;

Very patchy compliance by data controllers, no doubt reluctant to undertake changes in their existing practices to comply with what may seem complex and burdensome rules, when the risks of getting caught seem low;

An apparently low level of knowledge of their rights among data subjects, which may be at the root of the previous phenomenon.[17]

These conclusions suggest that one reason for poor compliance is the complexity of the regulatory requirements.[18] This could be caused by a lack of harmonization of the law, which makes it more difficult for individuals to know what law applies to the processing of their data, complicates the life of regulators by forcing them to deal with other regulatory systems, and gives rise to legal issues concerning cross-border enforcement. The European Commission has stated that there are significant differences in the compliance requirements that the EU Member States impose:

In some Member States adequacy is assessed in the first instance by the data controller which itself transfers personal data to a third country, sometimes under the ex-post supervision of the data protection supervisory authority. This situation may lead to different approaches to assessing the level of adequacy of third countries, or international organisations, and involves the risk that the level of protection of data subjects provided for in a third country is judged differently from one Member State to another. Also, the current legal instruments include no detailed, harmonised requirements as to which transfers can be considered lawful. This leads to practices which vary from Member State to Member State.[19]

One way to improve the level of compliance and enforcement would be to focus regulation more narrowly, by concentrating on situations where transborder data flows cause harm to individuals. Some jurisdictions limit the application of their data protection and privacy requirements to cases where harm has occurred or is likely to occur,[20] or explicitly require the regulator to consider harm as a factor in

---

[17] European Commission (n 14), at 12. See also European Commission, 'A comprehensive approach on personal data protection in the European Union', COM(2010) 609 final (4 November 2010), at 4, stating: 'As to international data transfers, many organisations considered that the current schemes are not entirely satisfactory and need to be reviewed and streamlined so as to make transfers simpler and less burdensome'.

[18] Regarding the negative effects that needless legal complexity can have on compliance with law, see Reed (n 2), at 131.

[19] European Commission (n 17), at 15.

[20] See APEC Privacy Framework (2005), <http://www.apec.org/Groups/Committee-on-Trade-and-Investment/~/media/Files/Groups/ECSG/05_ecsg_privacyframewk.ashx>, Principle I, Commentary, para. 14, at 14, stating: 'Hence, remedies for privacy infringements should be designed to prevent harms resulting from the wrongful collection or misuse of personal information, and should be proportionate to the likelihood and severity of any harm threatened by the collection or use of personal information.'

deciding whether to restrict transborder data flows.[21] However, under both EU law[22] and the European Convention on Human Rights,[23] data protection law applies irrespective of whether an individual has suffered any damage or harm, nor is it clear how 'harm' is to be defined in the context of transborder data flows.[24]

D. Compliance in practice

Transborder data flow regulation can influence important data processing decisions made by data controllers. The author is aware of many cases where it played a significant role in business decisions by companies in different sectors, such as financial services, pharmaceuticals, computing and IT services, and many others. Corporate governance legislation and a desire to avoid adverse publicity have, in particular, influenced the behaviour of multinational corporations, which now give increased attention to compliance with data protection law. The influence of transborder data flow regulation can extend to many types of corporate data processing decisions, and may arise, for example, in situations where a company is deciding whether to grant access to an internal database to employees in countries with stringent regulation of transborder data flows, or whether to locate data processing operations in a country where the law enforcement authorities frequently seek access to company databases.

In the author's experience, data controllers have a variable level of interest in compliance with transborder data flow regulation, with some devoting a great deal of attention and resources to it, while others do the minimum necessary. The attention that they pay to such regulation is often proportionate to the chance that they may lose business if they fail to comply. That is, even when formal enforcement by regulators is unlikely, in an increasing number of cases customers may simply refuse to deal with a company that cannot provide convincing evidence of

---

[21] See, eg, Bahamas Data Protection (Privacy of Personal Information) Act (11 April 2003), Section 17(2), stating: 'In determining whether to prohibit a transfer of personal data under this section, the Commissioner shall also consider whether the transfer would be likely to cause damage or distress to any person …'; Privacy (Cross-border Information) Amendment Bill 221-2 (2008), Part 11A, <http://www.legislation.govt.nz/bill/government/2008/0221/latest/DLM1362819.html>, Section 114B(2)(a), stating that in deciding whether to prohibit transborder data flows, the Privacy Commissioner of New Zealand must consider 'whether the transfer affects, or would be likely to affect, any individual'.

[22] Joined Cases C-465/00 and C-138/01 *Rechnungshof* [2003] ECR I-4989, para 75: 'To establish the existence of such an interference, it does not matter whether the information communicated is of a sensitive character or whether the persons concerned have been inconvenienced in any way'.

[23] See *Amann v Switzerland* (2000) ECHR 87, para. 70, stating: 'it is not for the Court to speculate as to whether the information gathered on the applicant was sensitive or not or as to whether the applicant had been inconvenienced in any way. It is sufficient for it to find that data relating to the private life of an individual were stored by a public authority to conclude that, in the instant case, the creation and storing of the impugned card amounted to an interference, within the meaning of Article 8, with the applicant's right to respect for his private life.'

[24] Regarding the difficulty of defining 'harm', particularly in the context of fundamental rights, see Roger Brownsword and Morag Goodwin, *Law and Technologies of the Twenty-First Century* (CUP 2012), at 208.

compliance, based on the customer's fear that the company's poor level of compliance may cause problems for the customer later on. For example, a data controller based outside the EU that offers data processing services to EU-based customers may well find that they demand a copy of a data protection audit, signature of the EU standard contractual clauses with regard to data transfers, or some other evidence of compliance before they will consider dealing with it. Such customer pressure can be more effective in forcing the company to focus attention on compliance with transborder data flow regulation than can the threat of potential action by DPAs.

To give another example, a company offering cloud computing services may find that its customers prefer that their data is stored in their home region, in order to minimize transborder data flows; some cloud computing service providers already grant customers the option of keeping data within a national or regional 'cloud'.[25] Customers may demand such services in order themselves to comply with transborder data flow regulation.[26] The issue of compliance can also arise in the context of corporate acquisitions, when companies being acquired routinely face questions from purchasers about whether their data transfer practices are compliant with applicable regulation.

The level of compliance also varies based on factors such as the size of the data controller and the amount of data transferred to other countries; thus, some large data controllers may have a high level of compliance, while smaller ones may lack the resources and the commercial motivation to attain such a standard. The importance of transborder data flow regulation as a strategic issue is also likely to be recognized more by larger data controllers with operations in other countries than by smaller ones.

Often decisions by companies are motivated not solely by transborder data processing regulation itself, but by such regulation in combination with other types of corporate governance law. US legal requirements exercise the greatest influence in this regard, since most leading Internet service, software, and IT hardware companies have their headquarters in the US (eg, Amazon, Apple, Facebook, Google, HP, Microsoft, IBM, Intel), and others still regard it as a key market and thus need to be in compliance with its requirements at least with regard to their US operations. In recent years, US corporate governance law has been significantly strengthened, and now requires that companies put in place compliance systems to prevent and detect legal violations of all types, with potential liability

---

[25] See, eg, Kevin J. O'Brien, 'Europe turns to the Cloud', *NY Times*, 24 July 2011, <http://www.nytimes.com/2011/07/25/technology/europe-turns-to-the-cloud.html?pagewanted=all>, reporting on a trend among cloud computing providers to set up local data centres in Europe.

[26] See, eg, Official Google Enterprise Blog, 'Google Apps to offer additional compliance options for EU data protection' (6 June 2012), <http://googleenterprise.blogspot.co.uk/2012/06/google-apps-to-offer-additional.html>, quoting Google global manager of global compliance Marc Crandall as saying that Google will sign the EU-approved standard contractual clauses for data transfers 'as an additional means of meeting the adequacy and security requirements of the European Commission's Data Protection Directive for our customers who operate within Europe'.

all the way up to the board of directors if this is not carried out.[27] For example, the US Federal Sentencing Guidelines[28] contain 'standards of effective compliance' that multinational companies have used as the basis for their global data protection programmes.[29] These obligations require companies to take compliance with all types of law seriously or face draconian penalties, which has resulted in greater attention being paid to compliance with transborder data flow regulation as well.

As data have become a valuable commercial asset, protecting them as they cross national borders is viewed as a way of securing a company's reputation. Companies have thus increased the financial and human resources invested in data protection compliance as it has become an area of greater strategic business importance. For example, the number of company data protection officers (DPOs) has grown in recent years,[30] and many companies have appointed global DPOs (in addition to those dealing with local compliance).

Regulation can also affect decisions taken by States. For example, some governments have become concerned about potential access by law enforcement to data transferred to foreign cloud computing providers, which has caused them either to avoid using such providers, or to build their own local cloud computing infrastructures.[31]

Companies are increasingly aware that violations of transborder data flow regulation can lead to adverse negative publicity that can cost them considerable amounts of money in loss of business, legal expenses, and lost productivity of employees. The business and financial implications of dealing with violations can have a powerful effect on motivating companies to comply with regulation.

[27] See American Bar Association, Committee on Corporate Laws, *Corporate Director's Guidebook* (ABA 2007), at 28–9, stating: 'The federal sentencing guidelines greatly increase the penalties for corporations found guilty of criminal violations, yet provide for significant fine reductions for corporations with appropriate programs in place to prevent and detect violations of law ... Companies should have formal written policies designed to promote compliance with law and corporate policy, which should be periodically monitored for effectiveness ...'

[28] United States Sentencing Commission, 2011 Federal Sentencing Guidelines Manual, <http://www.ussc.gov/Guidelines/2011_Guidelines/Manual_PDF/2011_Guidelines_Manual_Full.pdf>, at § 8B2.1.

[29] See Bojana Bellamy, 'Accenture's Client Data Protection Program' (February 2009), <http://www.hideproject.org/downloads/HIDE_PF-Outsourcing-Presentation_Bojana_Bellamy-20090206.pdf>.

[30] Eg, the membership of the International Association of Privacy Professionals (IAPP), the largest group worldwide of privacy officers and other privacy professionals, more than tripled between 2007 and 2012, and stands at over 10,000. See IAPP, 'International Association of Privacy Professionals Reaches 10,000 Member Mark' (7 March 2012), <https://www.privacyassociation.org/about_iapp/media/international_association_of_privacy_professionals_reaches_10000_member_mar>.

[31] See Kristina Irion, 'Government cloud computing and the policies of data sovereignty' (September 2011), <https://www.econstor.eu/dspace/bitstream/10419/52197/1/672481146.pdf>; 'Innenminister Friedrich will sichere "Bundescloud" aufbauen' (18 December 2011), <http://www.teltarif.de/bundes-cloud-friedrich-regierung-telekom-sichere-speicherung/news/45000.html>.

E. Example of EU data protection law

1. Introduction

EU data protection law provides a useful example for understanding how enforcement of transborder data flow regulation is structured and how it operates, and has been highly influential around the world. Moreover, considerable experience with enforcement has been built up in the EU, and significant changes to the system have been proposed.

2. Current rules

In the EU, enforcement actions are brought in national courts or by the national DPAs. The Article 29 Working Party has no formal enforcement power, but DPAs sometimes coordinate their enforcement activities under its auspices; for example, in October 2012 the Working Party sent a letter to Google signed by most of its members complaining about changes to its privacy policy.[32] Member State attitudes toward enforcement vary greatly, with some national DPAs taking a more proactive stance, while others reserve formal enforcement proceedings for particularly egregious cases. While Member State procedural and penal laws differ greatly, courts and DPAs can generally impose a variety of penalties, which can include the following.

- *Injunctive relief* For example, in March 2004, the DPA of the German federal state of Schleswig-Holstein ordered the global subsidiaries of a multinational corporation to delete the personal data of a former German employee. The employee had complained to the DPA about the fact that his former employer had a global HR database system hosted in the US which resulted in his data being transferred around the world, and that the multinational had not provided any legal basis for the HR database. Following an investigation, the DPA ordered the company to delete the employee's data in its subsidiaries around the world; the multinational complied with this request.

- *Refusal to authorize an international data transfer* In those countries that require authorization of transfers, a DPA may refuse it, or may request further information about the transfer such that it cannot be carried out in a timely fashion (in some cases such procedures may last months, or even years, by which time there may no longer be any point to the transfer).

- *Audits and inspections of company premises and data processing facilities* For example, the Spanish DPA has on at least one occasion conducted an audit of

---

[32] Article 29 Working Party, letter to Larry Page of Google (16 October 2012), <http://www.dataprotection.ie/documents/press/Letter_from_the_Article_29_Working_Party_to_Google_in_relation_to_its_new_privacy_policy.pdf>.

a third party data processor outside the EU (located in Colombia) regarding compliance with Spanish legal requirements for data transfers from Spain.[33] It seems that the audit by the Spanish DPA in Colombia was part of an ongoing programme to conduct such audits of data processors outside the EU,[34] and was carried out based on contractual clauses signed by the data importer which grant the DPA the same audit rights as it has in Spain.[35] Apparently the DPA obtained the consent and cooperation of the data exporter and data importer for the audits in Colombia.[36]

- *A monetary fine* For example, in 2009 the Berlin Data Protection Authority imposed a fine of over €1,123,000 on the national rail operator Deutsche Bahn for data protection violations.[37]

Private lawsuits are also possible,[38] but so far there have been few cases brought by private parties based on regulation of transborder data flows. Adverse publicity can also have a powerful effect on deterring abuses of transborder data flow regulation and on punishing them when they occur. One of the first high-profile examples of this in the context of data transfers from Europe occurred in 1996, when Citibank encountered criticism for transferring credit card data from Germany to a subsidiary in the US, until it finally worked with the Berlin data protection commissioner to adopt a contractual solution and provide a legal basis for the transfer.[39]

3. Proposed rules

In January 2012, the European Commission published proposals to replace the EU Data Protection Directive with a Regulation, which would also strengthen enforcement of data protection law and the rules on transborder data flows. The Proposed Regulation contains several provisions designed to realize these

---

[33] See Agencia Española de Protección de Datos, 'Report on International Data Transfers: Ex officio Sectorial Inspection of Spain-Colombia at Call Centres' (July 2007), <https://www.agpd. es/portalweb/jornadas/transferencias_internacionales_datos/common/pdfs/report_Inter_data_ transfers_colombia_en.pdf>.

[34] Agencia Española de Protección de Datos (n 33), at 7.

[35] Agencia Española de Protección de Datos (n 33), at 9, stating: 'the contracts signed between the telecommunications operators and the companies acting as processors include a clause that specifies the agreement by all parties that the Spanish Data Protection Agency is empowered to audit the importer to the same extent and under the same conditions as it would do with regard to the data exporter under Spanish law. Moreover, it stipulates that the data importer warrants that, at the request of the exporter and/or Agency, it shall make its data processing facilities available to the latter to carry out the audits deemed appropriate'.

[36] Agencia Española de Protección de Datos (n 33), at 11.

[37] See Berliner Beauftragter für Datenschutz und Informationsfreiheit, 'Deutsche Bahn akzeptiert hohe Geldbusse und will künftig Vorbild im Datenschutz sein' (23 October 2009), <http://www. datenschutz-berlin.de/attachments/627/PE_DB_AG.pdf?1256283223>.

[38] See Article 22 of the EU Directive, which obliges Member States to provide individuals with judicial remedies for breaches of their data protection rights.

[39] See Paul M. Schwartz, 'Managing Global Data Privacy: Cross-Border Information Flows in a Networked Environment' (2009), <http://theprivacyprojects.org/wp-content/uploads/2009/08/The-Privacy-Projects-Paul-Schwartz-Global-Data-Flows-20093.pdf>, at 11–12.

objectives, including a duty for DPAs to take action on request of another DPA within one month (Article 55(2)), and a provision empowering DPAs to conduct joint enforcement actions (Article 56). The proposal would also create a 'consistency mechanism', which is designed to ensure that the DPAs take a more consistent view of data protection questions of common interest, including cross-border enforcement questions. Under the mechanism, a DPA would communicate in advance to the Commission and a new European Data Protection Board (the successor to the Article 29 Working Party) certain enforcement and compliance measures it intended to take. The Board would then vote by a simple majority on the measure, and the DPA would be expected to 'take account' of the opinion of the Board, and communicate to it within two weeks whether it intended to take the measure (Article 58). The Commission would also adopt an opinion in relation to such measures, of which the DPAs would be expected to take the 'utmost account' (Article 59). The Commission would gain substantial powers to force the DPAs to take a more harmonized approach, since it may request that any matter is dealt with via the consistency mechanism (Article 58(4)), and may also adopt a reasoned decision requiring a DPA to suspend the adoption of a measure if it has 'serious doubts as to whether the draft measure would ensure the correct application of the Regulation or would otherwise result in its inconsistent application' (Article 60(1)). DPA decisions and measures are made enforceable in all Member States, except in cases where the DPA has not notified them to the Commission and the Board under the consistency mechanism (Article 63(2)).

The proposal contains some provisions that would create certain compliance burdens and enforcement mechanisms specifically directed at transborder data flows. For example, under Article 28(2), documentation of international data transfers would have to be kept, and certain types of international data transfers would require prior authorization by the DPA (Articles 34(1) and 42(4)).

Article 73(1) of the proposal provides that an individual in any Member State can lodge a complaint with any DPA, not only with the one where they reside. The draft also gives organizations and associations the right to bring claims before the DPAs, both on behalf of individuals (Article 73(2)) and on their own behalf (Article 73(3)), which types of collective action are already used in some Member States.[40] The Proposed Regulation would provide both natural and legal persons with the right to launch a judicial action against DPAs (Article 74(1)), including the possibility for an individual to request a DPA to initiate proceedings against another DPA (Article 74(4)). Member States are obliged to enforce final court decisions against DPAs (Article 74(5)) or against a data controller or processor (Article 75(4)) in any Member State, just as they are with regard to decisions of DPAs (Article 63(1)) (though with regard to DPA decisions, it is not clear if what is meant is that they are enforceable in court, or by other DPAs, or both).

Under the new regime for penalties and administrative fines, all controllers and processors involved in the data processing are jointly and severally liable for the

---

[40] Eg, in Austria (§ 29 Konsumentenschutzgesetz) and Germany (§ 3 Unterlassungsklagegesetz).

entire amount of any damage suffered, unless they can prove that they were not responsible for the event giving rise to the damage (Article 77(2) and (3)). The representative of a non EU-based data controller is also liable for any penalties assessed against the controller (Article 78(2)). The sanctions that may be imposed on companies under the Proposed Regulation are hugely increased over what was previously possible. They are to be imposed mandatorily for any intentional or negligent violation of certain provisions of the Proposed Regulation, and are divided into three categories, ranging from up to 0.5 per cent, 1 per cent, or 2 per cent of a company's annual worldwide turnover (ie, its worldwide revenues) respectively (Article 79(4)–(6)). To give an example of the potential maximum amount of such a fine, Google's annual revenues in 2010 were approximately $29 billion,[41] 2 per cent of which would be approximately $580 million (approximately €439 million). The text of Article 79 obliges the DPAs to impose administrative penalties ('*shall* impose a fine …', emphasis added), rather than merely allowing them to do so. Carrying out or instructing a data transfer to be carried out to other countries in violation of Articles 40–4 would carry the highest potential penalty (up to 2 per cent of overall turnover) under Article 79(6)(l).

The Proposed Regulation shows that the enforcement climate in the EU will become more stringent insofar as legal penalties are concerned. However, questions remain as to whether the new EU legal framework will actually lead to stronger enforcement in practice in light of factors such as the Internet and the globalization of data processing.

F. Conclusions

Compliance with regulation need not be perfect, and the fact that transborder data flow regulation is not always complied with is not, of itself, a reason for it not to be applied.[42] But if regulation is not enforced consistently, parties may wonder why they should comply with it, while those against whom it is enforced may ask why they are being singled out. A large gap between the scope of regulation and the possibility of enforcement can have a corrosive effect on trust in the regulatory framework.

The available evidence suggests that there is neither a high level of compliance with, nor sufficient enforcement of, transborder data flow regulation. One reason for this may be the complexity of the legal requirements; when regulation is unclear, it is difficult for parties to know how to comply. Another problem is a lack of resources for the DPAs.

But perhaps the biggest problem is the disproportionate relationship between the increasing flood of personal data now being transferred online, and the limited

---

[41] See <http://investor.google.com/financial/tables.html>.
[42] See Peter Blume, 'Transborder data flow: Is there a solution in sight?', 8 International Journal of Law and Information Technology 65, 82 (2000).

possibility of enforcing transborder data flow regulation by traditional means such as injunctions and lawsuits. The definition of transborder data flows is so broad that it can cover most acts of data processing on the Internet, and no national regulation could ever be consistently enforced with regard to such a vast amount of data processing on a global scale.

There is a need for penalties and enforcement mechanisms to be strengthened, but it is doubtful whether traditional means of enforcement will be sufficient to lead to a substantially increased level of compliance. Rather, it is likely that enforcement will continue to occur mainly in cases involving large-scale violations of the law. This could in itself be a strategy for regulators to follow—that is, it could be accepted that they will maximize their resources by intervening mainly in cases where there is a substantial chance of harm to a significant number of individuals, in order to encourage other data controllers to comply by making an example of particular incidences. However, if this is the case, then it should be stated openly and the law should be revised to concentrate on such instances.

Greater incentives should also be provided to 'build in' compliance to the technology by which data on the Internet are transferred, such as through principles like privacy by design.[43] Making greater use of such strategies would take some of the pressure off regulators and allow them to concentrate on cases where enforcement can have the greatest effect.

---

[43] See Chapter 4.D.

8

A Global Regulatory Framework for Transborder Data Flows

A. Major trends and issues

From its beginnings in the 1970s, transborder data flow regulation has been marked by tension between two different positions. The first one favours little or no regulation in order to further the free flow of data:

Be cautious with data flow controls; the liabilities that they bring may outweigh the advantages for the country involved.[1]

---

[1] Alden Heintz, 'The Dangers of Regulation', 29(3) Journal of Communications 129, 134 (1979).

The second position finds it necessary to regulate transborder data flows precisely in order to allow information to circulate freely:

The free and balanced international data flow must be regulated in order to remain balanced and free.[2]

This tension between the free flow of data and regulation of transborder data flows is based on a false dichotomy. Allowing data to flow freely across international borders is essential to freedom of expression, as well as to other important rights and values. At the same time, the increasing social and economic importance of data flows means that data should continue to receive protection when transferred.

There are considerable divergences in regulation among different States and regional systems, and no single institution or set of norms can perfectly reconcile them. The major trends over the past few decades can be summarized as follows.

- Before widespread use of the Internet began in the 1990s, it was assumed that transborder data flows were an exceptional occurrence,[3] and many data transferred were technical and not personal. The situation has come full circle, so that instead of being the exception, transborder flows of personal data are now the rule.

- Regulation of transborder data flows is now a subject of strategic importance, as data flows have become integral to economic and social development, free expression, cultural activities, and other basic social values.

- At a national level, the geographic spread of transborder data flow regulation has increased dramatically. From a handful of European countries, it has spread to all regions of the world, and to over 70 countries.

- Regulatory instruments promulgated by regional bodies are increasingly important, with the EU Data Protection Directive emerging as perhaps the single most influential piece of data protection legislation.

- At the international level, a number of organizations have been active in the area of transborder data flow regulation. However, there is a lack of detailed, legally binding standards that could apply on a global scale.

- The predominant motivation for enacting such regulation in its early years was a fear that without it, data processing would be transferred to countries without data protection laws, thus resulting in circumvention of the law.

- Regulation increasingly focuses on ensuring that adequate protections apply no matter where data are processed, which is often accomplished through the use of applicable law rules.

---

[2] Jan Freese, *International Data Flow* (Studentlitteratur 1979), at 70.

[3] See Frits W. Hondius, 'A Decade of International Data Protection', 30 Netherlands International Law Review 103, 119 (1983), stating: 'legislators have proceeded as if the entire phenomenon of automatic data processing was taking place within the borders.'

- Transborder data flow regulation has expanded beyond legislation to include a variety of non-binding and private sector instruments as well. In particular, instruments such as codes of practice, contractual clauses, and internal corporate policies have a growing influence on the way that personal data are transferred across national borders.

These trends have given rise to the following issues.

- There is confusion about what constitute 'transborder data flows', as well as concerning related questions such as how to define personal data and what the distinction should be between data controllers and data processors. In practice, this has meant that such terms are broadly construed, in order to avoid creating gaps in protection.
- There is a great diversity of regulation. Although based on the same high-level international instruments, national and regional regulations differ substantially.
- The broad application of regulation to the huge volume of data flows on the Internet means that its scope is disproportionate to the ability to enforce it.
- States have been unable to agree on a legally binding instrument of global scope that could provide a solid basis for regulation at an international level.
- The risks posed by transborder data flows have come to overshadow the benefits they can bring, particularly their role in facilitating freedom of expression.
- Private sector instruments regulate transborder data flows to an increasing extent, but are not sufficiently recognized across legal systems, and sometimes conflict with other legal norms.
- The role that technology can play in protecting and regulating transborder data flows has not been sufficiently recognized.
- The policies underlying regulation have shifted over the years, with some increasing in importance and others decreasing.
- The concept of territoriality has become problematic as a mechanism to determine applicable law and jurisdiction, and there is growing use of the principle of personality instead.
- Transborder data flow regulation has become entangled with rules on applicable law, and the two are often used in tandem for the same purpose, but without proper coordination between them.
- While regulation affects the way that transborder data flows are carried out in practice, the degree of compliance and enforcement seems to be small in relation to the volume of data flows.

There is tension between the nature of transborder data flow regulation as a topic of inherently global significance, and the fact that many States and regional organizations treat it mainly as a vehicle for exporting their own standards and values. Applying local standards extraterritorially to a global phenomenon will remain a Sisyphean endeavour, and the effort could be better used to facilitate interfaces (eg, through the use of mutual recognition[4]) between differing national and regional regulation.

The materials analysed herein indicate that the following are the most important interests underlying transborder data flow regulation:

- protection of fundamental rights or individual rights no matter where data are processed;
- avoiding data protection risks in other countries;
- protecting other important fundamental rights (eg the right to freedom of expression);
- furthering social and economic values that depend on global data flows;
- promoting transparency concerning transborder data flows;
- ensuring a reasonable degree of compliance and enforcement.

The question is, then, what conceptual framework best furthers these goals.

B. Transborder data flow regulation as a form of legal pluralism

1. Introduction

Transborder data flow regulation is best understood as a form of legal pluralism. Legal pluralism is not a strategy that can be enacted, but rather a description of a state of affairs that evolves over time. A pluralist approach is appropriate when there is no hierarchical legal structure that can provide an overall, authoritative governance framework, which is the case with regard to transborder data flow regulation. No single legal instrument, court, or tribunal can provide a normative structure for it, or adjudicate all disputes that arise under it. In such a situation, none of the various constituencies or layers of governance can adequately cope by themselves with all elements of regulation: national governance would be too parochial, international governance would not provide for sufficient public involvement, and technological or private sector solutions could lack democratic legitimation.[5]

Commentators have identified a wide variety of situations exhibiting characteristics of legal pluralism, including the following.

- *Conflicts of regimes in public international law* Issues in public international law often lack a clear hierarchy of norms and institutions, and thus present many examples of pluralistic situations, often involving conflicts between different legal regimes. Pluralism has been found to be one of the constitutive values of the current international legal system.[6]

---

[4] See Section C.6.
[5] See Nico Krisch, 'The pluralism of global administrative law', 17 European Journal of International Law 247, 269–70 (2006).
[6] ILC, 'Fragmentation of International Law: Difficulties arising from the Diversification and Expansion of International Law, Report of the Study Group of the International Law Commission finalized by Martti Koskenniemi', UN Doc. A/CN.4/L.682 (13 April 2006), <http://daccess-ods.un.org/access.nsf/Get?OpenAgent&DS=A/CN.4/L.682&Lang=E>, at 248.

- *Differing hierarchies in human rights law* Interactions between the European Court of Human Rights and the constitutional courts of the EU Member States, which are marked both by conflicts and cooperation, have been cited as an example of a pluralist approach.[7]

- *Conflict of laws on the Internet* The accessibility of information on the Internet can lead to conflicts between differing conceptions of fundamental rights, such as in the dispute that arose in 2004 based on the prosecution of Yahoo! in France because of the ability to download Nazi materials, which Yahoo! later challenged in court in California.[8] Theories have been developed under concepts of legal pluralism that would seek to resolve such conflicts based on the ties of the parties to the relevant community, rather than on territoriality.[9]

- *Transborder data flow scenarios* The EU–US Safe Harbor forms an intermediate plane between conflicting regulatory regimes which stops short of full harmonization, but which results in data importers in the US abiding by standards based on EU data protection law with regard to data imported from the EU.[10] It is thus based not on a clear hierarchy between the two systems, but on accommodation between them. The use of standard contractual clauses and binding corporate rules (BCRs), which are approved by EU regulators but implemented by companies, could be viewed as a similar example.

In a pluralist system, there is no overriding top-level norm (a *Grundnorm* or rule of recognition) that would allow resolution of conflicts,[11] which is precisely the situation with regard to regulation of transborder data flows. For example, what should be the result when corporate governance legislation mandates that data are disclosed to regulatory authorities in another country, but data transfer restrictions prohibit this; when a company privacy policy provides information about its international data transfer practices so as to comply with the legal requirements of one country, but such disclosure does not comply with the requirements of another one; or when law enforcement authorities in one country require a company in another one to transfer data to them in order to conduct an anti-terrorist investigation, but there is no legal basis for the transfer under the laws of the country where the data are stored? There is simply no overriding set of principles that can resolve such conflicts and take the legitimate interests of all the actors and affected parties into account.

---

[7] Nico Krisch, 'The open architecture of European human rights law', 71 Modern Law Review 183, 185 (2008).

[8] See Paul Schiff Berman, 'Global legal pluralism', 80 Southern California Law Review 1155, 1229–31 (2007).

[9] Schiff Berman (n 8), at 1229–34.   [10] Schiff Berman (n 8), at 1227.

[11] See Krisch (n 7), at 185.

2. A constitutional solution?

There is a natural wish for an overarching global solution to these issues that would simultaneously protect the data protection rights of individuals, not overburden data controllers, take into account fast-moving technological developments, and allow seamless enforcement of the law across national borders. Proposals have been made for a legally binding, global treaty covering data protection and transborder data flows.[12] This would be a *constitutional* solution, since it would be based on a binding, global legal framework, and thus on an agreed hierarchy among rules to resolve conflicts of authority.[13] However, beyond the fact that the odds of a treaty being agreed among numerous States are slight, there are strong reasons to believe that it would not by itself provide a solid legal foundation for transborder data flow regulation.

In order for a treaty to serve as the basis for regulation, the level at which it should be agreed would have to be decided. Stating that there should be a treaty 'at the international level' is insufficient, since this could refer to many different regional or global regulatory institutions.[14] There is no clear hierarchy between most international institutions, so that an instrument enacted by one need not have automatic legal validity with regard to others. The drafting of a convention would probably take many years: for example, it has been stated that the conclusion of a multilateral convention for legal harmonization takes a minimum of ten years,[15] and in some cases 50 years or more.[16] A convention can also be difficult to amend in the face of changing practices or technological evolution.[17]

Moreover, although a multilateral convention is binding under international law, it may still not produce a harmonized legal framework. In most countries, a convention must be implemented into national law, and may need to be measured against the standards of constitutional law,[18] which may result in significant

---

[12] See, eg, Peter Blume, 'Transborder data flow: Is there a solution in sight?', 8 International Journal of Law and Information Technology 65, 84 (2000).

[13] Gráinne de Búrca, 'The European Court of Justice and the International Legal Order after *Kadi*', 51 Harvard International Law Journal 1, 12 (2010), stressing the role of an agreed hierarchy in 'strong' versions of international constitutionalism.

[14] See Corien Prins, 'Should ICT regulation be undertaken at an international level?', in Bert-Jaap Koops, Miriam Lips, Corien Prins, and Maurice Shellekens (eds), *Starting Points for ICT Regulation: Deconstructing Prevalent Policy One-Liners* 151 (TMC Asser Press 2006), at 159.

[15] Roy Goode, 'Reflections on the Harmonisation of Commercial Law', (1991) Uniform Law Review 54, 62.

[16] Eg, the Vienna Convention on the Law of Sales of 1980 was the result of over 50 years' work. See John Goldring, 'Globalisation, National Sovereignty and the Harmonisation of Laws', (1998) Uniform Law Review 435, 448.

[17] See Souichirou Kozuka, 'The Economic Implications of Uniformity in Law', (2007) Uniform Law Review 683, 693, stating: 'ironically, the more popular a Convention is, the more difficult it is to amend the uniform law in a timely manner'.

[18] Eg, in the EU any treaty would have to meet the criteria of EU human rights law; see Joined Cases C-402 and 415/05 P *Kadi & Al Barakaat Int'l Found. v Council & Commission* [2008] ECR I-6351. See also de Búrca (n 13), at 27, describing the holding of the *Kadi* case as follows: 'The ECJ, while referring in general terms to the respect owed by the EC to international treaties including the U.N. Charter and to Security Council Resolutions, emphasized that no international treaty could affect the autonomy of the EC legal system, and that even if the Charter were to be ranked as part of EC law it would be ranked below the normative level of the EC treaties themselves and lower than the general principles of EC law.'

differences among national approaches. A treaty would also not necessarily take precedence over the multitude of national laws, regulations, private sector instruments, and codes of practice that currently exist. Implementation into domestic law has been found to be the most effective way of giving effect to human rights treaties,[19] and there is no guarantee that a treaty on transborder data flows would be implemented in similar ways (indeed, the experience thus far with divergences between national data protection laws suggests the opposite).

It is also not clear which international organization would be able to draft a global treaty on transborder data flow regulation. To take a few examples, the OECD does not have experience in producing legally binding documents in the area of data protection, and does not include members from less developed countries; the Council of Europe includes member States mainly from the European region; legal harmonization organizations like the United Nations Commission on International Trade Law (UNCITRAL) and the International Institute for the Unification of Private Law (UNIDROIT) do not have experience in data protection; and the ILC works much too slowly for such a fast-paced area. In the author's experience of discussing the issue with these organizations, most would not even want to assume the task of drafting such a treaty, which they see as resource-intensive and politically charged. Work of international organizations and legal harmonization bodies tends to be driven by what their member countries want, and at present the drafting of a treaty on transborder data flows does not seem to be a political priority; rather, States increasingly protect data transfers by applying their own national or regional standards extraterritorially.[20] The most promising initiative towards a global treaty on data protection and transborder data flows is the project to modernize Council of Europe Convention 108, which is legally binding and based on the long experience of the Council of Europe in human rights law and data protection; however, it is unclear what the result of the project will be, when it will be finalized, and whether it can gain widespread acceptance outside Europe.

Regulation can take many forms, including legislation, international treaties, and private sector instruments. The actors involved are in both the public and private sectors, and include States, data protection authorities (DPAs), companies and other data controllers, courts, and individuals. A variety of regulatory systems in different areas (eg, economic regulation, human rights, data protection) and in different countries may be involved with transborder data flows. There is no single legal instrument or mechanism that could satisfactorily reconcile the interests of so many norms, actors, and institutions in so many countries and legal systems.[21]

---

[19] See Christof Heyns and Frans Viljoen, 'The Impact of the United Nations Human Rights Treaties on the Domestic Level', 23 Human Rights Quarterly 483, 487 (2001), stating that the international human rights treaty system: 'has had its greatest impact where treaty norms have been made part of domestic law more or less spontaneously (for example as part of constitutional and legislative reform) ...'

[20] See Chapter 6.B.

[21] See Andreas Fischer-Lescano and Gunther Teubner, *Regime-Kollisionen* (Suhrkamp Verlag 2006), at 170; Krisch (n 7), at 185–6, stating that differences in fundamental policy positions may make it unachievable or even undesirable to seek a constitutional solution to conflicts and issues in pluralist regulatory systems.

International consensus on some of the individual questions involved in transborder data flow regulation would be useful,[22] but a binding international treaty cannot by itself be the entire solution.

3. A pluralist approach

Analysing transborder data flow regulation as a form of legal pluralism has a number of advantages, such as the following.

- *Allowing gradual harmonization over time* Accepting the fragmented legal structure of regulation allows the various norms and levels of authority to harmonize gradually over time, rather than raising unrealistic expectations that agreement on a global standard will solve the issues. Regulatory regimes for transborder data flows in one country or region can influence the level of protection in others, and thus grow together; for example, the EU Directive has influenced regulation adopted in other regions, and has caused increasing attention to be given to privacy protection by both the government and the business community in the US.[23]

- *Making more efficient use of resources* A constitutional solution such as an international treaty would require a massive amount of work over decades, whereas allowing the various levels of regulation to interact and gradually come into closer alignment (eg, through mutual recognition among various regional schemes) would allow a more efficient use of regulatory resources.

- *Avoiding the 'papering over' of disputes* International agreements can be used as tools to resolve issues in a pluralist legal framework, but States and regional organizations sometimes reach agreements governing transborder data flows as a way to legitimize in law actions taken for political reasons.[24] In such situations, concluding a treaty may resolve legal issues, but may also 'paper over' lingering disputes that are unlikely to go away just because a legal instrument has been agreed. The varying approaches to data protection in different legal systems are dependent on national cultural and social norms,[25] and a treaty purporting to establish a global standard would probably produce only the illusion of harmonization.

---

[22] See Section C.6.

[23] Gregory Shaffer, 'Globalization and Social Protection: the Impact of EU and International Rules in the Ratcheting Up of US Privacy Standards', 25 Yale Journal of International Law 1, 55, 80 (2000).

[24] See, eg, criticism of the agreement reached in 2012 between the EU and the US government for the transfer to the US of airline passenger name records (so-called PNR data) contained in European Data Protection Supervisor, 'Opinion of the European Data Protection Supervisor on the proposal for a Council Decision on the conclusion of the Agreement between the United States of America and the European Union on the use and transfer of Passenger Name Records to the United States Department of Homeland Security', 9 February 2012, [2012] OJ C35/16.

[25] See James Q. Whitman, 'The Two Western Cultures of Privacy: Dignity Versus Liberty', 113 Yale Law Journal 1153, 1219 (2004), stating: 'privacy law is not the product of logic ... It is the produce of local social anxieties and local ideals'.

An approach based on legal pluralism accepts conflicts between different levels and hierarchies of regulation as part of a process that can gradually lead to greater harmonization:

[Legal pluralism] … refrains from establishing a clearly structured institutional order and accepts that constituency contests will be played out in mutual challenges between different regimes and different levels in global regulatory governance. The connections between the parts of the overall order are heterarchical, not hierarchical, and often of a political rather than legal nature. Stability is thus created not by final decisions based on ultimate authority, but through processes of negotiation and compromise as well as challenge and concession between the different constituencies involved …[26]

Legal pluralism can also have disadvantages, such as limiting the bargaining power of weaker parties, putting a disorganized state of affairs in a more positive light than it deserves, and obscuring the role of powerful actors.[27] However, the implications of hegemonic acts, such as a powerful State exploiting its influence by attempting to block conclusion of a treaty, are less significant in an area like transborder data flow regulation that includes norms in many different areas and at different levels, and is hardly susceptible to a constitutional resolution in the first place.

The status of transborder data flow regulation as an example of legal pluralism does not mean that the current situation is ideal, or that nothing should be changed. On the contrary, the status quo evidences a number of problems, including States that do not adequately take into account the transborder nature of data protection regulation; governments that share data between themselves under murky legal rules; regulation that is overly complex and enacted without sufficient regard to its underlying policies; data controllers that use unclear privacy policies; and individuals who seem ambivalent about transborder data flows. Acceptance of a pluralist legal framework does not mean that constitutional mechanisms such as international agreements should never be pursued, but does demonstrate that they cannot provide a complete solution.

C. Suggestions for an improved regulatory framework

1. Introduction

It may be impossible to reconcile completely the competing interests of the various actors affected by transborder data flow regulation, but the issues it presents could be at least partially addressed if certain steps were taken. The search for regulatory perfection can be a chimera that leads only to frustration, and should not hinder the search for a framework that best furthers the six policy interests identified earlier.[28]

---

[26] Krisch (n 5), at 278.
[27] See Eyal Benvenisti and George W. Downs, 'The Empire's New Clothes: Political Economy and the Fragmentation of International Law', 60 Stanford Law Review 595, 597–8 (2007).
[28] See Section A.

International organizations, States, and governmental entities have the greatest responsibility for improving the current regulatory situation, but there are also some important steps that private sector data controllers should take. Some of the following ones could be implemented fairly quickly, while others would require continued efforts over a period of years. The goal would be gradually to achieve a better interface between different regulatory systems, a closer relationship between application of transborder data flow regulation and its enforcement, and a more coherent legal framework.

2. Default position allowing transborder data flows

Regulation should not require a separate legal basis for transborder data flows, or routinely subject them to prior regulatory approval or registration. However, data flows should be conducted in compliance with legal requirements applicable to data processing, and regulators should be able to suspend them or subject them to conditions in appropriate circumstances.

The default rule (ie, whether or not the transfer of personal data to another country should be permitted only if a legal basis is present) is crucial for determining the key elements of transborder data flow regulation, many of which will depend on whether data flows can operate without prior authorization. In particular, if the default position requires a legal basis before transfers are carried out, then there is likely to be greater regulatory oversight in advance, such as by a requirement to have transfers registered with or authorized by DPAs, and enforcement is more likely to take place after any violation of the law has occurred.

While the processing of personal data in another country can carry risks (eg, when the party to whom the data are transferred fails to provide adequate data security, or when the data are subject to access by the country's law enforcement authorities), these factors are not as a rule dependent on whether data flows across national borders; for example, poor data security or access to data by law enforcement can also occur if data are processed within the country. Thus, transborder data flows should not generally require a separate legal basis, authorization, or other regulatory approval. At the same time, regulators should have enhanced powers to suspend data flows, or subject them to conditions, if called for by the risks of particular data transfers. A duty of notification to regulators for certain types of data transfer that are particularly risky (eg, transfers of sensitive medical information) could also be provided.

It is true that transfer of data to another country deprives them of the protection of the national legal system, thus making it more difficult to assert individual rights; such arguments are often made with regard to the dangers of data transfers from the EU.[29] But when one reads that 'in France and Germany, according to a

---

[29] See, eg, Article 29 Working Party, 'Working Document: Transfers of personal data to third countries: Applying Article 26(2) of the EU Data Protection Directive to Binding Corporate Rules for International Data Transfers' (WP 74, 3 June 2003), at 10, stating: 'the enforcement of rights in transfrontier scenarios is always very complex and may involve disproportionate effort for the data subjects'.

recent study, telephones are tapped at ten to thirty times the rate they are tapped in the United States—and in the Netherlands and Italy, at 130 to 150 times the rate',[30] it can be seen that substantial data protection risks may exist in the home country notwithstanding the application of national law; an adequate level of data protection is not just a matter of what legal rules apply, but of what actually occurs in practice. Moreover, the increasing amount of informal cooperation between regulators can go a long way towards making up for the inability to assert formal enforcement jurisdiction in another country. Indeed, the fact that formal proceedings to enforce judgments across borders can be lengthy and expensive, and that many data protection violations do not involve a large economic loss, mean that in many cases there is a financial disincentive for parties to bring such proceedings through formal channels.

The risks of data processing in other countries are sometimes exaggerated, while those concerning processing within national borders may be underplayed. Much of the confusion concerning transborder data flow regulation results from the difficulty of separating the risks of transferring data to third parties in general from those of transferring data across borders. Indeed, so much data flows across borders via the Internet that there may no longer be any point in differentiating national data flows from transborder data flows. Other legal requirements for data processing should apply also in the case of transborder data flows; for example, if a particular type of data processing requires approval under national law, then such requirement should also apply if the data are to be transferred internationally. But an extra legal basis or authorization should not be required solely because the data are to be transferred across borders, absent some extra risk factor.

The existing legal bases seem insufficient to cope with the exponential growth and complexity of transborder data flows. Taking Articles 25 and 26 of the EU Directive as examples, the repertoire of adequacy decisions, consent, standard contractual clauses, BCRs, and other mechanisms requires the ability to define the roles of the actors involved in the transfers (eg, as data controllers or data processors) in a way that is becoming increasingly difficult in the context of phenomena such as cloud computing and online social networks. The steps involved in implementing such mechanisms (eg, the signature of contractual clauses) can also be impracticable in many common situations.

Some important data transfer situations also seem not to be covered by any possible legal bases. For example, the transfer of personal data across borders for 'big data' applications used for development purposes such as the identification of epidemics is clearly in the global public interest, but in some countries may not be regarded as falling within the exception for transfers necessary on 'important public interest grounds' under Article 26(1)(d) of the EU Directive.[31]

---

[30] Whitman (n 25), at 1159.
[31] See Article 29 Working Party, 'Working document on a common interpretation of Article 26(1) of Directive 95/46/EC of 24 October 1995' (WP 114, 25 November 2005), at 15, stating that only important public interests identified as such under applicable EU Member State legislation can fall under this exception.

Similarly, while it remains controversial whether data transfers initiated by individuals over the Internet are covered by transborder data flow regulation, they often result in application of the forum's law to the processing of data abroad, which usually produces the same result. And such transfers are difficult to legitimize by any of the existing mechanisms: consent can become meaningless when it is over-used, paper-based compliance such as under standard contractual clauses is difficult to implement and can lead to excessive bureaucracy, and large-scale compliance mechanisms such as BCRs are not appropriate for use by the many small and medium-sized enterprises with which individuals interact.

Not requiring an additional legal basis for *transborder* data flows also produces a better fit with the policies underlying transborder data flow regulation. Preventing circumvention of the law has declined in importance, and can be adequately taken into account by giving regulators the power to restrict data transfers if they are carried out in bad faith or if they would violate some important public policy of the forum. Protection against data processing risks abroad could likewise be covered by giving enhanced powers to regulators, and by international cooperation in compiling agreed catalogues of risks. Indeed, there is little evidence that existing authorization and registration requirements have had a significant benefit in improving the level of protection of personal data that are transferred abroad.

These considerations lead to the conclusions that in international instruments and national laws, mechanisms such as regulatory approvals and the filing of application and registration forms should be disfavoured; flexible instruments like codes of practice and targeted audits should be encouraged; and regulators should be given enhanced enforcement powers. This is the only way that the regulation of transborder data flows has a chance of keeping up with advances in technology and business processes.

The existence of a separate legal basis for transborder data flows is not by itself a requirement of fundamental rights law. Data protection must be considered in relation to its function in society, and must be balanced with other fundamental rights,[32] such as the right to free expression that is strongly implicated in cases involving transborder data flows. Moreover, transborder data flow regulation is not itself a core element of data protection, but rather functions as a conflict of laws rule that extends protections to data processed abroad. As long as transborder data flows are subject to general requirements for the processing of personal data, there is no reason that a default rule in favour of allowing the free flow of data, combined with the possibility of restricting such flows under certain conditions, cannot adequately protect data protection rights. Indeed, such a rule may enhance rights in some cases, by facilitating the flow of data from States with lower standards to ones with higher standards. The fact that data will be transferred across national borders

---

[32] See, eg, the decision of the European Court of Justice in Joined Cases C-92/09 and C-93/09 *Volker und Markus Schecke* [2010] ECR I-11063, at para. 48; Proposal for a Regulation of the European Parliament and of the Council on the protection of individuals with regard to the processing of personal data and on the free movement of such data (General Data Protection Regulation), COM(2012) 11 final, Recital 139.

is an element to be taken into account in an analysis of the risks of data processing, but should not by itself require an extra legal basis.

Weighing the impact of transborder data flows on data protection rights requires a balancing test to ensure that the result does not go beyond what is necessary for the legitimate aims pursued, having particular regard to the resulting interference with any rights.[33] Under EU law, this essentially requires that the arrangement in question is proportionate, meaning that the measures must be appropriate for attaining the objective pursued and not exceed what is necessary to achieve it.[34] Allowing transborder data flows as a default rule is proportionate, since it can provide appropriate protection for personal data transferred abroad through mechanisms such as obliging data exporters to comply with legal requirements that apply to data processing in general, and granting regulators sufficient powers to intervene.

This default rule also takes better account of freedom of expression, which has so far received insufficient attention in discussion of transborder data flow regulation. The freedom to communicate across borders is a key component of the freedom of expression, as is made clear by the Universal Declaration of Human Rights of 1948 (UDHR) and the International Covenant on Civil and Political Rights of 1966 (ICCPR), both of which mention the freedom to transfer data 'regardless of frontiers'.[35] The UN Human Rights Council has affirmed that offline rights must also be protected online, mentioning in particular freedom of expression under the UDHR and ICCPR.[36]

Requiring an additional legal basis for transborder data flows also increases the risk that States will use transborder data flow regulation not to protect the processing of personal data, but to advance their own national sovereignty. There is an increasing amount of rhetoric suggesting that measures to protect sovereignty and economic interests may be carried out in the guise of privacy protection.[37]

---

[33] See Joined Cases C-92/09 and C-93/09 *Volker und Markus Schecke* [2010] ECR I-0000, at para. 79.

[34] Joined Cases C-92/09 and C-93/09 (n 33), at para. 74.

[35] See UDHR, Article 19, and ICCPR, Article 19(2). See Anne W. Branscomb, 'Global Governance of Global Networks: A Survey of Transborder Data Flow in Transition', 36 Vanderbilt Law Review 985, 1030–34 (1983), arguing that these provisions could be the basis for an emerging international right to communicate across borders.

[36] UN Human Rights Council, 'The promotion, protection, and enjoyment of human rights on the Internet', UN Doc. A/HRC/20L.13 (29 June 2012), stating: 'the same rights that people have offline must also be protected online, in particular freedom of expression, which is applicable regardless of frontiers and through any media of one's choice, in accordance with articles 19 of the Universal Declaration of Human Rights and the International Covenant on Civil and Political Rights'.

[37] See European Commission, 'Communication from the Commission to the European Parliament, the Council, the European Economic and Social Committee and the Committee of the Regions, Safeguarding Privacy in a Connected World—A European Data Protection Framework for the 21st Century', COM(2012) 9/3, 25 January 2012, at 7, stating regarding the proposed EU Data Protection Regulation: 'the new rules will also give EU companies an advantage in global competition. Under the reformed regulatory framework, they will be able to assure their customers that valuable personal information will be treated with the necessary care and diligence. Trust in a coherent EU regulatory regime will be a key asset for service providers and an incentive for investors looking for optimal conditions when locating services.'

Adopting a default rule to allow transborder data flows without a separate legal basis means that data transfers would generally take place without prior regulatory oversight, and that most enforcement would take place 'after the fact' (ie, after transfers have taken place). This makes it imperative that the other individual steps advocated in this section are carried out, so that compliance takes place proactively as well as reactively. Particularly important is the adoption of strong accountability mechanisms to hold data exporters responsible once data have been transferred;[38] the adoption of technological protections for data flows, such as through the use of privacy by design;[39] the development of standardized compliance mechanisms (eg, audit checklists, and agreement on the risks presented by various scenarios);[40] and a greater willingness by governments themselves to comply with transborder data flow regulation.[41]

3. Organizational approach with geography as a relevant factor

Transborder data flow regulation should be based on an organizational approach, with geography taken into account.

The approaches to regulation vary, with some jurisdictions favouring ones based on geography (eg, those dependent on the 'adequacy' of data protection in foreign jurisdictions), and others preferring those based on the practices of the organizations exporting and importing the data (eg, under the concept of accountability). There is an inherent tension between the liberalization of restrictions on the flow of capital and transborder services, on the one hand, and the regulation of transborder data flows, on the other hand.

The first regulation of transborder data flows enacted in the 1970s was based mainly on geography, but there has been a gradual trend towards regulation that focuses on the organization processing the data. One reason for this is the difficulty of determining whether a particular privacy regime is 'adequate', 'comparable', or 'equivalent' based on the standards of the country of export. For example, the procedures used in the EU to reach decisions on adequacy are widely viewed as inefficient,[42] and since the Directive was adopted the European Commission has issued a relatively small number of such decisions. There is also a risk that political considerations may come into play when determining the adequacy of data protection and privacy regimes.

Geography remains relevant in the regulation of transborder data flows, since 'human beings tend to cluster geographically, based on shared cultures, languages, tastes, wealth, and values'.[43] There will always be cases where individuals may

---

[38] See Section C.4.   [39] See Section C.5.   [40] See Section C.6.   [41] See Section C.9.

[42] See regarding problems with the EU system for reaching adequacy determinations, Article 29 Working Party, 'The Future of Privacy' (WP 168, 1 December 2009), at 10–11, stating that the process for reaching adequacy decisions should be 'redesigned'.

[43] Jack Goldsmith and Tim Wu, *Who Controls the Internet? Illusions of a Borderless World* (OUP 2008), at 183. See also Pankaj Ghemawat, 'Why the World Isn't Flat', 159 Foreign Policy 54, 58 (2007), stating: 'clearly, the borders in our seemingly "borderless world" still matter to most people.'

become concerned about the processing of their personal data outside the borders of their country, based, for example, on a perceived risk of access to the data by foreign law enforcement, the chance of a breach of data security, or some other potential danger. Data controllers may also prefer to keep data within a particular region, and some cloud computing service providers already grant customers the option of keeping data within a national or regional 'cloud'. Technological factors may also gradually cause an increase in the amount of data being processed locally rather than transferred across the globe; for example, response speed for many types of Internet services (so-called 'latency') is generally increased with the geographical proximity of the user to the data centre storing or processing the data.[44] This indicates that customer demand may lead to routing data via local and regional hubs for reasons of cost, performance, and reliability.[45] Thus, the market for data processing services, driven by demand from both data controllers and individuals, will increasingly allow them to choose whether to restrict the transborder transfer of their personal data. Geography will also remain important with regard to law enforcement access to data, since more governments are likely to demand that entities offering communications in their countries also maintain equipment there, in order to facilitate such access.[46]

But the location of data processing (ie, geography) is not in itself determinative of the level of data protection. Take the example of a company that transfers personal data of customers to a database at its headquarters in another country, and that regards compliance with data protection requirements as crucial to its business success. The company could outsource processing of the data to a third party located in the country of its customers, and could conclude contractual clauses with the third party to obligate it to comply with relevant data protection requirements. But the fact that the data are processed in the country of the customers might even lower the level of data protection: no matter what legal protections the company applies, in practical terms it will never be able to oversee and audit the third party's compliance as well as it can that of its own employees at its headquarters, and by outsourcing the processing it is turning over to a third party an operation that it has a strong business incentive to operate securely. Thus, in such a case any theoretical increase in the level of data protection by processing the data in the country of the customers might be outweighed in practice by allowing a third party to have access to the data.

---

[44] W. Kuan Hon and Christopher Millard, 'Data Export in Cloud Computing—How can Personal Data be Transferred outside the EEA? (The Cloud of Unknowing, Part 4)', Queen Mary University of London, School of Law (4 April 2012), <http://www.cloudlegal.ccls.qmul.ac.uk/Research/researchpapers/55649.html>, at 26 fn 116.

[45] See, eg, Steve Gibbard, 'Geographic Implications of DNS Infrastructure Distribution', <http://www.cisco.com/web/about/ac123/ac147/archived_issues/ipj_10-1/101_dns-infrastructure.html>; Steve Gibbard, 'Internet Mini-Cores', <http://www.pch.net/resources/papers/Gibbard-mini-cores.pdf>.

[46] See, eg, 'India says BlackBerry agrees to give it real-time access to corporate messages', (6 September 2010) Bloomberg BNA Privacy & Security Law Report 1241, quoting the Indian Home Secretary as stating: 'All people who operate communications services in India should have a server in India ...'

The adequacy or geographical approach is sometimes misunderstood as an element of fundamental rights, whereas actually it is an applicable law rule that is one of several possible mechanisms to take account of the risks of the transfer of personal data across national borders. Fundamental rights law in some countries requires that the State takes measures to ensure that data are not deprived of all protection when transferred beyond national borders, but does not mandate use of a particular approach to attain this goal. It has been stated that 'if we call the right to protection of personal data, a fundamental right with some essential elements, we should be careful not to move forward and call all provisions of a particular law, or a particular draft regulation all fundamental rights ...'[47] An organizational approach can protect data, and fundamental rights, perfectly well if it is structured properly.

The geographical and organizational approaches could be combined—that is, an organizational approach could consider geography as a factor when deciding whether the transfer of personal data abroad is appropriate. An example is provided by the Guidance Document on contracting decisions published by the Treasury Board of Canada, which applies the principle of accountability,[48] but also allows the locations to which the data are to be transferred to be considered as a factor in the analysis. Under this approach, the location to which data are exported is not the sole consideration in determining whether a transfer is appropriate, but is one factor to be considered in a risk analysis based on the sensitivity of the personal information, the expectations of the individuals to whom the information relates, and the potential injury if personal information is wrongly disclosed or misused.[49]

An organizational approach can also help to defuse some of the complex questions posed by the geographical approach to transborder data flow regulation (eg, when and whether personal data cross national borders). The existence of protections throughout the organization processing the data also helps to avoid the excessive use of consent to legitimize data processing.

Such an approach should include a requirement of transparency towards individuals, so that they can learn the purposes of the transfer as well as the place to which their data are being transferred. A default rule in favour of allowing transborder data flows also requires a strong enforcement regime with real 'teeth'. This means that data controllers should have to document compliance with applicable law; that regulators should have enhanced powers to oversee and compel compliance; and that there should be greater cooperation between regulators across national borders.

---

[47] Peter Hustinx, Concluding Remarks made at 3rd Annual Symposium of the European Union Agency for Fundamental Rights, Vienna (10 May 2012), <http://www.edps.europa.eu/EDPSWEB/webdav/site/mySite/shared/Documents/EDPS/Publications/Speeches/2012/12-05-10_Speech_Vienna_EN.pdf>, at 5.

[48] Treasury Board of Canada, 'Taking Privacy into Account Before Making Contracting Decisions' (2006), at 2: 'Each institution is responsible and accountable for any personal information under its care'.

[49] Treasury Board of Canada (n 48), at 7 and Annex A.

4. Continued accountability of data controllers

Data exporters should remain accountable and responsible for personal data once they are transferred, and sufficient penalties for violations should be provided.

Regulation should require that data exporters take the risks of transborder data flows into account before data are transferred, and implement appropriate measures to minimize them. The growing strategic importance of transborder data flow regulation means that responsibility should not stop at national borders, and data exporters should be accountable and responsible for personal data after transfer. The measures taken to implement such a system can vary, as is demonstrated by the difference between those contained in the APEC Privacy Framework,[50] which are quite high level, and those in the General Data Protection Regulation proposed by the European Commission,[51] which are more specific. But transborder data flow regulation should contain at least the following accountability mechanisms.

- The responsibility of the data exporter to investigate the risks of data transfer, in light of factors such as the sensitivity of the data, the country to which the data will be exported, the measures taken to protect the data by the data importer, etc.

- Steps by the data exporter to ameliorate any risks associated with the transfer across borders. In cases where risks are low, this may require no further action by the exporter, while in others it might need to carry out extensive actions (eg, having the data importer sign contractual clauses protecting the data, or asking the importer to perform a data protection audit).

- Documentation of the steps the data exporter has taken to reduce the risks.

- Information about the transfer that should be provided to individuals in a clear and transparent fashion.

The extent of these measures should differ based on the risks of the transfer; for instance, in some routine cases an investigation of the risks could be cursory, whereas in others it might have to be quite extensive. Limits should also be placed on the legal liability of data controllers, so they do not remain responsible for all processing of the data by third parties.

---

[50] See, eg, APEC Privacy Framework (2005), <http://www.apec.org/Groups/Committee-on-Trade-and-Investment/~/media/Files/Groups/ECSG/05_ecsg_privacyframewk.ashx>, at para. 26, stating: 'A personal information controller should be accountable for complying with measures that give effect to the Principles stated above. When personal information is to be transferred to another person or organization, whether domestically or internationally, the personal information controller should obtain the consent of the individual or exercise due diligence and take reasonable steps to ensure that the recipient person or organization will protect the information consistently with these Principles.'

[51] See, eg, Proposal for a Regulation of the European Parliament and of the Council (n 32), Article 5(f), which strengthens the accountability of data controllers by requiring that personal data be processed under the responsibility and liability of the controller, and Article 28, requiring data controllers and processors, with some exceptions, to keep detailed documentation of all data processing operations, which must be produced upon request to DPAs.

Increased accountability will require parties transferring personal data, both in the private and public sectors, to increase their level of compliance. The present low level of compliance is to some extent caused by regulation that is vaguely drafted and overly ambitious, as well as by the fact that the wide jurisdictional scope of transborder data flow regulation often requires compliance with foreign law with which data controllers may be unfamiliar. But some controllers also exploit this situation to avoid complying when they know there is only a small chance that regulation will be enforced against them. A reform of transborder data flow regulation based on a default rule in favour of allowing data flows and applying an accountability standard cannot be an excuse for reducing the level of protection; indeed, the hope is that it can increase the standard of compliance.

Transborder data flow regulation can only be effective if regulators have strong enforcement powers, which they should be able to exercise both proactively (ie, before a violation occurs) and reactively (ie, when there has been a violation of law or policy), and if they are provided with adequate resources. National laws need to be strengthened to increase the powers of regulators, and States should enhance their cooperation to improve the prospects for cross-border enforcement.

5. Adjusting regulation to technological realities

Transborder data flow regulation should be adjusted to the realities of modern technology. For example, the conditions under which data processing for personal and household purposes are exempted from regulation should be specified. The distinction between 'data transfer' and 'data transit' should be clarified. And legal incentives should be provided to reduce the risks of transborder data flows through technological means.

The Internet and other technological developments have complicated the application of transborder data flow regulation, which should better take technology into account.

If the definition of a 'data transfer' is made dependent on the state of technology at a particular point in time, it will quickly become outdated. Rather than defining a data transfer based on factors such as whether data were passively 'made available' or actively 'transmitted', the applicability of transborder data flow regulation should be triggered by whether personal data will be processed outside the country where they were originally collected. This test would focus on the need to protect personal data no matter where in the world they are processed, which fits the nature of transborder data flow regulation as a form of applicable law rule. The applicability of regulation can then be limited by factors such as those mentioned in the *Bodil Lindqvist* case so that it is not construed to apply to the entire Internet without limitation. This means that the applicability of transborder data flow regulation should be conditioned on there being a sufficient connection with the State in question.

Technology has also complicated application of the 'personal and household' exemption contained in many data protection laws. It would be counterproductive to subject data processing by individuals concerning their intimate activities to the full panoply of data protection requirements, while at the same time data controllers such as social networks should not be exempted from all responsibility just because individuals use them for their personal communications. The exemption should be applied in a more nuanced way, in order to focus it on the cases for which it is intended (ie, data processing that is inherently personal and confidential), and so that it does not exempt data controllers from responsibility.

Likewise, the distinction between 'data transfer' and 'data transit' is becoming increasingly difficult to sustain as the line between data controllers and data processors is blurred. Mere transit of personal data should not be regarded as an exception to the definition of a data transfer, since data in transit are still flowing. Rather, the focus should be on the fact that mere transit does not pose a substantial risk of harm to the data, since they are simply being passed on to the next connection point. The fact that data are merely in transit should be an element to be taken into account when a risk analysis of transborder data flows is performed.

Transborder data flow regulation has focused too much on legal and administrative measures, and too little on the possibility of using technology to protect data that are transferred, such as through the use of privacy by design. For example, certain regulatory requirements could be relaxed or not applied in cases where personal data transferred across borders are encrypted so that only the parties to the transfer or authorized third parties would have access to the plaintext. This would require agreement between regulators and governments on matters such as the types of encryption that can benefit from such relaxation, how use of it is to be verified, etc., which might not be easy to attain. But just as technology brings increased risks to data protection, it can provide new solutions as well, and these have not been sufficiently explored.

6. Promoting international legal interoperability

States should enhance intergovernmental cooperation and ensure that regulatory standards and mechanisms they develop are interoperable with those in other legal systems.

International cooperation regarding transborder data flow regulation has so far not been particularly successful. States have worked together to produce some important international instruments, such as Council of Europe Convention 108 and the OECD Guidelines. But they have had more trouble agreeing on steps that are practically useful. For example, despite the fact that the EU framework for data protection is supposed to result in a level of harmonization that is 'generally complete',[52] the Article 29 Working Party has been labouring since 2004 towards a procedure whereby BCRs authorized by one EU DPA could be legally recognized by others, and still not all DPAs have accepted it.[53] This indicates that data protection and transborder data flow regulation are still viewed too often as matters

---

[52] See the *Lindqvist* case, C-101/01 [2003] ECR I-12971, at para. 96, in which the European Court of Justice held that harmonization of national data protection laws by the EU Directive is 'not limited to minimal harmonisation but amounts to harmonisation which is generally complete.'

[53] See <http://ec.europa.eu/justice/policies/privacy/binding_rules/index_en.htm>.

of local or national significance. At the regional level, legal frameworks are being amended to force regulators to cooperate more (eg, in the EU[54]), and voluntary cooperation mechanisms between data protection regulators are being developed by organizations such as APEC and the OECD. However, more should be done in this regard.

There is a need to build bridges between different systems of transborder data flow regulation, which can be referred to as the concept of 'legal interoperability'. There is no general agreement about the meaning of this term, but it can be understood broadly to refer to measures taken to facilitate the interaction between regulatory systems across national borders.[55] Such techniques have been used by organizations such as UNCITRAL and UNIDROIT to harmonize 'interface laws'—that is, the laws that affect transactions between persons in different States[56]—which has also been referred to as the most successful type of legal harmonization.[57] This suggests that measures such as the following should be taken.

- *Recognition of BCRs and similar accountability mechanisms (eg, standard contractual clauses) between different regions* Different States and regions could agree to recognize each other's legal mechanisms for transferring personal data internationally. An example would be BCRs in the EU and Cross-Border Privacy Rules (CBPRs) in the APEC region, which could interact through the concept of mutual recognition (see the following section); informal discussions between the Article 29 Working Party and APEC have begun,[58] with a view to reaching agreement on the conditions under which mutual recognition could occur.

- *Agreement on specific transborder data flow situations where extra protection is required* There is confusion about the risks specific to the transborder flow of personal data. Greater coordination in this regard would help States to adopt better laws and assist regulators in reaching decisions about data transfers. Regional regulatory groups such as the Article 29 Working Party have already opined on the international data transfer situations that pose the greatest risks, and such work could be internationalized, with more detail and description of the risks involved and how they can be dealt with. This could result in instruments being drafted on an international level, such as codes of practice and security measures.

- *Agreement on technical measures that can create incentives to protect data transferred internationally* As has already been discussed, greater agreement on technical measures to protect data transferred internationally (eg, lists of

---

[54] See Proposal for a Regulation of the European Parliament and of the Council (n 32), Articles 55 and 56, setting forth the details of proposed mutual assistance and cooperation procedures that would force the EU DPAs to work together more closely.

[55] See John Palfrey and Urs Gasser, *Interop, The Promise and Perils of Highly Interconnected Systems* (Basic Books 2012), at 178.

[56] See Goldring (n 16), at 437.   [57] Goldring (n 16), at 450.

[58] Information known to the author through contacts with data protection regulators.

approved encryption technologies) could both increase the level of protection and facilitate relaxation of regulatory requirements.

• *Greater cooperation between privacy regulatory authorities* In view of the length and complexity of procedures to enforce rights through formal channels, informal cooperation between regulatory authorities provides one of the most promising avenues for bridging the gaps between legal systems.[59] Such cooperation is already underway under the auspices of groups such as the Global Privacy Enforcement Network (GPEN) and the APEC Cross-border Privacy Enforcement Arrangement, but should be intensified. In some cases this may require governments to amend their laws in order to allow the cross-border sharing of information between regulatory authorities.[60]

• *Preparation of an international model law on transborder data flows* At present, States tend to base transborder data flow regulation on various regional or national models, and then add their own national variations. Many countries, particularly those without much prior experience of data protection law, would benefit from a globally-oriented model law dealing with transborder data flows, so that they do not have to start from scratch or use a regional or national model when preparing regulation.

The variable quality of current regulation demonstrates the need for such a model law. For example, consent is used too often as a legal basis for transborder data flows, particularly in the online context, often without giving the individual a clear understanding of what he or she is consenting to. Some data protection laws encourage this trend by requiring consent in virtually all cases when data are to be transferred to other countries,[61] which can devalue its use and create less transparency for individuals rather than more. A model law on transborder data flows drafted by a group of experts under the auspices of an international organization could help to raise the quality of national legislation and promote international harmonization.

The details of such a model law would be subject to negotiation and may be difficult to agree on, given the differences between the various privacy regimes around the world. However, the following could be the main elements:

1. A requirement that personal data receive protection no matter where in the world they are processed. The details of such protection could be based on an

---

[59] See OECD, 'Report on the Cross-Border Enforcement of Privacy Laws' (2006), <http://www.oecd.org/dataoecd/17/43/37558845.pdf>, at 19–26, giving examples of such informal cooperation.
[60] See OECD, 'Recommendation on Cross-border Co-operation in the Enforcement of Laws Protecting Privacy' (2007), at 7, 9, 11; Law Commission of New Zealand, 'Review of the Privacy Act 1993' (March 2010), <http://www.lawcom.govt.nz/sites/default/files/publications/2010/03/Publication_129_460_Part_17_Chapter-14-Trans-border%20Data%20Flows.pdf>, at 398–9.
[61] See, eg, Costa Rica Law No. 8968/2011 on the Protection of Personal Data, Article 14; South Korea Personal Information Protection Act, Law 10465 (2011), Article 17(3).

internationally agreed model, either one already existing (such as Council of Europe Convention 108 or the Madrid Resolution) or a newly drafted one.

2. A commitment by the data exporter to take steps ensuring that such protection is given, which should be proportionate to the risks presented by the transfer. Factors relevant to determining the risks could be listed, such as the protections present in the organizations to which the data will be processed; any particular risks associated with the processing; and the countries in which the data will be processed and accessed. This would include the accountability obligations described earlier.[62]

3. A listing of mechanisms that can be used to protect the data, which could include audit or due diligence procedures, contractual clauses, security measures, etc.

4. A duty of the data exporter to notify the DPA in the case of data transfers posing a particularly high degree of risk to the interests and rights of the individuals whose data are transferred.

5. A grant of power to regulators to intervene should any questions or problems arise, together with a duty on them to cooperate with other ones and to determine which regulator is best placed to deal with any complaints.

6. A commitment by the data exporter to cooperate with regulators (including facilitation of contact with the data importer), and with individuals should they have questions or complaints about the export of their data.

The availability of such a model law would allow States to consult an internationally-oriented template, rather than one based on the law of a specific jurisdiction, if they choose to enact legal regulation of transborder data flows. As is the case with similar model laws drafted by organizations such as UNCITRAL, it would constitute 'a suggested pattern for law-makers in national governments to consider adopting as part of their domestic legislation'[63] that could be enacted voluntarily.

(a) Use of the concept of mutual recognition

Mutual recognition involves retaining separate regulatory standards for internally produced products or services, but agreeing to recognize those produced under standards from other jurisdictions subject to conditions.[64] It is often used with regard to goods, and is embedded in certain legal systems (eg, in EU law[65]). Both

---

[62] See Section C.4.   [63] See <http://www.uncitral.org/uncitral/en/uncitral_texts_faq.html>.
[64] See Gregory Shaffer, 'Reconciling trade and regulatory goals: prospects and limits of new approaches to transatlantic governance through mutual recognition and safe harbour agreements', 9 Columbia Journal of European Law 29, 32–3 (2002).
[65] See Consolidated version of the Treaty on the Functioning of the European Union, [2010] OJ C83/47, Article 26(2), setting forth the principle of the free movement of goods within the EU. See also Adrienne Héritier, 'Mutual recognition: comparing policy areas', 14 Journal of European Public Policy 800 (2007).

the EU and the US have negotiated a number of mutual recognition agreements with third countries with regard to standards for goods and services.[66]

So-called 'safe harbour' agreements between States can act as a form of mutual recognition, by requiring data controllers in other countries to abide by some of the standards of a foreign community in order to receive certain legal benefits; the EU–US Safe Harbor agreement, which is based on private sector certification of companies' privacy practices, backed up by enforcement by the US Federal Trade Commission (FTC),[67] is the best-known example in the data protection field.[68]

Mutual recognition could be profitably used in areas such as cross-border recognition of data protection audits, and certification of seal programmes. In some cases private bodies can enter into agreements with regulatory agencies regarding recognition of privacy practices from other jurisdictions, or be the main implementers of such regimes;[69] an example is an agreement reached in 2001 between the US-based trust seal provider BBB OnLine and a Japanese counterpart involving certification of companies' online privacy practices.[70] The US government has endorsed mutual recognition as a way to create greater international interoperability of transborder data flow regimes, and has plans to develop further international instruments for this purpose.[71]

The beginnings of a global mutual recognition approach can be discerned in certain data protection regulation that at least partially recognizes the laws of other countries and regions; examples are the data protection laws of Israel and Russia, which both recognize as 'adequate' countries that have ratified Council of Europe Convention 108. Even if accession to an instrument such as Convention 108 will probably not be widely recognized by itself as providing sufficient data protection until the Convention is modernized (ie, since Convention 108 currently lacks a provision ensuring 'quality control' of the national legislation of countries that enact it), membership in it and similar international legal instruments should give countries that enact them a 'fast track' towards being recognized as providing sufficient protection, thus advancing international legal interoperability.

Codes of conduct drawn up by regulators or by the private sector could also be used as a form of mutual recognition. Such codes could contain standards for transborder data flows that would be applied by parties in various countries, and

---

[66] For a discussion of such agreements, see Kalypso Nicolaidis and Gregory Shaffer, 'Transnational mutual recognition regimes: governance without global government', 68 Law and Contemporary Problems 263, 278–80 (2005); Shaffer (n 64), at 36.

[67] In 2011, the FTC announced its first substantive enforcement action for specific violations of the Safe Harbor Principles, in the context of a settlement agreement concerning the online service Google Buzz. See US FTC, *In the Matter of Google Inc.*, Docket No. C-4336, 13 October 2011.

[68] Regarding the Safe Harbor agreement as a form of mutual recognition, see Schiff Berman (n 8), at 1227.

[69] See Nicolaidis and Shaffer (n 66), at 279, stating: 'Hybrid public–private administration is widespread in mutual recognition regimes, which can involve the outsourcing of monitoring, certification, and assessment functions'.

[70] Nicolaidis and Shaffer (n 66), at 279.

[71] White House, 'Consumer Data Privacy in a Networked World' (February 2012), <http://www.whitehouse.gov/sites/default/files/privacy-final.pdf>, at 31, 33.

could also receive regulatory approval, so that parties abiding by them would automatically be able to satisfy legal requirements. The Proposed Regulation of the European Commission would encourage the drawing up of such codes covering transborder data flow regulation.[72]

The use of mutual recognition in the context of data protection presents special issues. For instance, there is greater need to consider the protection of individual rights in a mutual recognition system impacting fundamental rights than in a system involving goods.[73] Existing mutual recognition systems used in data protection have also provoked concerns about the lowering of standards (eg, in the context of the EU–US Safe Harbor agreement).[74] However, the decision-making process determines the level of the regulatory standards in a mutual recognition system,[75] so that a transparent system allowing for sufficient input from stakeholders and an efficient decision-making process need not lead to a 'race to the bottom'. A mutual recognition system can also cause higher regulatory standards from one system gradually to influence another system; for example, the author is aware from his personal experience of many companies based in the US that have adapted their privacy practices to become closer to EU standards after having joined the Safe Harbor mechanism. This can occur because it is often easier and less costly to adopt a single data processing standard throughout a company, even if it is at a higher level, than to apply several different ones.[76]

(b) Use of internationally agreed tools for transborder data flows

States and regional organizations have adopted different sets of tools for transborder data flows, and apply varying legal standards to them. This makes it difficult for parties transferring personal data to use the same mechanisms to protect personal data transferred to different regions. Certain tools seem on the way to becoming an international standard; for example, in the author's experience, some countries outside the EU now informally allow data transfers to be carried out under contractual clauses based on the EU model clauses. Greater global agreement on such tools (ie, incorporating input from beyond one or two legal systems and geographic regions) would be helpful in improving the general level of compliance, which is particularly important if the default rule is set to allow data transfers without a separate legal basis.[77] An example could be the standardized contracts accepted globally in fields like the construction industry (eg, the standard contracts of FIDIC, the International Federation of Consulting Engineers[78]).

[72] Proposal for a Regulation of the European Parliament and of the Council (n 32), Article 38(1)(f).
[73] See Sandra Lavenex, 'Mutual recognition and the monopoly of force: limits of the single market analogy', 14 Journal of European Public Policy 762, 763 (2007); Susanne K. Schmidt, 'Mutual recognition as a new mode of governance', 14 Journal of European Public Policy 667, 676 (2007).
[74] For differing views of the efficacy of the Safe Harbor, see (attacking Safe Harbor) Galexia, 'The US Safe Harbor: fact or fiction?' (2008), <http://www.galexia.com/public/research/assets/safe_harbor_fact_or_fiction_2008/safe_harbor_fact_or_fiction-Detailed.html>; and (defending it) Damon Greer, 'Safe Harbor—a framework that works', 1 International Data Privacy Law 143 (2011).
[75] See Miguel Poiares Maduro, 'So close and yet so far: the paradoxes of mutual recognition', 14 Journal of European Public Policy 814, 817 (2007).
[76] See Shaffer (n 23), at 78.   [77] See Section C.2.   [78] See <http://www.fidic.org>.

7. Jurisdictional restraint and greater acceptance of international values

Governments and regulators should be cautious in asserting jurisdiction and application of their national transborder data flow regulation, and in appropriate circumstances should recognize important values that are of concern to the entire international community as grounds for transferring personal data.

States, regulators, courts, and other authorities should be cautious in asserting jurisdiction and application of their national transborder data flow regulation. The risk of conflict of laws is increasing, owing to the fact that States are extending the scope of their law as a way to protect personal data processed abroad. In addition, there are more clashes between data protection law and other types of law, such as when a regulatory authority orders that personal data are transferred to its country in violation of transborder data flow regulation.

Legal pluralism assumes the existence of conflicts between regulatory systems, and sometimes an open conflict of laws can help to resolve an international controversy more meaningfully than can an international agreement that leaves a dispute to simmer under the surface.[79] However, this does not mean that conflict of laws is always to be encouraged; many of them are caused by an assertion of jurisdiction over data processing or data transfers that have closer ties to another State, or that could more efficiently be handled by another regulator. These types of undesirable conflict lead to unnecessary international tensions, as well as a waste of resources, as regulators deal with issues that could be better handled in a different jurisdiction.

There is need for a 'safety valve' allowing regulators and courts to refrain from engaging in 'regulatory overreaching', which has been defined as a 'situation in which rules are expressed so generally and non-discriminatingly that they apply prima facie to a large range of activities without having much of a realistic chance of being enforced'.[80] The fact that data flow on the Internet without regard to national borders means that transborder data flow regulation could apply to nearly every act of data processing on it. There seems to be no bar in customary international law to more than one State exercising jurisdiction over the same activity;[81] however, this does not mean that they are always *required* to do so, or that the law could not be structured to refrain from doing so, as set forth in the following non-binding declaration agreed by OECD member countries urging States to exercise restraint in asserting jurisdiction:

1. In contemplating new legislation, action under existing legislation or other exercise of jurisdiction which may conflict with the legal requirements or established

---

[79] See Section B.3.

[80] See Lee Bygrave, 'Determining applicable law pursuant to European Data Protection Legislation', 16 Computer Law and Security Report 252, 255 (2000).

[81] See, eg, Case C-366/10 *The Air Transport Association of America and Others* [2011] ECR 0000, Opinion of AG Kokott, para. 158.

policies of another Member country and lead to conflicting requirements being imposed on multinational enterprises, the Member countries concerned should:

a) Have regard to relevant principles of international law;

b) Endeavour to avoid or minimise such conflicts and the problems to which they give rise by following an approach of moderation and restraint, respecting and accommodating the interests of other Member countries;

c) Take fully into account the sovereignty and legitimate economic, law enforcement and other interests of other Member countries ... '[82]

Situations often arise in which a number of different States and regulators can have jurisdiction over the same data processing; in such situations it can be appropriate for one regulator to refrain from exercising jurisdiction, as long as there is another one that can take action.[83] It was the consequences of such a conclusion that caused the European Court of Justice in the *Bodil Lindqvist* case to interpret the data transfer rules of the EU Directive restrictively and find that they should not be applied to activities that could result in EU data protection law being applied indiscriminately to the entire Internet.[84]

Parties are increasingly being compelled to transfer personal data to other countries based on foreign legal requirements. A few laws provide exceptions that allow data transfers based on compulsion under foreign law.[85] But despite the presence in data protection laws of exceptions allowing transborder data flows based on 'public interest grounds' or for the 'defence of legal claims',[86] there is a general reluctance to allow data transfers based on foreign law or public policy, as this could allow a foreign State to mandate circumvention of the home State's regulation.[87]

It is understandable that a State would not allow its laws to be automatically overridden by those of a foreign State. However, this misses the point, which is not that such conflicts should automatically lead to an exemption from data transfer regulation, but that international and foreign laws and policies should be taken into account in specific cases, and should provide a legal basis for transborder data flows under the right circumstances. The EU Directive allows foreign legal requirements to be recognized as a legal basis for data transfers, when the legal compulsion deals with a matter that is of concern to the EU Member State from which the data

---

[82] OECD, Annex 2 to the Declaration on International Investment and Multinational Enterprises, 'Conflicting Requirements Imposed on Multinational Enterprises' (1991), <http://www.oecd.org/daf/internationalinvestment/investmentpolicy/conflictingrequirementsimposedonmultinationalenterprises.htm>.

[83] See Schiff Berman (n 8), at 1215.   [84] C-101/01 [2003] ECR I-12971, para. 69.

[85] See, eg, DIFC, Law No. 1 of 2007, Article 12(1)(j), allowing data transfers abroad when 'the transfer is necessary to comply with any regulatory requirements, auditing, accounting, anti-money laundering or counter terrorist financing obligations or the prevention or detection of any crime that apply to a Data Controller'.

[86] EU Data Protection Directive, Article 26(1)(d).

[87] See Article 29 Working Party, 'Working document on a common interpretation of Article 26(1) of Directive 95/46/EC of 24 October 1995' (WP 114, 25 November 2005), at 14, stating: 'the drafters of the Directive clearly did envisage that only important public interests identified as such by the national legislation applicable to data controllers established in the EU are valid in this connection. Any other interpretation would make it easy for a foreign authority to circumvent the requirement for adequate protection in the recipient country laid down in Directive 95/46.'

would be transferred as well as the one whose law seeks to compel the transfer.[88] This suggests that foreign law should be more widely recognized as a legal basis for transborder data flows in areas that are of concern to the entire international community (eg, anti-corruption, disaster relief, money laundering, and certain law enforcement measures), and that data protection laws should give courts and regulators the ability to consider foreign law and policy on a case-by-case basis. The use of international public policy as a basis for transborder data flows can still be balanced against the rights of individuals, in order to ensure that the latter are sufficiently taken into account. An example of such an approach is provided by a provision of the Data Protection Law of the Dubai International Financial Centre (DIFC), which allows transfers under the following circumstances:

(i) the transfer is necessary to uphold the legitimate interests of the Data Controller recognised in the international financial markets, provided that such is pursued in accordance with international financial standards and except where such interests are overridden by legitimate interests of the Data Subject relating to the Data Subject's particular situation …[89]

In many data protection laws, an important public interest can only be used as a basis for transferring data if it is recognized as such in the legislation of the country of data export,[90] which may result in some important interests not being recognized. For example, data analytic techniques for the prevention of disease and disaster relief may have great benefit for the international community as a whole, but may not provide a basis under national law for the transfer of data, since they are only of indirect benefit for the country from which data are transferred. As it is based on fundamental rights law in many countries, data protection law should be oriented more towards the protection of universal values, and not just those that are local or national. This should be seen not as a weakening of local values, but as a strengthening of fundamental rights at a global level.

Too often the question of whether transborder data flows to a particular country should be allowed is seen as a 'black or white' dichotomy—that is, either they are regarded as wholly permissible or wholly impermissible. It would be preferable to use a more nuanced approach, under which restriction of data transfers would depend on various factors that impact the risk involved in particular transfers. Such factors could include the legal and political system of the country involved; the purposes for which the data will be processed; and the degree of international consensus on the purposes of data processing and transfer. Considerations of fundamental rights may prevent foreign legal requirements from overriding data transfer regulation of the forum in particular cases.[91] But evidence of an international

---

[88] See EU Data Protection Directive, Recital 58, recognizing that the 'important public interest' exception could apply for transfers 'between tax or customs administrations in different countries' or 'between services competent for social security matters'.

[89] DIFC Data Protection Law 2007, Law No. 1 of 2007, Article 12(1)(i).

[90] See Article 29 Working Party (n 87), at 15.

[91] Eg, in the EU. See Joined Cases C-402 and 415/05 P *Kadi & Al Barakaat Int'l Found. v Council & Commission* [2008] ECR I-6351.

consensus on the purposes of the transfer should be taken into account when determining if it is permissible; this could include indicia such as whether the particular purpose has been the subject of international treaties, resolutions of international organizations, and similar evidence. The pluralistic nature of transborder data flow regulation makes it ill-suited to a 'black or white' approach, and calls for one that takes international norms into account.

8. Increased transparency

Both States and data controllers should increase transparency regarding transborder data flow regulation.

Greater transparency needs to be created for individuals regarding transborder data flows. This means that privacy notices giving information about them should be drafted in clearer language, and that cross-border regulatory cooperation should be increased, so that individuals can more easily assert their rights with regard to data that have been transferred to other countries. More information should be provided regarding the entities used to process and store personal data, and data controllers should appoint internal privacy officers who are tasked with providing information about data processing and responding to complaints.

Despite pledges by States to 'seek transparency in regulations and policies relating to information, computer and communications services affecting transborder data flows',[92] much more needs to be done in this regard. It can be difficult to obtain reliable and timely information on transborder data flow regulation, since many countries seem to view the subject as one of mainly national importance, whereas in a globalized world there is often a need for persons and organizations outside the jurisdiction to obtain such information.

A lack of transparency concerning regulation frustrates data controllers and confuses individuals. The steps that States could take include making available on the Internet the current text of any national regulation of transborder data flows, in multiple languages; providing regular updates in a timely fashion regarding any new or revised regulation, relevant case law, and guidance; and designating a contact point in the government (eg, in a ministry or DPA) to which questions could be addressed. Countries and other governmental entities should cooperate in disseminating information about regulation; this could be done, for example, by making information available in a central repository maintained on the website of an international organization. Because of the global nature of transborder data flow regulation, States and regulators should realize that persons outside their own country also have an interest in information about it.[93]

---

[92] Declaration on Transborder Data Flows (Adopted by the Governments of the OECD Member Countries on 11th April 1985), <http://www.oecd.org/document/32/0,3343,en_2649_34255_1888 153_1_1_1,00.html>.

[93] See Nicolaidis and Shaffer (n 66), at 301, stating with regard to mutual recognition: 'In the mutual recognition context, domestic regulators must give notice of proposed standards, make explicit the extent to which home or host state rules will apply, and give notice of changes to standards that

9. Better regulatory compliance by States

States and governments should themselves comply with transborder data flow regulation.

States should abide by the same regulation that they impose on other parties. Too many laws regulating transborder data flows include broad exemptions for government purposes such as law enforcement activities;[94] while the specific context of government activities may require adaptation of the rules in certain cases, it is difficult to see why regulation should not generally apply to them. EU data protection law, which formerly provided a broad exemption for the processing of data for law enforcement purposes but eliminated it under the Lisbon Treaty,[95] can serve as an example in this regard.

Governments should also improve legal standards with regard to data transferred between them. A substantial amount of personal data is routinely exchanged between governments under various international treaties, and informal discussions with data protection regulators and diplomats indicate that the majority of such agreements pay little or no attention to providing protections for data transferred. It would set a good example if standard data protection clauses or protocols were agreed internationally, and routinely included in agreements providing protections for data shared between governments.[96] Having such standardized clauses accepted by governments around the world could also help to further the acceptance of global data protection standards.

Much more transparency, and greater legal protection, are also necessary with regard to government access to data held by the private sector. A serious dialogue should be undertaken between governments, private sector data controllers, individuals, and privacy advocates in order to produce stronger legal frameworks with regard to government access of such data transferred across national borders.[97] This could include steps such as agreeing on conditions of data access; security measures

---

have already been considered equivalent. Foreign states and individuals are to have a right to be heard by national administrators, whether directly or indirectly. In sum, national authorities must "take account," even if only through transparent procedures, of consumers and citizens outside their national territories if they are to be more accountable to those on whom their decisions have an effect.'

[94] See, eg, Macau Personal Data Protection Act (Act 8/2005), Article 20(3); Peru Law No. 29733/2011 on the Protection of Personal Data, Article 15.3; Federal Law of the Russian Federation of 27 July 2006 No. 152-FZ on Personal Data (as amended by Law of 25 July 2011 No. 261-FZ), Article 12.4.3; Tunisia Law No. 2004-63 of 27 July 2004, on the Protection of Personal Data (2004), Article 50.

[95] See Consolidated version of the Treaty on the Functioning of the European Union (n 65), Article 16(2).

[96] See, eg, Franziska Boehm, *Information Sharing and Data Protection in the Area of Freedom, Security and Justice* (Springer 2012), at 407, proposing harmonized criteria for the exchange of personal data among law enforcement authorities in the EU. For a suggested standardized agreement that could be used internationally based on the US Fair Information Practices (FIP), see John W. Kropf, 'The Golden Rule of Privacy: A Proposal for a Global Privacy Policy on Government-to-Government Sharing of Personal Information', (15 January 2007) Bloomberg BNA Privacy & Security Law Report 90.

[97] See Fred H. Cate, James X. Dempsey, and Ira S. Rubenstein, 'Systematic government access to private-sector data', 2 International Data Privacy Law 195, 199 (2012).

applicable to providing data to law enforcement bodies; the rights of individuals; and redress mechanisms.[98]

D. Concluding remarks

Both the beneficial and the harmful aspects of globalization, the Internet, and online communication involve the international transfer of personal data, which has become an indispensible part of modern life. It is increasingly difficult to discuss transborder data flow regulation as a phenomenon distinct from regulation of the Internet in general.

There is a natural desire to find a single, high-level solution to the legal issues raised by transborder data flow regulation, and the inability to do so is frustrating. But the search for an overarching solution may in itself be problematic, since it can give rise to unrealistic expectations and detract from the various issues identified here that can be addressed individually.[99]

The world is currently witnessing two contradictory phenomena, namely an ever-increasing globalization of the economy and of society (much of which is made possible by the Internet and the ability to communicate online), together with a growth in regulation and restriction of the means (ie, the transfer of personal data) necessary to realize them. Such tensions are not easily resolved, since they reflect fundamental differences in the conception of data protection and privacy in different legal systems, as well as the fact that there is currently no international hierarchy of actors, norms, and institutions to resolve them. An overarching, high-level international consensus on these questions is unlikely any time soon, but steps could be taken to deal with the conflicts caused by the current plurality of legal rules, as set forth in this chapter.

The transfer of personal data across borders is often assumed to be inherently risky. This leads to an undervaluation of the benefits of data flows, which are central to many important fundamental rights, economic benefits, and social values. The emphasis should be not only on protecting against the risks, but also on maximizing the benefits, of transborder data flows.

Regulation has also focused too much on securing application of local standards to personal data transferred outside national borders, while neglecting policies that are in the interest of the international community as a whole. States, individuals, and regulators will have to come to terms with the fact that a regulatory system offering a good level of protection in most cases is probably the best that can be achieved in a fragmented world. The goal of transborder data flow regulation

---

[98] See European Data Protection Supervisor, 'Opinion of the European Data Protection Supervisor on the Commission's Communication on "Unleashing the potential of Cloud Computing in Europe"' (16 November 2012), at 23.

[99] For an analogous argument regarding the pointlessness of a search for a 'grand blueprint' to solve coherency problems in public international law, see Martti Koskenniemi, *From Apology to Utopia* (CUP 2006), at 602–5.

should be to promote the universality of fundamental rights, not just to ensure the application of local values outside national borders.

Data controllers want to be able to operate globally under a single legal standard; individuals expect to be able to assert their rights in other countries under the law of their home State; and governments enact an increasing volume of transborder data flow regulation, while themselves engaging in data access and data sharing that is often untransparent and legally questionable. Data protection and privacy law cannot wholly resolve these tensions, since they reflect the hypocrisies of a world that is simultaneously fascinated by the benefits of globalization and the Internet, and frightened by the insecurities they bring. The way that we deal with the issues raised by transborder data flow regulation will ultimately reflect what kind of an Internet we want, and what sort of a world we choose to live in.

Data Protection and Privacy Law Instruments Regulating Transborder Data Flows (as of January 2013)

Author's note

The following tables contain English versions of provisions in data protection and privacy law instruments from around the world that specifically regulate transborder data flows (ie, instruments and provisions dealing with data transfers in general are not included, except in a few cases). It is current as of 1 January 2013. Unless otherwise noted, only legally binding instruments that are currently in force (in most cases legislation), or influential non-binding instruments promulgated by leading international institutions, have been included. While substantial effort has been made regarding the accuracy of the citations and the translations, and official sources have been used for the latter when available, no guarantees are made in this regard, and in some cases it has been necessary to rely on unofficial translations. The text is a quotation from the relevant provision, except in a few cases where it has been summarized (listed as a 'paraphrase'). The formatting and numeration is that used in the original text of the provisions.

A. International instruments (binding and non-binding)

Name	Provisions	Text or translation (excerpts; notes are given in italics)
APEC	APEC Privacy Framework (can be voluntarily implemented in the 21 APEC Member Economies: Australia; Brunei Darussalam; Canada; Chile; the People's Republic of China; Hong Kong, China; Indonesia; Japan; Republic of Korea; Malaysia; Mexico; New Zealand; Papua New Guinea; Peru; The Philippines; Russia; Singapore; Chinese Taipei; Thailand; the United States of America; and Vietnam)	**Principle IX (Accountability)** A personal information controller should be accountable for complying with measures that give effect to the Principles stated above. When personal information is to be transferred to another person or organization, whether domestically or internationally, the personal information controller should obtain the consent of the individual or exercise due diligence and take reasonable steps to ensure that the recipient person or organization will protect the information consistently with these Principles.

Name	Provisions	Text or translation (excerpts; notes are given in italics)
Council of Europe	Convention for the Protection of Individuals with regard to Automatic Processing of Personal Data, 28 January 1981, ETS 108 (1981)	**Article 12 Transborder flows of personal data and domestic law** 1. The following provisions shall apply to the transfer across national borders, by whatever medium, of personal data undergoing automatic processing or collected with a view to their being automatically processed. 2. A Party shall not, for the sole purpose of the protection of privacy, prohibit or subject to special authorisation transborder flows of personal data going to the territory of another Party. 3. Nevertheless, each Party shall be entitled to derogate from the provisions of paragraph 2: a. insofar as its legislation includes specific regulations for certain categories of personal data or of automated personal data files, because of the nature of those data or those files, except where the regulations of the other Party provide an equivalent protection; b. when the transfer is made from its territory to the territory of a non-contracting State through the intermediary of the territory of another Party, in order to avoid such transfers resulting in circumvention of the legislation of the Party referred to at the beginning of this paragraph. *NOTE: For the states that have ratified or acceded to Convention 108, see* <http://conventions.coe.int/Treaty/Commun/ChercheSig.asp?NT=108&CM=1&DF=&CL=ENG>
	Additional Protocol	**Article 2 Transborder flows of personal data to a recipient which is not subject to the jurisdiction of a Party to the Convention** 1. Each Party shall provide for the transfer of personal data to a recipient that is subject to the jurisdiction of a State or organisation that is not Party to the Convention only if that State or organisation ensures an adequate level of protection for the intended data transfer. 2. By way of derogation from paragraph 1 of Article 2 of this Protocol, each Party may allow for the transfer of personal data: a. if domestic law provides for it because of: – specific interests of the data subject, or – legitimate prevailing interests, especially important public interests, or

Name	Provisions	Text or translation (excerpts; notes are given in italics)
		b. if safeguards, which can in particular result from contractual clauses, are provided by the controller responsible for the transfer and are found adequate by the competent authorities according to domestic law. *NOTE: For the states that have ratified or acceded to the Additional Protocol, see* <http://conventions.coe.int/Treaty/Commun/ChercheSig.asp?NT=181&CM=2&DF=&CL=ENG>
	Recommendation No. R(87)15 of the Committee of Ministers to Member States regulating the use of personal data in the police sector (17 September 1987)	**5.4. International communication** Communication of data to foreign authorities should be restricted to police bodies. It should only be permissible: a. if there exists a clear legal provision under national or international law, b. in the absence of such a provision, if the communication is necessary for the prevention of a serious and imminent danger or is necessary for the suppression of a serious criminal offence under ordinary law, and provided that domestic regulations for the protection of the person are not prejudiced.
Economic Community of West African States (ECOWAS)	Supplementary Act A/SA.1/01/10 on Personal Data Protection within ECOWAS (16 February 2010)	**Article 36** 1) The data controller shall transfer personal data to a non-member ECOWAS country only where such a country provides an adequate level of protection for privacy, freedoms and the fundamental rights of individuals in relation to the processing or possible processing of such data. 2) The data controller shall inform the Data Protection Authority prior to any transfer of personal data to such a third country.
European Union	Directive 95/46/EC of the European Parliament and of the Council of 24 October 1995 on the protection of individuals with regard to the processing of personal data and on the free movement of such data, [1995] OJ L281/31 (binding on the 27 EU and the three EEA Member States, see under Section B.)	**Article 25** 1. The Member States shall provide that the transfer to a third country of personal data which are undergoing processing or are intended for processing after transfer may take place only if, without prejudice to compliance with the national provisions adopted pursuant to the other provisions of this Directive, the third country in question ensures an adequate level of protection.

Name	Provisions	Text or translation (excerpts; notes are given in italics)
		2. The adequacy of the level of protection afforded by a third country shall be assessed in the light of all the circumstances surrounding a data transfer operation or set of data transfer operations; particular consideration shall be given to the nature of the data, the purpose and duration of the proposed processing operation or operations, the country of origin and country of final destination, the rules of law, both general and sectoral, in force in the third country in question and the professional rules and security measures which are complied with in that country.
		3. The Member States and the Commission shall inform each other of cases where they consider that a third country does not ensure an adequate level of protection within the meaning of paragraph 2.
		4. Where the Commission finds, under the procedure provided for in Article 31(2), that a third country does not ensure an adequate level of protection within the meaning of paragraph 2 of this Article, Member States shall take the measures necessary to prevent any transfer of data of the same type to the third country in question.
		5. At the appropriate time, the Commission shall enter into negotiations with a view to remedying the situation resulting from the finding made pursuant to paragraph 4.
		6. The Commission may find, in accordance with the procedure referred to in Article 31(2), that a third country ensures an adequate level of protection within the meaning of paragraph 2 of this Article, by reason of its domestic law or of the international commitments it has entered into, particularly upon conclusion of the negotiations referred to in paragraph 5, for the protection of the private lives and basic freedoms and rights of individuals. Member States shall take the measures necessary to comply with the Commission's decision.

Name	Provisions	Text or translation (excerpts; notes are given in italics)

Article 26

1. By way of derogation from Article 25 and save where otherwise provided by domestic law governing particular cases, Member States shall provide that a transfer or a set of transfers of personal data to a third country which does not ensure an adequate level of protection within the meaning of Article 25(2) may take place on condition that:

   (a) the data subject has given his consent unambiguously to the proposed transfer; or

   (b) the transfer is necessary for the performance of a contract between the data subject and the controller or the implementation of precontractual measures taken in response to the data subject's request; or

   (c) the transfer is necessary for the conclusion or performance of a contract concluded in the interest of the data subject between the controller and a third party; or

   (d) the transfer is necessary or legally required on important public interest grounds, or for the establishment, exercise or defence of legal claims; or

   (e) the transfer is necessary in order to protect the vital interests of the data subject; or

   (f) the transfer is made from a register which according to laws or regulations is intended to provide information to the public and which is open to consultation either by the public in general or by any person who can demonstrate legitimate interest, to the extent that the conditions laid down in law for consultation are fulfilled in the particular case.

2. Without prejudice to paragraph 1, a Member State may authorize a transfer or a set of transfers of personal data to a third country which does not ensure an adequate level of protection within the meaning of Article 25(2), where the controller adduces adequate safeguards with respect to the protection of the privacy and fundamental rights and freedoms of individuals and as regards the exercise of the corresponding rights; such safeguards may in particular result from appropriate contractual clauses.

Name	Provisions	Text or translation (excerpts; notes are given in italics)
		3. The Member State shall inform the Commission and the other Member States of the authorizations it grants pursuant to paragraph 2. If a Member State or the Commission objects on justified grounds involving the protection of the privacy and fundamental rights and freedoms of individuals, the Commission shall take appropriate measures in accordance with the procedure laid down in Article 31(2). Member States shall take the necessary measures to comply with the Commission's decision. 4. Where the Commission decides, in accordance with the procedure referred to in Article 31(2), that certain standard contractual clauses offer sufficient safeguards as required by paragraph 2, Member States shall take the necessary measures to comply with the Commission's decision.
	Regulation (EC) No 45/2001 of the European Parliament and of the Council of 18 December 2000 on the protection of individuals with regard to the processing of personal data by the institutions and bodies of the Community and on the free movement of such data, [2001] OJ L8/1 (applies to the EU institutions)	**Article 9** 1. Personal data shall only be transferred to recipients, other than Community institutions and bodies, which are not subject to national law adopted pursuant to Directive 95/46/EC, if an adequate level of protection is ensured in the country of the recipient or within the recipient international organisation and the data are transferred solely to allow tasks covered by the competence of the controller to be carried out. 2. The adequacy of the level of protection afforded by the third country or international organisation in question shall be assessed in the light of all the circumstances surrounding a data transfer operation or set of data transfer operations; particular consideration shall be given to the nature of the data, the purpose and duration of the proposed processing operation or operations, the recipient third country or recipient international organisation, the rules of law, both general and sectoral, in force in the third country or international organisation in question and the professional rules and security measures which are complied with in that third country or international organisation.

Name	Provisions	Text or translation (excerpts; notes are given in italics)
		3. The Community institutions and bodies shall inform the Commission and the European Data Protection Supervisor of cases where they consider the third country or international organisation in question does not ensure an adequate level of protection within the meaning of paragraph 2.
		4. The Commission shall inform the Member States of any cases as referred to in paragraph 3.
		5. The Community institutions and bodies shall take the necessary measures to comply with decisions taken by the Commission when it establishes, pursuant to Article 25(4) and (6) of Directive 95/46/EC, that a third country or an international organisation ensures or does not ensure an adequate level of protection.
		6. By way of derogation from paragraphs 1 and 2, the Community institution or body may transfer personal data if:
		(a) the data subject has given his or her consent unambiguously to the proposed transfer; or
		(b) the transfer is necessary for the performance of a contract between the data subject and the controller or the implementation of pre-contractual measures taken in response to the data subject's request; or
		(c) the transfer is necessary for the conclusion or performance of a contract entered into in the interest of the data subject between the controller and a third party; or
		(d) the transfer is necessary or legally required on important public interest grounds, or for the establishment, exercise or defence of legal claims; or
		(e) the transfer is necessary in order to protect the vital interests of the data subject; or
		(f) the transfer is made from a register which, according to Community law, is intended to provide information to the public and which is open to consultation either by the public in general or by any person who can demonstrate a legitimate interest, to the extent that the conditions laid down in Community law for consultation are fulfilled in the particular case.

Name	Provisions	Text or translation (excerpts; notes are given in italics)
		7. Without prejudice to paragraph 6, the European Data Protection Supervisor may authorise a transfer or a set of transfers of personal data to a third country or international organisation which does not ensure an adequate level of protection within the meaning of paragraphs 1 and 2, where the controller adduces adequate safeguards with respect to the protection of the privacy and fundamental rights and freedoms of individuals and as regards the exercise of the corresponding rights; such safeguards may in particular result from appropriate contractual clauses. 8. The Community institutions and bodies shall inform the European Data Protection Supervisor of categories of cases where they have applied paragraphs 6 and 7.
	Council Framework Decision 2008/977/JHA of 27 November 2008 on the protection of personal data processed in the framework of police and judicial cooperation in criminal matters, [2008] OJ L350/60	**Article 13 Transfer to competent authorities in third States or to international bodies** 1. Member States shall provide that personal data transmitted or made available by the competent authority of another Member State may be transferred to third States or international bodies, only if: (a) it is necessary for the prevention, investigation, detection or prosecution of criminal offences or the execution of criminal penalties; (b) the receiving authority in the third State or receiving international body is responsible for the prevention, investigation, detection or prosecution of criminal offences or the execution of criminal penalties; (c) the Member State from which the data were obtained has given its consent to transfer in compliance with its national law; and (d) the third State or international body concerned ensures an adequate level of protection for the intended data processing. 2. Transfer without prior consent in accordance with paragraph 1(c) shall be permitted only if transfer of the data is essential for the prevention of an immediate and serious threat to public security of a Member State or a third State or to essential interests of a Member State and the prior consent cannot be obtained in good time. The authority responsible for giving consent shall be informed without delay.

Name	Provisions	Text or translation (excerpts; notes are given in italics)
		3. By way of derogation from paragraph 1(d), personal data may be transferred if: (a) the national law of the Member State transferring the data so provides because of: (i) legitimate specific interests of the data subject; or (ii) legitimate prevailing interests, especially important public interests; or (b) the third State or receiving international body provides safeguards which are deemed adequate by the Member State concerned according to its national law. 4. The adequacy of the level of protection referred to in paragraph 1(d) shall be assessed in the light of all the circumstances surrounding a data transfer operation or a set of data transfer operations. Particular consideration shall be given to the nature of the data, the purpose and duration of the proposed processing operation or operations, the State of origin and the State or international body of final destination of the data, the rules of law, both general and sectoral, in force in the third State or international body in question and the professional rules and security measures which apply.
	Excerpts from Proposal for a Regulation of the European Parliament and of the Council on the protection of individuals with regard to the processing of personal data and on the free movement of such data (General Data Protection Regulation), COM(2012) 11 final, proposed by the European Commission on 25 January 2012	**Article 40 General principle for transfers** Any transfer of personal data which are undergoing processing or are intended for processing after transfer to a third country or to an international organisation may only take place if, subject to the other provisions of this Regulation, the conditions laid down in this Chapter are complied with by the controller and processor, including for onward transfers of personal data from the third country or an international organisation to another third country or to another international organisation. **Article 41 Transfers with an adequacy decision** 1. A transfer may take place where the Commission has decided that the third country, or a territory or a processing sector within that third country, or the international organisation in question ensures an adequate level of protection. Such transfer shall not require any further authorisation. 2. When assessing the adequacy of the level of protection, the Commission shall give consideration to the following elements: (a) the rule of law, relevant legislation in force, both general and sectoral, including

Name	Provisions	Text or translation (excerpts; notes are given in italics)
		concerning public security, defence, national security and criminal law, the professional rules and security measures which are complied with in that country or by that international organisation, as well as effective and enforceable rights including effective administrative and judicial redress for data subjects, in particular for those data subjects residing in the Union whose personal data are being transferred; (b) the existence and effective functioning of one or more independent supervisory authorities in the third country or international organisation in question responsible for ensuring compliance with the data protection rules, for assisting and advising the data subjects in exercising their rights and for co-operation with the supervisory authorities of the Union and of Member States; and (c) the international commitments the third country or international organisation in question has entered into. 3. The Commission may decide that a third country, or a territory or a processing sector within that third country, or an international organisation ensures an adequate level of protection within the meaning of paragraph 2. Those implementing acts shall be adopted in accordance with the examination procedure referred to in Article 87(2). 4. The implementing act shall specify its geographical and sectoral application, and, where applicable, identify the supervisory authority mentioned in point (b) of paragraph 2. 5. The Commission may decide that a third country, or a territory or a processing sector within that third country, or an international organisation does not ensure an adequate level of protection within the meaning of paragraph 2 of this Article, in particular in cases where the relevant legislation, both general and sectoral, in force in the third country or international organisation, does not guarantee effective and enforceable rights including effective administrative and judicial redress for data subjects, in particular for those data subjects residing in the Union whose personal data are being transferred. Those implementing acts shall be adopted in accordance with the examination

Name	Provisions	Text or translation (excerpts; notes are given in italics)
		procedure referred to in Article 87(2), or, in cases of extreme urgency for individuals with respect to their right to personal data protection, in accordance with the procedure referred to in Article 87(3).

6. Where the Commission decides pursuant to paragraph 5, any transfer of personal data to the third country, or a territory or a processing sector within that third country, or the international organisation in question shall be prohibited, without prejudice to Articles 42 to 44. At the appropriate time, the Commission shall enter into consultations with the third country or international organisation with a view to remedying the situation resulting from the Decision made pursuant to paragraph 5 of this Article.

7. The Commission shall publish in the Official Journal of the European Union a list of those third countries, territories and processing sectors within a third country and international organisations where it has decided that an adequate level of protection is or is not ensured.

8. Decisions adopted by the Commission on the basis of Article 25(6) or Article 26(4) of Directive 95/46/EC shall remain in force, until amended, replaced or repealed by the Commission.

Article 42 Transfers by way of appropriate safeguards

1. Where the Commission has taken no decision pursuant to Article 41, a controller or processor may transfer personal data to a third country or an international organisation only if the controller or processor has adduced appropriate safeguards with respect to the protection of personal data in a legally binding instrument.

2. The appropriate safeguards referred to in paragraph 1 shall be provided for, in particular, by:
   (a) binding corporate rules in accordance with Article 43; or
   (b) standard data protection clauses adopted by the Commission. Those implementing acts shall be adopted in accordance with the examination procedure referred to in Article 87(2); or

Name	Provisions	Text or translation (excerpts; notes are given in italics)
		(c) standard data protection clauses adopted by a supervisory authority in accordance with the consistency mechanism referred to in Article 57 when declared generally valid by the Commission pursuant to point (b) of Article 62(1); or (d) contractual clauses between the controller or processor and the recipient of the data authorised by a supervisory authority in accordance with paragraph 4. 3. A transfer based on standard data protection clauses or binding corporate rules as referred to in points (a), (b) or (c) of paragraph 2 shall not require any further authorisation. 4. Where a transfer is based on contractual clauses as referred to in point (d) of paragraph 2 of this Article the controller or processor shall obtain prior authorisation of the contractual clauses according to point (a) of Article 34(1) from the supervisory authority. If the transfer is related to processing activities which concern data subjects in another Member State or other Member States, or substantially affect the free movement of personal data within the Union, the supervisory authority shall apply the consistency mechanism referred to in Article 57. 5. Where the appropriate safeguards with respect to the protection of personal data are not provided for in a legally binding instrument, the controller or processor shall obtain prior authorisation for the transfer, or a set of transfers, or for provisions to be inserted into administrative arrangements providing the basis for such transfer. Such authorisation by the supervisory authority shall be in accordance with point (a) of Article 34(1). If the transfer is related to processing activities which concern data subjects in another Member State or other Member States, or substantially affect the free movement of personal data within the Union, the supervisory authority shall apply the consistency mechanism referred to in Article 57. Authorisations by a supervisory authority on the basis of Article 26(2) of Directive 95/46/EC shall remain valid, until amended, replaced or repealed by that supervisory authority.

Name	Provisions	Text or translation (excerpts; notes are given in italics)
		Article 43 Transfers by way of binding corporate rules

1. A supervisory authority shall in accordance with the consistency mechanism set out in Article 58 approve binding corporate rules, provided that they:
   - (a) are legally binding and apply to and are enforced by every member within the controller's or processor's group of undertakings, and include their employees;
   - (b) expressly confer enforceable rights on data subjects;
   - (c) fulfil the requirements laid down in paragraph 2.
2. The binding corporate rules shall at least specify:
   - (a) the structure and contact details of the group of undertakings and its members;
   - (b) the data transfers or set of transfers, including the categories of personal data, the type of processing and its purposes, the type of data subjects affected and the identification of the third country or countries in question;
   - (c) their legally binding nature, both internally and externally;
   - (d) the general data protection principles, in particular purpose limitation, data quality, legal basis for the processing, processing of sensitive personal data; measures to ensure data security; and the requirements for onward transfers to organisations which are not bound by the policies;
   - (e) the rights of data subjects and the means to exercise these rights, including the right not to be subject to a measure based on profiling in accordance with Article 20, the right to lodge a complaint before the competent supervisory authority and before the competent courts of the Member States in accordance with Article 75, and to obtain redress and, where appropriate, compensation for a breach of the binding corporate rules;
   - (f) the acceptance by the controller or processor established on the territory of a Member State of liability for any breaches of the binding corporate rules by any member of the group of undertakings not established in the Union; the controller

Name	Provisions	Text or translation (excerpts; notes are given in italics)
		or the processor may only be exempted from this liability, in whole or in part, if he proves that that member is not responsible for the event giving rise to the damage; (g) how the information on the binding corporate rules, in particular on the provisions referred to in points (d), (e) and (f) of this paragraph is provided to the data subjects in accordance with Article 11; (h) the tasks of the data protection officer designated in accordance with Article 35, including monitoring within the group of undertakings the compliance with the binding corporate rules, as well as monitoring the training and complaint handling; (i) the mechanisms within the group of undertakings aiming at ensuring the verification of compliance with the binding corporate rules; (j) the mechanisms for reporting and recording changes to the policies and reporting these changes to the supervisory authority; (k) the co-operation mechanism with the supervisory authority to ensure compliance by any member of the group of undertakings, in particular by making available to the supervisory authority the results of the verifications of the measures referred to in point (i) of this paragraph. 3. The Commission shall be empowered to adopt delegated acts in accordance with Article 86 for the purpose of further specifying the criteria and requirements for binding corporate rules within the meaning of this Article, in particular as regards the criteria for their approval, the application of points (b), (d), (e) and (f) of paragraph 2 to binding corporate rules adhered to by processors and on further necessary requirements to ensure the protection of personal data of the data subjects concerned. 4. The Commission may specify the format and procedures for the exchange of information by electronic means between controllers, processors and supervisory authorities for binding corporate rules within the meaning of this Article. Those implementing acts shall be adopted in accordance with the examination procedure set out in Article 87(2).

Name	Provisions	Text or translation (excerpts; notes are given in italics)

Article 44 Derogations

1. In the absence of an adequacy decision pursuant to Article 41 or of appropriate safeguards pursuant to Article 42, a transfer or a set of transfers of personal data to a third country or an international organisation may take place only on condition that:

   (a) the data subject has consented to the proposed transfer, after having been informed of the risks of such transfers due to the absence of an adequacy decision and appropriate safeguards; or

   (b) the transfer is necessary for the performance of a contract between the data subject and the controller or the implementation of pre-contractual measures taken at the data subject's request; or

   (c) the transfer is necessary for the conclusion or performance of a contract concluded in the interest of the data subject between the controller and another natural or legal person; or

   (d) the transfer is necessary for important grounds of public interest; or

   (e) the transfer is necessary for the establishment, exercise or defence of legal claims; or

   (f) the transfer is necessary in order to protect the vital interests of the data subject or of another person, where the data subject is physically or legally incapable of giving consent; or

   (g) the transfer is made from a register which according to Union or Member State law is intended to provide information to the public and which is open to consultation either by the public in general or by any person who can demonstrate legitimate interest, to the extent that the conditions laid down in Union or Member State law for consultation are fulfilled in the particular case; or

   (h) the transfer is necessary for the purposes of the legitimate interests pursued by the controller or the processor, which cannot be qualified as frequent or massive, and where the controller or processor has assessed all the circumstances surrounding the data transfer operation or the set of data transfer

Name	Provisions	Text or translation (excerpts; notes are given in italics)
		operations and based on this assessment adduced appropriate safeguards with respect to the protection of personal data, where necessary.

2. A transfer pursuant to point (g) of paragraph 1 shall not involve the entirety of the personal data or entire categories of the personal data contained in the register. When the register is intended for consultation by persons having a legitimate interest, the transfer shall be made only at the request of those persons or if they are to be the recipients.

3. Where the processing is based on point (h) of paragraph 1, the controller or processor shall give particular consideration to the nature of the data, the purpose and duration of the proposed processing operation or operations, as well as the situation in the country of origin, the third country and the country of final destination, and adduced appropriate safeguards with respect to the protection of personal data, where necessary.

4. Points (b), (c) and (h) of paragraph 1 shall not apply to activities carried out by public authorities in the exercise of their public powers.

5. The public interest referred to in point (d) of paragraph 1 must be recognised in Union law or in the law of the Member State to which the controller is subject.

6. The controller or processor shall document the assessment as well as the appropriate safeguards adduced referred to in point (h) of paragraph 1 of this Article in the documentation referred to in Article 28 and shall inform the supervisory authority of the transfer.

7. The Commission shall be empowered to adopt delegated acts in accordance with Article 86 for the purpose of further specifying 'important grounds of public interest' within the meaning of point (d) of paragraph 1 as well as the criteria and requirements for appropriate safeguards referred to in point (h) of paragraph 1.

Article 45

International co-operation for the protection of personal data

1. In relation to third countries and international organisations, the Commission and supervisory authorities shall take appropriate steps to:
   (a) develop effective international co-operation mechanisms to facilitate the enforcement

Name	Provisions	Text or translation (excerpts; notes are given in italics)
		of legislation for the protection of personal data; (b) provide international mutual assistance in the enforcement of legislation for the protection of personal data, including through notification, complaint referral, investigative assistance and information exchange, subject to appropriate safeguards for the protection of personal data and other fundamental rights and freedoms; (c) engage relevant stakeholders in discussion and activities aimed at furthering international co-operation in the enforcement of legislation for the protection of personal data; (d) promote the exchange and documentation of personal data protection legislation and practice. 2. For the purposes of paragraph 1, the Commission shall take appropriate steps to advance the relationship with third countries or international organisations, and in particular their supervisory authorities, where the Commission has decided that they ensure an adequate level of protection within the meaning of Article 41(3).
	Proposal for a Directive of the European Parliament and of the Council on the protection of individuals with regard to the processing of personal data by competent authorities for the purposes of prevention, investigation, detection or prosecution of criminal offences or the execution of criminal penalties, and the free movement of such data, COM(2012) 10/3, proposed by the European Commission on 25 January 2012	**Article 33** General principles for transfers of personal data Member States shall provide that any transfer of personal data by competent authorities that is undergoing processing or is intended for processing after transfer to a third country, or to an international organisation, including further onward transfer to another third country or international organisation, may take place only if: (a) the transfer is necessary for the prevention, investigation, detection or prosecution of criminal offences or the execution of criminal penalties; and (b) the conditions laid down in this Chapter are complied with by the controller and processor. **Article 34** Transfers with an adequacy decision 1. Member States shall provide that a transfer of personal data to a third country or an international organisation may take place where the Commission has decided in accordance with Article 41 of Regulation (EU) ..../2012 or in

Appendix

Name	Provisions	Text or translation (excerpts; notes are given in italics)
		accordance with paragraph 3 of this Article that the third country or a territory or a processing sector within that third country, or the international organisation in question ensures an adequate level of protection. Such transfer shall not require any further authorisation.
		2. Where no decision adopted in accordance with Article 41 of Regulation (EU) .... /2012 exists, the Commission shall assess the adequacy of the level of protection, giving consideration to the following elements:
		(a) the rule of law, relevant legislation in force, both general and sectoral, including concerning public security, defence, national security and criminal law as well as the security measures which are complied with in that country or by that international organisation; as well as effective and enforceable rights including effective administrative and judicial redress for data subjects, in particular for those data subjects residing in the Union whose personal data are being transferred;
		(b) the existence and effective functioning of one or more independent supervisory authorities in the third country or international organisation in question responsible for ensuring compliance with the data protection rules, for assisting and advising the data subject in exercising their rights and for co-operation with the supervisory authorities of the Union and of Member States; and
		(c) the international commitments the third country or international organisation in question has entered into.
		3. The Commission may decide, within the scope of this Directive, that a third country or a territory or a processing sector within that third country or an international organisation ensures an adequate level of protection within the meaning of paragraph 2. Those implementing acts shall be adopted in accordance with the examination procedure referred to in Article 57(2).
		4. The implementing act shall specify its geographical and sectoral application, and, where applicable, identify the supervisory authority mentioned in point (b) of paragraph 2.

Name	Provisions	Text or translation (excerpts; notes are given in italics)

5. The Commission may decide within the scope of this Directive that a third country or a territory or a processing sector within that third country or an international organisation does not ensure an adequate level of protection within the meaning of paragraph 2, in particular in cases where the relevant legislation, both general and sectoral, in force in the third country or international organisation, does not guarantee effective and enforceable rights including effective administrative and judicial redress for data subjects, in particular for those data subjects whose personal data are being transferred. Those implementing acts shall be adopted in accordance with the examination procedure referred to in Article 57(2), or, in cases of extreme urgency for individuals with respect to their right to personal data protection, in accordance with the procedure referred to in Article 57(3).

6. Member States shall ensure that where the Commission decides pursuant to paragraph 5, that any transfer of personal data to the third country or a territory or a processing sector within that third country, or the international organisation in question shall be prohibited, this decision shall be without prejudice to transfers under Article 35(1) or in accordance with Article 36. At the appropriate time, the Commission shall enter into consultations with the third country or international organisation with a view to remedying the situation resulting from the Decision made pursuant to paragraph 5 of this Article.

7. The Commission shall publish in the Official Journal of the European Union a list of those third countries, territories and processing sectors within a third country or an international organisation where it has decided that an adequate level of protection is or is not ensured.

8. The Commission shall monitor the application of the implementing acts referred to in paragraphs 3 and 5.

Article 35

Transfers by way of appropriate safeguards

1. Where the Commission has taken no decision pursuant to Article 34, Member States shall provide that a transfer of personal data to a

Name	Provisions	Text or translation (excerpts; notes are given in italics)
		recipient in a third country or an international organisation may take place where: (a) appropriate safeguards with respect to the protection of personal data have been adduced in a legally binding instrument; or (b) the controller or processor has assessed all the circumstances surrounding the transfer of personal data and concludes that appropriate safeguards exist with respect to the protection of personal data. 1. The decision for transfers under paragraph 1 (b) must be made by duly authorised staff. These transfers must be documented and the documentation must be made available to the supervisory authority on request.

Article 36

Derogations

By way of derogation from Articles 34 and 35, Member States shall provide that a transfer of personal data to a third country or an international organisation may take place only on condition that: (a) the transfer is necessary in order to protect the vital interests of the data subject or another person; or (b) the transfer is necessary to safeguard legitimate interests of the data subject where the law of the Member State transferring the personal data so provides; or (c) the transfer of the data is essential for the prevention of an immediate and serious threat to public security of a Member State or a third country; or (d) the transfer is necessary in individual cases for the purposes of prevention, investigation, detection or prosecution of criminal offences or the execution of criminal penalties; or (e) the transfer is necessary in individual cases for the establishment, exercise or defence of legal claims relating to the prevention, investigation, detection or prosecution of a specific criminal offence or the execution of a specific criminal penalty.

Article 37

Specific conditions for the transfer of personal data

Member States shall provide that the controller informs the recipient of the personal data of any processing restrictions and takes all reasonable steps to ensure that these restrictions are met.

Article 38

International co-operation for the protection of personal data

Name	Provisions	Text or translation (excerpts; notes are given in italics)
		1. In relation to third countries and international organisations, the Commission and Member States shall take appropriate steps to: (a) develop effective international co-operation mechanisms to facilitate the enforcement of legislation for the protection of personal data; (b) provide international mutual assistance in the enforcement of legislation for the protection of personal data, including through notification, complaint referral, investigative assistance and information exchange, subject to appropriate safeguards for the protection of personal data and other fundamental rights and freedoms; (c) engage relevant stakeholders in discussion and activities aimed at furthering international co-operation in the enforcement of legislation for the protection of personal data; (d) promote the exchange and documentation of personal data protection legislation and practice. 2. For the purposes of paragraph 1, the Commission shall take appropriate steps to advance the relationship with third countries or with international organisations, and in particular their supervisory authorities, where the Commission has decided that they ensure an adequate level of protection within the meaning of Article 34(3).
OECD	Guidelines on the Protection of Privacy and Transborder Flows of Personal Data (1980)	15. Member countries should take into consideration the implications for other Member countries of domestic processing and re-export of personal data. 16. Member countries should take all reasonable and appropriate steps to ensure that transborder flows of personal data, including transit through a Member country, are uninterrupted and secure. 17. A Member country should refrain from restricting transborder flows of personal data between itself and another Member country except where the latter does not yet substantially observe these Guidelines or where the re-export of such data would circumvent its domestic privacy legislation. A Member country may also impose restrictions in respect of certain categories of personal data for which its

Name	Provisions	Text or translation (excerpts; notes are given in italics)
		domestic privacy legislation includes specific regulations in view of the nature of those data and for which the other Member country provides no equivalent protection. 18. Member countries should avoid developing laws, policies and practices in the name of the protection of privacy and individual liberties, which would create obstacles to transborder flows of personal data that would exceed requirements for such protection.

B. National data protection and privacy legislation in force

Country	Source	Text or translation (excerpts; notes are given in italics)
EU and EEA Member States	EU Data Protection Directive 95/46/EC, Articles 25 and 26 (see under 'European Union' in Section A)	The 27 EU Member States (Austria, Belgium, Bulgaria, Cyprus, Czech Republic, Denmark, Estonia, Finland, France, Germany, Greece, Hungary, Ireland, Italy, Latvia, Lithuania, Luxembourg, Malta, the Netherlands, Poland, Portugal, Romania, Slovakia, Slovenia, Spain, Sweden, and the United Kingdom) and the three EEA Member States (Iceland, Liechtenstein, and Norway) have all adopted the provisions of the EU Data Protection Directive (including restrictions on transborder data flows) and implemented them into their national laws. Croatia is expected to join the EU on 1 July 2013.
	Local or regional data protection laws in many EU Member States regulate transborder data flows	For example: German federal state of Hessen, Hessisches Datenschutzgesetz (applies only to the public law sector and entities subject to public law): § 17: (1) The provisions of this Act apply to the permissibility of transferring personal data within the area of application of the EU Data Protection Directive. (2) A transfer to recipients outside the area listed in para. 1 is only permissible based on this Act if it exclusively accrues to the benefit of the individual or an adequate level of data protection with the recipient is assured. The DPA of Hessen is to be consulted before any decision about adequacy is made. If an adequate level of protection is not assured, then personal data may only be transferred if: 1. the individual has consented; 2. the transfer is necessary for protection of an overriding public interest or to assert, exercise or defend legal claims before a court;

Country	Source	Text or translation (excerpts; notes are given in italics)
		3. the transfer is necessary to protect the vital interests of the individual, or 4. the transfer is conducted from a register designed for the information of the public and that is accessible either by the public or by all persons who can show a legitimate interest in consulting it, insofar as the legal requirements are fulfilled in a particular case. The recipient to whom the data are transferred must be informed that the transferred data may only be processed for purposes that are consistent with those for the fulfilment of which the data are being transferred.
Albania	Law No. 9887 on the Protection of Personal Data (10 March 2008)	**Article 8 International transfer** 1. The international transfer of personal data is done with recipients from states which have an adequate level of personal data protection. The level of personal data protection for a state is established by assessing all circumstances related to processing, nature, purpose and duration of processing, country of origin and final destination, legal provisions and security standards in force in the recipient state. States that have an adequate level of data protection are specified by a decision of the Council of Ministers. 2. International transfer of personal data with a state that does not have an adequate level of personal data protection may be done when: a) it is authorised by international acts ratified by the Republic of Albania and are directly applicable [sic]; b) data subject has given his/her consent for the international transfer; c) it constitutes a contractual obligation concluded between the controller and data subject or a third party to the interest of the data subject; ç) [sic] it is a legal obligation of the controller; d) it is necessary for protecting vital interests of the data subject; dh) [sic] it is necessary or constitutes a legal requirement over an important public interest or for exercising and protecting a legal right; e) transfer is done from a register that is open for consultation and provides information to the general public. 3. Exchange of personal data to the diplomatic representations of foreign governments or international institutions in the Republic of Albania shall be considered an international transfer of data.

Country	Source	Text or translation (excerpts; notes are given in italics)
		Article 9 International transfer of data that need to be authorized 1. In cases other than those provided for in Article 8 herein, the international transfer of personal data with a state that does not have an adequate level of data protection, shall be carried out upon an authorization from the Commissioner. 2. The Commissioner, after making an assessment, may give the authorisation for transfer of personal data to the recipient State by defining conditions and obligations. 3. The Commissioner issues instructions in order to allow certain categories of personal data international transfer to a state that does not have an adequate level of personal data protection. In these cases, the controller is exempted from the authorisation request. 4. The controller shall submit a request for authorisation to the Commissioner prior to the data transfer. In the authorization request, the controller shall guarantee the observance of the interests of the data subject to protection of confidentiality outside the Republic of Albania.
Andorra	Qualified Law 15/2003 of December 18, on the Protection of Personal Data, 2003 ('LQPDP')	**Article 35** International data communications may not take place when the destination country of the data does not establish, in its regulations, a level of protection for personal data equivalent, at least, to that established by this Law.
Angola	Law No. 22/11 on the Protection of Personal Data	**Article 33 Data transfers to countries that ensure an adequate level of protection** 1. The international transfer of data to countries that ensure adequate protection is subject to notification to the Data Protection Agency. 2. It is acknowledged that foreign countries ensure an adequate level of protection when they guarantee, at minimum, a level of protection as the one provided in this law. 3. The Data Protection Agency decides by opinion whether a country ensures adequate protection. 4. The adequacy of the level of data protection appreciated by the Data Protection Agency as a function of all the circumstances surrounding the data transfer or set of data transfers, takes account especially of the nature of the data, the purpose and duration of the intended processing activity, the countries of final destination and their laws, both general and sector-specific, that are in force in the state concerned, including the professional rules and security measures which are complied with in that state.

Country	Source	Text or translation (excerpts; notes are given in italics)

Article 34 Data transfers to countries that do not ensure an adequate level of protection

1. The international transfer of data to a country that does not ensure adequate protection is subject to authorization by the Data Protection Agency, which may be granted only under one of the following circumstances or based on other specific legislation:
   a) if the data subject has given unambiguous, expressed and written consent;
   b) if the international data transfer occurs during the application of international treaties or agreements where the Republic of Angola is a party;
   c) if the data transfer has the sole purpose of responding to or requesting humanitarian aid;
   d) if the data transfer is necessary for the performance of a contract between the data subject and the data controller or the implementation of precontractual measures taken in response to the data subject's request;
   e) if the data transfer is necessary for the conclusion or performance of the contract concluded in the interest of the data subject between the controller and a third party;
   f) if the data transfer is necessary or legally required to protect public interest or for the establishment, exercise or defence of legal claims;
   g) if the data transfer is necessary to protect the vital interests of the data subject or for the purpose of medical prevention, treatment or diagnosis if the data subject is physically or legally incapable of giving consent;
   h) if the data transfer is performed from publicly accessible sources;
   i) if the recipient of the data guarantees to the data exporter by contractual clauses, an adequate level of protection for the data transferred.

2. The Data Protection Agency determines the specific conditions required for the contract referred to in subsection i) above.

3. In the event of international transfers of data between companies of the same group, an adequate level of protection can be achieved by laying down uniform rules on internal privacy and data protection with which compliance is mandatory.

Country	Source	Text or translation (excerpts; notes are given in italics)

Argentina	Personal Data Protection Act (4 October 2000), Act No. 25,326	**Section 12 International transfer**
		
		1. Transfer of personal data of any kind to any country or international or supranational organisation is hereby forbidden if adequate protection is not provided.
		2. This shall not apply in the following events:
		  a) International judicial cooperation;
		  b) Exchange of medical data, if required by the patient's treatment, or by an epidemiological research, provided that it is carried out under the terms of sub Article e) of the previous Article;
		  c) Bank or stock exchange transfers, relating to the respective transactions and in accordance with applicable laws;
		  d) Whenever transfer has been agreed upon within the framework of international treaties signed by the Argentine Republic;
		  e) Whenever the purpose of the transfer is international cooperation among intelligence organisations to fight against organized crime, terrorism and drug-trafficking.

Armenia	Law of the Republic of Armenia on Personal Data (8 October 2002)	**Article 6 Legality of Personal Data Processing**
		
		1. Processing of personal data is considered legal:
		  1) When the personal data is processed with the consent of the data subject;
		  2) When the personal data is processed for the protection of data subject's critical interests when there is no basis to assume that he/she will disagree when being informed about the processing;
		  3) When the processing of the personal data is envisaged by legislation or is necessary for execution of law requirements;
		  4) When processing of the personal data is required for the protection of state and public security from immediate peril.
		2. The consent of the data subject is the absolute voluntary permission to process his/her personal data expressed in any form. The data subject may withdraw his/her consent at any time. The withdrawal of consent has no retrospective [*sic*] effect.
		
		Article 13 Transfer of Personal Data to Foreign Countries
		
		Personal data are transferred to foreign countries according to international treaties of Armenia and on the basis stipulated under Article 6 of this Law.

Country	Source	Text or translation (excerpts; notes are given in italics)

Australia	Privacy Act 1988, as amended on 14 September 2006
	
	NOTE: Amendments to the Privacy Act regarding transborder data flows are being considered by the Australian government, see Parliament of the Commonwealth of Australia, House of Representatives, 'Privacy Amendment (Enhancing Privacy Protection) Bill 2012', Section 16C
		Schedule 3, Principle 9—Transborder data flows
		
		An organisation in Australia or an external Territory may transfer personal information about an individual to someone (other than the organisation or the individual) who is in a foreign country only if:
		
		(a) the organisation reasonably believes that the recipient of the information is subject to a law, binding scheme or contract which effectively upholds principles for fair handling of the information that are substantially similar to the National Privacy Principles; or
		(b) the individual consents to the transfer; or
		(c) the transfer is necessary for the performance of a contract between the individual and the organisation, or for the implementation of pre-contractual measures taken in response to the individual's request; or
		(d) the transfer is necessary for the conclusion or performance of a contract concluded in the interest of the individual between the organisation and a third party; or
		(e) all of the following apply:
		  (i) the transfer is for the benefit of the individual;
		  (ii) it is impracticable to obtain the consent of the individual to that transfer;
		  (iii) if it were practicable to obtain such consent, the individual would be likely to give it; or
		(f) the organisation has taken reasonable steps to ensure that the information which it has transferred will not be held, used or disclosed by the recipient of the information inconsistently with the National Privacy Principles.

Bahamas	Data Protection (Privacy of Personal information) Act (11 April 2003)	**Section 17 Prohibition on the transfer of personal data outside Bahamas** (1) The Commissioner may, subject to the provisions of this section, prohibit the transfer of personal data from The Bahamas to a place outside The Bahamas, in such cases where there is a failure to provide protection either by contract or otherwise equivalent to that provided under this Act. (2) In determining whether to prohibit a transfer of personal data under this section, the Commissioner shall also consider whether the transfer would be likely to cause damage or distress to any person and have regard to the desirability of facilitating international transfers of data. (3) A prohibition under subsection (1) shall be effected by the service of a notice (referred to in this Act as a prohibition notice) on the person proposing to transfer the data concerned..... .

Country	Source	Text or translation (excerpts; notes are given in italics)
Benin	Law No. 2009–09 on the Protection of Personal Data (27 April 2009)	**Article 9** The data controller shall not transfer any personal data abroad unless the foreign country provides a sufficient level of protection for privacy rights and the rights and freedoms of data subjects in relation to the processing of personal data. The level of protection provided by the country shall be assessed in light of data protection laws and security measures that are applied in the foreign country, such as for the purpose, duration, nature, origin and the intended destination of the personal data. … **Article 43(h)** The following processing activities are subject to prior approval and investigation by the DPA due to concerns about rights and freedoms, or circumstances where the nature or the purpose of the processing activity may have an impact on the privacy of the data subject: … (h) Any processing activity involving the transfer of personal data to foreign countries when the process ensures a sufficient level of protection for privacy rights, rights and freedoms of data subjects, in particular standard contractual clauses or binding corporate rules.
Bosnia and Herzegovina	Law on the Protection of Personal Data (27 July 2001)	**Article 8 Data Transfer Abroad** Personal data shall not be transferred from the country to a data controller or data processor abroad, whatever the data medium or the mode of transmission is, unless the conditions of Article 5 of this Law are complied with and provided that the same principles of data protection are obeyed by the foreign controller in respect of the data. *NOTE: The proposed transfer abroad of special categories of data requires prior notification to the DPA (Article 11 (h)).*
Burkina Faso	Law No. 010–2004/An Regarding the Protection of Personal Data (20 April 2004)	**Article 24** The transfer of personal data from the territory of Burkina Faso abroad, which is subject to automatic processing as prescribed by Article 19, is possible only if it complies with the requirements of this Act. However, in exceptional circumstances, a transfer may be authorized by decree with the approval of the DPA.

Country	Source	Text or translation (excerpts; notes are given in italics)
Canada	Federal level: Personal Information Protection and Electronic Documents Act (PIPEDA) and interpretation of it by Canadian courts and regulators	**Personal Information Protection and Electronic Documents Act (PIPEDA), Schedule 1, section 4.1 Principle 1: Accountability** An organization is responsible for personal information under its control and shall designate an individual or individuals who are accountable for the organization's compliance with the following principles … *See Office of the Privacy Commissioner of Canada, 'Guidelines for Processing Personal Data across Borders' (2009) 5, <http://www.priv.gc.ca/information/guide/2009/gl_dab_090127_e.pdf>:* 'PIPEDA does not prohibit organizations in Canada from transferring personal information to an organization in another jurisdiction for processing. However under PIPEDA, organizations are held accountable for the protection of personal information transfers under each individual outsourcing arrangement'.
	Provincial level:	<u>Alberta</u>: Personal Information Protection and Electronic Documents Act, § 40(1)(g)—permits the disclosure of personal information controlled by a public body in response to a subpoena, warrant, or order issued by a court only when the court has 'jurisdiction in Alberta'. <u>British Columbia</u>: Freedom of Information and Protection of Privacy Amendment Act, § 30.1—requires each public body to ensure that 'personal information in its custody or under its control is stored only in Canada and accessed only in Canada'; some exceptions are provided. <u>Nova Scotia</u>: Personal Information International Disclosure Protection Act (2006), § 5(1)—requires that a public body ensure that 'personal information in its custody or under its control … is stored only in Canada and accessed only in Canada'; some exceptions are provided. <u>Québec</u>: 1. Act Respecting Access to Documents Held by Public Bodies and the Protection of Personal Information (2006), § 70.1—requires that before 'releasing personal information outside Québec or entrusting a person or a body outside Québec with the task of holding, using or releasing such information on its behalf', public bodies must ensure that the information receives protection 'equivalent' to that afforded under provincial law. 2. Act Respecting the Protection of Personal Information in the Private Sector, § 17—provides that an organization doing business in Québec that entrusts a person outside Québec with 'holding, using or communicating such information on its behalf' must take 'all reasonable steps to ensure' that the information will be used only for the purposes for which consent was obtained and will not be 'communicated to third parties' without such consent.

Country	Source	Text or translation (excerpts; notes are given in italics)
Colombia	Law 1266 of 2008	**Article 5 Circulation of information** The personal information collected or provided as established by law to the operators, which is part of the managed data bank, may be provided orally, in writing, or placed at the disposal of the following individuals and in the following terms: … (f) …If the receiver of the information were a foreign data bank, the delivery without authorization of the data subject may only be made leaving written evidence of the delivery of the information and upon prior verification by the operator that the laws of the respective country or the receiver provide sufficient guarantees for the protection of the rights of the data subject.
	Law 1581 of 17 October 2012	**Transfer of data to third countries** **Article 26 Prohibition** The transfer of personal data to countries that do not provide an adequate level of data protection is prohibited. It is acknowledged that a country provides an adequate level of data protection when it complies with the relevant standards set by the Industry and Commerce Superintendence, which in no case shall be lower than this law requires for the data recipients. This prohibition shall not apply in the case of: a) Information for which the data subject has given its express and unambiguous consent to the transfer; b) The exchange of medical data, when required for medical reasons related to the data subject or for public health; c) Stock exchange or banking transfers, according to applicable legislation; d) Transfers agreed in the framework of international treaties where the Republic of Colombia is a party, based on the principle of mutuality; e) Transfers necessary for the performance of a contract between the data subject and the controller, or the implementation of precontractual measures as long as there is permission of the data subject; f) Transfers necessary or legally required on public interest grounds or for the establishment, exercise or defense of a right in judicial proceedings; Paragraph 1. For cases not covered by the derogations of this Article, the Industry and Commerce Superintendence shall declare whether compliance concerning the international transfer of personal data is ensured. For this purpose, the Superintendent is empowered to require information and implement the measures designed to establish compliance with the budget ensuring the viability of the operation.

Country	Source	Text or translation (excerpts; notes are given in italics)
		Paragraph 2. The provisions of this Article shall apply to all personal data, including those covered by Law 1266 of 2008.
Costa Rica	Law No. 8968/2011 on the Protection of Personal Data	**Article 14 Transfer of personal data** The controller of a public or private database may only transfer data containing in them when the data subject has explicitly and validly provided its consent and the transfer was made without violating the principles and rights under this law. **Article 31 Serious Violations** Serious violations for the purposes of this Act are considered: … f) The transfer of personal information of Costa Ricans or foreigners residing in the country to databases in third countries without the consent of the data subjects.
Croatia	Act on Personal Data Protection (12 June 2003), No. 1364–2003 (as amended by Act on Amendments to the Personal Data Protection Act, No. 2616–2006) *NOTE: Croatia is expected to join the EU on 1 July 2013, in which case EU law will apply*	**Article 13 Personal data transfer abroad from the Republic of Croatia** Personal data filing systems or personal data contained in personal data filing systems may be transferred abroad from the Republic of Croatia for further processing only if the state or the international organisation the personal data is being transferred to have adequately regulated the legal protection of personal data and have ensured an adequate level of protection. Prior to transferring personal data abroad from the Republic of Croatia, the personal data filing system controller shall, in case of reasonable doubt regarding the existence of adequate personal data protection system or whether an adequate level of protection is in place, obtain an opinion regarding this issue from the Personal Data Protection Agency. The adequate level of protection which is provided by the state or by an international organisation shall be evaluated in terms of the circumstances connected with the presentation of personal data, and in particular in terms of the type of the data concerned, the purpose and duration of the processing thereof, the country to which the data refer, the legal provisions in force in the country in question, and the professional rules and security measures applicable in the country concerned. By way of derogation from paragraph 1 of this Article, personal data forming part of personal data filing systems may be taken out of the Republic of Croatia to states or to international organisations which do not provide for an adequate level of protection within

Country	Source	Text or translation (excerpts; notes are given in italics)
		the meaning of paragraph 2 of this Article only in the following cases:

the meaning of paragraph 2 of this Article only in the following cases:
- if the data subject consents to the transfer of the personal data,
- if the transfer is essential to protect the life or the physical well-being of the data subject, or
- if the personal data filing system controller provides sufficient guarantees regarding the protection of privacy and the fundamental rights and freedoms of individuals, which might arise from the contractual provisions, for which the Personal Data Protection Agency establishes that they are appropriate in accordance with the valid regulations which regulate the protection of personal data.

Article 34 Notification requirement

If during supervision the Agency determines that legal provisions establishing personal data processing have been violated, it shall be entitled to warn or notify the personal data filing system controller about the irregularities in the personal data processing and issue a decision prohibiting the transfer of personal data abroad from the Republic of Croatia ...

Country	Source
Dubai International Financial Centre (DIFC, a self-legislating free financial zone administered by the government of Dubai)	DIFC Data Protection Law 2007, Law no. 1 of 2007 (applicable only to the Dubai International Financial Centre)

Article 11 Transfers out of the DIFC—Adequate Level of Protection

(1) A transfer of Personal Data to a Recipient located in a jurisdiction outside the DIFC may take place only if:
  (a) an adequate level of protection for that Personal Data is ensured by laws and regulations that are applicable to the Recipient, as set out in Article 11(2); or
  (b) in accordance with Article 12.
(2) For the purposes of Article 11(1), a jurisdiction has an adequate level of protection for that Personal Data if that jurisdiction is listed as an acceptable jurisdiction under the Regulations or with the written approval of the Commissioner of Data Protection.

Article 12 Transfers out of the DIFC in the Absence of an Adequate Level of Protection

(1) A transfer or a set of transfers of Personal Data to a Recipient which is not subject to laws and regulations which ensure an adequate level of protection within the meaning of Article 11 may take place on condition that:
  (a) the Commissioner of Data Protection or his delegate has granted a permit or written authorisation for the transfer or the set of transfers and the Data Controller applies

Country	Source	Text or translation (excerpts; notes are given in italics)
		adequate safeguards with respect to the protection of this Personal Data;
		(b) the Data Subject has given his written consent to the proposed transfer;
		(c) the transfer is necessary for the performance of a contract between the Data Subject and the Data Controller or the implementation of pre-contractual measures taken in response to the Data Subject's request;
		(d) the transfer is necessary for the conclusion or performance of a contract concluded in the interest of the Data Subject between the Data Controller and a Third Party;
		(e) the transfer is necessary or legally required on grounds important in the interests of the DIFC, or for the establishment, exercise or defence of legal claims;
		(f) the transfer is necessary in order to protect the vital interests of the Data;
		(g) the transfer is made from a register which according to laws or regulations is intended to provide information to the public and which is open to consultation either by the public in general or by any person who can demonstrate legitimate interest, to the extent that the conditions laid down in law for consultation are fulfilled in the particular case;
		(h) the transfer is necessary for compliance with any legal obligation to which the Data Controller is subject or the transfer is made at the request of a regulator, police or other government agency;
		(i) the transfer is necessary to uphold the legitimate interests of the Data Controller recognised in the international financial markets, provided that such is pursued in accordance with international financial standards and except where such interests are overridden by legitimate interests of the Data Subject relating to the Data Subject's particular situation; or
		(j) the transfer is necessary to comply with any regulatory requirements, auditing, accounting, anti-money laundering or counter terrorist financing obligations or the prevention or detection of any crime that apply to a Data Controller.

Country	Source	Text or translation (excerpts; notes are given in italics)
Faroe Islands	Act on Processing of Personal Data, Act No. 73 of 8 May 2001, as amended by Act No. 24 of 17 May 2004	**Article 16 Transfer of personal data to foreign countries** Transfer to a foreign country of personal data may take place only if the foreign country in question ensures an adequate level of protection. The adequacy of the level of protection afforded by a foreign country shall be assessed in the light of all the circumstances surrounding a data transfer operation, the purpose and duration of the processing operation, the nature of the data, the rules of law in force in the foreign country in question and the professional rules and security measures which are complied with in that country. Permission is required from the Data Protection Agency cf. Article 35, Part 6. Part 2. In spite of Part 1, the Minister of Justice may, after having received a statement from the Data Protection Agency, decide provisions for, to [*sic*] which foreign countries personal data can be transferred without permission from the Data Protection Agency. **Article 17 Exceptions** The Data Protection Agency may authorize a transfer of personal data to foreign countries, cf. Article 35, Part 6 even if the foreign country in question do [*sic*] not ensures an adequate level of protection if: 1) the data subject has given his explicit consent to the transfer, 2) the transfer is required by international conventions or because of membership in an international community, 3) the transfer is necessary for the performance of a contract with the data subject or to do what is required, to implement pre-contractual measures taken in response to the data subject's request, 4) the transfer is necessary for the conclusion or performance of a contract concluded in the interest of the data subject with a third party, 5) the transfer is necessary in order to protect the vital interests of the data subject, 6) the transfer is necessary in order to identify, submit in to force or protect a legal claim, 7) the transfer is necessary or legally required on important public interest grounds, or 8) Statutory authority exists when data is required from a public register. Part 2. The Data Protection Agency may authorise a transfer of personal data to a foreign country, which does not comply with the provisions laid down in Part 1, where the controller adduces adequate safeguards with respect to the protection of the rights of the data subject. More detailed conditions may be laid down for the transfer....

Country	Source	Text or translation (excerpts; notes are given in italics)
Gabon	Law No. 001/2011 (25 September 2011) on the Protection of Personal Data	**Transfer of personal data** **Article 94** The data controller may only transfer personal data to another State if that State ensures an adequate level of protection of privacy, and the freedoms and fundamental rights of individuals with regard to the processing of personal data. The adequacy of the level of protection provided by a State is notably assessed taking into account the provisions in force in that State, the implemented security measures, the characteristics of the processing, such as its purpose and duration, as well as the nature, the origin and the destination of the processed data. The National Commission for the Protection of Personal Data guarantees and publishes a list of States providing an adequate level of protection with respect to any transfer of personal data. **Article 95** The data controller may also transfer personal data to a State not meeting the requirements of section 99 below if the data subject has expressly consented to the transfer or the transfer is necessary for one of the following purposes: – The protection of the data subject's life; – The protection of public interest; – To comply with obligations ensuring the establishment, exercise or defence of legal claims; – For consulting, under legitimate grounds, a register which, under law or regulations is intended to provide information to the public and is open to consultation by any person who can demonstrate legitimate interest; – The performance of a contract between the data controller and the data subject, or the implementation of pre-contractual measures taken in response to the data subject's request; – The conclusion or performance of a current or a future contract between the data controller and a third party concluded in the interest of the data subject. An exception to the prohibition mentioned in Article 94 above can be made by decision of the National Commission for the Protection of Personal Data or, in case of the processing mentioned in Article 55 above, by a decree following a reasoned and public opinion of the Commission, when the processing ensures a sufficient level of the protection of privacy as well as the freedoms and fundamental rights of individuals, particularly on the basis of contractual clauses or internal regulations pertaining to the processing. The Commission shall inform

Country	Source	Text or translation (excerpts; notes are given in italics)
		the recipient States about any decisions authorizing the transfer of personal data that it takes under the preceding paragraph.

Article 96

If the National Commission for the Protection of Personal Data has found that a State does not ensure an adequate level of protection with regard to a transfer of personal data, it shall issue a note prohibiting the data transfer. For this purpose, it shall promptly inform the official authorities and the public. Upon receipt by the Commission of a notification filed under section 52 or 53 above, demonstrating that personal data are being transferred to that State, the Commission shall deliver a note and order the data controller to suspend or cancel the data transfer, depending on the case. If the Commission later observes that the State to which the transfer is intended now ensures an adequate level of protection, it notifies the data controller of the end of the suspension of the transfer.

Ghana — Data Protection Act 2012

Section 18

(2) A data controller or processor shall in respect of foreign data subjects ensure that personal data is processed in compliance with data protection legislation of the foreign jurisdiction of that subject where personal data originating from that jurisdiction is sent to this country for processing.

Section 47

(1) An application for registration as a data controller shall be made in writing to the Commission and the applicant shall furnish the following particulars:

...

(g) the name or description of the country to which the applicant may transfer the data ...

Guernsey — Data Protection (Bailiwick of Guernsey) Law (2001), as amended by the Data Protection (Bailiwick of Guernsey) (Amendment) Ordinance (2010)

8th principle Transfer of data abroad

Personal data shall not be transferred to a country or territory outside the Bailiwick unless that country or territory ensures an adequate level of protection for the rights and freedoms of data subjects in relation to the processing of personal data.

...

Section 13

An adequate level of protection is one which is adequate in all the circumstances of the case, having regard in particular to:

(a) the nature of the personal data;
(b) the country or territory of origin of the information contained in the data;

Country	Source	Text or translation (excerpts; notes are given in italics)
		(c) the country or territory of final destination of that information; (d) the purposes for which and period during which the data are intended to be processed; (e) the law in force in the country or territory in question; (f) the international obligations of that country or territory; (g) any relevant codes of conduct or other rules which are enforceable in that country or territory (whether generally or by arrangement in particular cases); and (h) any security measures taken in respect of the data in that country or territory. **Section 14** The eighth principle does not apply to a transfer falling within any paragraph of Schedule 4, except in such circumstances and to such extent as the Committee may by Order provide.
India	Information Technology (Reasonable security practices and procedures and sensitive personal data or information) Rules (2011)	**Rule 7 Transfer of information** A corporate body or any person on its behalf may transfer sensitive personal data or information to any other corporate body or person located in India or in another country that ensures the same level of data protection as the one that the corporate body adheres to, as provided under these Rules. The transfer is allowed only if it is necessary for the performance of a lawful contract between the corporate body or a person on its behalf and the provider of information or where the data subject has consented to the data transfer.
Isle of Man	Data Protection Act (2002)	**8th Principle** Personal data shall not be transferred to a country or territory outside the Island unless that country or territory ensures an adequate level of protection for the rights and freedoms of data subjects in relation to the processing of personal data. **Section 21** An adequate level of protection is one which is adequate in all the circumstances of the case, having regard in particular to – (a) the nature of the personal data, (b) the country or territory of origin of the information contained in the data, (c) the country or territory of final destination of that information, (d) the purposes for which and period during which the data are intended to be processed,

Country	Source	Text or translation (excerpts; notes are given in italics)
		(e) the law in force in the country or territory in question, (f) the international obligations of that country or territory, (g) any relevant codes of conduct or other rules which are enforceable in that country or territory (whether generally or by arrangement in particular cases), and (h) any security measures taken in respect of the data in that country or territory.
Israel	Protection of Privacy Law, 5741–1981 (2001)	**Article 36(2)** The Minister of Justice is charged with the implementation of this Law and may, with the approval of the Constitution, Law and Justice Committee of the Knesset, make regulations as to any matter relating to its implementation, and inter alia— … (2) conditions of transmitting information to or from databases outside the boundaries of the State.
	Privacy Protection (Transfer of Data to Databases Abroad) Regulations, 5761–2001—implementing Article 36(2) of the Protection of Privacy Law, 5741–1981	<u>Limitation on transfer of data</u> 1. A person shall not transfer, nor shall he enable, the transfer abroad of data from databases in Israel, unless the law of the country to which the data is transferred ensures a level of protection no lesser, mutatis mutandis, than the level of protection of data provided for by Israeli Law, and the following principles shall apply: (1) Data shall be gathered and processed in a legal and fair manner; (2) Date shall be held, used and delivered only for the purpose for which it was received; (3) Data gathered shall be accurate and up to date; (4) The right of inspection is reserved to the data subject; (5) The obligation to take adequate security measures to protect data in databases is mandatory. <u>Conditions to the transfer of data abroad</u> 2. Notwithstanding Regulation 1, a database owner may transfer data or enable the transfer of data from his database in Israel abroad, provided that one of the following conditions is met: (1) The data subject has consented to the transfer; (2) The consent of the data subject cannot be obtained and the transfer is vital to the protection of his health or physical wellbeing;

Country	Source	Text or translation (excerpts; notes are given in italics)
		(3) The data is transferred to a corporation under the control of the owner of the database from which the data is transferred, and he has guaranteed the protection of privacy after the transfer; In this Paragraph, the meaning of 'control' is as defined in the Securities Law, 5728–1968;
		(4) The data is transferred to a person bound by an agreement with the owner of the database from which the data is transferred, to comply with the conditions for the ownership and use of the data applying to a database in Israel, mutatis mutandis;
		(5) The data was made available to the public or was opened for public inspection by legal authority;
		(6) The transfer of data is vital to public safety or security;
		(7) The transfer of data is mandatory according to Israeli Law;
		(8) The data is transferred to a database in a country—
		(1) which is a Party to the European Convention for the Protection of Individuals with Regard to Automatic Processing of Sensitive Data;
		(2) which receives data from Member States of the European Community, under the same terms of acceptance;
		(3) in relation to which the Registrar of Databases announced, in an announcement published in the Official Gazette ('Reshumot'), that it has an authority for the protection of privacy, after reaching an arrangement for cooperation with the said authority.
		Guarantee to ensure privacy
		3. When transferring data according to Regulation 1 or Regulation 2, the owner of the database shall ensure, in a written guarantee by the recipient of the data, that recipient of the data is taking adequate measures to ensure the privacy of the data subjects....
Jersey	Data Protection (Jersey) Law, 2005 (L.2/2005)	**8th Principle** Personal data shall not be transferred to a country or territory outside the European Economic Area unless that country or territory ensures an adequate level of protection for the rights and freedoms of data subjects in relation to the processing of personal data. ...

Country	Source	Text or translation (excerpts; notes are given in italics)
		Section 13 Eighth principle: what is adequate protection in foreign country

For the purposes of the eighth principle, an adequate level of protection is one that is adequate in all the circumstances of the case, having regard in particular to –

(a) the nature of the personal data;

(b) the country or territory of origin of the information contained in the data;

(c) the country or territory of final destination of that information;

(d) the purposes for which and period during which the data are intended to be processed;

(e) the law in force in the country or territory in question;

(f) the international obligations of that country or territory;

(g) any relevant codes of conduct or other rules that are enforceable in that country or territory (whether generally or by arrangement in particular cases); and

(h) any security measures taken in respect of the data in that country or territory.

Section 14 Exceptions to eighth principle

The eighth principle does not apply to a transfer falling within any of paragraphs 1–9 of Schedule 4, except in such circumstances and to such extent as may be prescribed by Regulations …

Macau (Macau Special Administrative Region (MSAR) of the People's Republic of China)

Personal Data Protection Act (Act 8/2005)

Article 19 Principles

1. The transfer of personal data to a destination outside the MSAR may only take place subject to compliance with this Act and provided the legal system in the destination to which they are transferred ensures an adequate level of protection.

2. The adequacy of the level of protection referred to in the previous number shall be assessed in the light of all the circumstances surrounding a data transfer operation or set of data transfer operations; particular consideration shall be given to the nature of the data, the purpose and duration of the proposed processing operation or operations, the place of origin and place of final destination, the rules of law, both general and sectoral, in force in the destination in question and the professional rules and security measures which are complied with in that destination.

Country	Source	Text or translation (excerpts; notes are given in italics)

3. It is for the public authority to decide whether a legal system ensures an adequate level of protection referred to in the previous number.

Article 20 Derogations

1. A transfer of personal data to a destination in which the legal system does not ensure an adequate level of protection within the meaning of No. 2 of the previous article may be allowed on condition that the public authority is notified, and that the data subject has given his consent unambiguously to the proposed transfer, or if that transfer:

   (1) is necessary for the performance of a contract between the data subject and the controller or the implementation of pre-contractual measures taken in response to the data subject's request;

   (2) is necessary for the performance or conclusion of a contract concluded or to be concluded in the interests of the data subject between the controller and a third party;

   (3) is necessary or legally required on important public interest grounds, or for the establishment, exercise of defence of legal claims;

   (4) is necessary in order to protect the vital interests of the data subject;

   (5) is made from a register which according to laws or administrative regulations is intended to provide information to the public and which is open to consultation either by the public in general or by any person who can demonstrate legitimate interest, provided the conditions laid down in law for consultation are fulfilled in the particular case.

2. Without prejudice to No. 1 the public authority may authorise a transfer or a set of transfers of personal data to a destination in which the legal system does not ensure an adequate level of protection within the meaning of No. 2 of the previous article, provided the controller adduces adequate safeguards with respect to the protection of the privacy and fundamental rights and freedoms of individuals and with respect to their exercise, particularly by means of appropriate contractual clauses.

3. A transfer of personal data which is necessary for the protection of defence, public security and public health, and for the prevention, investigation and prosecution of criminal offences, shall be governed by special legal provisions or by the international conventions and regional agreements to which the MSAR is party.

Country	Source	Text or translation (excerpts; notes are given in italics)
The former Yugoslav Republic of Macedonia	Law on Personal Data Protection (25 January 2005)	**Article 27** The controller shall keep records of each personal data collection which shall contain: … 8) transfer of personal data to other states …

VII. Transfer of personal data to other states

Article 31

The personal data transfer to other countries may be carried out only if the other state provides adequate degree of personal data protection.

During the evaluation of degree of appropriateness of the personal data protection, all circumstances will be separately addressed which refer to the operation or operations for personal data transmitted, especially the nature and the origin of personal data which are transmitted, the goals and duration of operational processing, the state where they are transmitted, the rules regulating for personal data protection in that state and regulations regulating the rules of the profession and the security measures. The degree of appropriateness of the personal data protection of other states is estimated by the Directorate.

Article 32

If the state where the data are to be transmitted does not provide appropriate degree of personal data protection, the Directorate shall not allow transmission of personal data.

Article 33

As an exception to the Article 31 of this Law, the transmission of personal data transfer may be realized in the following cases:

– if the personal data subject had given explicit written consent on the data transmission;
– when the transmission is necessary for realization of the contract between the personal data subject and the controller or realization of the pre-agreed measures undertaken as a reply to the personal data subject's request;
– the transmission is necessary for signing or realization of the contract concluded in the interest of the personal data subject, the controller and a third party;
– the transmission is necessary for protection of the public interest or protection of the fundamental freedoms and rights of the citizens, and

Country	Source	Text or translation (excerpts; notes are given in italics)
		– the transmission is necessary for protection of the life or the physical and moral integrity of the personal data subject. – The Directorate may allow personal data transmission in other state which does not provide appropriate degree of their protection if the controller states the existence of adequate restrictions for privacy protection, the fundamental rights and freedom of the personal data subject, arising from valid provisions of the contract.
Mauritius	Data Protection Act 2004, Act No. 13 of 2004	**Article 31—Transfer of personal data** (1) Subject to subsection (2), no data controller shall, except with the written authorization of the Commissioner, transfer personal data to a third country. (2) The Eighth data protection principle specified in the First Schedule shall not apply where— (a) the data subject has given his consent to the transfer; (b) the transfer is necessary— (i) for the performance of a contract between the data subject and the data controller, or for the taking of steps at the request of the data subject with a view to his entering into a contract with the data controller; (ii) for the conclusion of a contract between the data controller and a person, other than the data subject, which is entered at the request of the data subject, or is in the interest of the data subject, or for the performance of such a contract; (iii) in the public interest, to safeguard public security or national security. (c) the transfer is made on such terms as may be approved by the Commissioner as ensuring the adequate safeguards for the protection of the rights of the data subjects. (3) For the purpose of subsection (2)(c), the adequacy of the level of protection of a country shall be assessed in the light of all the circumstances surrounding the data transfer, having regards in particular to— (a) the nature of the data; (b) the purpose and duration of the proposed processing; (c) the country of origin and country of final destination;

Country	Source	Text or translation (excerpts; notes are given in italics)
		(d) the rules of law, both general and sectoral, in force in the country in question; and (e) any relevant codes of conduct or other rules and security measures which are complied with in that country.
Mexico	Decree issuing the Federal Law on Protection of Personal Data Held by Private Parties (2010)	**Article 36** Where the data controller intends to transfer personal data to domestic or foreign third parties other than the data processor, it must provide them with the privacy notice and the purposes to which the data owner has limited data processing. Data processing will be done as agreed in the privacy notice, which shall contain a clause indicating whether or not the data owner agrees to the transfer of his data; moreover, the third party receiver will assume the same obligations as the data controller that has transferred the data. **Article 37** Domestic or international transfers of data may be carried out without the consent of the data owner in the following cases: I. Where the transfer is pursuant to a Law or Treaty to which Mexico is party; II. Where the transfer is necessary for medical diagnosis or prevention, health care delivery, medical treatment or health services management; III. Where the transfer is made to holding companies, subsidiaries or affiliates under common control of the data controller, or to a parent company or any company of the same group as the data controller, operating under the same internal processes and policies; IV. Where the transfer is necessary by virtue of a contract executed or to be executed in the interest of the data owner between the data controller and a third party; V. Where the transfer is necessary or legally required to safeguard public interest or for the administration of justice; VI. Where the transfer is necessary for the recognition, exercise or defense of a right in a judicial proceeding; and VII. Where the transfer is necessary to maintain or fulfil a legal relationship between the data controller and the data owner.

Country	Source	Text or translation (excerpts; notes are given in italics)
Moldova	Law No. 17-XVI of 15 February 2007 on the Protection of Personal Data (modified by Law No. 141-XVI of 26.06.2008, in force as of 1 August 2008)	**Article 16 Transborder transfer of personal data** (1) The present Article is applied in the case of transfer across national borders, whatever support is used, of personal data, which are subject to processing or are collected with the purpose to be subject of such processing. (2) Personal data, that are on the territory of the Republic of Moldova and destined to be transferred to other states, are protected in accordance with the present law. (3) The transborder transfer of personal data, that are subject to a processing or are going to be processed after the transfer, can be made in the case when the respective state ensures an adequate level of protection of the rights of personal data subjects and of the data destined for the transfer, as well as in other cases according to the international agreements the Republic of Moldova is party of. (4) The level of protection is established by the Center, taking into consideration the conditions in which the data transfer is performed, especially the nature of the data, the purpose of the data transfer and processing, the country of final destination, the legislation of the requesting state. (5) In the case when the Center concludes that the level of protection offered by the state of destination is unsatisfactory, it may prohibit the data transfer. (6) The transfer of personal data to the states that do not ensure an adequate level of protection, can be made only: (a) with the written consent of the personal data subject; (b) in case of the need to sign or execute an agreement or a contract between the personal data subject and their holder, or between the holder of these data and a third party in the interest of the personal data subject; (c) if the transfer is necessary to protect the rights, freedoms or interests of the personal data subject; (d) in case when personal data are accessible to the public.
Monaco	Law No. 1.165—Act Concerning the Processing of Nominal Information (23 December 1993)	**Article 8 (8)** To be admissible, the declaration envisaged in the first subparagraph of Article 6 … must include: (8) mention, when necessary, that the data processing is intended for the communication of data abroad, even if it results from operations previously carried out outside Monaco.

Country	Source	Text or translation (excerpts; notes are given in italics)
		NOTE: Article 6 refers to the obligation that persons or entities under private law must file a declaration of their processing activities with the DPA.
Morocco	Law No. 09–08 Relative to the Protection of Individuals with regards to their Personal Data (5 March 2009)	**Chapter 5, Article 43 The transfer of data to a foreign country** The data controller shall not transfer any personal data to a foreign country unless that country ensures a sufficient level of protection for privacy rights and freedoms. The level of protection provided by the foreign country shall be assessed in light of the regulations and security measures applicable in that country, the characteristics of the processing such as the purpose, duration, nature, origin and intended destination of personal data. The DPA has established a list of countries that comply with the provisions mentioned above. **Article 44** As an exception to the provisions of Article 43 above, the data controller may transfer personal data to a foreign country that does not fulfil the requirements mentioned if the data subject gave its express consent for such a transfer or: 1. if the transfer is justified by one of the following conditions: a) for the protection of the data subject's life; b) in the public's interest; c) for reasons of contractual obligations between the data controller and the data subject; d) at the conclusion or execution of a contract in the interest of the data subject by the data controller and a third party; e) at the conclusion or execution of a contract or a contract to be concluded, in the interest of the data subject, between the data controller and a third party; f) at the execution of an international mutual assistance agreement on judicial matters; g) for the prevention, diagnosis and treatment of medical diseases. 2. If the transfer is made in compliance with a bilateral or multilateral agreement to which Morocco is a party. 3. At the express authority of the DPA, when the processing ensures a sufficient level of protection for privacy rights, rights and freedoms of data subjects, such as through standard contractual clauses or binding corporate rules.

Country	Source	Text or translation (excerpts; notes are given in italics)
New Zealand	Privacy Act 1993 (as amended in 2010 by the Privacy (Cross-Border Information) Amendment Bill, excerpts only)	See below

Part 11A Transfer of personal information outside New Zealand

114A Interpretation.

In this Part, unless the context otherwise requires,—
    'OECD Guidelines' means the Organisation for Economic Co-operation and Development Guidelines Governing the Protection of Privacy and Transborder Flows of Personal Data
    'State' includes any State, territory, province, or other part of a country
    'transfer prohibition notice' means a notice given under section 114B prohibiting the transfer of personal information from New Zealand to another State.

114B Prohibition on transfer of personal information outside New Zealand

(1) The Commissioner may prohibit a transfer of personal information from New Zealand to another State if the Commissioner is satisfied, on reasonable grounds, that—

(a) the information has been, or will be, received in New Zealand from another State and is likely to be transferred to a third State where it will not be subject to a law providing comparable safeguards to this Act; and

(b) the transfer would be likely to lead to a contravention of the basic principles of national application set out in Part Two of the OECD Guidelines and set out in Schedule 5A.

(2) In determining whether to prohibit a transfer of personal information, the Commissioner must also consider, in addition to the matters set out in subsection (1) and section 14, the following:

(a) whether or not the transfer affects, or would be likely to affect, any individual; and

(b) the general desirability of facilitating the free flow of information between New Zealand and other States; and

(c) any existing or developing international guidelines relevant to transborder data flows, including (but not limited to)—

(i) the OECD Guidelines:

(ii) the European Union Directive 95/46/EC on the Protection of Individuals with Regard to the Processing of Personal Data and on the Free Movement of Such Data.

Country	Source	Text or translation (excerpts; notes are given in italics)
		(3) Subsection (1) does not apply if the transfer of the information, or the information itself, is— (a) required or authorised by or under any enactment; or (b) required by any convention or other instrument imposing international obligations on New Zealand …
Peru	Law No. 29733/2011 on the Protection of Personal Data	**Article 11. Principle of adequate level of protection** In the event of trans-border data flows, the recipient country must have an adequate level of protection for the personal data to be processed or at least a level of protection comparable to the one provided by this Law. The scope of the adequate level of protection in the recipient country must at least ensure compliance with the guiding principles for the protection of personal data under this Title and an effective system of guarantees. **Article 15. Trans-border flow of personal data** The data controller and the data processor of the database including personal data may engage in trans-border flows of personal data only if the recipients guarantee an adequate level of protection in accordance with this Law. The National Authority for the Protection of Personal Data will supervise the compliance with this requirement. The provisions of the previous paragraph do not apply in the following cases: 15.1 Agreements under international treaties where the Republic of Peru is a party. 15.2 International judicial cooperation. 15.3 International cooperation between intelligence agencies for the fight against terrorism, illegal drug trafficking, money laundering, corruption, human trafficking and other forms of organized crime. 15.4 When the personal data are necessary to perform a contract to which the data subject is a party. 15.5 In case of bank or stock exchange transfers, concerning the respective transactions in accordance with applicable Law. 15.6 When the trans-border flow of personal data takes place for the prevention, diagnosis or medical or surgical treatment of the data subject or when it is necessary to carry out epidemiological or similar studies, provided that adequate dissociation procedures are applied. 15.7 When the data subject has given his prior, informed, express and unambiguous consent. 15.8 In others cases established by regulation of this Law.

Country	Source	Text or translation (excerpts; notes are given in italics)
Russia	Federal Law of the Russian Federation of 27 July 2006 No. 152-FZ on Personal Data (as amended by Law of 25 July 2011 No. 261-FZ)	**Article 12** 1. Cross-border transfer of personal data to foreign countries that are parties of the Convention for the Protection of Individuals with regard to Automatic Processing of Personal Data [Council of Europe Convention 108], as well as to the territory of foreign States that ensure adequate protection of the rights of subjects of personal data is performed in accordance with the present Federal Law and may be forbidden or restricted with the aim of protecting the principles of the constitutional regime of the Russian Federation, morality, health and the rights and lawful interests of citizens, and ensuring the country's defence and the State's security. 2. The competent authority for the protection of the rights of subjects of personal data shall approve the list of foreign States that are not parties of the Convention for the Protection of Individuals with regard to Automatic Processing of Personal Data but ensure adequate protection of the rights subjects of personal data. A foreign State that is not a party of the Convention for the Protection of Individuals with regard to Automatic Processing of Personal Data may be included in the list of foreign States that ensure adequate protection of the rights of subjects of personal data, if that State ensures that its law complies with the provisions of the Convention and provides appropriate data security guarantees. 3. Before commencing cross-border transfer of personal data the operator is obliged to assure himself that the foreign State to the territory of which personal data is being transferred ensures adequate protection of the rights of subjects of personal data. 4. Cross-border transfer of personal data to the territory of States which do not ensure adequate protection of the rights of subjects of personal data may be performed in the following cases: 1) with the written consent of the subject of personal data; 2) in the cases provided by international treaties of the Russian Federation; 3) in the cases provided by Federal Laws, if this is necessary for the purpose of protection of the principles of the constitutional regime of the Russian Federation, ensuring the country's defence and the State's security, as well as the security of stable and safe operation of the transport sector, the interests of the individual, the society and State in the transport industry against acts of unlawful intervention;

Country	Source	Text or translation (excerpts; notes are given in italics)
		4) for fulfilment of a contract, to which the subject of personal data is a party; 5) for protection of the life, health or other vital interests of the subject of personal data or of other persons when it is impossible to obtain the written consent of the subject of personal data.
San Marino	Act on Collection, Elaboration and Use of Computerised Personal Data, 1983, as amended by Act No. 70/95 (1995)	**Article 4** The transfer abroad of data concerning San Marino fiscal or legal persons is subject to the prior and reasoned authorization of the data protection authority under Article 15.
Senegal	Law No. 2008–12 of 25 January 2008, on the Protection of Personal Data	**Article 49** The data controller shall not transfer any personal data abroad unless the foreign country ensures a sufficient level of protection for privacy rights, rights and freedoms of data subjects in relation to the processing of personal data. Before any transfer of personal data to a foreign country, the data controller shall inform the DPA. Before any process of personal data coming from abroad, the DPA shall ensure that the data controller provides a sufficient level of protection for privacy rights, rights and freedoms of data subjects in relation to the processing of personal data. The level of protection provided by the data controller shall be assessed in light of security measures which are applied in compliance with the Act, and criteria of the process such as its purposes, duration, nature, origin and destination of data. **Article 50** The data controller may transfer personal data to a foreign country that does not fulfil the requirements mentioned in the article above if the transfer is limited, not substantial and if the data subject gave its express consent to the transfer or if the transfer is justified by one of the following conditions: 1) protection of data subject's life; 2) protection of public interest; 3) compliance with mandatory rules regarding judicial process; or 4) contractual obligations between the data controller and the data subject. **Article 51** The DPA may authorize, upon request, the transfer of personal data or a group of transfers to a foreign country that does not provide an adequate level of protection if the data controller offers guarantees regarding privacy rights, rights and freedoms of data subjects and their ability to exercise those rights.

Country	Source	Text or translation (excerpts; notes are given in italics)
Serbia	Law on Personal Data Protection (October 2008)	**Article 53** Data can be transferred from the Republic of Serbia to a state party to the Council of Europe Convention for the Protection of Individuals with regard to Automatic Processing of Personal Data. Data may be transferred from the Republic of Serbia to a state that is not a party to the Convention referred to in paragraph 1 of this Article or an international organization if such state or international organization has a regulation or a data transfer agreement in force which provides a level of data protection equivalent to that envisaged by the Convention. In cases of transborder transfer of data referred to in paragraph 2 of this Article, the Commissioner shall determine whether the requirements are met and safeguards put in place for the transfer of data from the Republic of Serbia and shall authorize such transfer.
South Korea	Personal Information Protection Act, Law 10465 (2011)	**Article 17(3)** When a personal information manager provides a third person at any overseas location with personal information, he/she shall notify the subject of information of the matters referred to in each subparagraph or paragraph (2) and obtain the consent thereto, and shall not enter into a contract concerning the trans-border transfer of personal information stipulating any details contravening this Act.
St Lucia	Data Protection Act 2011	**Article 28** 1. Subject to subsection (2), a data controller shall not transfer personal data to a country or territory outside Saint Lucia unless— a. with the written consent of the Commissioner; and b. that country or territory ensures an adequate level of protection for the rights and freedoms of data subjects in relation to the processing of personal data. 2. Subsection (1)(b) shall not apply where— a. the data subject has given his or her consent to the transfer; b. the transfer is necessary— – for the performance of a contract between the data subject and the data controller, or for the taking of steps at the request of the data subject with a view to the data subject entering into a contract with the data controller;

Country	Source	Text or translation (excerpts; notes are given in italics)

		– for the conclusion of a contract between the data controller and a person, other than the data subject, which is entered at the request of the data subject, or is in the interest of the data subject, or for the performance of such a contract;
		   – it is in the public interest or section 34 applies;
		  c. the transfer is made on such terms as may be approved by the Commissioner as ensuring the adequate safeguards for the protection of the rights of the data subject.
		3. For the purposes of subsection (2)(c), the adequacy of the level of safeguards of a country or territory shall be assessed in the light of all the circumstances surrounding the transfer of personal data, having regard in particular to—
		  a. the nature of the personal data:
		  b. the purpose and duration of the proposed processing;
		  c. the country or territory of origin and country of final destination;
		  d. the rules of law in force in the country or territory in question; and
		  e. any relevant codes of conduct or other rules and security measures which are complied with in that country or territory.
		
		NOTE: The only official source available for this Act is the Privacy and Data Protection Bill of 17 March 2010, but authoritative sources have confirmed that the Bill was passed in December 2011.

Switzerland	Federal Act on Data Protection (19 June 1992) (as amended on 1 January 2008)	**Art. 6 Cross-border disclosure**
		1. Personal data may not be disclosed abroad if the privacy of the data subjects would be seriously endangered thereby, in particular due to the absence of legislation that guarantees adequate protection.
		2. In the absence of legislation that guarantees adequate protection, personal data may be disclosed abroad only if:
		  a. sufficient safeguards, in particular contractual clauses, ensure an adequate level of protection abroad;
		  b. the data subject has consented in the specific case;
		  c. the processing is directly connected with the conclusion or the performance of a contract and the personal data is that of a contractual party;

Country	Source	Text or translation (excerpts; notes are given in italics)
		d. disclosure is essential in the specific case in order either to safeguard an overriding public interest or for the establishment, exercise or enforcement of legal claims before the courts; e. disclosure is required in the specific case in order to protect the life or the physical integrity of the data subject; f. the data subject has made the data generally accessible and has not expressly prohibited its processing; g. disclosure is made within the same legal person or company or between legal persons or companies that are under the same management, provided those involved are subject to data protection rules that ensure an adequate level of protection. 3. The Federal Data Protection and Information Commissioner (the Commissioner, Art. 26) must be informed of the safeguards under paragraph 2 letter a and the data protection rules under paragraph 2 letter g. The Federal Council regulates the details of this duty to provide information.
Trinidad & Tobago	Act No. 13/2011 on the Protection of Personal Privacy and Information	**Section 72 Cross border disclosure of personal information** (1) Where a mandatory code of conduct is developed pursuant to section 71, it shall require at a minimum that personal information under the custody or control of an organization shall not be disclosed by that organization to any third party without the consent of the individual to whom it relates, except in general, where such information is disclosed for the purposes (a) for which the information was collected or for use consistent with that purpose; (b) of a Court Order; or (c) of complying with any written law. (2) Where personal information under the custody and control of an organization is to be disclosed to a party residing in another jurisdiction, the organization shall inform the individual to whom it relates of the (a) purpose for which the information is being collected once that purpose is known to the organisation; (b) identity of – the person requesting the information; and – the relevant public body with responsibility for Data Protection in the other jurisdiction, and obtain his consent before disclosing the information.

Country	Source	Text or translation (excerpts; notes are given in italics)
		(3) Where a person under subsection (2) does not consent to the release of his personal information, the organization shall not so disclose.
		(4) Where a person under subsection (2) consents to the disclosure of his information and the organization is
		(a) satisfied that the jurisdiction to which the information is being sent has comparable safeguards as provided by this Act, the organization shall disclose the personal information;
		(b) not satisfied that the jurisdiction to which the information is being sent has comparable safeguards, the organization shall refer the matter to the Commissioner for a determination as to whether the other jurisdiction has comparable safeguards as provided by this Act and inform the individual to whom the personal information relates of the referral.
		(5) Upon a referral under subsection (4), the Commissioner shall make a determination whether the other jurisdiction has or does not have comparable safeguards as provided by this Act, and inform the organization accordingly.
		(6) Where the organization is informed that the jurisdiction to which the information is being sent
		(a) has comparable safeguards, the organization shall inform the person concerned and disclose the personal information; or
		(b) does not have comparable safeguards, the organization shall inform the person concerned and obtain his consent for the disclosure
		– without limitation on the personal information; or
		– with limitation on the personal information sharing to the extent necessary to ensure the protection of personal privacy and information.
Tunisia	Law No. 2004–63 of 27 July 2004, on the Protection of Personal Data (2004)	**Article 50** The transfer of personal data to a foreign country is prohibited when it may endanger public security or Tunisia's vital interests.

Country	Source	Text or translation (excerpts; notes are given in italics)
		### Article 51
		The transfer of personal data to a foreign country for the purpose of processing or for the future purpose of processing, is not permitted if the country does not provide an adequate level of protection. The adequate level of protection shall be assessed in light of the nature, purpose for which and period during which the personal data are intended to be processed; where the data shall be transferred to; and the security measures taken to ensure the safety of the personal data. In any case, the transfer of personal data must be carried out in accordance with the provisions of the Act.
		### Article 52
		In any case, the DPA's authorization is required before the transfer of personal data abroad. The DPA shall issue its decision within one month from the date of receipt of the application.
		Whenever the personal data to be transferred concerns minors, an application for authorization must be made before a juvenile and family court judge.
Ukraine	Law of Ukraine No. 2297-VI of 1 June 2010 on Protection of Personal Data	### Article 29(3)
		Transfer of personal data to foreign subjects of relations related to personal data shall be performed on conditions of providing appropriate protection of personal data and with an appropriate permission in cases established by law or international treaty of Ukraine and according to the rules stipulated by national legislation. Personal data shall not be transferred for a purpose other than the purpose for which they have been collected.
Uruguay	Data Protection Act, No. 18.331 (2008)	### Article 23 Data transferred internationally
		It is prohibited to transfer personal data of any type to countries or international bodies that do not provide adequate levels of protection in accordance with the standards of international or regional law in this regard. The prohibition shall not apply in cases of:
		1) international judicial cooperation, in conformity with the respective international instrument, such as a treaty or a convention, according to the circumstances of the case;
		2) exchange of medical data, when the situation demands that the affected person be treated for reasons of public health or hygiene;
		3) banking or stock-market information transfers, in relation to the respective transactions and in conformity with the legislation applicable to such transfers;

Country	Source	Text or translation (excerpts; notes are given in italics)
		4) agreements within the framework of international treaties to which the Oriental Republic of Uruguay is party; 5) international cooperation between intelligence agencies for combating organised crime, terrorism and drug trafficking. The international transfer of data shall also be permissible in the following circumstances: A) the interested party has given his/her unequivocal consent to the proposed transfer; B) the transfer is necessary for the performance of a contract between the interested party and the data controller or for the execution of precontractual measures taken at the request of the interested party; C) the transfer is necessary for the execution or performance of a contract entered into, or to be entered into, in the interests of the interested party, between the data controller and a third party; D) the transfer is necessary or legally required for the safeguarding of an important public interest, or for the recognition, exercise or defence of a right in a judicial proceeding; E) the transfer is necessary for the safeguarding of the vital interest of the interested party. F) The transfer is made from a register which, by virtue of legal or regulatory provisions, is designed to facilitate the provision of information to the public and is open to consultation by the general public or by any person who can demonstrate a legitimate interest, provided, in each individual case, the conditions established by law for its consultation are satisfied. Without prejudice to the provisions of the first paragraph of this article, the *Unidad Reguladora y de Control de Protección de Datos Personales [Data Protection Authority]* may authorise a transfer or a series of transfers of personal data to a third-party country that does not guarantee an adequate level of protection when the data controller offers sufficient guarantees regarding the protection of privacy, fundamental human rights and liberties, and regarding the exercise of the respective rights. These guarantees may derive from appropriate contractual clauses.

C. Other important instruments

Name	Source	Text or translation (excerpts; notes are given in italics)
European Union (**voluntary measures**)	Binding Corporate Rules: Article 29 Working Party, 'Working Document setting up a framework for Binding Corporate Rules' (WP 154, 24 June 2008), at 7	*Paraphrase:* Binding corporate rules must contain 'an explanation of the measures in place to restrict transfers and onward transfers outside of the group', and a commitment that all transfers to external controllers and processors located outside of the EU must respect EU rules on transborder data flows.
	Standard Contractual Clauses: Commission Decision 2010/87/EU of 5 February 2010 on standard contractual clauses for the transfer of personal data to processors established in third countries under Directive 95/46/EC of the European Parliament and of the Council, [2010] OJ L39/5	*Paraphrase:* Clause 11: The non-EU data importer must not transfer the data to a subprocessor unless EU-based legal standards are complied with.
	Commission Decision 2004/915/EC of 27 December 2004 amending Decision (EC) 2001/497 as regards the introduction of an alternative set of standard contractual clauses for the transfer of personal data to third countries, [2004] OJ L385/74	*Paraphrase:* Clause II(h): The non-EU data importer must process the personal data transferred in accordance with EU-based legal standards. *Paraphrase:* Clause II(i): The non-EU data importer must not transfer the data to a third party located outside the EEA unless EU-based legal standards are complied with.
	Safe Harbor Privacy Principles issued by the US Department of Commerce on 21 July 2000, and recognized as 'adequate' under European Commission Decision 2000/520/EC of 26 July 2000, [2000] OJ L215/7	**ONWARD TRANSFER:** To disclose information to a third party, organizations must apply the Notice and Choice Principles. Where an organization wishes to transfer information to a third party that is acting as an agent, as described in the endnote, it may do so if it first either ascertains that the third party subscribes to the Principles or is subject to the Directive or another adequacy finding or enters into a written agreement with such third party requiring that the third party provide at least the same level of privacy protection as is required by the relevant Principles. If the organization complies with these requirements, it shall not be held responsible (unless the organization agrees otherwise) when a third party to

Name	Source	Text or translation (excerpts; notes are given in italics)
		which it transfers such information processes it in a way contrary to any restrictions or representations, unless the organization knew or should have known the third party would process it in such a contrary way and the organization has not taken reasonable steps to prevent or stop such processing.
European Union and Australia	Agreement between the European Union and Australia on the processing and transfer of European Union-sourced passenger name record (PNR) data by air carriers to the Australian Customs Service, [2008] OJ L213/49	**Article 3** Compliance with this Agreement by Customs shall, within the meaning of relevant EU data-protection law, constitute an adequate level of protection for EU-sourced PNR data transferred to Customs for the purpose of this Agreement.
European Union and United States	Agreement between the United States of America and the European Union on the use and transfer of passenger name records to the United States Department of Homeland Security, [2012] OJ L215/5	**Article 19** In consideration of this Agreement and its implementation, DHS shall be deemed to provide, within the meaning of relevant EU data protection law, an adequate level of protection for PNR processing and use. In this respect, carriers which have provided PNR to DHS in compliance with this Agreement shall be deemed to have complied with applicable legal requirements in the EU related to the transfer of such data from the EU to the United States.
	Agreement between the European Union and the United States of America on the processing and transfer of Financial Messaging Data from the European Union to the United States for purposes of the Terrorist Finance Tracking Program, [2010] OJ L8/11	*Paraphrase: see Article 5, proving protections to personal data transferred from the EU to the US for the purposes of the Terrorist Finance Tracking Program.*
	Reports by the High Level Contact Group (HLCG) on information sharing and privacy and personal data protection (23 November 2009), <http://register.consilium.europa.eu/pdf/en/09/st15/st15851.en09.pdf>	**Principle 12** Where personal information is transmitted or made available by a competent authority of the sending country or by private parties in accordance with the domestic law of the sending country to a competent authority of the receiving country, the competent authority of the receiving country may only authorise or carry out an onward transfer of this information to a competent authority of a third country if permitted under its domestic

Name	Source	Text or translation (excerpts; notes are given in italics)
		law and in accordance with existing applicable international agreements and international arrangements between the sending and receiving country. In the absence of such international agreements and international arrangements, such transfers should moreover support legitimate public interests consisting of: national security, defence, public security, the prevention, investigation, detection and prosecution of criminal offences, breaches of ethics of regulated professions, or the protection of the data subject. In all cases transfers should be fully consistent with these common principles, especially the limitation/purpose specification.
Infocomm Development Authority of Singapore (IDA) and the National Trust Council of Singapore (NTC)	Voluntary Model Data Protection Code for the Private Sector (Version 1.3 final)	**Principle 4.1.1** Where data are to be transferred to someone (other than the individual or the organisation or its employees), the organisation shall take reasonable steps to ensure that the data which is to be transferred will not be processed inconsistently with this Model Code. *NOTE: The Implementation and Operational Guidelines to the provision explain that 'the restrictions on the onward transfers of personal data under this principle apply to transfers to another organisation whether the organisation is located in Singapore or not'.*
Madrid Resolution	International Standards on the Protection of Personal Data and Privacy (non-binding)	**15 International Transfers** 1. As a general rule, international transfers of personal data may be carried out when the State to which such data are transmitted affords, as a minimum, the level of protection provided for in this Document. 2. It will be possible to carry out international transfers of personal data to States that do not afford the level of protection provided for in this document where those who expect to transmit such data guarantee that the recipient will afford such level of protection; such guarantee may for example result from appropriate contractual clauses. In particular, where the transfer is carried out within corporations or multinational groups, such guarantees may be contained in internal privacy rules, compliance with which is mandatory.

Name	Source	Text or translation (excerpts; notes are given in italics)
		3. Moreover, national legislation applicable to those who expect to transmit data may permit an international transfer of personal data to States that do not afford the level of protection provided for in this Document, where necessary and in the interest of the data subject in the framework of a contractual relationship, to protect the vital interests of the data subject or of another person, or when legally required on important public interest grounds.
		Applicable national legislation may confer powers on the supervisory authorities referred to in section 23 to authorize some or all of the international transfers falling within their jurisdiction, before they are carried out. In any case, those who expect to carry out an international transfer of personal data should be capable of demonstrating that the transfer complies with the guarantees provided for in this Document and in particular where required by the supervisory authorities pursuant to the powers laid down in paragraph 23.2.
Treasury Board of Canada	Taking Privacy into Account before Making Contracting Decisions (2006)	Guidance which requires public bodies when contracting (including situations when this will result in personal data being transferred outside of Canada) to apply a context-specific test regarding the risk to privacy, under which agencies are to evaluate the following factors: – the sensitivity of the personal information, including whether the information is detailed or highly personal, and the context in which it was collected; – the expectations of the individuals to whom the personal information relates; and – the potential injury if personal information is wrongfully disclosed or misused, including the potential for identity theft or access by foreign governments.

D. Data protection and privacy legislation not yet fully in force

Country	Source and Status	Text or translation (excerpts; notes are given in italics)
Barbados	Data Protection Act—draft bill, still in the legislative process	**Section 4(2)(h) Eighth Principle** (2) The data protection principles referred to under subsection (1) are as follows: … (h) Eighth Principle: personal data shall not be transferred to a country or territory outside Barbados unless that country or territory ensures an adequate level of protection for the rights and freedoms of data subjects in relation to the processing of personal data.

Hong Kong (Special Administrative Region of the People's Republic of China)	Personal Data (Privacy) Ordinance (Chapter 486)—the Ordinance is in force, but Section 33 on transborder data flows is not	**Section 33 Prohibition against transfer of personal data to place outside Hong Kong except in specified circumstances**
		
		(1) This section shall not apply to personal data other than personal data the collection, holding, processing or use of which—
		(a) takes place in Hong Kong; or
		(b) is controlled by a data user whose principal place of business is in Hong Kong.
		(2) A data user shall not transfer personal data to a place outside Hong Kong unless—
		(a) the place is specified for the purposes of this section in a notice under subsection (3);
		(b) the user has reasonable grounds for believing that there is in force in that place any law which is substantially similar to, or serves the same purposes as, this Ordinance;
		(c) the data subject has consented in writing to the transfer;
		(d) the user has reasonable grounds for believing that, in all the circumstances of the case—
		  – the transfer is for the avoidance or mitigation of adverse action against the data subject;
		  – it is not practicable to obtain the consent in writing of the data subject to that transfer; and
		  – if it was practicable to obtain such consent, the data subject would give it;

Country	Source and Status	Text or translation (excerpts; notes are given in italics)
		(e) the data are exempt from data protection principle 3 by virtue of an exemption under Part VIII; or
		(f) the user has taken all reasonable precautions and exercised all due diligence to ensure that the data will not, in that place, be collected, held, processed or used in any manner which, if that place were Hong Kong, would be a contravention of a requirement under this Ordinance.
		(3) Where the Commissioner has reasonable grounds for believing that there is in force in a place outside Hong Kong any law which is substantially similar to, or serves the same purposes as, this Ordinance, he may, by notice in the Gazette, specify that place for the purposes of this section.
		(4) Where the Commissioner has reasonable grounds for believing that in a place specified in a notice under subsection (3) there is no longer in force any law which is substantially similar to, or serves the same purposes as, this Ordinance, he shall, either by repealing or amending that notice, cause that place to cease to be specified for the purposes of this section....
Malaysia	Personal Data Protection Bill (2010)—enacted by royal assent on 2 June 2010, but not yet in force	**Transfer of personal data to places outside Malaysia** 129. (1) A data user shall not transfer any personal data of a data subject to a place outside Malaysia unless to such place as specified by the Minister, upon the recommendation of the Commissioner, by notification published in the *Gazette*. (2) For the purposes of subsection (1), the Minister may specify any place outside Malaysia if— *(a)* there is in that place in force any law which is substantially similar to this Act, or that serves the same purposes as this Act; or

Country	Source and Status	Text or translation (excerpts; notes are given in italics)
		(b) that place ensures an adequate level of protection in relation to the processing of personal data which is at least equivalent to the level of protection afforded by this Act.

(3) Notwithstanding subsection (1), a data user may transfer any personal data to a place outside Malaysia if—

(a) the data subject has given his consent to the transfer;

(b) the transfer is necessary for the performance of a contract between the data subject and the data user;

(c) the transfer is necessary for the conclusion or performance of a contract between the data user and a third party which—

   (i) is entered into at the request of the data subject; or

   (ii) is in the interests of the data subject;

(d) the transfer is for the purpose of any legal proceedings or for the purpose of obtaining legal advice or for establishing, exercising or defending legal rights;

(e) the data user has reasonable grounds for believing that in all circumstances of the case—

   (i) the transfer is for the avoidance or mitigation of adverse action against the data subject;

   (ii) it is not practicable to obtain the consent in writing of the data subject to that transfer; and

   (iii) if it was practicable to obtain such consent, the data subject would have given his consent;

Country	Source and Status	Text or translation (excerpts; notes are given in italics)
		(f) the data user has taken all reasonable precautions and exercised all due diligence to ensure that the personal data will not in that place be processed in any manner which, if that place is Malaysia, would be a contravention of this Act;
		(g) the transfer is necessary in order to protect the vital interests of the data subject; or
		(h) the transfer is necessary as being in the public interest in circumstances as determined by the Minister.
		(4) Where the Commissioner has reasonable grounds for believing that in a place as specified under subsection (1) there is no longer in force any law which is substantially similar to this Act, or that serves the same purposes as this Act—
		(a) the Commissioner shall make such recommendations to the Minister who shall, either by cancelling or amending the notification made under subsection (1), cause that place to cease to be a place to which personal data may be transferred under this section; and
		(b) the data user shall cease to transfer any personal data of a data subject to such place with effect from the time as specified by the Minister in the notification.
		(5) A data user who contravenes subsection (1) commits an offence and shall, on conviction, be liable to a fine not exceeding three hundred thousand ringgit or to imprisonment for a term not exceeding two years or to both.
		(6) For the purposes of this section, 'adverse action', in relation to a data subject, means any action that may adversely affect the data subject's rights, benefits, privileges, obligations or interests.

Country	Source and Status	Text or translation (excerpts; notes are given in italics)

Singapore	Personal Data Protection Bill (Bill No 24/2012)—still in the legislative process	**Transfer of Personal Data outside Singapore**
		
		26.—(1) An organization shall not transfer any personal data to a country or territory outside Singapore except in accordance with the requirements prescribed under this Act to ensure that the organisations provide a standard of protection to personal data so transferred that is comparable to the protection under this Act.
		(2) The Commission may, under the application of any organization, by notice in writing exempt the organization from any requirement prescribed pursuant to subsection (1) in respect of any transfer of personal data by that organization.
		(3) An exemption under subsection (2)—
		  (a) may be granted subject to such conditions as the Commission may specify in writing; and
		  (b) need not be published in the Gazette and may be revoked at any time by the Commission.
		(4) The Commission may at any time add to, vary or revoke any condition imposed under this section.

South Africa	Protection of Personal Information Bill (2012)—still in the legislative process	**Chapter 9, Clause 72 Transfers of personal information outside Republic**
		
		72. (1) A responsible party in the Republic may not transfer personal information about a data subject to a third party who is in a foreign country unless—
		  (a) the third party who is the recipient of the information is subject to a law, binding corporate rules, binding agreement or a memorandum of understanding entered into between two or more public bodies, which provide an adequate level of protection that—
		    (i) effectively upholds principles for reasonable

Country	Source and Status	Text or translation (excerpts; notes are given in italics)
		processing of the information that are substantially similar to the conditions for the lawful processing of personal information relating to a data subject who is a natural person and, where applicable, a juristic person; and (ii) includes provisions, that are substantially similar to this section, relating to the further transfer of personal information from the recipient to third parties who are in a foreign country; (b) the data subject consents to the transfer; (c) the transfer is necessary for the performance of a contract between the data subject and the responsible party, or for the implementation of pre-contractual measures taken in response to the data subject's request; (d) the transfer is necessary for the conclusion or performance of a contract concluded in the interest of the data subject between the responsible party and a third party; or (e) the transfer is for the benefit of the data subject, and— (i) it is not reasonably practicable to obtain the consent of the data subject to that transfer; and (ii) if it were reasonably practicable to obtain such consent, the data subject would be likely to give it. (2) Where the transfer of personal information, as referred to in subsection (1), is made in terms of a non-binding memorandum of understanding the public body

Country	Source and Status	Text or translation (excerpts; notes are given in italics)
		remains accountable for purposes of this Act for the protection of the personal information.

(3) For the purpose of this section—

(a) 'accountable' means that where the recipient of the information, who is a party to a non-binding memorandum of understanding, processes the personal information of a data subject in a manner that would have constituted an interference with the privacy of the data subject in terms of this Act had the information been processed in the Republic, the processing will be regarded as an interference with the privacy of the data subject in terms of this Act and will be regarded as having been processed by the responsible party;

(b) 'binding corporate rules' means personal information processing policies, within a group of undertakings, which are adhered to by a responsible party or operator within that group of undertakings when transferring personal information to a responsible party or operator within that same group of undertakings in a foreign country; and

(c) 'group of undertakings' means a controlling undertaking and its controlled undertakings.

Bibliography

Note: some types of material are in alphabetical and others in chronological order; URLs are only included for Sources that are primarily available online

1. LEGISLATION

(i) Multilateral conventions

General Agreement on Trade in Services, 15 April 1994, Marrakesh Agreement Establishing the World Trade Organization, Annex 1B, The legal texts: The results of the Uruguay Round of multilateral trade negotiations 284 (1999), 1869 UNTS 183, 33 International Legal Materials 1167 (1994)

Convention on the law applicable to contractual relations (the 'Rome Convention'), [2005] OJ C334/1

Convention implementing the Schengen Agreement of 14 June 1995 between the Governments of the States of the Benelux Economic Union, the Federal Republic of Germany and the French Republic on the gradual abolition of checks at their common borders, [2000] OJ L239/19

Council of Europe Convention for the Protection of Individuals with regard to Automatic Data Processing of Personal Data, 28 January 1981, ETS 108 (1981)

Vienna Convention on the Law of Treaties (adopted on 23 May 1969, entered into force on 27 January 1980) 1155 UNTS 331

International Covenant of Civil and Political Rights (1966)

European Convention on Human Rights (1953)

Universal Declaration of Human Rights (1948)

(ii) Bilateral agreements

Agreement between the United States of America and the European Union on the use and transfer of passenger name records to the United States Department of Homeland Security, [2012] OJ L215/5

Agreement between the European Union and the United States of America on the processing and transfer of Financial Messaging Data from the European Union to the United States for purposes of the Terrorist Finance Tracking Program, [2010] OJ L8/11

Agreement between the European Union and Australia on the processing and transfer of European Union sourced passenger name record (PNR) data by air carriers to the Australian customs service, [2008] OJ L213/49

US–German Social Security Agreement, 7 January 1976

(iii) EU law (including proposed legislation)

Commission Implementing Decision 2012/484/EU of 21 August 2012 pursuant to Directive 95/46/EC of the European Parliament and of the Council on the adequate protection of personal data by the Eastern Republic of Uruguay with regard to automated processing of personal data, [2012] OJ L227/11

Proposal for a Regulation of the European Parliament and of the Council on the protection of individuals with regard to the processing of personal data and on the free movement of such data (General Data Protection Regulation), COM(2012) 11 final

Proposal for a Directive of the European Parliament and of the Council on the protection of individuals with regard to the processing of personal data by competent authorities for the purposes of prevention, investigation, detection or prosecution of criminal offences or the execution of criminal penalties, and the free movement of such data, COM(2012) 10/3

Commission Decision 2011/61/EU of 31 January 2011 pursuant to Directive 95/46/EC of the European Parliament and of the Council on the adequate protection of personal data by the State of Israel with regard to automated processing of personal data, [2011] OJ L27/39

Commission Decision of 19 October 2010 pursuant to Directive 95/46/EC of the European Parliament and of the Council on the adequate protection of personal data in Andorra, [2010] OJ L277/27

Commission Decision of 5 March 2010 pursuant to Directive 95/46/EC of the European Parliament and of the Council on the adequate protection provided by the Faeroese Act on the processing of personal data, [2010] OJ L58/17

Commission Decision 2010/87/EU of 5 February 2010 on standard contractual clauses for the transfer of personal data to processors established in third countries under Directive 95/46/EC of the European Parliament and of the Council, [2010] OJ L39/5

Consolidated version of the Treaty on the Functioning of the European Union (TFEU), [2010] OJ C83/47

Charter of Fundamental Rights of the European Union, [2010] OJ C83/2

Directive 2002/58/EU of the European Parliament and of the Council of 12 July 2002 concerning the processing of personal data and the protection of privacy in the electronic communications sector, [2002] OJ L201/37, amended by Directive 2009/136/EC of the European Parliament and of the Council of 25 November 2009, [2009] OJ L337/11

Council Framework Decision 2008/977/JHA of 27 November 2008 on the protection of personal data processed in the framework of police and judicial cooperation in criminal matters, [2008] OJ L350/60

Council Decision 2008/651/CFSP/JHA of 30 June 2008 on the signing, on behalf of the European Union, of an Agreement between the European Union and Australia on the processing and transfer of European Union-sourced passenger name record (PNR) data by air carriers to the Australian Customs Service, [2008] OJ L213/47

Commission Decision 2008/393/EC of 8 May 2008 pursuant to Directive 95/46/EC of the European Parliament and of the Council on the adequate protection of personal data in Jersey, [2008] OJ L138/21

Treaty of Lisbon amending the Treaty on European Union and the Treaty establishing the European Community, [2007] OJ C306/1

Directive 2006/24/EC of the European Parliament and of the Council of 15 March 2006 on the retention of data generated or processed in connection with the provision of publicly available electronic communications services or of public communications networks and amending Directive (EC) 2002/58, [2006] OJ L105/54

Commission Decision 2006/253/EC of 6 September 2005 on the adequate protection of personal data contained in the Passenger Name Record of air passengers transferred to the Canada Border Services Agency, [2005] OJ L91/49

Commission Decision 2004/915/EC of 27 December 2004 amending Decision (EC) 2001/497 as regards the introduction of an alternative set of standard contractual clauses for the transfer of personal data to third countries, [2004] OJ L385/74

Commission Decision 2004/411/EC of 28 April 2004 on the adequate protection of personal data in the Isle of Man, [2004] OJ L151/1

Commission Decision 2003/821/EC of 21 November 2003 on the adequate protection of personal data in Guernsey, [2003] OJ L308

Commission Decision C (2003) 1731 of 30 June 2003 pursuant to Directive 95/46/EC of the European Parliament and of the Council on the adequate protection of personal data in Argentina, [2003] OJ L168

Commission Decision 2002/2/EC of 20 December 2001 pursuant to Directive 95/46/EC of the European Parliament and of the Council on the adequate protection of personal data provided by the Canadian Personal Information Protection and Electronic Documents Act, [2002] OJ L2/13

Regulation (EC) No 45/2001 of the European Parliament and of the Council of 18 December 2000 on the protection of individuals with regard to the processing of personal data by the institutions and bodies of the Community and on the free movement of such data, [2001] OJ L8/1

Commission Decision 2001/497/EC of 15 June 2001 on standard contractual clauses for the transfer of personal data to third countries, under Directive 95/46/EC, [2001] OJ L181/19

Council Regulation (EC) 44/2001 of 22 December 2000 on jurisdiction and the recognition and enforcement of judgments in civil and commercial matters, [2001] OJ L12/1

Commission Decision 2000/520/EC of 26 July 2000 pursuant to Directive 95/46 of the European Parliament and of the Council on the adequacy of the protection provided by the safe harbor privacy principles and related frequently asked questions issued by the US Department of Commerce, [2000] OJ L215/7

Decision of the EEA Joint Committee No 83/1999 of 25 June 1999 amending Protocol 37 and Annex XI (Telecommunication services) to the EEA Agreement, [2000] OJ L296/41

Commission Decision 2000/518/EC of 26 July 2000 pursuant to Directive 95/46/EC of the European Parliament and of the Council on the adequate protection of personal data provided in Switzerland, [2000] OJ L215/1

Directive 95/46/EC of the European Parliament and of the Council of 24 October 1995 on the protection of individuals with regard to the processing of personal data and on the free movement of such data, [1995] OJ L281/31

European Commission, Amended Proposal for a Council Directive on the protection of individuals with regard to the processing of personal data and on the free movement of such data, COM(92) 422 final, 15 October 1992

(iv) **National constitutions**

Belgian Constitution of 7 February 1831, last revised in July 1993
Portuguese Constitution of 2 April 1976
Spanish Constitution of 27 December 1978
Swedish Constitution of 1 January 1975

(v) **National law and regulation**

Albania: Law No. 9887 on the Protection of Personal Data (10 March 2008)
Andorra: Qualified Law 15/2003 of December 18, on the Protection of Personal Data, 2003

Angola: Law No. 22/11 on the Protection of Personal Data

Argentina: Personal Data Protection Act (4 October 2000), Act No. 25,326

Armenia: Law on Personal Data (8 October 2002)

Australia: Privacy Act 1988, as amended on 14 September 2006; Australian Privacy Principles, Companion Guide (June 2010)

Austria: Data Protection Act 2000; Verordnung des Bundeskanzlers vom 18. Dezember 1980 über die Gleichwertigkeit ausländischer Datenschutzbestimmungen, Bundesgesetzblatt für die Republik Österreich, 30 December 1980, at 3403; Österreichisches Datenschutzgesetz vom 18.10.1978; Konsumentenschutzgesetz

Azerbaijan: Law on Personal Data No. 998-IIIQ (2010)

Bahamas: Data Protection (Privacy of Personal Information) Act (11 April 2003)

Benin: Law No. 2009-09 on the Protection of Personal Data (27 April 2009)

Bosnia and Herzegovina: Law on the Protection of Personal Data (27 July 2001)

Burkina Faso: Law No. 010-2004/AN Regarding the Protection of Personal Data (20 April 2004); Assemblée Nationale, Dossier No. 06 relatif au projet de loi portant sur la protection des données à caractère personnel

Colombia: Law 1581 of 17 October 2012; Law 1266 of 2008

Costa Rica: Law No. 8968/2011 on the Protection of Personal Data

Croatia: Act on Personal Data Protection (12 June 2003), no. 1364-2003 (as amended by Act on Amendments to the Personal Data Protection Act, No. 2616-2006)

Dubai International Financial Centre (DIFC): Data Protection Law 2007, Law no. 1 of 2007

Faroe Islands: Act on Processing of Personal Data, Act No. 73 of 8 May 2001, as amended by Act No. 24 of 17 May 2004

Finland: Personal Data File Act and Personal Data File Decree, 30 April 1987

France: Data Protection Act

Gabon: Law No. 001/2011 (25 September 2011) on the Protection of Personal Data

Germany: Federal Data Protection Act (Bundesdatenschutzgesetz); Unterlassungsklagegesetz

Greece: Data Protection Act

Bailiwick of Guernsey: Data Protection Law (2001), as amended by the Data Protection (Bailiwick of Guernsey) (Amendment) Ordinance (2010)

Hong Kong: Personal Data (Privacy) Ordinance

India: Indian Ministry of Communications and Information Technology, Information Technology (Reasonable security practices and procedures and sensitive personal data or information) Rules (2011) (issued under Section 43 of the Information Technology Act 2000)

Ireland: Data Protection Bill, 1987

Isle of Man: Data Protection Act (2002)

Israel: Protection of Privacy Law, 5741-1981 (2001); and Privacy Protection (Transfer of Data to Databases Abroad) Regulations, 5761-2001

Japan: Kojinjoho no hogo ni kansuru horitsu [Japanese Personal Information Protection Act], Law No. 57 of 2003

Jersey: Data Protection Law, 2005 (L.2/2005)

Luxembourg: Data Protection Act of 31 March 1979

Macau (Macau Special Administrative Region (MSAR) of the People's Republic of China): Personal Data Protection Act (Act 8/2005)

Former Yugoslav Republic of Macedonia: Law on Personal Data Protection (25 January 2005)

Mauritius: Data Protection Act 2004, Act No. 13 of 2004; Debate No. 12 of 01.06.04, Second Reading of the Data Protection Bill (No. XV of 2004)

Mexico: Decree issuing the Federal Law on Protection of Personal Data Held by Private Parties (2010)

Monaco: Law No. 1.165—Act Concerning the Processing of Nominal Information (23 December 1993)

Morocco: Law No. 09-08 Relative to the Protection of Individuals with regard to their Personal Data (5 March 2009)

Netherlands: Data Protection Act

New Zealand: Privacy (Cross-border Information) Amendment Bill 221-2 (2008), Part 11A; Privacy Act 1993; Law Commission of New Zealand, 'Review of the Privacy Act 1993' (March 2010)

Peru: Law No. 29733/2011 on the Protection of Personal Data

Poland: Data Protection Act

Russia: Federal Law of 27 July 2006 No. 152-FZ on Personal Data (as amended by Law of 25 July 2011 No. 261-FZ)

San Marino: Act on Collection, Elaboration and Use of Computerised Personal Data, 1983, as amended by Act No. 70/95 (1995)

Senegal: Law No. 2008-12 of 25 January 2008, on the Protection of Personal Data; Rapport sur le projet de loi No. 32/2007 portant sur la protection des données à caractère personnel

Serbia: Law on Personal Data Protection (October 2008)

South Korea: Personal Information Protection Act, Law 10465 (2011)

St Lucia: Data Protection Act 2011

Sweden: Data Act of 1973

Switzerland: Federal Act on Data Protection (as amended April 2011)

Trinidad and Tobago: Act No. 13/2011 on the Protection of Personal Privacy and Information

Tunisia: Law No. 2004-63 of 27 July 2004, on the Protection of Personal Data (2004)

Ukraine: Law No. 2297-VI of 1 June 2010 on Protection of Personal Data

Uruguay: Data Protection Act, no. 18.331 (2008)

United States: Foreign Account Tax Compliance Act (FATCA)

(vi) Proposed national law and regulation not yet in force

Barbados: Data Protection Act (draft bill)

Malaysia: Personal Data Protection Bill (2010) (enacted but not yet in force)

Singapore: Personal Data Protection Bill (Bill No. 24/2012)

South Africa: Protection of Personal Information Bill (2012) (still in the legislative process)

(vii) Provincial and state law

Alberta Freedom of Information and Protection of Privacy Act

British Columbia Freedom of Information and Protection of Privacy Amendment Act

Hessisches Datenschutzgesetz, 7 October 1970

Massachusetts Standards for the Protection of Personal Information of Residents of the Commonwealth, 201 Mass. Code Regs 17.00–17.05

Québec Act Respecting Access to Documents Held by Public Bodies and the Protection of Personal Information (2006)

Québec Act Respecting the Protection of Personal Information in the Private Sector

2. CASE LAW

(i) International Court of Justice and Permanent Court of International Justice

Case concerning Barcelona Traction, Light and Power Co. Ltd (*Belgium v Spain*), [1970] ICJ Reports 65

SS Lotus (*France v Turkey*), PCIJ Reports, Series A, No. 10 (1927)

(ii) Court of Justice of the European Union (European Court of Justice)

Reference for a preliminary ruling from the Audiencia Nacional (Spain) lodged on 9 March 2012—Case C-131/12 *Google Spain, SL, Google Inc. v Agencia Española de Protección de Datos, Mario Costeja González*

Case C-366/10 *The Air Transport Association of America and Others* [2011] ECR 0000

Joined Cases C-468/10 and C-469/10 *ASNEF and FECEMD v Administración del Estado* [2011] ECR I-0000

Joined Cases C-92/09 and C-93/09 *Volker und Markus Schecke* [2010] ECR I-0000

Joined Cases C-402 and 415/05 P *Kadi & Al Barakaat Int'l Found. v Council & Commission* [2008] ECR I-6351

Case T-194/04 *Bavarian Lager v Commission* [2007] ECR-II 04523, (partially reversed by the ECJ, Case C-28/08 P *Bavarian Lager* [2010] ECR I-06055)

Case C-255/02 *Halifax plc* [2006] ECR I-1609

Case C-101/01 *Bodil Lindqvist* [2003] ECR I-12971

Joined Cases C-465/00, C-138/01 and C-139/01 *Rechnungshof* [2003] ECR I-4989

Case 110/99 *Emsland-Stärke v Hauptzollamt Hamburg-Jonas* [2000] ECR-I-11569

Case C-212/97 *Centros Ltd v Erhvervs- og Selskabsstyrelsen* [1999] ECR I-1459

(iii) European Court of Human Rights

Al-Jedda v United Kingdom (2011)] ECHR 1092

Al-Skeini v United Kingdom (2011) 53 EHRR 18

Case of Dickson v United Kingdom (2008) 46 EHRR 927

Kudla v Poland (2002) 35 EHRR 198

Z v United Kingdom (2002) 34 EHRR 97

Rotaru v Romania (2000) ECHR 191

Amann v Switzerland (2000) ECHR 87

Z v Finland (1997) 25 EHRR 371

Handyside v United Kingdom (1976) 1 EHRR 737

(iv) US cases

US Federal Trade Commission, *In the Matter of Google Inc.*, Docket No. C-4336, 13 October 2011

Columbia Pictures, Inc. v Bunnell, 245 FRD 443, 69 FedRServ3d 173 (C.D. Cal. 2007)

Volkswagen v Valdez, 909 SW2d 900 (Tex. 1995)

3. BOOKS AND BOOK CHAPTERS

Philip Alston, 'The "not-a-cat" syndrome: can the international human rights regime accommodate non-state actors?', in Philip Alston (ed), *Non-State Actors and Human Rights* 3 (OUP 2005)

American Bar Association, Committee on Corporate Laws, *Corporate Director's Guidebook* (ABA 2007)

Maria Véronica Pérez Asinari, 'International Aspects of Personal Data Protection: *Quo Vadis EU?*', in Maria Véronica Pérez Asinari and Pablo Palazzi (eds), *Challenges of Privacy and Data Protection Law* 381 (31 Cahiers du CRID) (Bruylant 2008)

Robert Baldwin, Martin Cave, and Martin Lodge, *Understanding Regulation: Theory, Strategy, and Practice* (2nd edn, OUP 2012)

Colin J. Bennett and Charles D. Raab, *The Governance of Privacy* (MIT Press 2006)

Franziska Boehm, *Information Sharing and Data Protection in the Area of Freedom, Security and Justice* (Springer 2012)

Katharina Boele-Woelki, 'Unifying and Harmonizing Substantive Law and the Role of Conflict of Laws', 340 *Recueil des Cours de l'Académie de Droit International* 271 (2009)

Michael Bothe and Wolfgang Kilian, *Rechtsfragen grenzüberschreitender Datenflüsse* (Verlag Dr Otto Schmidt 1992)

Ian Brownlie, *Principles of Public International Law* (7th edn, OUP 2008)

Roger Brownsword and Morag Goodwin, *Law and Technologies of the Twenty-First Century* (CUP 2012)

Lee Bygrave, 'Privacy Protection in a Global Context—A Comparative Overview', in Peter Wahlgren (ed), *Scandinavian Studies in Law* 319 (Stockholm Institute for Scandinavian Law 2004)

Lee Bygrave, *Data Protection Law: Approaching its Rationale, Logic and Limits* (Kluwer Law International 2002)

Fred H. Cate, 'The Failure of Fair Information Practice Principles', in Jane K. Winn (ed), *Consumer Protection in the Age of the Information Economy* 341 (Ashgate 2006), also online at <http://papers.ssrn.com/sol3/papers.cfm?abstract_id=1156972>

F.A. Mann, unpublished manuscript, quoted in Lawrence Collins, 'F.A. Mann', in Jack Beatson and Reinhard Zimmerman (eds), *Jurists Uprooted: German-Speaking Émigré Lawyers in Twentieth-century Britain* 381 (OUP 2004)

Els De Busser, *Data Protection in EU and US Criminal Cooperation* (Maklu 2009)

Paul De Hert and Serge Gutwirth, 'Data Protection in the Case law of Strasbourg and Luxembourg: Constitutionalisation in Action', in Serge Gutwirth et al. (eds), *Reinventing Data Protection?* 3 (Springer 2009)

Andreas Fischer-Lescano and Gunther Teubner, *Regime-Kollisionen* (Suhrkamp Verlag 2006)

Jan Freese, *International Data Flow* (Studentlitteratur 1979)

Lon L. Fuller, *The Morality of Law* (2nd edn, Yale University Press 1969)

Jack Goldsmith and Tim Wu, *Who Controls the Internet? Illusions of a Borderless World* (OUP 2008)

James Griffin, *On Human Rights* (OUP 2008)

Dieter Grimm, 'The Protective Function of the State', in Georg Nolte (ed), *European and US Constitutionalism* 137 (CUP 2005)

Lauri Hannikainen and Kristian Myntti, 'Article 19', in Asbjørn Eide et al. (eds), *The Universal Declaration of Human Rights: A Commentary* (Scandinavian University Press 1992)

Mika Hayashi, 'The Information Revolution and the Rules of Jurisdiction in Public International Law', in Myriam Dunn, Sai Felicia Krishna-Hensel, and Victor Mauer (eds), *The Resurgence of the State* 59 (Ashgate 2007)

Jonathan Hill, 'The Exercise of Jurisdiction in Private International Law', in Patrick Capps, Malcolm Evans, and Stratos Konstadinidis (eds), *Asserting Jurisdiction: International and European Legal Perspectives* 39 (Hart 2003)

Frits W. Hondius, *Emerging Data Protection in Europe* (North-Holland 1975)

Bert-Jaap Koops, 'Criteria for normative technology: the acceptability of "code as law" in light of democratic and constitutional values', in Roger Brownsword and Karen Yeung (eds), *Regulating Technologies: Legal Futures, Regulatory Frames and Technological Fixes* 161 (Hart 2008)

Martti Koskenniemi, *From Apology to Utopia* (CUP 2006)

John W. Kropf, *Guide to U.S. Government Practice on Global Sharing of Personal Information* (American Bar Association 2012)

Christopher Kuner, *European Data Protection Law: Corporate Compliance and Regulation* (2nd edn, OUP 2007)

Lawrence Lessig, *Code (version 2.0)* (Basic Books 2006), <http://codev2.cc/download+remix/Lessig-Codev2.pdf>

Kurt Lipstein, 'The General Principles of Private International Law', 135 *Recueil des Cours de l'Académie de Droit International* 72 (1972)

Miguel Poiares Maduro, 'Foreword', in Rita de la Feria and Stefan Vogenauer (eds), *Prohibition of Abuse of Law: A New General Principle of EU Law?* vii (Hart 2011)

F.A. Mann, 'The Doctrine of Jurisdiction in International Law', 111 *Recueil des Cours de l'Académie de Droit International* 9 (1964)

Christopher Marsden, *Internet Co-Regulation: European Law, Regulatory Governance and Legitimacy in Cyberspace* (CUP 2011)

Hans-Joachim Mengel, *Internationale Organisationen und transnationaler Datenschutz* (Wissenschaftlicher Autoren-Verlag 1984)

Marko Milanovic, *Extraterritorial Application of Human Rights Treaties* (OUP 2011)

Lokke Moerel, *Binding Corporate Rules: Corporate Self-Regulation of Global Data Transfers* (OUP 2012)

Manfred Nowak, *UN Covenant on Civil and Political Rights (CCPR Commentary)* (N.P. Engel 1993)

John Palfrey and Urs Gasser, *Interop, The Promise and Perils of Highly Interconnected Systems* (Basic Books 2012)

Coleman Phillipson, *The International Law and Custom of Ancient Greece and Rome* (Macmillan 1911)

Edward W. Ploman, *International Law Governing Communications and Information* (Frances Pinter Ltd 1982)

Corien Prins, 'Should ICT regulation be undertaken at an international level?', in Bert-Jaap Koops, Miriam Lips, Corien Prins, and Maurice Shellekens (eds), *Starting Points for ICT Regulation: Deconstructing Prevalent Policy One-Liners* 151 (TMC Asser Press 2006)

Charles D. Raab and Paul De Hert, 'Tools for Technology Regulation: Seeking Analytical Approaches Beyond Lessig and Hood' in Roger Brownsword and Karen Yeung (eds), *Regulating Technologies: Legal Futures, Regulatory Frames and Technological Fixes* 263 (Hart 2008)

Chris Reed, *Making Laws for Cyberspace* (OUP 2012)

Restatement of the Law (Third), The Foreign Relations Law of the United States (American Law Institute Publishers 1987)

Hannes Rössler, 'Interpretation of EU Law', in Jürgen Basedow, Klaus J. Hopt, Reinhard Zimmermann, and Andreas Stier (eds), *Max Planck Encyclopedia of European Private Law* (OUP 2012)

Cedric Ryngaert, *Jurisdiction in International Law* (OUP 2008)

Dag Wiese Schartum, 'Norway', in Peter Blume (ed), *Nordic Data Protection Law* (DJØF 2001)

Sara Schoonmaker, *High-Tech Trade Wars: US–Brazilian Conflicts in the Global Economy* (University of Pittsburgh Press 2002)

Paul M. Schwartz and Daniel Solove, *Privacy Law Fundamentals* (International Association of Privacy Professionals 2011)

Spiros Simitis and Ulrich Dammann, *EU-Datenschutzrichtlinie* (Nomos-Verlag 1997)

Dan Jerker B. Svantesson, *Private International Law and the Internet* (Kluwer Law International 2007)

Peter P. Swire and Robert E. Litan, *None of Your Business: World Data Flows, Electronic Commerce, and the European Privacy Directive* (Brookings Institution Press 1998)

Takis Tridimas, *The General Principles of EU Law* (2nd edn, OUP 2009)

Nicola Vennemann, 'Application of International Human Rights Conventions to Transboundary State Acts', in Rebecca M. Bratspies and Russell A. Miller (eds), *Transboundary Harm in International Law: Lessons from the Trailsmelter Arbitration* 295 (CUP 2006)

Alan Westin, *Privacy and Freedom* (Atheneum 1970)

Robin C.A. White and Claire Ovey, *The European Convention on Human Rights* (5th edn, OUP 2010)

Lucius N. Wochner, *Der Persönlichkeitsschutz im grenzüberschreitenden Datenverkehr* (Schulthess Polygraphischer Verlag 1981)

4. LEGAL ARTICLES AND STUDIES

Maria Verónica Perez Asinari, 'Is there any Room for Privacy and Data Protection within the WTO Rules?', 9 Electronic Commerce Law Review 249 (2002)

Theodore P. Augustinos and Socheth Sor, 'March 1 Compliance Deadline Looms for Companies With Personal Information of Massachusetts Residents', (20 February 2012) Bloomberg BNA Privacy & Security Law Report 317

Eyal Benvenisti and George W. Downs, 'The Empire's New Clothes: Political Economy and the Fragmentation of International Law', 60 Stanford Law Review 595 (2007)

Paul Schiff Berman, 'Global legal pluralism', 80 Southern California Law Review 1155 (2007)

Jon Bing, 'Data Protection, Jurisdiction and the Choice of Law', [1999] Privacy Law & Policy Reporter 92, also available at <http://www.austlii.edu.au/au/journals/PLPR/1999/65.html>

Jon Bing, 'Transnational Data Flows and the Scandinavian Data Protection Legislation', 24 Scandinavian Studies in Law 65 (1980)

W. Scott Blackmer, 'Transborder data flows at risk', Lexology (20 February 2012), <http://www.infolawgroup.com/2012/02/articles/cloud-computing-1/transborder-data-flows-at-risk/>

Peter Blume, 'Transborder data flow: Is there a solution in sight?', 8 International Journal of Law and Information Technology 65 (2000)

Jane Bortnick, 'International Information Flow: The Developing World Perspective', 14 Cornell International Law Journal 333 (1981)

Anne W. Branscomb, 'Global Governance of Global Networks: A Survey of Transborder Data Flow in Transition', 36 Vanderbilt Law Review 985 (1983)

Ian Brown, 'Government Access to Private-Sector Data in the United Kingdom', 2(4) International Data Privacy Law 230 (2012)

Ulf Brühann, 'Die Veröffentlichung personenbezogener Daten im Internet als Datenschutzproblem', (2004) Datenschutz und Datensicherheit 201

Paula J. Bruening and K. Krasnow Waterman, 'Data tagging for new models of information governance', 8 IEEE Security & Privacy 64 (Sept.–Oct. 2010)

Paula Bruening and Bridget Treacy, 'Privacy, Security Issues Raised by Cloud Computing', (9 March 2009) Bloomberg BNA Privacy & Security Law Report 425

Gráinne de Búrca, 'The European Court of Justice and the International Legal Order after *Kadi*', 51 Harvard International Law Journal 1 (2010)

Mark Burdon, Jason Reid, and Rouhshi Low, 'Encryption safe harbours and data breach notification laws', 26 Computer Law and Security Review 520 (2010)

Lee Bygrave, 'Determining applicable law pursuant to European Data Protection Legislation', 16 Computer Law and Security Report 252 (2000)

Paolo G. Carozza, 'Subsidiarity as a structural principle of international human rights law', 97 American Journal of International Law 38 (2003)

J.M. Carroll, 'The Problem of Transnational Data Flows', in *Policy Issues in Data Protection and Privacy, Proceedings of the OECD Seminar 24th to 26th June 1974*, at 201

Fred H. Cate, James X. Dempsey, and Ira S. Rubenstein, 'Systematic government access to private-sector data', 2 International Data Privacy Law 195 (2012)

Fred H. Cate, 'Government data mining: the need for a legal framework', 43 Harvard Civil Rights-Civil Liberties Law Review 435 (2008)

Fred H. Cate, 'Provincial Canadian Geographic Restrictions on Personal Data in the Public Sector' (2008), <http://www.hunton.com/files/tbl_s47Details/FileUpload265/2312/cate_patriotact_white_paper.pdf>

Fred H. Cate, 'The First Amendment and the International "Free Flow" of Information', 30 Virginia Journal of International Law 371 (1989)

Cayman Islands, Consultation on the draft Data Protection Bill 2012, September 2012, <http://www.dataprotection.ky/images/downloads/general%20public%20consultation%20paper.pdf>

Malcolm Crompton, Christine Cowper, and Christopher Jefferis, 'The Australian *Dodo* Case: An Insight for Data Protection Regulation', (26 January 2009) Bloomberg BNA Privacy & Security Law Report 180

Ronald Dworkin, 'Is Wealth a Value?', (1980) 9 Journal of Legal Studies 191

John M. Eger, 'Emerging Restrictions on Transnational Data Flows: Privacy Protection or Non-Tariff Trade Barriers?', 10 Law and Policy in International Business 1055 (1978)

European Commission (DG Justice), 'Comparative Study on Different Approaches to New Privacy Challenges in Particular in the Light of Technological Developments' (20 January 2010), <http://ec.europa.eu/justice/policies/privacy/docs/studies/new_privacy_challenges/final_report_working_paper_2_en.pdf>

European Group on Tort Law, 'Principles of European Tort Law' (2005), <http://civil.udg.edu/php//templates/PUBLIC/img/egtl/icon_doc.gif>

J.J. Fawcett, 'Evasion of Law and Mandatory Rules in Private International Law', 49 Cambridge Law Journal 44 (1990)

Andreas Fischer-Lescano and Gunther Teubner, 'Regime-Collisions: the Vain Search for Legal Unity in the Fragmentation of Global Law', 25 Michigan Journal of International Law 999 (2003)

William L. Fishman, 'Introduction to Transborder Data Flows', 16 Stanford Journal of International Law 3 (1980)

A. Michael Froomkin, 'Of governments and governance', 14 Berkeley Technology Law Journal 617 (1999)

Galexia, 'The US Safe Harbor: fact or fiction?' (2008), <http://www.galexia.com/public/research/assets/safe_harbor_fact_or_fiction_2008/safe_harbor_fact_or_fiction-Detailed.html>

Robert Gellman, *Privacy in the Clouds: Risks to Privacy and Confidentiality from Cloud Computing* (World Privacy Forum, 23 February 2009), <http://www.worldprivacyforum.org/pdf/WPF_Cloud_Privacy_Report.pdf>

Pankaj Ghemawat, 'Why the World Isn't Flat', 159 Foreign Policy 54 (2007)

John Goldring, 'Globalisation, National Sovereignty and the Harmonisation of Laws', (1998) Uniform Law Review 435

Jack Goldsmith, 'Against Cyberanarchy', 65 University of Chicago Law Review 1199 (1998)

Roy Goode, 'Reflections on the Harmonisation of Commercial Law', (1991) Uniform Law Review 54

Allan Gotlieb, Charles Dalfen, and Kenneth Katz, 'The Transborder Transfer of Information by Communications and Computer Systems: Issues and Approaches to Guiding Principles', 68 American Journal of International Law 227 (1974)

Damon Greer, 'Safe Harbor—a framework that works', 1 International Data Privacy Law 143 (2011)

Graham Greenleaf, 'Global data privacy laws: 89 countries, and accelerating', Queen Mary University of London, School of Law Legal Studies Research Paper No. 98/2012 (2012), <http://ssrn.com/abstract=2000034>

Graham Greenleaf, 'Promises and illusions of data protection in Indian Law', 1 International Data Privacy Law 47 (2011)

Graham Greenleaf, 'Five Years of the APEC Privacy Framework: Failure or Promise?', 25 Computer Law and Security Review 28 (2009)

Hague Conference on Private International Law, 'Cross-Border Data Flows and Protection of Privacy' (13 March 2010), <http://www.hcch.net/upload/wop/genaff2010pd13e.pdf>

Dara Hallinan, Michael Friedewald, and Paul McCarthy, 'Citizens' perceptions of data protection and privacy in Europe', 28 Computer Law and Security Review 263 (2012)

Alden Heintz, 'The Dangers of Regulation', 29(3) Journal of Communications 129 (1979)

Adrienne Héritier, 'Mutual recognition: comparing policy areas', 14 Journal of European Public Policy 800 (2007)

Christof Heyns and Frans Viljoen, 'The Impact of the United Nations Human Rights Treaties on the Domestic Level', 23 Human Rights Quarterly 483 (2001)

W. Kuan Hon and Christopher Millard, 'Data Export in Cloud Computing—How can Personal Data be Transferred outside the EEA? (The Cloud of Unknowing, Part 4)', Queen Mary University of London, School of Law (4 April 2012), <http://www.cloudlegal.ccls.qmul.ac.uk/Research/researchpapers/55649.html>

Frits W. Hondius, 'A Decade of International Data Protection', 30 Netherlands International Law Review 103 (1983)

Frits W. Hondius, 'International Data Protection Action', in *Policy Issues in Data Protection and Privacy, Proceedings of the OECD Seminar 24th to 26th June 1974*, 208

International Chamber of Commerce (ICC), 'Cross-border law enforcement access to company data—current issues under data protection and privacy law', Document No. 373/507 (7 February 2012), <http://www.iccwbo.org/Data/Policies/2012/Cross-border-law-enforcement-access-to-company-data-current-issues-under-data-protection-and-privacy-law/>

International Chamber of Commerce (ICC), 'Privacy Toolkit, An International Business Guide for Policymakers' (2003), <http://intgovforum.org/Substantive_1st_IGF/privacy_toolkit.pdf>

International Monetary Fund, 'Capital Controls: Country Experiences with their Use and Liberalization' (17 May 2000), <http://www.imf.org/external/pubs/ft/op/op190/index.htm>

Katie W. Johnson, 'APEC Cross-Border Data Transfer Rules Aren't a Safe Harbor, FTC's Ramirez Says', (19 March 2012) Bloomberg BNA Privacy & Security Law Report 503

Chris Jones (Statewatch Analysis), 'Making fundamental rights flexible: the European Commission's Approach to negotiating agreements on the transfer of passenger name record (PNR) data to the USA and Australia' (March 2012), <http://www.statewatch.org/analyses/no-169-eu-pnr-us-aus-comparison.pdf>

Shalom Kassan, 'Extraterritorial Jurisdiction in the Ancient World', 29 American Journal of International Law (1935)

Michael Kirby, 'The history, achievement and future of the 1980 OECD guidelines on privacy', 1 International Data Privacy Law 6 (2011)

Michael D. Kirby, 'Transborder Data Flows and the "Basic Rules of Data Privacy"', 16 Stanford Journal of International Law 27 (1980)

Souichirou Kozuka, 'The Economic Implications of Uniformity in Law', (2007) Uniform Law Review 683

Nico Krisch, 'The open architecture of European human rights law', 71 Modern Law Review 183 (2008)

Nico Krisch, 'The pluralism of global administrative law', 17 European Journal of International Law 247 (2006)

John W. Kropf, 'The Golden Rule of Privacy: A Proposal for a Global Privacy Policy on Government-to-Government Sharing of Personal Information', (15 January 2007) Bloomberg BNA Privacy & Security Law Report 90

Christopher Kuner, 'The European Commission's Proposed Data Protection Regulation: A Copernican Revolution in European Data Protection Law', (6 February 2012) Bloomberg BNA Privacy & Security Law Report 6

Christopher Kuner, 'Data Protection Law and International Jurisdiction on the Internet' (Parts 1 and 2), 18 International Journal of Law and Information Technology (2010) 18(2) 176 and 18(3) 227

Christopher Kuner, 'An International Legal Framework for Data Protection: Issues and Prospects', 25 Computer Law and Security Review 307 (2009)

Christopher Kuner, 'Onward Transfers of Personal Data under the US Safe Harbor Framework', (17 August 2009) Bloomberg BNA Privacy & Security Law Report 1211

Sandra Lavenex, 'Mutual recognition and the monopoly of force: limits of the single market analogy', 14 Journal of European Public Policy 762 (2007)

Miguel Poiares Maduro, 'So close and yet so far: the paradoxes of mutual recognition', 14 Journal of European Public Policy 814 (2007)

Theodor Meron, 'Extraterritoriality of Human Rights Treaties', 89 American Journal of International Law 78 (1995)

Ralf Michaels and Joost Pauwelyn, 'Conflict of Norms or Conflict of Laws? Different Techniques in the Fragmentation of International Law', Duke Law Scholarship Repository, 4/2012, <http://scholarship.law.duke.edu/cgi/viewcontent.cgi?article=2933&context=faculty_scholarship>

Alex Mills, 'The Private History of International Law', 55 International and Comparative Law Quarterly 1 (2006)

Hiroshi Miyashita, 'The evolving concept of data privacy in Japanese law', 1 International Data Privacy Law 229 (2011)

Ved P. Nanda, 'The Communication Revolution and the Free Flow of Information in a Transnational Setting', 30 American Journal of Comparative Law Supplement (1982)

Kalypso Nicolaidis and Gregory Shaffer, 'Transnational mutual recognition regimes: governance without global government', 68 Law and Contemporary Problems 263 (2005)

Paul Ohm, 'Broken Promises of Privacy: Responding to the Surprising Failure of Anonymization', 57 UCLA Law Review 1701 (2010)

G. Russell Pipe, 'National Policies, International Debates', 29(3) Journal of Communications 114 (1979)

Jörg Polakiewicz, 'Corporate Responsibility to Respect Human Rights: Challenges and Opportunities for Europe and Japan', CALE Discussion Paper No. 9 (October 2012), <http://cale.law.nagoya-u.ac.jp/_src/sc618/CALE20DP20No.209-121010.pdf>

Chris Reed, 'How to Make Bad Law: Lessons from Cyberspace', 73 Modern Law Review 903 (2010)

Joel Reidenberg, 'Technology and Internet Jurisdiction', 153 University of Pennsylvania Law Review 1951 (2004–05)

Joel R. Reidenberg, 'E-commerce and transatlantic privacy', 38 Houston Law Review 717 (2001)

Joel R. Reidenberg, 'Lex Informatica: the Formulation of Information Policy Rules through Technology', 76 Texas Law Review 553 (1998)

Susanne K. Schmidt, 'Mutual recognition as a new mode of governance', 14 Journal of European Public Policy 667 (2007)

Olivier De Schutter, 'Globalization and jurisdiction: lessons from the European Convention on Human Rights', 6 Baltic Yearbook of International Law 185 (2006)

Paul M. Schwartz, 'The E.U.–U.S. Privacy Collision: A Turn to Institutions and Procedures', Harvard Law Review Symposium 2012: Privacy & Technology, <http://www.harvard-lawreview.org/symposium/papers2012/schwartz.pdf>

Paul M. Schwartz, 'Systematic Government Access to Private-Sector Data in Germany', 2(4) International Data Privacy Law 289 (2012)

Paul M. Schwartz and Karl-Nikolaus Peifer, 'Prosser's Privacy and the German Right of Personality: Are Four Privacy Torts Better than One Unitary Concept?', 98 California Law Review 1925 (2010)

Paul M. Schwartz, 'Managing Global Data Privacy: Cross-Border Information Flows in a Networked Environment' (2009), <http://theprivacyprojects.org/wp-content/uploads/2009/08/The-Privacy-Projects-Paul-Schwartz-Global-Data-Flows-20093.pdf>

Paul M. Schwartz, 'European Data Protection Law and Restrictions on International Data Flows', 80 Iowa Law Review 471 (1995)

William Seltzer and Margo Anderson, 'The Dark Side of Numbers: The Role of Population Data Systems in Human Rights Abuses', 68(2) Social Research 481 (2001)

Gregory Shaffer, 'Reconciling trade and regulatory goals: prospects and limits of new approaches to transatlantic governance through mutual recognition and safe harbour agreements', 9 Columbia Journal of European Law 29 (2002)

Gregory Shaffer, 'Globalization and Social Protection: the Impact of EU and International Rules in the Ratcheting Up of US Privacy Standards', 25 Yale Journal of International Law 1 (2000)

Surveillance Studies Network for the UK Information Commissioner, A Surveillance Society (September 2006), <http://www.ico.gov.uk/~/media/documents/library/Data_Protection/Practical_application/SURVEILLANCE_SOCIETY_FULL_REPORT_2006.ashx>

Dan Jerker B. Svantesson, 'Privacy, the Internet and Transborder Data Flows: An Australian Perspective', 4 Masaryk University Journal of Law and Technology (2010)

Dan Jerker B. Svantesson, 'How does the accuracy of geolocation technologies affect the law?', 7 Masaryk University Journal of Law and Technology 11 (2008)

Systematic Government Access to Private Sector Data (special issue), 2(4) International Data Privacy Law (2012)

Omer Tene and Jules Polenetsky, 'Big Data for All: Privacy and User Control in the Age of Analytics' (20 September 2012), <http://papers.ssrn.com/sol3/papers.cfm?abstract_id=2149364>

Cecile de Terwagne and Sophie Louveaux, 'Data Protection and Online Networks', 13 Computer Law and Security Report 234 (1997)

Robert Uerpmann-Wittzack, 'Internetvölkerrecht', 47 Archiv des Völkerrechts 261 (2009)

Ye Diana Wang and Henry H. Emurian, 'An overview of online trust: Concepts, elements, and implications', 21 Computers in Human Behavior 105 (2005)

Rolf H. Weber, 'Regulatory Autonomy and Privacy Standards under GATS', 7 Asian Journal of WTO and International Health Law and Policy 25 (2012)

James Q. Whitman, 'The Two Western Cultures of Privacy: Dignity Versus Liberty', 113 Yale Law Journal 1153 (2004)

Zack Whittaker, 'Blackberry encryption "too secure"; national security vs. consumer privacy', ZDNet (29 July 2010), <http://www.zdnet.com/blog/igeneration/blackberry-encryption-too-secure-national-security-vs-consumer-privacy/5732>

Yesha Yadav, 'Separated by a common language? An examination of the transatlantic dialogue on data privacy law and policy in the fight against terrorism', 36 Rutgers Computer and Technology Law Journal 73 (2009)

5. PAPERS OF DATA PROTECTION AUTHORITIES

(i) International

27th International Conference of Data Protection and Privacy Commissioners, 'The protection of personal data and privacy in a globalised world: a universal right respecting diversities' (2005)

(ii) EU

Article 29 Working Party, 'Opinion 05/2012 on Cloud Computing' (WP 196, 1 July 2012)

Article 29 Working Party, 'Opinion 8/2010 on applicable law' (WP 179, 16 December 2010)

Article 29 Working Party, 'Opinion 3/2010 on the principle of accountability' (WP 173, 13 July 2010)

Article 29 Working Party, 'Opinion 1/2010 on the concepts of "controller" and "processor"' (WP 169, 16 February 2010)

Article 29 Working Party, 'The Future of Privacy' (WP 168, 1 December 2009)

Article 29 Working Party, 'Opinion 5/2009 on online social networking' (WP 163, 12 June 2009)

Article 29 Working Party, 'Working Document 1/2009 on pre-trial discovery for cross border civil litigation' (WP 158, 11 February 2009)

Article 29 Working Party, 'Working Document on Frequently Asked Questions (FAQs) related to Binding Corporate Rules' (WP 155 rev. 4, 24 June 2008)

Article 29 Working Party, 'Working Document setting up a framework for the structure of Binding Corporate Rules' (WP 154, 25 June 2008)

Article 29 Working Party, 'Working Document setting up a table with the elements and principles to be found in Binding Corporate Rules' (WP 153, 24 June 2008)

Article 29 Working Party, 'Recommendation 1/2007 on the Standard Application for Approval of Binding Corporate Rules for the Transfer of Personal Data' (WP 133, 10 January 2007)

Article 29 Working Party, 'Opinion 10/2006 on the processing of personal data by the Society for Worldwide Interbank Financial Telecommunication (SWIFT)' (WP 128, 22 November 2006)

Article 29 Working Party, 'Opinion 1/2006 on the application of EU data protection rules to internal whistleblowing schemes in the fields of accounting, internal accounting controls, auditing matters, fight against bribery, banking and financial crime' (WP 117, 1 February 2006)

Article 29 Working Party, 'Working document on a common interpretation of Article 26(1) of Directive 95/46/EC of 24 October 1995' (WP 114, 25 November 2005)

Article 29 Working Party, 'Working Document Establishing a Model Checklist Application for Approval of Binding Corporate Rules' (WP 108, 14 April 2005)

Article 29 Working Party, 'Working Document Setting Forth a Co-Operation Procedure for Issuing Common Opinions on Adequate Safeguards Resulting From "Binding Corporate Rules"' (WP 107, 14 April 2005)

Article 29 Working Party, 'Model Checklist, Application for approval of Binding Corporate Rules' (WP 102, 25 November 2004)

Article 29 Working Party, 'Working Document on Transfers of personal data to third countries: Applying Article 26(2) of the EU Data Protection Directive to Binding Corporate Rules for International Data Transfers' (WP 74, 3 June 2003)

Article 29 Working Party, 'Opinion 4/2002 on the level of protection of Personal Data in Argentina' (WP 63, 3 October 2002)

Article 29 Working Party, 'Opinion 2/2002 on the use of unique identifiers in telecommunication terminal equipments: the example of IPv6' (WP 58, 30 May 2002)

Article 29 Working Party, 'Working document on determining the international application of EU data protection law to personal data processing on the Internet by non-EU based websites' (WP 56, 30 May 2002)

Article 29 Working Party, 'Opinion 7/2001 on the Draft Commission Decision (version 31 August 2001) on Standard Contractual Clauses for the Transfer of Personal Data to Data Processors Established in Third Countries under Article 26(4) of Directive 95/46' (WP 47, 13 September 2001)

Article 29 Working Party, 'Working Document: Transfers of personal data to third countries: Applying Articles 25 and 26 of the EU data protection directive' (WP 12, 24 July 1998)

Article 29 Working Party, 'First orientations on Transfers of Personal Data to Third Countries—Possible Ways Forward in Assessing Adequacy' (WP 4, 26 June 1997)

European Data Protection Supervisor, 'Opinion of the European Data Protection Supervisor on the Commission's Communication on "Unleashing the potential of Cloud Computing in Europe"' (16 November 2012)

European Data Protection Supervisor, 'Opinion of the European Data Protection Supervisor on the data protection reform package' (7 March 2012)

European Data Protection Supervisor, 'Opinion of the European Data Protection Supervisor on the proposal for a Council Decision on the conclusion of the Agreement between the United States of America and the European Union on the use and transfer of Passenger

Name Records to the United States Department of Homeland Security', 9 February 2012, [2012] OJ C35/16

European Data Protection Supervisor, 'Opinion of the European Data Protection Supervisor on the Proposal for a Council Decision on the conclusion of the Agreement between the United States of America and the European Union on the use and transfer of Passenger Name Records to the United States Department of Homeland Security' (9 December 2011)

European Data Protection Supervisor, 'Opinion of the European Data Protection Supervisor on the Communication from the Commission to the European Parliament, the Council, the Economic and Social Committee and the Committee of the Regions—"A comprehensive approach on personal data protection in the European Union"' (14 January 2011)

(iii) Latin America

'Recommendation Directly Pertaining to Transborder Data Flows Adopted by the Third Conference of Latin American Informatics Authorities, Recommendation Number 12', reprinted in United Nations Centre on Transnational Corporations, 'Transnational Corporations and Transnational Data Flows: A Technical Paper', ST/CTC/23, 1982, Annex III

(iv) Belgium

Belgian Privacy Commission, Decision of 9 December 2008 in the SWIFT Affair, unofficial English translation at <http://www.privacycommission.be/sites/privacycommission/files/documents/swift_decision_en_09_12_2008.pdf>

(v) Canada

Office of the Privacy Commissioner of Canada, 'Guidelines for Processing Personal Data Across Borders' (2009)

Office of the Privacy Commissioner of Canada, 'Revisiting the Privacy Landscape a Year Later' (March 2006)

Information & Privacy Commissioner for British Columbia, 'Privacy and the USA Patriot Act: Implications for British Columbia Public Sector Outsourcing' (October 2004)

(vi) Denmark

Datatilsynet, 'Processing of sensitive personal data in a cloud situation' (3 February 2011), <http://www.datatilsynet.dk/english/processing-of-sensitive-personal-%20data-in-a-cloud-solution/>

(vii) France

CNIL, Délibération no. 2005-305 du 8 décembre 2005 portant autorisation unique de traitements automatisés de données à caractère personnel mis en œuvre dans le cadre de dispositifs d'alerte professionnelle

CNIL, Délibération no. 2005-111 du 26 mai 2005 relative à une demande d'autorisation de la Compagnie européenne d'accumulateurs pour la mise en œuvre d'un dispositif de ligne éthique

CNIL, Délibération no. 2005-110 du 26 mai 2005 relative à une demande d'autorisation de McDonald's France pour la mise en œuvre d'un dispositif d'intégrité professionnelle

CNIL, 10e rapport d'activité (1989)

(viii) Germany

Der Bundesbeauftragte für den Datenschutz und die Informationsfreiheit, 'Deutsche und kanadische Datenschutzbehörden schaffen Grundlage für verstärkte Zusammenarbeit' (15 October 2012), <http://www.bfdi.bund.de/DE/Oeffentlichkeitsarbeit/Pressemitteilungen/2012/21_DCANDSBehoerdenSchaffenGrundlageZurZusammenarbeit.html?nn=408908>

Berliner Beauftragter für Datenschutz und Informationsfreiheit, 'Deutsche Bahn akzeptiert hohe Geldbusse und will künftig Vorbild im Datenschutz sein' (23 October 2009), <http://www.datenschutz-berlin.de/attachments/627/PE_DB_AG.pdf?1256283223>

Abgestimmte Positionen der Aufsichtsbehörden in der AG 'Internationaler Datenverkehr' am 12./13. Februar 2007—Bezug: Protokoll der Sitzung mit Wirtschaftsvertretern am 23. Juni 2006 (28 March 2007)

Düsseldorfer Kreis, 'Fallgruppen zur Internationalen Auftragsdatenverarbeitung, Handreichung des Düsseldorfer Kreises zur rechtlichen Bewertung' (28 March 2007)

(ix) the Netherlands

M.A.H. Fontein-Bijnsdorp, 'Article 4 WBP revisited: Some comments regarding the applicability of the Wet bescherming persoonsgegevens (WBP) [Dutch Data Protection Act]', <http://www.dutchdpa.nl/downloads_art/art_afo_2009_applicability_of_dutch_dp_act.pdf?refer=true&theme=purple>

(x) New Zealand

New Zealand Privacy Commissioner, 'Privacy amendment important for trade and consumer protection' (26 August 2010)

(xi) Spain

Agencia Española de Protección de Datos, 'Report on International Data Transfers: Ex officio Sectorial Inspection of Spain-Colombia at Call Centres' (July 2007)

Spanish Data Protection Agency, 'Report on International Data Transfers' (July 2007)

(xii) Switzerland

Eidgenössischer Datenschutz- und Öffentlichkeitsbeauftragter, '19. Tätigkeitsbericht 2011/2012' [19th annual report of the Swiss Federal Data Protection Commissioner]

(xiii) United Kingdom

UK Information Commissioner, 'The Eighth Data Protection Principle and international data transfers' (30 May 2006)

6. DOCUMENTS ISSUED BY INTERNATIONAL ORGANIZATIONS

APEC Privacy Framework (2005)

Consultative Committee of the Convention for the Protection of Individuals with regard to Automatic Processing of Personal Data [ETS No. 108], 'Opinion on Uruguay's request to be invited to accede to Convention 108 and its additional Protocol', T-PD (2011) 08 rev en (26 May 2011)

'Consultative Committee of the Convention for the Protection of Individuals with regard to Automatic Processing of Personal Data (ETS No. 108) (T-PD)—Abridged report of the 24th plenary meeting' (2 July 2008)

'Convention for the Protection of Individuals with regard to Automatic Processing of Personal Data (ETS No. 108)—Request by Uruguay to be invited to accede, 6 July 2011'

Council of Europe, Recommendation No. R(87)15 of the Committee of Ministers to Member States regulating the use of personal data in the police sector (17 September 1987)

International Organization of Securities Commissions (IOSCO), 'Multilateral Memorandum of Understanding (MMOU) concerning Consultation and Cooperation and the Exchange of Information', <http://www.iosco.org/library/index.cfm?section=mou_siglist>

Memorandum of Understanding between the Council of Europe and the European Union (May 2007)

OAS, Department of International Law Newsletter, 'Department of International Law Advances Cooperation with Organizations and Authorities on Privacy and Data Protection' (November 2011), <http://www.oas.org/dil/Newsletter/newsletter_api_ppd_NOV-2011.html>.

OECD, Declaration on Transborder Data Flows (Adopted by the Governments of the OECD Member Countries on 11th April 1985)

OECD, Recommendation of the Council concerning Guidelines governing the Protection of Privacy and Transborder Flows of Personal Data (23 September 1980)

OECD, Guidelines on the Protection of Privacy and Transborder Flows of Personal Data (1980)

Parliamentary Assembly of the Council of Europe, Resolution 428 (1970)

Permanent Council of the Organization of American States, Committee on Juridical and Political Affairs, Draft: Preliminary Principles and Recommendations on Data Protection (The Protection of Personal Data), CP/CAJP-2921/10 (19 November 2010)

UN Guidelines concerning Computerized Personal Data Files of 14 December 1990, UN Doc. E/CN.4/1990/72

UN Doc. A/RES/45/95 (14 December 1990)

7. OTHER REPORTS AND STUDIES

'The 9/11 Commission Report' (2004)

APEC Data Privacy Pathfinder Projects Implementation Work Plan (Revised), APEC doc. 2009/SOM1/ECSG/SEM/027

Bojana Bellamy, 'Accenture's Client Data Protection Program' (February 2009), <http://www.hideproject.org/downloads/HIDE_PF-Outsourcing-Presentation_Bojana_Bellamy-20090206.pdf>

Carnegie Endowment for International Peace, 'The World Order in 2050' (April 2010)

The Conference Board, 'Global Economic Outlook 2012'

Eurobarometer Study (for the European Commission), 'Data Protection in the European Union—Data Controllers' Perceptions—Analytical Report' (February 2008), <http://ec.europa.eu/public_opinion/flash/fl_226_en.pdf>

Eurobarometer Study (for the European Commission), 'Data Protection in the European Union—Citizens' Perceptions—Analytical Report' (February 2008), <http://ec.europa.eu/public_opinion/flash/fl_225_en.pdf>

European Commission, 'EU approves New Zealand's data protection standards in step to boost trade' (EU RAPID press release) (19 December 2012), <http://europa.eu/rapid/press-release_IP-12-1403_en.htm>

European Commission, 'Communication from the Commission to the European Parliament, the Council, the European Economic and Social Committee and the Committee of the Regions, Safeguarding Privacy in a Connected World—A European Data Protection Framework for the 21st Century', COM(2012) 9/3 (25 January 2012)

European Commission, 'A comprehensive approach on personal data protection in the European Union', COM(2010) 609 final (4 November 2010)

European Commission, 'Working Paper No. 2: Data protection laws in the EU' (20 January 2010)

Commission of the European Communities, 'Communication to the European Parliament, the Council, the European Economic and Social Committee and the Committee of the Regions: The Internet of Things—An Action Plan for Europe', COM(2009) 278 final (18 June 2009)

European Commission, 'Comparative study on the situation in the 27 Member States as regards the law applicable to non-contractual obligations arising out of violations of privacy and rights relating to personality', JLS/2007/C4/028, Final Report (February 2009)

European Commission, 'Data Protection in the European Union: Citizens Perceptions, Analytical Report' (February 2008)

European Commission, 'Analysis and impact study on the implementation of Directive EC 95/46 in Member States' (2003)

European Commission, 'First Report on the implementation of the Data Protection Directive (95/46/EC)' COM(2003) 265 final (15 May 2003)

European Commission, 'Commission decisions on the adequacy of the protection of personal data in third countries', <http://ec.europa.eu/justice/data-protection/document/international-transfers/adequacy/index_en.htm>

European Union Agency for Fundamental Rights, 'Data Protection in the European Union: the Role of National Data Protection Authorities' (2010)

Galway Project and Centre for Information Policy Leadership, 'Data Protection Accountability: The Essential Elements, A Document for Discussion' (2009)

Global Pulse, 'Big Data for Development: Challenges and Opportunities' (May 2012)

International Law Commission, 'Report on the Work of its Fifty-Eighth Session' (1 May–9 June and 3 July–11 August 2006) UN Doc. A/61/10, Annex D

International Law Commission, 'Fragmentation of International Law: Difficulties arising from the Diversification and Expansion of International Law, Report of the Study Group of the International Law Commission finalized by Martti Koskenniemi', UN Doc. A/CN.4/L.682 (13 April 2006)

The Madrid Resolution, 'International Standards on the Protection of Personal Data and Privacy' (2009)

McKinsey Global Institute, 'Big data: the next frontier for innovation, competition, and productivity' (May 2011)

Law Commission of New Zealand, 'Review of the Privacy Act 1993' (March 2010)

State Services Commission of New Zealand, 'Government Use of Offshore Information and Communication Technologies (ICT) Service Providers: Advice on Risk Management' (2009)

OECD, 'Recommendation on Cross-border Co-operation in the Enforcement of Laws Protecting Privacy' (2007)

OECD, 'Report on the Cross-Border Enforcement of Privacy Laws' (2006)

OECD, 'Report on Compliance with, and Enforcement of, Privacy Protection Online' (12 February 2003)

OECD, Annex 2 to the Declaration on International Investment and Multinational Enterprises, 'Conflicting Requirements Imposed on Multinational Enterprises' (1991), <http://www.oecd.org/daf/internationalinvestment/investmentpolicy/conflictingre-quirementsimposedonmultinationalenterprises.htm>

Zachary N.J. Peterson, Mark Gondree, and Robert Beverly, 'A Position Paper on Data Sovereignty: The Importance of Geolocating Data in the Cloud', <http://rbeverly.net/research/papers/soverign-hotcloud11.pdf>

Parliament of the Commonwealth of Australia, House of Representatives, 'Privacy Amendment (Enhancing Privacy Protection) Bill 2012, Explanatory Memorandum'

Ponemon Institute, '2011 Global Encryption Trends Survey'

RAND Europe, 'Review of the European Data Protection Directive' (2009)

Reports by the High Level Contact Group (HLCG) on information sharing and privacy and personal data protection (23 November 2009)

Report of the Commission on Transnational Corporations of the UN Economic and Social Council of 6 July 1981, reprinted in Hans-Joachim Mengel, *Internationale Organisationen und transnationaler Datenschutz* (Wissenschaftlicher Autoren-Verlag 1984), at 185–207

'Routing 101: the Basics', <http://www.cisco.com/en/US/netsol/ns339/ns392/ns399/ns400/networking_solutions_white_paper0900aecd802d5489.shtml>

'The Sedona Conference International Principles on Discovery, Disclosure & Data Protection' (December 2011)

Treasury Board of Canada, 'Taking Privacy into Account Before Making Contracting Decisions' (2006)

UN Human Rights Council 'The promotion, protection, and enjoyment of human rights on the Internet', UN Doc. A/HRC/20L.13 (29 June 2012)

United Nations Commission on International Trade Law (UNCITRAL), Report of the Working Group IV (Electronic Commerce) on the work of its fortieth session, Vienna, 14-18 October 2002, UN Doc. A/CN.9/527

White House, 'Consumer Data Privacy in a Networked World' (February 2012)

World Economic Forum, 'Global Information Technology Report 2009–2010'

8. CODES OF PRACTICE

Infocomm Development Authority of Singapore (IDA) and the National Trust Council of Singapore (NTC), Voluntary Model Data Protection Code for the Private Sector (Version 1.3 final)

9. NEWS ARTICLES

Bill Hinchberger, 'European banks shut Americans out over U.S. tax rules' (27 September 2012), <http://www.usatoday.com/story/money/business/2012/09/27/american-expats/1594695/>

Gillian Tett, 'Big data is watching you', *Financial Times*, 10 August 2012, <http://www.ft.com/cms/s/2/97cffaf0-e1b5-11e1-92f5-00144feab49a.html>

Official Google Enterprise Blog, 'Google Apps to offer additional compliance options for EU data protection' (6 June 2012), <http://googleenterprise.blogspot.co.uk/2012/06/google-apps-to-offer-additional.html

Amiti Sen and Harsimran Julka, 'India seeks "Data Secure Nation" status, more Hi-end business from European Union', *The Economic Times*, 16 April 2012, <http://articles. economictimes.indiatimes.com/2012-04-16/news/31349813_1_data-security-council-data-protection-laws-standard-contractual-clauses>

Journalist's Resource, 'The Arab Spring and the Internet: Research Roundup' (22 March 2012), <http://journalistsresource.org/studies/society/internet/research-arab-spring-internet-key-studies/>

'Innenminister Friedrich will sichere "Bundescloud" aufbauen' (18 December 2011), <http://www.teltarif.de/bundes-cloud-friedrich-regierung-telekom-sichere-speicherung/news/45000.html>

Kristina Irion, 'Government cloud computing and the policies of data sovereignty' (September 2011), <https://www.econstor.eu/dspace/bitstream/10419/52197/1/672481146.pdf>

Kevin J. O'Brien, 'Europe turns to the Cloud', *NY Times*, 24 July 2011, <http://www. nytimes.com/2011/07/25/technology/europe-turns-to-the-cloud.html?pagewanted=all>

Charles Arthur, 'What's a zettabyte? By 2015 the Internet will know, says Cisco', *The Guardian*, 29 June 2011, <http://www.guardian.co.uk/technology/blog/2011/jun/29/zettabyte-data-internet-cisco>

Ryan Singel, 'Report: Egypt Shut Down Net with Big Switch, Not Phone Calls', Wired (10 February 2011), <http://www.wired.com/threatlevel/2011/02/egypt-off-switch/>

'India says BlackBerry agrees to give it real-time access to corporate messages', (6 September 2010) BNA Privacy & Security Law Report 1241

Margaret Coker, Tim Falconer and Phred Dvorak, 'UAE Puts the Squeeze on Blackberry', *Wall Street Journal*, 31 July 2010, <http://online.wsj.com/article/SB10001424052748704702304575402493300698912.html?mod=WSJEUROPE_hpp_LEFTTopStories>

'Ireland blocks EU data sharing with Israel' (8 July 2010), <http://jta.org/news/article/2010/07/08/2739965/ireland-backs-out-of-data-sharing-with-israel>

Symantec Corp., 'Internet Security Threat Report, Volume XV' (April 2010), <http://www4.symantec.com/Vrt/wl?tu_id=SUKX1271711282503126202>

'Data, data everywhere—A special report on managing information', *The Economist*, 27 February 2010, at 3

Jonathan Zittrain, 'Lost in the Cloud', *New York Times*, 19 July 2009, <http://www.nytimes.com/2009/07/20/opinion/20zittrain.html?_r=1>

Luke O'Brien, 'Yahoo betrayed my husband', Wired (15 March 2007), <http://www.wired.com/politics/onlinerights/news/2007/03/72972>

Patrick Ross, 'Congress fears European privacy standards' CNET News (8 March 2001), <http://news.cnet.com/2100-1023-253826.html>

Steve Gibbard, 'Geographic Implications of DNS Infrastructure Distribution', <http://www.cisco.com/web/about/ac123/ac147/archived_issues/ipj_10-1/101_dns-infrastructure.html>

Steve Gibbard, 'Internet Mini-Cores', <http://www.pch.net/resources/papers/Gibbard-mini-cores.pdf>

10. LETTERS AND SPEECHES

Article 29 Working Party, letter to Larry Page of Google (16 October 2012), <http://www.dataprotection.ie/documents/press/Letter_from_the_Article_29_Working_Party_to_Google_in_relation_to_its_new_privacy_policy.pdf>

Peter Hustinx, Concluding Remarks made at 3rd Annual Symposium of the European Union Agency for Fundamental Rights, Vienna (10 May 2012), at 5, <http://www.edps.

europa.eu/EDPSWEB/webdav/site/mySite/shared/Documents/EDPS/Publications/
Speeches/2012/12-05-10_Speech_Vienna_EN.pdf>
Letter from Swiss Federal Data Protection and Information Commissioner FDPIC
Hans-Peter Thür of 9 December 2008, <http://export.gov/static/sh_swiss_FDP_
Commissioner_Latest_eg_main_018520.pdf>
Letter from Timothy J. Muris, Chairman, Federal Trade Commission, to Congressman
Edward J. Markey, United States House of Representatives (7 May 2004), p 3
(unpublished)

Index